Improbable Diplomats

In 1971, Americans made two historic visits to China that would transform relations between the two countries. One was by US official Henry Kissinger; the other, earlier, visit was by the US table tennis team. Historians have mulled over the transcripts of Kissinger's negotiations with Chinese leaders. However, they have overlooked how, alongside these diplomatic talks, a rich program of travel and exchange had begun with ping-pong diplomacy. *Improbable Diplomats* reveals how a diverse cast of Chinese and Americans – athletes and physicists, performing artists and seismologists – played a critical, but to-date overlooked, role in remaking US-China relations. Based on new sources from more than a dozen archives in China and the United States, Pete Millwood argues that the significance of cultural and scientific exchanges went beyond reacquainting the Chinese and American people after two decades of minimal contact; exchanges also powerfully influenced Sino-American diplomatic relations and helped transform post-Mao China.

Pete Millwood is a Postdoctoral Fellow in the Society of Fellows in the Humanities at The University of Hong Kong. His writing has appeared in *History Today* and *The Washington Post*. This is his first book.

Cambridge Studies in US Foreign Relations

Edited by

Paul Thomas Chamberlin
Columbia University
Lien-Hang T. Nguyen
Columbia University

This series showcases cutting-edge scholarship in US foreign relations that employs dynamic new methodological approaches and archives from the colonial era to the present. The series will be guided by the ethos of transnationalism, focusing on the history of American foreign relations in a global context rather than privileging the US as the dominant actor on the world stage.

Also in the Series

R. Joseph Parrott and Mark Atwood Lawrence (eds.), *The Tricontinental Revolution: Third World Radicalism and the Cold War*

Aaron Donaghy, *The Second Cold War: Carter, Reagan, and the Politics of Foreign Policy*

Amanda C. Demmer, *After Saigon's Fall: Refugees and US-Vietnamese Relations, 1975–1995*

Heather Marie Stur, *Saigon at War: South Vietnam and the Global Sixties*

Seth Jacobs, *Rogue Diplomats: The Proud Tradition of Disobedience in American Foreign Policy*

Sarah Steinbock-Pratt, *Educating the Empire: American Teachers and Contested Colonization in the Philippines*

Walter L. Hixson, *Israel's Armor: The Israel Lobby and the First Generation of the Palestine Conflict*

Aurélie Basha i Novosejt, *"I Made Mistakes": Robert McNamara's Vietnam War Policy, 1960–1964*

Greg Whitesides, *Science and American Foreign Relations since World War II*

Jasper M. Trautsch, *The Genesis of America: US Foreign Policy and the Formation of National Identity, 1793–1815*

Hideaki Kami, *Diplomacy Meets Migration: US Relations with Cuba during the Cold War*

Shaul Mitelpunkt, *Israel in the American Mind: The Cultural Politics of US-Israeli Relations, 1958–1988*

Pierre Asselin, *Vietnam's American War: A History*

Lloyd E. Ambrosius, *Woodrow Wilson and American Internationalism*

Geoffrey C. Stewart, *Vietnam's Lost Revolution: Ngô Đình Diệm's Failure to Build an Independent Nation, 1955–1963*

Michael E. Neagle, *America's Forgotten Colony: Cuba's Isle of Pines*

Elisabeth Leake, *The Defiant Border: The Afghan-Pakistan Borderlands in the Era of Decolonization, 1936–1965*

Tuong Vu, *Vietnam's Communist Revolution: The Power and Limits of Ideology*

Renata Keller, *Mexico's Cold War: Cuba, the United States, and the Legacy of the Mexican Revolution*

Improbable Diplomats

How Ping-Pong Players, Musicians, and Scientists Remade US-China Relations

PETE MILLWOOD

The University of Hong Kong

CAMBRIDGE
UNIVERSITY PRESS

CAMBRIDGE
UNIVERSITY PRESS

University Printing House, Cambridge CB2 8BS, United Kingdom

One Liberty Plaza, 20th Floor, New York, NY 10006, USA

477 Williamstown Road, Port Melbourne, VIC 3207, Australia

314–321, 3rd Floor, Plot 3, Splendor Forum, Jasola District Centre,
New Delhi – 110025, India

103 Penang Road, #05–06/07, Visioncrest Commercial, Singapore 238467

Cambridge University Press is part of the University of Cambridge.

It furthers the University's mission by disseminating knowledge in the pursuit of
education, learning, and research at the highest international levels of excellence.

www.cambridge.org
Information on this title: www.cambridge.org/9781108837439
DOI: 10.1017/9781108935982

© Pete Millwood 2023

First published 2023

A catalogue record for this publication is available from the British Library.

Library of Congress Cataloging-in-Publication Data
NAMES: Millwood, Pete, 1989– author.
TITLE: Improbable diplomats : how ping-pong players, musicians, and scientists
remade US–China relations / Pete Millwood, University of Hong Kong.
OTHER TITLES: How ping-pong players, musicians, and scientists remade
US-China relations
DESCRIPTION: Cambridge ; New York, NY : Cambridge University Press, 2023. |
SERIES: Cambridge Studies in US foreign relations | Includes
bibliographical references and index.
IDENTIFIERS: LCCN 2022025396 | ISBN 9781108837439 (hardback) |
ISBN 9781108935982 (ebook)
SUBJECTS: LCSH: United States – Relations – China. | China – Relations – United
States. | China – Foreign relations – 1976- | Cultural diplomacy. | United
States – Foreign relations – 1969–1974. | United States – Foreign
relations – 1974–1977. | BISAC: HISTORY / United States / General
CLASSIFICATION: LCC E183.8.C5 .M488 2022 | DDC 327.73051–dc23/eng/20220531
LC record available at https://lccn.loc.gov/2022025396

ISBN 978-1-108-83743-9 Hardback

Contents

Figures

Acknowledgments

My foremost debt of gratitude in writing this book is to my Oxford doctoral supervisor, Rana Mitter. Rana provided invaluable input at every stage and much encouragement but also asked important, tough questions and did his best to dissuade me from writing anything boring. Arne Westad expertly guided this project in its early stages and has provided much wisdom since. Several people that offered valuable feedback on my doctoral thesis continued to guide me as I worked toward transforming the thesis into a book, in particular Rana, Andrew Preston, Micah Muscolino, and Matthew Jones. Artemy Kalinovsky's insights into how to pitch a book made for not only a better proposal but a better book, too.

My other primary debt is to the many individuals who lived this history and then shared their experiences with me: Anne Solomon, Douglas Murray, Mary Brown Bullock, Orville Schell, Robert Keatley, Paul Pickowicz, Susan Shirk, and others. Many of these people are featured in the text, but some are not, and in all cases their contribution to the project goes beyond what I could directly include in the text. Hearing their stories but also their analysis nurtured my excitement about this project and my commitment to writing an account of US-China relations that went beyond government records. I look forward to some of them reading this book and am sad that others will not get the chance to. Particular thanks go to Jan Berris, who, among many other things, provided access to the National Committee on US-China Relations' files before they were formally archived, put me in touch with a host of people who played critical roles in the exchange program, and, far from least importantly, shared her own memories of being at the heart of US cultural exchanges with China for half a century. If I have told the history of Sino-American exchange half as well as she does, I will be satisfied indeed.

Financial support for this project was provided, first and foremost, by the UK Arts and Humanities Research Council. Research in China and the United States was made possible by further funding from the AHRC, a Chinese government scholarship, and grants from the Rockefeller Archive Center, New York University's Tamiment Cold War Center, and the Bentley Library, University of Michigan, as well as smaller grants from Oxford and the London School of Economics (LSE). Archivists and librarians at these institutions and more provided valuable help, and I am particularly thankful for the generous assistance of Mary Ann Quinn at the Rockefeller Archive Center. Niu Dayong and Deng Liman did much to facilitate my research in China.

During my doctoral research and as I worked to transform the thesis into a book, critical feedback was provided at seminars at the Kluge Center, at LSE, Oxford, Tokyo, Cambridge, Berkeley, and at conferences hosted by, among others, the Max Planck Institute in Berlin and the Niels Bohr Institute in Copenhagen, and at panels at the conferences of the Association for Asian Studies and the Society for Historians of American Foreign Relations. The scholars that provided feedback at those venues are too numerous to list in full, but particularly generous and insightful comments were made by Zuoyue Wang, Jennifer Miller, Hans van de Ven, and Masaya Inoue. Colleagues at LSE kindly read parts of a draft manuscript and offered useful comments and encouragement.

Several people read large parts or even the entirety of the draft manuscript and provided invaluable feedback and corrections, including Jan Berris, Tom Gold, Mary Bullock, and Federico Pachetti. Critical to the final shape of the book were the two anonymous reviews of the draft manuscript. I am indebted to both reviewers for their thoughtful and engaged responses to the manuscript that had the detail and depth to allow me to, I think, significantly improve the final version. The Society of Fellows in the Humanities at the University of Hong Kong (HKU) provided the ideal environment for me to do so. I have the Society (and, perhaps, COVID-19) to thank for a year entirely dedicated to revising the manuscript. I was sped on the way to doing so by supportive colleagues within the fellowship, and in the HKU History Department.

I'm grateful for the work of Cecelia Cancellaro and Victoria Phillips at Cambridge University Press for bringing this work into print and in guiding a first-time author through that process and to Deborah

Gershonowitz for her enthusiasm for the project while she was based at Cambridge University Press.

I couldn't have written the book without Julia Kukiewicz's unwavering support. Her contribution to the project went far beyond tolerating our lives being built around the exigences of research. She read endless iterations of the text, insisted I write something others would want to read, and shared her eye for the story in the history, all of which were critical to bringing a book out of a thesis. I dedicate this book to my parents, Chrissie and Jon Millwood, from whom a lifetime of love and support has done everything to gift me the privilege of spending my time researching and writing.

These many sources of assistance notwithstanding, any remaining errors are of my making.

Abbreviations

ACLS	American Council of Learned Societies
AFSC	American Friends Service Committee
CAS	Chinese Academy of Sciences
CCAS	Committee of Concerned Asian Scholars
CCP	Chinese Communist Party
CCPIT	China Council for the Promotion of International Trade
CFR	Council on Foreign Relations
CIA	Central Intelligence Agency
CPIFA	Chinese People's Institute of Foreign Affairs
CPUSA	Communist Party of the United States of America
CSCPRC	Committee on Scholarly Communication with the People's Republic of China
FAS	Federation of American Scientists
FBI	Federal Bureau of Investigation
IPR	Institute of Pacific Relations
IREX	International Research and Exchanges Board
MFN	Most Favored Nation
MIT	Massachusetts Institute of Technology
NAS	National Academy of Sciences
NCUSCR	National Committee on United States-China Relations
NCUSCT	National Council for United States-China Trade
NSC	National Security Council
NSSM	National Security Study Memorandum
PRC	People's Republic of China

PRCLO	People's Republic of China Liaison Office
ROC	Republic of China
SSRC	Social Science Research Council
STAPRC	Scientific and Technical Association of the People's Republic of China
UK	United Kingdom
UN	United Nations
US	United States
USCPFA	US-China Peoples Friendship Association
USG	United States government
USLO	United States Liaison Office
USTTA	United States Table Tennis Association
ZGZYWXYJS	Zhonggong zhongyang wenxian yanjiushi [CCP Central Committee Document Research Office]

Introduction

In May 1970, Chairman Mao Zedong shared with the Chinese people his most recent thoughts on the United States of America. The chairman had come to rule China in 1949 after a bloody civil war that had raged on-and-off for more than twenty years. He had led his Communist forces against not only their domestic opponents – the Kuomintang – but also foreign enemies. After his founding of the People's Republic of China (PRC) at the end of the civil war, Mao singled out the United States (US) as the worst of these enemies, decrying the American arch-imperialists for invading Korea in 1950 and frustrating Chinese attempts to liberate the Kuomintang's redoubt on Taiwan. Time had not tempered his rhetoric: now, Mao claimed that President Richard Nixon had committed fascist atrocities and massacred both whites and blacks at home, while bombing southeast Asia and masterminding coups to topple legitimate leaders abroad. The chairman hailed an emerging global wave of furious resistance to American imperialism. Mao was confident that a mass movement of protest would overthrow Nixon and international resistance would blunt US aggression abroad.[1]

Mao's invitation for Nixon to visit China less than two years later came, then, as a shock to the Chinese populace. The chairman beamed as he shook hands with the man for whom he had predicted a sticky end. Nixon looked equally thrilled at the meeting, in spite of having made his

[1] "Quan shijie renmin tuanjie qilai, dabai Meiguo qinluezhe jiqi yiqie zougou!" [People of the world, unite and defeat the US aggressors and all their running dogs!], *Renmin Ribao* [People's Daily], May 21, 1970.

political career hounding "reds" and championing the Cold War containment of Communism. The two men met during "the week that changed the world" and began a process of settling the differences that had divided their countries for more than two decades: US involvement in a war against China's Communist neighbor, Vietnam; the presence of American troops and nuclear weapons on Taiwan; Washington's insistence that the Kuomintang government on that island spoke for all Chinese. These negotiations took time. Nixon's chief foreign policy aide, Henry Kissinger, got into the habit of visiting China twice a year and, in 1975, Nixon's successor Gerald Ford followed in his predecessor's footsteps and met Mao in Beijing. The process of negotiation was ultimately successful: the establishment of diplomatic relations between China and the United States occurred on January 1, 1979. That agreement was marked by another summit visit, this time by a Chinese leader: President Jimmy Carter welcomed Mao's ultimate successor, Deng Xiaoping, to the United States for the first state visit to that country by a Chinese leader.

This potted history is how the rapprochement between the United States and China has been remembered: as a series of summits.[2] This book takes a different approach. It looks beyond great men such as Mao and Nixon to focus on a neglected story: how the American and Chinese *people* reconnected. Many of the most significant moments in this story are also visits – but not by government officials. The first of these was by the US amateur table tennis team. Their sensational ping-pong diplomacy of April 1971 preceded – and, this book shows, helped precipitate – Kissinger and Nixon's visits to China. It also reawakened the American public's interest in China. A year later, the return leg of this ping-pong diplomacy constituted the first official delegation of PRC citizens to the United States and brought Chinese Communists into American stadiums, colleges, and living rooms – not to mention to Disneyland.[3] Deng's US summit visit of 1979 was preceded, six months earlier, by the most high-powered delegation of scientists to be sent by the United States

---

[2] Margaret MacMillan builds her lively book around the Nixon–Mao summit, but she is far from alone in focusing her narrative and analysis on Sino-American summit interactions. Other accounts are discussed later in this introduction. Margaret MacMillan, *Seize the Hour: When Nixon Met Mao* (London: John Murray, 2006).

[3] Chinese officials refused to travel to the United States while Chiang Kai-shek's Republic of China maintained an embassy there. Chinese diplomats had transited through New York to attend the United Nations after the PRC had been seated there on November 15, 1971. In addition, some PRC citizens had fled to the United States after 1949. The ping-pong return leg was the first official delegation of PRC citizens to visit the United States.

to any country. Led by Frank Press, a brilliant scientist who had discovered how to measure earthquakes at sea and on the Moon, that visit paved the way not only for the establishment of diplomatic relations between the United States and China but also for large-scale American scientific assistance to China's miraculous post-Mao development. In between, many dozens of exchange visits in both directions reacquainted the Chinese and American people after more than two decades of near-hermetic isolation, reviving the deep interaction that had stretched back for more than a century preceding the 1949 Chinese revolution – and that would subsequently come to be a defining feature of our era.

Improbable Diplomats argues that exchange visits between Americans and Chinese did more than just reconnect these two peoples, however. It shows that these interactions also exerted a powerful influence on the diplomatic relationship between the two governments – and, indeed, on the negotiations that took place in summit meetings. The cultural and scientific exchange program of athletes, musicians, physicists, and many others was, this book contends, a critical factor in the successes and failures, the progress and setbacks, that marked the eight years of negotiations during Washington and Beijing's rapprochement, culminating in diplomatic recognition in 1979. Exchange visits were, naturally enough, shaped by developments in high-level diplomacy – but, in turn, exchanges also influenced relations between the two governments. These two tracks of diplomacy were, this book reveals, deeply connected and mutually constitutive.

The role of ping-pong diplomacy in instigating Sino-American rapprochement and Nixon's China summit is well known and has been widely recognized by historians: that episode was perhaps the example par excellence of cultural exchange diplomacy during the Cold War. What has received less attention is the continuing influence of exchange visits and transnational contacts on Sino-American diplomatic talks after Nixon's 1972 visit and through to the final agreement to establish formal relations made in 1978.[4] Having been both cause and consequence of Nixon's visit, the expanding exchange program of the 1970s was one of the foremost means by which both governments looked to maintain and

---

[4] An important recent study of Sino-European contacts in the 1950s and 1960s stated, for example, that "the actual official and substantial development of Sino-American relations only started at the end of the [1970s]." This book explores the substance that was in fact evident before 1979. Angela Romano and Valeria Zanier, "Circumventing the Cold War: The Parallel Diplomacy of Economic and Cultural Exchanges between Western Europe and Socialist China in the 1950s and 1960s: An Introduction", *Modern Asian Studies* 51, no. 1 (2017): 2–3.

deepen rapprochement during the eight-year road to "normalizing" relations, the term used to refer to the establishment of full diplomatic ties.

Exchanges influenced the Sino-American relationship in two critical ways: by having an immediate, tangible effect at key make-or-break junctures in the relationship, and by gradually and cumulatively contributing to the overall condition of ties. The following chapters will feature a range of critical moments where exchange contacts made the difference between the relationship moving forward or breaking down. In 1971 and 1972, the two legs of ping-pong diplomacy constituted the first reciprocal exchange visits between US and PRC citizens; in 1973, deepening exchanges prompted the creation of de facto embassies in Washington and Beijing; in 1978, Frank Press's marquee scientific delegation helped convinced Chinese leaders to urgently conclude normalization negotiations in order to upgrade their access to advanced American scientific expertise. In all these instances and more, contact through cultural and scientific interaction acted as an impetus for major change in the diplomatic relationship – change that would not have been realized, certainly when it was, without the input of actors outside of either government.

Perhaps as important, however, was the long-term contribution of exchange contacts in rebuilding a Sino-American relationship that had all but completely dissolved during the twenty years after China's Communist revolution. As will be shown in this book's prologue, the number of Americans that had traveled to China since 1949 numbered in the dozens. During that time, almost no PRC citizens had officially set foot in the United States and certainly there had been nothing like the Chinese exchange delegations that began to visit the country in 1972.[5] High-level diplomatic contact had hardly been deeper: ambassadorial negotiations held in Geneva and then Warsaw had been frosty and led to almost no agreements – in spite of more than one hundred meetings.[6] In the absence of contact, both ignorance and suspicion had bred. Before Nixon traveled to Beijing, he hastily crammed information about Mao's China by

---

[5] One of the few exceptions was the visit of PRC diplomat Wu Xiuquan to New York in 1950. Wu travelled to the United States as the head of a PRC delegation to the United Nations but used his presence to visit New York and meet with Americans seen by Beijing as friendly to the PRC, including the Black singer Paul Robeson, who was unable to accept Xu's invitation to travel to the PRC. Wu Xiuquan, *Zai waijiaobu ba nian de jingli, 1950.1–1958.10: Waijiao huiyilu* [Eight Years in the Foreign Ministry: Memoirs of Diplomacy] (Beijing: Shijie zhishi chubanshe, 1983), 59–63.

[6] Yafeng Xia, *Negotiating with the Enemy: U.S.-China Talks during the Cold War, 1949–1972* (Bloomington, IN: Indiana University Press, 2006).

reading books by some of the few Westerners to have directly experienced the country, calling some of the authors to the White House for personal conversations.[7] Chinese leaders relied on similar – sometimes even the same – individuals for information on the United States: leftist Americans like Edgar Snow that visited or sojourned in the PRC were considered some of the few reliable conduits of information about the United States by top Chinese leaders like Mao and Premier Zhou Enlai.

As rapprochement began in 1971, Americans outside of government also needed to learn about – and to care about – China if rapprochement was to be successful. The direct experience of participating in rapprochement by interacting with Chinese people through the medium of exchanges was perhaps the most important way in which trust and understanding was rebuilt. This process of restoring empathy was, then, simultaneously undertaken by Americans working in the West Wing and those living unremarkable lives on the West Coast, and a broad and durable bilateral relationship could only be constructed if Americans in and out of office reconnected to China – a fact not lost on Kissinger and his colleagues in Washington. Exchanges did not always produce positive sentiments or genuine understanding, however: although the vast majority of Americans that directly encountered China and its people in the 1970s were glad to have done so, many developed simplistic or stereotyped readings of China that were inaccurate but nonetheless influential. Emotion often trumped information in how Americans perceived China. Nonetheless, the piecemeal and cumulative work of exchange contact made a critical contribution to restoring a relationship between the two societies, just as did periodic moments of breakthrough via exchange diplomacy.

Sino-American exchanges generally had a salutary influence on the diplomatic relationship. After the first ping-pong trip paved the way for Kissinger and Nixon to visit China, further exchange visits amplified American popular enthusiasm for Nixon's new China policy and provided the public with substance to accompany the pomp and secret discussions of the presidential summit and Kissinger's visits. High-level relations between Washington and Beijing deteriorated in the wake of the Watergate scandal that absorbed the White House from 1973 and culminated in Nixon's resignation in 1974. During this fraught period, exchange contacts were

---

[7] See, for example, Nixon's meeting with André Malraux. Steven E. Phillips, ed., *Foreign Relations of the United States, 1969–1976*, vol. XVII, China, 1969–1972 (Washington, DC: United States Government Printing Office, 2006), Document 192.

one of the few facets of the US-China relationship that remained active despite deadlocked diplomatic talks – even as the impact of the breakdown and tension in high-level ties was powerfully felt in the exchange program. Finally, the expansion of Sino-American scientific and technological cooperation in the years leading up to 1978 – largely realized through exchange visits and transnational scientific cooperation – played a critical role in convincing Deng Xiaoping to offer Washington the compromise deal that unlocked the final normalization agreement of that year.

Nonetheless, diplomacy via the exchange program was also the venue for political conflict between the American and Chinese people and governments. In one instance in 1975, a major tour by a Chinese performing arts troupe was called off at the last minute after US hosts learned of the visitors' intention to sign a song that called for the "liberation" of Taiwan, adding strain to an already tense Sino-American diplomatic relationship under Ford. At other times, antagonism over the program of exchange visits developed gradually. American visitors chafed at the strict controls they were subject to while in China, particularly as Chinese guests were welcome almost anywhere in the United States – from private homes to the most cutting-edge scientific laboratories. Indeed, resentment at imbalances of access ultimately prompted frustrated US nongovernmental organizations to impose their own limits on Chinese delegations – an action that alarmed governments in both capitals. Exchange contacts could, then, threaten the diplomatic relationship just as easily as they could strengthen it.

This book thus shows that, before normalization, the unofficial diplomats who organized and participated in exchange visits were at the vanguard of negotiating China and America's transition from their mutual isolation in the 1950s and 1960s to the cooperation of the 1970s and the decades that followed. In this way, *Improbable Diplomats* seeks to broaden our understanding of Sino-American history: rather than a relationship determined by a few oversized individuals – Kissinger, Zhou, Nixon, Mao, Carter, and Deng – this book shows that the rapprochement was a far wider interaction between Americans and Chinese both inside and outside of government.

EXCHANGE DIPLOMACY AND ITS PRACTITIONERS

This book employs the term "exchange diplomacy" to encompass three layers of diplomacy that were all critical to the Sino-American exchange program and, this book argues, to the US-China relationship more broadly. First, negotiations between the Chinese and US governments over the exchange program. The importance of exchange visits to Sino-American ties was enshrined in the Shanghai Communiqué signed during the Nixon–Mao 1972 summit. That document, which became a charter of the relationship before normalization, stated that, "The two sides agreed that it is desirable to broaden the understanding between the two peoples. To this end, they discussed specific areas in such fields as science, technology, culture, sports and journalism, in which people-to-people contacts and exchanges would be mutually beneficial. Each side undertakes to facilitate the further development of such contacts and exchanges."[8] While the two governments did indeed discuss "specific areas" for such visits during the 1972 summit, thereafter government-to-government exchange diplomacy was typically concerned with the overall structure of visits in each direction: their number and broad focus – cultural, scientific, or commercial, for example.

The closer details of exchange contact were negotiated at the second layer of exchange diplomacy: that between US nongovernmental organizations and their counterparts in China. As will be discussed below, the Chinese interlocutors of US private organizations concerned with exchanges were under state control: US nongovernmental organizations worked with state-run institutions like the Chinese Academy of Sciences or the Chinese People's Institute of Foreign Affairs (CPIFA) as well as directly with the Chinese Foreign Ministry. It was at this level that the specifics of exchange contacts were typically negotiated: the precise topics of exchange visits and the principles that would govern the behavior of Chinese visiting the United States and Americans visiting the PRC, for example. Moreover, it was at this second layer that most disagreements or controversies over exchanges typically played out (even if the US government was an interested party in such talks and frequently sought to influence their outcome).

The third – and by no means least important – layer of exchange diplomacy happened on the ground, between Chinese and Americans participating in exchange visits. Careful planning and choreography by the two governments and by US nongovernmental organizations meant nothing without the participation of individual Americans and Chinese involved in visiting and hosting. As we shall see throughout this book, the exchange diplomacy conducted at the two aforementioned layers was

---

[8] Shanghai Communiqué, February 27, 1972, *FRUS, 1969–1976*, vol. XVII, Document 203.

only as effective as the individual transnational encounters that occurred in sports stadiums, laboratories, and theatres – and around dining tables and on the tour buses that took participants between the more structured, performative moments of exchange visits. Here, there was agency for Chinese actors beyond state control: the PRC government carefully selected and trained participants in exchanges in this period, but Beijing could not exert control over every moment of visits and the primary role and identity of exchange participants remained athletes, artists, or scientists.

The agency of Chinese individuals participating in exchange encounters was demonstrated in the run-up to the very first exchange of this book's narrative. The first leg of ping-pong diplomacy was, as argued in Chapter 1, a carefully planned initiative by Mao, Zhou, and the Chinese government. But even this most important moment in Sino-American exchange diplomacy involved individual agency on the ground: Mao only learned of Chinese player Zhuang Zedong's famous greeting of the American hippie Glenn Cowan from his digest of Western newspapers. Upon reading of Zhuang's spontaneous interaction with Cowan and the Chinese player's presentation of a silk-scroll painting to the American as a token of friendship, Mao remarked, "Zhuang Zedong is not only very good at ping-pong but also quite diplomatic. This man is quite politically minded."[9] Mao and his colleagues would, on many other occasions, have cause to be satisfied with the initiative taken by Chinese participants in exchanges to ensure such interactions met the goals of the state – but we will also see that, on other occasions, the PRC state looked to countermand decisions made by individual Chinese participants in exchanges. We should not ignore the agency of the Chinese people that participated in exchange diplomacy or the challenge this agency could pose to Beijing's carefully orchestrated diplomacy.[10]

Other terms have been used by historians to refer to these layers of exchange diplomacy: as shown in the quotation from the Shanghai Communiqué above, one such term was "people-to-people diplomacy" (民间外交) or sometimes simply "people's diplomacy" (人民外交). The term

---

[9] Li Gong, "Chinese Decision Making and the Thawing of U.S.–China Relations," in *Re-examining the Cold War: U.S.-China Diplomacy, 1954–1973*, ed. Robert Ross and Jiang Changbin (Cambridge, MA: Harvard University Press, 2002), 342–43; Xu Guoqi, *Olympic Dreams: China and Sports, 1895–2008* (Cambridge, MA: Harvard University Press, 2008), 133.

[10] Gordon Barrett makes a similar point regarding Chinese scientists participating in earlier transnational exchanges and contacts. Gordon Barrett, "China's 'People's Diplomacy' and the Pugwash Conferences, 1957–1964," *Journal of Cold War Studies* 20, no. 1 (April 2018): 168.

people-to-people diplomacy had been used by the Chinese Communist Party (CCP) in earlier periods to refer specifically to the attempts of the Party and, after the 1949 establishment of the PRC, the state, to bypass foreign governments and conduct diplomacy with the populations of other countries directly.[11] The practice of people-to-people diplomacy had earlier Soviet precedents – closely studied by China during the Sino-Soviet Alliance – and, like similar initiatives from Moscow, was focused on influencing foreign public opinion, especially in the West. (After the Sino-Soviet Split, any reference to Soviet inspiration in China's foreign affairs was, of course, expunged).[12]

People-to-people diplomacy continued to be a feature of Beijing's relations with the United States in the 1970s and certainly the PRC's approach to exchange visits was in part intended to shape American public perceptions of China and to cultivate friends of China among Americans. The term can be misleading, however. The PRC state's use of a term that implies unmediated interactions between people was always deliberately deceptive because of the central role of the PRC state in putting such interactions toward its political ends; as Anne-Marie Brady puts it, the term refers to how the Chinese "government makes use of a wide range of officially nonofficial contacts with other countries to expand its influence."[13] The term should certainly not confuse us into thinking that the Chinese state was uninterested in such contacts, or saw them as unimportant: as Zhou Enlai commented in 1957, the PRC state's diplomacy incorporated official, semi-official, and nongovernmental diplomacy.[14] The PRC state was no less interested in controlling the Chinese population's diplomatic interactions with people outside China as it was any other aspect of their lives (even if, in both instances, this control could never be, in practice, total).[15] I employ the term people-to-people

---

[11] For further discussion of these terms, see Barrett, 140–41. The PRC continues to highlight "people-to-people" exchanges and diplomacy in its foreign policy. These constitute one of the five pillars of the contemporary Belt and Road Initiative (BRI) launched in 2013.

[12] Beverley Hooper, *Foreigners under Mao: Western Lives in China, 1949–1976* (Hong Kong: Hong Kong University Press, 2016), 24; Anne-Marie Brady, *Making the Foreign Serve China: Managing Foreigners in the People's Republic* (Lanham, MD: Rowman & Littlefield, 2003), 190.

[13] Brady, *Making the Foreign Serve China*, 23.

[14] Zhao Qizheng, "You minjian waijiao dao gonggong waijiao [From People's Diplomacy to Public Diplomacy]," *Waijiao pinglun* 26, no. 5 (2009): 1.

[15] The use of the term people-to-people diplomacy in the specialized historiography of China's foreign relations is specific to this strategy but can nonetheless be confusing to those not already familiar with that literature.

diplomacy in this book in its specific historical context: the PRC's state-led direct appeals to Americans beyond government. However, I prefer the term exchange diplomacy when analyzing the broader category of all exchange contacts between China and the United States between 1971 and 1978 because I believe it better represents the involvement and agency of both non-state and state actors, in both China and the United States, in the Sino-American exchanges of this period.[16]

Exchange visits of the sort examined in this book are also often referred to as public or cultural diplomacy. Public diplomacy has been defined by historian Nicholas J. Cull as "the conduct of foreign policy through engagement with foreign publics." This was indeed an important objective of both Chinese and US sides in the exchanges of the 1970s, which was particularly apparent in some categories of exchanges such as Beijing's courting of American congressmen and of members of the US-China Peoples Friendship Association, to give two examples. Nonetheless, while this book analyzes in some detail Chinese attempts to share US public opinion through exchange contacts, the difficulty in gauging the reception of American exchanges in China in the 1970s – then and now – as well as the multiple other objectives of exchanges has led me to avoid focusing of exchanges primarily as a form of public diplomacy.[17] I have avoided the term "cultural diplomacy" for a more practical reason: not only because it is, as Michael L. Krenn has argued, a "slippery term" that has lacked clear definition in the historiography, but also to distinguish between exchanges of arts and culture on the one hand and, on the other hand, visits focused on science, trade, and other topics (one of the definitional problems highlighted by Krenn).[18] These various foci for exchanges are often considered together under the rubric of cultural diplomacy. Here, I delineate explicitly cultural exchanges from scientific, commercial, and other exchange visits.

The significance of exchange visits in Sino-American relations was enhanced before 1979 by the absence of full, "normalized" diplomatic relations between the two governments. This lack of official relations made exchange contact both more significant – one of the only shows

---

[16] Tellingly, the Chinese state has itself more recently moved away from the term "people-to-people diplomacy" (民间外交) and toward the term "public diplomacy" (公共外交) for initiatives aimed at foreign populations. Zhao, "You minjian waijiao dao gonggong waijiao."

[17] Nicholas J. Cull, "How We Got Here," in *Toward a New Public Diplomacy: Redirecting U.S. Foreign Policy*, ed. Philip Seib (New York: Palgrave Macmillan, 2009), 23.

[18] Michael L. Krenn, *The History of United States Cultural Diplomacy: 1770 to the Present Day* (New York: Bloomsbury Academic, 2017), 1–2.

in town in the bilateral relationship – and less easily managed by the two governments, particularly on account of the PRC's insistence that exchanges be conducted exclusively by nongovernmental organizations (at least on the US side). This was a combination that at times alarmed the US government. Kissinger found impromptu meetings of Americans and Chinese during the first ping-pong trip to China unnerving, fearing that the table tennis players might undo the hard work that he and Nixon had put into opening secret backchannels to Beijing (when the reality was quite the opposite). During the remainder of his eight years in power, Kissinger retained his suspicion of nongovernmental involvement in the rapprochement. He initially attempted to have exchanges brought under the direct management of the State Department. The Chinese government rebuffed this suggestion, however, saying that contact between Chinese and American societies must remain unofficial for as long as the relationship between the two governments was not normalized. Normalization required Washington switching diplomatic recognition from its ally, the Republic of China (ROC) on Taiwan, to the Communist People's Republic on the Chinese mainland – a step the US government found hard to swallow during the 1970s. The PRC's position thus forced Kissinger to accept that the direct management of exchanges on the US side would have to be by nongovernmental organizations.

The two most important American nongovernmental organizations in exchange contacts with China of this period play a central role in this book's narrative. The National Committee on United States-China Relations (NCUSCR, or simply National Committee) and the Committee on Scholarly Communication with the People's Republic of China (CSCPRC, or the Committee on Scholarly Communication for short) were both founded in 1966.[19] The two Committees shared the common purpose of encouraging the American populace to have direct, personal contact with China. In the early 1970s, China initially favored continuing contacts with left-leaning American organizations and individuals as it had done in the 1950s and 1960s. Nonetheless, with US government assistance, both Committees came to be central to the Sino-American exchange program of the rapprochement era and together oversaw almost all of the most significant individual exchange visits of that decade, as well as a steady stream of lower profile trips.

---

[19] Originally known as the Committee on Scholarly Communication with Mainland China, and much later the Committee on Scholarly Communication with China.

The National Committee arranged "cultural" exchanges, a broad mandate that ran the gamut from groups of acrobats to journalists, an orchestra to delegations of local mayors and city officials. The Committee on Scholarly Communication facilitated cooperation between American and Chinese scientists and academics. Before 1979, this was achieved primarily through exchange visits, with the addition of some ongoing academic research and cooperation, such as the sharing of data and the joint authorship of research publications. Other US nongovernmental organizations were involved in exchange contacts with China during this period – and are accordingly featured in the chapters ahead – but none had as much influence on the changing nature of the overall Sino-American relationship as the National Committee and the Committee on Scholarly Communication.

One important reason for the influence of the NCUSCR and CSCPRC on that relationship was the support and privilege ultimately afforded to the two organizations by both the US and Chinese governments and the political importance their exchanges thus took on. Less than a year after Nixon's 1972 summit visit, the NCUSCR and CSCPRC had been designated by the US government as the two organizations responsible for a program of "facilitated exchanges," a designation briefly resisted but ultimately accepted by Beijing. As the following pages will show, this elevation of the two Committees was deeply political: they were selected for this important role because Washington trusted them to play a constructive role in building the rapprochement envisioned by Nixon and Kissinger. Their exchange visits were "facilitated" through yearly government-to-government negotiations over the broad contours of the program – including the total number of such visits – and through funding and advice to both organizations provided by the US government. Visits organized by other US nongovernmental groups were not included in this program of "facilitated exchanges" and did not receive US governmental support, although, as discussed below, any visit to the PRC in this period necessitated Chinese state involvement, and often gratis official hospitality.[20]

Before the Sino-American normalization of 1979, facilitated exchanges were the most formal contacts in an exchange program that

---

[20] A small number of exchanges overseen by the National Council for United States-China Trade were also considered "facilitated exchanges," and are discussed in this book. Exchange visits were only a limited aspect of the trade council's organizational remit, however.

was ostensibly conducted on an unofficial basis (with the exception of a handful of congressional delegations invited to China before 1978). The political involvement of both governments in these facilitated exchanges was both cause and consequence of their political importance: the visits overseen by the NCUSCR and CSCPRC were intended to be a corollary to the developing diplomatic relationship, and the success or otherwise of such visits therefore influenced the relationship between the two governments in a more direct manner than the exchanges organized outside of the facilitated exchange program (even as these, too, contributed to the thickening of the ties between the two countries). Recently declassified government documents from the Chinese and US governments reveal the extent to which both governments, recognizing the influence of nongovernmental actors in the rapprochement, sought to co-opt or control exchange organizations such as the NCUSCR and CSCPRC.

These efforts notwithstanding, *Improbable Diplomats* argues for the agency of these nongovernmental actors and their influence on the Sino-American relationship. The leadership of both the National Committee and the Committee on Scholarly Communication were broadly committed to the US government's central objective in its China policy throughout this period: improving relations with Beijing and realizing Sino-American normalization. (This is not to say, however, that this was either organization's primary objective or that either group formally lobbied for normalization.) This concord in long-term mission, however, did not stop the two Committees dissenting from official policy about the best means to achieve the goal of normalizing relations. Nor did it mean that the two organizations always agreed with American officials about what compromises were appropriate in order to develop ties with the PRC – indeed, this was sometimes a cause of significant dissent from within the ranks of the two groups. Thus, this book shows how these nongovernmental actors frequently took a different approach to the US government toward rebuilding the American relationship with China and argues that this constituted an alternative American approach to US-China relations in this formative decade.

While the NCUSCR and CSCPRC supported the overall objective of US foreign policy toward Beijing after 1972 – achieving normalization – the two organizations each had their own distinct individual missions. The goal of the National Committee on US-China Relations in this period was to bring as much of American society as possible into direct contact with China and the Chinese people.[21] That meant sending a diverse range of Americans to China and then receiving Chinese visitors – not only in Washington but also in Texas, Detroit, Memphis, and Williamsburg; not only in seats of power and at national institutions from Juilliard to Hollywood, but also in schools and at family dining tables.

The Committee on Scholarly Communication's objective was, like the National Committee's, promoting direct contact, but within the narrower and more specific constituency of scientists and academics. Moreover, while the CSCPRC, like the National Committee, believed that contact would build mutual understanding, the organization also sought a more tangible outcome: sharing scientific knowledge transnationally and thus advancing academic research in both countries. When contradictions emerged between governmental diplomacy and the NCUSCR or CSCPRC's own organizational missions – a not infrequent occurrence, this book will show – both nongovernmental groups proved willing and able to clash with Chinese and US officials to forward their own agendas, even if this brought tension into the diplomatic relationship.

If both organizations took as their core objective bringing a widening canvas of Americans into contact with China, the two groups were themselves elite and tightly knit. The National Committee was an invite-only organization that had only a few hundred members through the 1970s, carefully selected from the highest levels of American business, academia, media, industry, and public service. The Committee on Scholarly Communication was an even smaller organization: truly a committee, it consisted of a rotating membership or twenty or so high-ranking academicians and operated within the nongovernmental National Academy of Sciences (NAS), having been established by that organization in coordination with two other leading nongovernmental academic institutions, the American Council of Learned Societies (ACLS) and the Social Science Research Council (SSRC).

The National Committee and the Committee on Scholarly Communication were closely linked from an early stage: the chairman of the National Committee, for example, held a seat as an ex officio member of the Committee on Scholarly Communication, and, over the 1970s, a host of influential individuals from American academia, public policy circles, and industry

---

[21] As explored in the prologue, the NCUSCR was initially a public-education organization. The National Committee became focused on exchanges after hosting the return leg of the ping-pong diplomacy exchange in 1972.

were influential in both groups simultaneously. Together, then, the two Committees represented a core part of American civil society's engagement with China, even as they were far from mass organizations. Their activities appealed to a much broader audience – to the American scientific community at large, and to an even wider and diverse audience for cultural exchanges – but their social make-up conditioned how and why they interacted with China. (The elite status of the NCUSCR and CSCPRC was representative of a broader trend in early Sino-American exchange contacts: the leftist Committee of Concerned Asian Scholars made radical critiques of US Asian policy but was made up of academics trained at the best American universities, and even more ostensibly grass roots organizations such as the US-China Peoples Friendship Association knew that the prohibitive cost of their trips to China – which included a $500 mark-up to support the Association – "was hypocritical and contradictory" to the organization's attempts to "reach out to working class and minority peoples."[22])

Despite their high-profile role in building support for rapprochement, the National Committee, Committee on Scholarly Communication, and the exchange visits with China that they oversaw have been conspicuously absent from existing historical accounts of US-China relations in the 1970s. This has been in part due to the inaccessibility of the records of the two Committees: this book is the first to make a thorough use of the archival records of both organizations, much of which have only been made public in the last few years. Where cultural and scientific exchanges have been discussed in existing works on the Sino-American relations of the 1970s, the ties they constructed between the United States and China have been assumed to be derivative of the diplomatic relationship between the two governments.[23] By contrast, this book uses internal documents from both

---

[22] Fabio Lanza, *The End of Concern: Maoist China, Activism, and Asian Studies* (Durham, NC: Duke University Press, 2017), 86; George to National Steering Committee members, undated [but likely written soon after May 7, 1977], Folder 7, Box 1, US-China Peoples Friendship Association records (USCPFAR), New York Public Library Archives and Manuscripts Division (NYPLAMD), New York, United States.

[23] Such a depiction is explicit or implicit in many of the leading works on Sino-American relations in this period and the memoirs of many of the leading US government officials from that period. See, for example, Patrick Tyler, *A Great Wall: Six Presidents and China: An Investigative History* (New York: Public Affairs, 1999); James Mann, *About Face: A History of America's Curious Relationship with China from Nixon to Clinton* (New York: Alfred Knopf, 1999); Chris Tudda, *A Cold War Turning Point: Nixon and China, 1969–1972* (Baton Rouge, LA: Louisiana State University Press, 2012), especially 191–92; Henry Kissinger, *White House Years* (Boston, MA: Little, Brown and Company, 1979); Henry Kissinger, *Years of Upheaval* (London: Weidenfeld & Nicolson, 1982).

Committees, the personal papers of some of the leading individuals involved in the two organizations, and oral and written accounts of many of the exchange visits that they oversaw, to give a voice to these nongovernmental actors and the individual Americans that they sought to represent, and to show how cultural and scientific exchanges were far from simply derivative of the high-diplomatic Sino-American relationship.

Comprehensive statistics for the number of Chinese and American visitors to travel in each direction in the 1970s are not available. It is clear, however, that by the late 1970s, the flows of people were substantial: around 8,000 Americans traveled to China between 1972 and the end of 1974; in 1977 alone, 4,000 Americans visited the PRC and approximately 10,000 more traveled in 1978, the final year before normalized relations. This was an infinitesimally small proportion of those that sought to travel: the National Committee estimated that *several million* Americans had applied to visit China between 1971 and 1978.[24] The vast disparity between the number of people who sought and acquired visas was due to the extreme difficulties in gaining permission to enter China. The PRC government exclusively selected "influential individuals" for early travel, providing invitations only to public figures and those with an existing connection to the Chinese government or a recommendation from an organization with such a relationship – such as (but not exclusively) the NCUSCR or CSCPRC.[25] Thus, initially, most Americans and practically all Chinese traveled to the other country in organized delegations (with the significant exception of Chinese Americans who had preexisting ties to the PRC and could obtain permission for travel through family members who were PRC citizens). By the mid- to late-1970s, some Americans were making their way to China more or less under their own steam, with tourism resuming in the wake of Mao's death in 1976. Private Chinese travel to the United States was yet more

---

[24] The NCUSCR's documents held in the organization's offices in New York are not catalogued and organized only at document level. They are referenced as "NCUSCR office collection" (NCUSCROC). NCUSCR Annual Report, 1976–77, National Committee on United States-China Relations office collection, New York, United States; NCUSCR letter to members of women's volleyball delegation, May 22, 1978, Folder 91, Box 12, Series 3, Record Group (RG) 4, NCUSCR records, Rockefeller Archive Center, Sleepy Hollow, NY, United States (RAC); Mike Mansfield, *China: A Quarter Century after the Founding of the People's Republic: A Report* (Washington, DC: United States Government Printing Office, 1975), 29.

[25] Memcon: Yue and Yost, October 22, 1977, Folder 98, Box 13, Series 3, RG4, NCUSCR records, RAC.

limited: by 1975, the National Committee believed that only around 190 Chinese had traveled to the country on individual private visits, almost all on commercial business.[26]

In numerical terms, the NCUSCR and CSCPRC only facilitated the minority of travel by Americans to China or Chinese to the United States in the 1970s. This book does not attempt to offer a comprehensive history of travel between China and the United States in this period; instead, a focus on exchange visits allows us to explore in depth the most politically important contacts – and those that included many of the most remarkable Sino-American encounters. Nonetheless, both the NCUSCR and CSCPRC oversaw a substantial share of contacts in their respective fields. As of 1977, the Committee on Scholarly Communication had overseen 90 percent of the Chinese science delegations to the United States and 25 percent of such trips to China since 1972 (with many other trips also receiving direct assistance from the Committee).[27] Most of the CSCPRC's delegations had around a dozen participants and, by the end of 1978, the organization had overseen thirty American delegations that traveled to the PRC and thirty-seven Chinese delegations that traveled to the United States, together including more than 700 individual scientists.[28] It is harder to assess proportions of cultural exchanges: the category is broader, and such contacts were less regulated than scientific contacts and thus involved a wider array of American hosts and organizers.[29] The National Committee ran fewer but much larger exchanges than the Committee on Scholarly Communication and was directly or indirectly involved in the vast majority of the most high-profile cultural exchanges between the United States and China in this period. Between ping-pong diplomacy and normalization, the NCUSCR was involved in

---

[26] "Exchanges with the People's Republic of China," May 21, 1975, Folder 76, Box 6, Series 1, Douglas P. Murray papers (DPMP), RAC.

[27] CSCPRC working paper, "The importance of expanding US-China scientific and technical relations," March 23, 1977, "1977 – Exchange Agreement – Negotiations," Committee on Scholarly Communication with the PRC papers (CSCPRCP), National Academy of Sciences archives, Washington, DC, United States (NAS).

[28] *CEN*, Vol. 7, No. 1, February 1979; Zhou Peiyuan, *Zhou Peiyuan wenji* [Collected Works of Zhou Peiyuan] (Beijing: Daxue chubanshe, 2002), 438.

[29] The Chinese People's Association for Friendship with Foreign Countries, an ostensibly nongovernmental Chinese organization that oversaw some Sino-American cultural exchanges claims to have received "eight or nine American groups with about two hundred guests [in total]" in each of the years following 1972. Gu Zixin, "Why Your Devotion to People-to-People Diplomacy – An Interview with CPAFFC Vice President Li Xiaolin," *Voice of Friendship*, no. 4 (2005): 18–23.

sending nineteen delegations to China and receiving fourteen in the United States.[30] The number of participants in the trips organized by the group during this period together totaled 1,062, almost evenly split between 538 Americans traveling to China and 524 Chinese to the United States.[31]

As the exchange programs they managed grew over the course of the 1970s, so did the budgets of the two groups. In its first year managing exchange visits, the National Committee had $310,632 to spend on all programming; that year, the CSCPRC had a budget of $216,185.[32] By the mid-1970s, both groups were spending more than half a million dollars a year.[33] By 1978, the Committee on Scholarly Communication's budget growth had outpaced that of the NCUSCR; the group was expecting to have $1.5 million at its disposal the following year.[34] Hundreds of thousands of these dollars came from the government. The National Committee first accepted State Department funding in 1972 and, in the 1972–1973 financial year, received $76,600 in government funds, some 21 percent of the organization's income. In the 1977–1978 year, the group received some $290,000 in government support – 55 percent of its overall income.[35] The NCUSCR kept a balance between public support and funds raised privately. The organization had prided itself on its private fundraising in the 1960s and early 1970s – donations from large foundations, corporations, and individual donors – and, as will be discussed, only reluctantly began accepting state financial support; thus, until 1978, private funding outweighed support from the government.[36] The Committee on Scholarly Communication likewise combined funds from private and public sources, receiving hundreds of thousands of dollars of federal funding from the National Science Foundation and smaller amounts from the State Department, while also winning major grants from private philanthropic sources. National Science Foundation

[30] Of these, four trips had been assisted by the NCUSCR, rather than directly sponsored.
[31] "NCUSCR exchanges, 1972–79," September 14, 1979, Folder 16, Box 1, Series 1, DPMP, RAC.
[32] Provisional statement on income and expenditure for 1971–72, Folder 71, Box 6, Series 1, DPMP, RAC; Office of the NAS Foreign Secretary to NAS Council, October 15, 1972, "1972 – General," CSCPRCP, NAS.
[33] NCUSCR revenues and expenses, 1974–75, Folder 77, Box 6, Series 1, DPMP, RAC; Keatley, "Proposal for Partial Support of the CSCPRC," October 1974, "1974 – Request for funds," CSCPRCP, NAS.
[34] NAS council minutes, "Report of the foreign secretary," October 29, 1978, "1978 – Student Exchange Program – General," CSCPRCP, NAS.
[35] NCUSCR Annual Reports, 1972–73 and 1977–78, NCUSCROC.
[36] NCUSCR Annual Reports, 1977–78, NCUSCROC.

funding covered approximately half of the CSCPRC's operating costs between 1972 and 1975, with $775,000 in total funding from the Foundation in that period.[37] If we follow the money, we again come to the conclusion that the two Committees occupied a liminal position between the public and private.

The historical importance of the CSCPRC and NCUSCR to exchange contacts in this period went beyond just the visits that the two organizations directly oversaw. As the most influential and best-connected nongovernmental organizations focused on Sino-American exchanges, both Committees took an active interest in contacts between the Chinese and American populations more broadly, negotiating with both governments the structure and substance of all Sino-American exchanges, as well as actively promoting and publicizing exchanges that were not under their direct remit. As we shall see, their role in doing so was sometimes challenged by other American organizations and individuals. Nonetheless, in part because both governments came to look to the two Committees as the primary representatives of those Americans that did and might travel to China, they exercised a powerful influence on the overall landscape of Sino-American exchange contacts before normalization.

Despite the Chinese government's insistence that the US government not directly manage American participation in people-to-people exchange, the top leadership of the Beijing government was deeply involved in exchange diplomacy. Premier Zhou Enlai and even Chairman Mao himself were sometimes directly involved in critical decisions about Sino-American exchanges, although for the most part the management of these contacts was delegated to a range of institutions that broadly mirrored the division of labor between American exchange organizations – but that had little of the independence of US nongovernmental groups. The NCUSCR's counterpart organization was the Chinese People's Institute of Foreign Affairs, the main function of which was receiving politically important visitors.[38] The CSCPRC worked with the Scientific and Technical Association of the PRC (STAPRC) and the Chinese Academy of Sciences (CAS). The Scientific and Technical Association of the PRC was formed in 1958

---

[37] Hughes to Proxmire, May 13, 1975, "1975 – Inquiries," CSCPRC, NAS.
[38] Priscilla Roberts, "Bringing the Chinese Back In: The Role of Quasi-Private Institutions in Britain and the United States," in *China, Hong Kong, and the Long 1970s: Global Perspectives*, ed. Priscilla Roberts and Odd Arne Westad (Cham: Palgrave Macmillan, 2017), 307.

through a merger of China's scientific societies and its membership consisted of all such organizations, with a national-level leadership of 100
members. Given the political importance of exchanges, other relevant
organs of the Chinese government often played a role in Sino-American
exchanges too, including the International Department of the CCP Central Committee, which was tasked with winning influential friends for the
PRC abroad, in particular among leftists.[39]

Exchange contacts overseen by other American organizations are also
examined in the pages ahead. These include cultural exchanges arranged
through left-leaning groups such as the US-China Peoples Friendship
Association (USCPFA) and the Committee of Concerned Asian Scholars (CCAS), commercial contacts facilitated by the National Council for
United States-China Trade (NCUSCT) that was founded in 1973, and
congressional delegations, or CoDels, that were the only form of regular official, government-sponsored exchanges before 1978. These other
organizations and their constituencies encouraged contact with China
for reasons that sometimes overlapped with and sometimes differed from
those of the NCUSCR and the CSCPRC. Some organizations – particularly the Friendship Association and the Committee of Concerned Asian
Scholars – also overtly challenged the centrality of the elite-led NCUSCR
and CSCPRC in the most politically symbolic of exchanges and their
cooperation with the US government, as analyzed in the pages below.
Two of these organizations – the Committee of Concerned Asian Scholars
and the National Council for United States-China Trade – have been the
subject of recent dedicated studies, by Fabio Lanza and Christian Talley,
respectively.[40] *Improbable Diplomats* does not seek to duplicate these
valuable works or to offer a comprehensive history of all US nongovernmental organizations involved in exchanges with China, although the
book does seek to reveal the varied texture of Sino-American exchange
in this period and give some sense of the experiences of Americans and

[39] Shanghai People's Publishing House, "Jiedai Meiguo 'Zhongguo Shukan She' zongjingli
Hengli Nuoyisi qingkuang tongbao" [Briefing on reception of Henry Noyce, general
manager of US China Books and Periodicals], May 27, 1975, Folder B244-3-657-42,
SHMA; Julia Lovell, "The Uses of Foreigners in Mao-Era China: 'Techniques of Hospitality' and International Image-Building in the People's Republic, 1949–1976," *Transactions of the Royal Historical Society* 25 (2015): 141.
[40] Lanza, *End of Concern*; Christian Talley, *Forgotten Vanguard: Informal Diplomacy
and the Rise of United States-China Trade, 1972–1980* (Notre Dame, IN: University of
Notre Dame Press, 2018).

Chinese participating in exchange visits irrespective of host or sender; it is the first book to attempt to do so.[41]

POSITIONING EXCHANGE DIPLOMACY WITHIN
AN HISTORIOGRAPHICAL CONTEXT

The summitry and high-diplomacy of the Sino-American relationship has been the subject of many detailed and compelling studies, initially by political scientists and then, too, by historians. *Improbable Diplomats* is not seeking to replicate the rich work already completed by both Western and Chinese historians: it is not another history of rapprochement exclusively or even primarily from the perspective of the White House or the Chinese Foreign Ministry. This book primarily seeks to expand upon this existing historiography, adding a further layer to previous narratives focused on high diplomacy.[42] Nonetheless, by examining Sino-American diplomacy that took place below the level of summit diplomacy, this book also reveals limitations in the arguments of existing works. One such limitation is the overwhelming emphasis placed on the importance of grand strategy and anti-Soviet "triangular diplomacy" in forging Sino-American relations. Diplomatic historians have argued that Sino-American rapprochement was motivated by the need for both Washington and Beijing to gain leverage over Moscow. This book shows that there are limitations to such an explanation for changes in the US-China relationship in the 1970s: while fear of the Soviet threat motivated both sides to begin rapprochement (although in fact Nixon was as interested in Beijing's help ending the Vietnam War, and Chinese

---

[41] Perhaps the book that comes closest to this is He Hui's recent study in Chinese, though He takes a substantially different approach to my own. He Hui, *Dangdai Zhong Mei minjian jiaoliu shi: 1969–2008 nian* [Contemporary Chinese and American Folk Exchange History (1969–2008)] (Beijing: Kexue chubanshe, 2017).

[42] Some of the best international histories of the rapprochement include Harry Harding, *A Fragile Relationship: The United States and China since 1972* (Washington, DC: Brookings Institution, 1992); Robert Ross, *Negotiating Cooperation: The United States and China, 1969–1989* (Stanford, CA: Stanford University Press, 1995); William Kirby, Robert Ross, and Gong Li, eds., *Normalization of U.S.-China Relations: An International History* (Cambridge, MA: Harvard University Asia Center, 2007); Chen Jian, *Mao's China and the Cold War* (Chapel Hill, NC: University of North Carolina Press, 2001); MacMillan, *Seize the Hour*; Robert Ross and Jiang Changbin, eds., *Re-Examining the Cold War: U.S.-China Diplomacy, 1954–1973* (Cambridge, MA: Harvard University Press, 2001); Xia, *Negotiating with the Enemy*; Evelyn Goh, *Constructing the U.S. Rapprochement with China, 1961–1974: From "Red Menace" to "Tacit Ally"* (Cambridge: Cambridge University Press, 2004); Tudda, *Cold War Turning Point*.

leaders in US withdrawal from Taiwan), it does little to explain the development of the Sino-American relationship from 1972 through 1978.[43]

After all, first contact immediately achieved what both sides most fundamentally wanted in their relationship with Moscow: Nixon won a May
1972 meeting with Soviet leader Leonid Brezhnev that solidified détente,
and Mao ensured there would be no US collusion in a Soviet attack on the
PRC – and even pocketed the suggestion of American military assistance in
China's struggle against Moscow, as well as the sharing of classified intelligence by Kissinger. As the following chapters will document, after 1972,
Kissinger continued his attempts to build the Sino-American relationship on
a foundation of collusion against Moscow. But this did not work. Mao and
Zhou had other objectives in seeking rapprochement that had no connection
to the Soviets – most notably US withdrawal from Taiwan – and they told
Kissinger as much. Anti-Soviet security collaboration again helped bring
progress in 1978 under Deng and Zbigniew Brzezinski, but we nonetheless
need to look elsewhere to explain nearly seven years of meandering Sino-
American high-level negotiations – but significantly developing ties in other
areas of the relationship – between Nixon's 1972 summit and the normalization agreement of December 1978. One important factor to consider
alongside these waxing and waning talks is the exchange program and the
transnational relationship between the Chinese and American people.

Western historians are not alone in having focused on grand strategy
and high-level politics as the drivers of rapprochement: Chinese historians of Sino-American relations such as Xia Yafeng, Yang Kuisong, and
Chen Jian have done so, too. These historians have seen Mao, Zhou,
and Deng as exercising near-total control over Chinese foreign policy
and have thus focused their attention on understanding the motivations
of these leaders. *Improbable Diplomats* does not dispute this characterization of decision-making in Beijing. In fact, it offers a further example of
this control in the form of the Chinese government's active involvement
in exchange contacts and Beijing's attempts to ensure that exchanges
served the PRC's foreign policy ends.[44]

---

[43] Among the many works that place anti-Soviet collusion at the center of their explanation for rapprochement are Ross, *Negotiating Cooperation*; MacMillan, *Seize the Hour*;
Tyler, *A Great Wall*; Mann, *About Face*.

[44] Kuisong Yang and Yafeng Xia, "Vacillating between Revolution and Détente: Mao's
Changing Psyche and Policy toward the United States, 1969–1976," *Diplomatic History*
34, no. 2 (April 2010): 395–423; Chen, *Mao's China and the Cold War*. Xia also focuses
on high-level talks in his comprehensive account of the Sino-American Warsaw talks.
Xia, *Negotiating with the Enemy*.

A few early studies of the Sino-American relationship have looked beyond highpolitics to consider the role of the broader American populace in rapprochement. Richard Madsen and Harry Harding highlighted the role that US civil society played in supporting rapprochement and speculated that Chinese leaders' engagement with the United States was also partially motivated by a desire to restore economic and social contacts between the two countries. American groups that had a long-standing historical connection to China played a particular role: missionaries, Sinologists, and businessmen who had been involved in trade with pre-revolution China. Madsen, Harding, and Evelyn Goh have shown how, together, these groups helped shift public discourse from seeing Communist China as an implacable enemy to perceiving the PRC as a modernizing country with which the United States could establish a mutually beneficial relationship, a point explored further in this book's prologue. Madsen argues that Nixon understood (even if Kissinger did not) that this process of changing American public perception of China must continue beyond his summit: "A successful geopolitical gambit between top government officials would have to become a successful encounter between ... two hitherto estranged peoples."[45]

In recent years, scholarly interest in how rapprochement was encouraged and experienced by the American and Chinese populace has increased. Xu Guoqi has offered the broadest consideration of this experience in his study of that relationship over the longue durée (although the breadth of Xu's study means that only a part of one chapter of his book covers the 1970s), while He Hui has provided a useful Chinese-language account of Sino-American people-to-people contacts from 1969 through 2008.[46] One theme present in Xu's work but explored in greater detail by other scholars has been American fascination with the elusive China market. As also recently explored by Christian Talley and Kazushi Minami, rapprochement took American businessmen back to China alongside the country's diplomats and reawakened the dream that Chinese consumption would make Americans rich. There was a political importance to this trade, too, as will be discussed in this book.

---

[45] Both Harding and in particular Madsen recognize the NCUSCR as a critical locus of these groups efforts to change perceptions of China and, in turn, US China policy. Harding, *Fragile Relationship*, 4–5; Richard Madsen, *China and the American Dream: A Moral Inquiry* (Berkeley, CA: University of California Press, 1995), 63, 68; Goh, *Constructing the U.S. Rapprochement with China*, 4.

[46] Xu Guoqi, *Chinese and Americans: A Shared History* (Cambridge, MA: Harvard University Press, 2014); He, *Dangdai Zhong Mei minjian jiaoliu shi*.

Talley calls trade a "diplomatic backchannel" and argues that promoting commercial exchange required actors beyond the two governments: "formal diplomacy, especially in light of the lack of diplomatic recognition, was underequipped to handle the multifaceted problems of the Sino-American relationship. To realize the full benefits of rapprochement, the United States would have to look to nontraditional forms of diplomacy to grapple with ... issues, including the question of bilateral trade."[47] As this book shows, a similar dynamic was at work in cultural and scientific exchanges.

If politics and trade were connected, other nongovernmental interactions had a more obvious political importance. These included contacts with China overseen by what Priscilla Roberts calls "quasi-private" US institutions such as the Council on Foreign Relations and the NCUSCR or the role of American and other "foreign friends" who were resident in the PRC and who also, as explored by Beverley Hooper and Brady, played a role in the Sino-American transnational contacts of the 1970s.[48] Gordon H. Chang's recent survey of Sino-American history also reflects the historiographical trend toward recognizing Sino-American relations beyond those between the two governments, although Chang includes the period of 1971 through 1978 in what he calls a "great interregnum" in the relationship for the first thirty years of the PRC's history. Chang states that there were only "a few rare exceptions" to the total lack of contact between the two sides during that period.[49] As this book will show, this characterization underplays, among other interactions, the active exchange of contact that took place in the eight years after ping-pong diplomacy. If there was an interregnum in Sino-American contact, this

---

[47] Talley, *Forgotten Vanguard*, 3, 44; Kazushi Minami, "Oil for the Lamps of America? Sino-American Oil Diplomacy, 1973–1979," *Diplomatic History* 41, no. 5 (2017): 959–84.

[48] I argue that the term "quasi-private" overemphasizes the role of the state in these groups. As discussed in the following pages, at least the NCUSCR (and the CSCPRC, too, an organization not examined by Roberts) were private organizations that were supported by, and worked with, the government, but were not compelled to answer to official backers and often dissented from government policy. One of the subsidiary arguments of this book, as discussed in the conclusion, is that such a relationship with the state is not in fact remarkable for a nongovernmental organization that has relevance to government policy. Nonetheless, Roberts's recognition of these organizations' ties to the state is an important point recognized in this work. Roberts, "Bringing the Chinese Back In"; Hooper, *Foreigners under Mao*; Brady, *Making the Foreign Serve China*.

[49] Gordon H. Chang, *Fateful Ties: A History of America's Preoccupation with China* (Cambridge, MA: Harvard University Press, 2015), 203.

book suggests a more appropriate periodization would be 1950 through 1971 – although, as the prologue shows (and Chang acknowledges), even that period saw some level of contact between the two societies. This book draws on these recent studies of the connection between nongovernmental institutions and rapprochement. While pathbreaking, none of these works have offered a full account of the cultural and scientific exchange program of the 1970s, nor combined non-state and governmental sources to trace the direct and interactive connection between high-level and exchange diplomacy, as this book seeks to do.

Other recent scholarly interest in nongovernmental, transnational contact between the United States and China in the 1970s and before has focused on political radicals, whether students and scholars critical of the Vietnam War or Black activists looking for an example of revolutionary praxis. As explored in detail in the prologue, political radicals were effectively the only Americans to have access to the PRC in the 1950s and 1960s and, as the following chapters will document, were still favored by Beijing as rapprochement began in 1971 and 1972. However, the priorities of Chinese foreign policy changed markedly from 1972 onwards, with Beijing transferring its patronage to politically centrist American elites in order to cultivate support for Sino-American rapprochement among the broad American populace. The body of the book then takes up where studies of radical engagement with China by Fabio Lanza, Robeson Taj Frazier, and others turn to epilogue and thus documents the next phase of Sino-American transnational contact that followed the revolutionary decade of the 1960s.[50]

The uptick in the number of transnational histories of Sino-American relations reflects recent broader interest in such a methodology felt, for example, in studies of US foreign relations and of Sino-European relations.[51] This growing transnational historiography offers several

[50] Lanza, *End of Concern*; Robeson Taj Frazier, *The East Is Black: Cold War China in the Black Radical Imagination* (Durham, NC: Duke University Press, 2015); Matthew D. Johnson, "From Peace to the Panthers: PRC Engagement with African-American Transnational Networks, 1949–1979," *Past & Present* 218, Supplement 8 (January 2013): 233–57. For earlier works on this subject, see David Caute, *The Fellow-Travellers: Intellectual Friends of Communism*, revised edition (London: Yale University Press, 1988); Paul Hollander, *Political Pilgrims: Travels of Western Intellectuals to the Soviet Union, China, and Cuba, 1928–1978* (New York: University Press of America, 1990).
[51] Meredith Oyen, *The Diplomacy of Migration: Transnational Lives and the Making of U.S.-Chinese Relations in the Cold War* (Ithaca, NY: Cornell University Press, 2015), 8; Romano and Zanier, "Circumventing the Cold War."

important insights that are useful when considering the case study of Sino-American relations in the 1970s. The first of these concerns defining "exchanges." As discussed above, this was the contemporary term for cross-border visits that was employed by the protagonists of the coming chapters. As Paul Kramer has highlighted in his examination of US student exchanges in the twentieth century, not all exchanges were equal, however; instead, many were "deeply asymmetrical."[52] Indeed, imbalances in the exchange program were a wellspring of tension in Sino-American relations. China favored symmetry in exchanges – when they sent biologists, they expected to receive biologists – but Americans resented the corollary of this: the PRC's refusal to receive the Americans that most wanted to travel to China, while sending delegation after delegation of those Chinese that would gain most from visits to the United States.[53] As the following chapters will discuss in detail, these differing interpretations of what was being exchanged for what were a cause of a simmering tension through the 1970s – tension that sometimes erupted into open confrontation. Nonetheless, the term is also a useful reminder that, even as interactions included hierarchies and imbalances, they were also intended to be reciprocal and of mutual benefit. This fundamental assumption, held by Chinese and American actors alike, underpinned the logic of the Sino-American exchange program – including complaints about its sometimes-lopsided benefits.[54]

Perhaps the most important recent debate within transnational historiography has been over the role of the state in nongovernmental contacts. Transnational history was originally set against the power of the state. Early work in the field offered a corrective against classical diplomatic history that had portrayed relations between countries as dominated entirely by governments. Transnational historians showed that, in fact, relationships between societies – but also between states – are determined by a much broader and more diverse range of actors. More recently, historians in this field have acknowledged that this influence

---

[52] Paul Kramer, "Is the World Our Campus? International Students and U.S. Global Power in the Long Twentieth Century," *Diplomatic History* 33, no. 5 (November 2009): 779.

[53] As with many aspects of their approach to exchanges, this approach may have been learned from the Soviets, who also favored "mechanically observed" equality in Sino-Soviet exchanges – even in areas in which the two sides have vastly diverging expertise. Austin Jersild, *The Sino-Soviet Alliance: An International History* (Chapel Hill, NC: University of North Carolina Press, 2014), 197.

[54] Christina Klein, *Cold War Orientalism: Asia in the Middlebrow Imagination, 1945–1961* (Berkeley, CA: University of California Press, 2003), 13.

runs both ways: if nongovernmental actors can influence state-to-state relations, governments also hold sway over private cross-border relationships between civil society groups, businesses, and nongovernmental organizations. This dynamic is powerfully clear in the Cold War-era cultural diplomacy of both the United States and the PRC, as further explored in this book's prologue.[55] This argument for the influence of governments on transnational contacts is not a reversion to the previous assumption that governments are omnipotent in international relations. Instead, it is a recognition of the simultaneous agency of state and non-state actors; that, in the words of Andrew Preston and Doug Rossinow's leading recent text in this field, "governments and nonstate actors were never sealed off from one another in the modern world."[56] Or, as Penny Von Eschen wrote in another field-defining handbook, "we need to consider state, non-state, and transnational formations and actors as intersecting and rarely, if ever, entirely independent entities."[57]

States always hold influence over transnational contacts, then. But not all states hold the same level of influence. This is certainly true in the case of the Sino-American contacts of the 1970s. The US and Chinese governments took two very different approaches to their people's contacts with the other society. The US government, this book shows, was deeply interested in exchange and other nongovernmental contacts with China. Nonetheless, many of those working in the State Department believed that these contacts would be most productive if non-state actors were afforded meaningful (although not total) independence – even if this pained the ever-controlling Kissinger. After Kissinger's departure from office, even Carter's National Security Advisor, Zbigniew Brzezinski, shared this belief in the value of distance between government and exchange organizations.

---

[55] Krenn, *United States Cultural Diplomacy*, in particular, for example, p. 129.
[56] Quotation from Andrew Preston and Douglas Rossinow, "Introduction," in *Outside in: The Transnational Circuitry of U.S. History*, ed. Andrew Preston and Douglas Rossinow (New York: Oxford University Press, 2017), abstract to electronic version of chapter; Thomas Risse-Kappen, "Introduction," in *Bringing Transnational Relations Back In: Non-State Actors, Domestic Structures and International Institutions*, ed. Thomas Risse-Kappen (Cambridge: Cambridge University Press, 1995), 3–33; Thomas W. Zeiler, "The Diplomatic History Bandwagon: A State of the Field," *The Journal of American History* 95, no. 4 (2009): 1053–73; C. A. Bayly et al., "AHR Conversation: On Transnational History," *The American Historical Review* 111, no. 5 (January 12, 2006): 1441–64.
[57] Penny Von Eschen, "Locating the Transnational in the Cold War," in *The Oxford Handbook of the Cold War*, ed. Richard H Immerman and Petra Goedde (Oxford: Oxford University Press, 2013), 458.

The Chinese government did not share this view. While American transnational contacts with the PRC were with Chinese organizations somewhat distant from the central nucleus of state power, these Chinese groups were nonetheless indisputably under the control of PRC leaders and had little real autonomy. In accordance with Thomas Risse-Kappen's widely cited, foundational definition of transnational relations – "regular interactions across national boundaries when at least one actor is a non-state agent or does not operate on behalf of a national government" – the Sino-American exchange contacts of the 1970s were transnational. Moreover, in many ways, exchanges had close similarities with other classic contemporary examples of transnational contact: the (re)building of epistemic communities between Chinese and American scientists but also other skilled professionals – educators, journalists, and others – bore similarities with similar Soviet-American transnational interactions analyzed by Matthew Evangelista, for example.[58] But Sino-American exchange diplomacy was also a case of transnational contact in which the importance of the state is powerfully clear, and where there was, on the Chinese side, little distinction between governmental and nongovernmental actors.[59] This work thus draws on Meredith Oyen's insight that we should recognize the "importance of ... state-to-people relations as well" when examining diplomacy.[60] State-to-state, state-to-people, people-to-state, and people-to-people contacts all played a role in Sino-American exchange diplomacy in the 1970s.

Exchange visits and transnational contact have often been assumed to help build understanding and friendship between countries – an idea encouraged by organizations that facilitate such contact and are eager for funding and support. Studies of transnational contacts, however, have shown that the historical reality has rarely been so simple.[61] Direct

---

[58] Matthew Evangelista, "Transnational Organizations and the Cold War," in *The Cambridge History of the Cold War*, ed. Melvyn P. Leffler and Odd Arne Westad, vol. 3 (Cambridge: Cambridge University Press, 2010), 400–21; Matthew Evangelista, *Unarmed Forces: The Transnational Movement to End the Cold War* (Ithaca, NY: Cornell University Press, 1999).

[59] Risse-Kappen, "Bringing Transnational Relations Back In," 3.

[60] Oyen, *Diplomacy of Migration*, 248.

[61] Sam Lebovic, "From War Junk to Educational Exchange: The World War II Origins of the Fulbright Program and the Foundations of American Cultural Globalism, 1945–1950," *Diplomatic History* 37, no. 2 (April 2013): 280–312; Deborah Cohn, "'In between Propaganda and Escapism': William Faulkner as Cold War Cultural Ambassador," *Diplomatic History* 40, no. 3 (2016): 392–420; Matt Loayza, "'A Curative and

experience of endemic and violent racism, for example, alienated people of color on exchange visits from the Third World to the United States in the 1950s and 1960s (even as other aspects of US society impressed them).[62] This book will argue that the experience of Sino-American exchange left a similarly complex impression on visitors in both directions. Undertaken with the same lofty but sincerely held goals as other exchange programs, transnational contact excited Americans and Chinese and did often help the two peoples garner a more accurate understanding of the other. But this heightened awareness revealed differences as often as it did commonalities, and greater interaction also brought conflict. Indeed, this book argues that Sino-American transnational contact did not automatically breed empathy or cooperation: in many cases, contact confirmed stereotypes or misperceptions of the other – and increased confidence that such views were justified – and fed narratives of societal superiority on both sides. Exchanges were at their most constructive when carefully planned and coordinated between organizers in both countries who trusted one another and were prepared to speak frankly about the differences between the United States and China (and, even then, were not always smooth sailing). The implications of this for the contemporary Sino-American relationship will be reflected on in the conclusion of the book.

Improbable Diplomats draws together tools and insights from the cutting edge of the methodologies of transnational history and of international and diplomatic history. Indeed, the book seeks to demonstrate that these fields – overlapping in subject matter but often with contesting analytical interpretations – are, in fact, productively compatible. This is also the argument of Preston and Rossinow's state-of-the-field work. "At their most fundamental level," that work posits, "both international history and transnational history focus on topics that both cross and transcend national borders. The key difference between them is that, while international history privileges relations among states, transnational history examines relations among peoples below the state level."[63]

Creative Force': The Exchange of Persons Program and Eisenhower's Inter-American Policies, 1953–1961," *Diplomatic History* 37, no. 5 (November 2013): 946–70; Klein, *Cold War Orientalism*; Jessica C. E. Gienow-Hecht, "The World Is Ready to Listen: Symphony Orchestras and the Global Performance of America," *Diplomatic History* 36, no. 1 (January 2012): 17–28.

[62] Kramer, "Is the World Our Campus?"; Mary L. Dudziak, *Cold War Civil Rights: Race and the Image of American Democracy* (Princeton, NJ: Princeton University Press, 2000), 59–60.

[63] Preston and Rossinow, "Introduction," 4.

In recognition of the synergy between transnational and international history, this book declines to privilege either relations among states or those between peoples. Instead, it examines the interactive connection between these two tracks of diplomacy.

This is an approach that also draws on insights from scholarship on China's relationship with the outside world. In particular, it has been argued that the Chinese term *waishi* (外事) has a different, broader meaning than its typical English translation, "foreign affairs." *Waishi* incorporates not only the actions of governments but also of citizens. It includes a range of interactions with those outside of China, including contact that takes place within the spatial confines of the country's borders – not least, exchange visits such as those considered in this book. The concept of *waishi* thus avoids a hard distinction between official, state-to-state foreign policy and a society's broader relationship with other societies. In accordance with this idea, this book will emphasize the continuum and connections between interactions with the outside world by governments and their citizens and posits a deep connection between high-level governmental diplomacy and transnational interactions via exchanges.[64]

SOURCES AND AN OVERVIEW OF THE TEXT

Improbable Diplomats draws upon records from nearly twenty archives from across the United States and China, combining documents from government archives with an array of sources that shed light on the role of the exchange organizations and individuals that are at the center of this narrative. As previously mentioned, the vast majority of documents from the NCUSCR and CSCPRC, and from the personal papers of individuals connected to these two organizations, have not yet been examined by historians; many of these documents have only recently been made available for research. Governmental and nongovernmental documents have been supplemented with oral history interviews with leading figures who served in both nongovernmental groups, with some of the earliest American visitors to the PRC, and with US government officials who oversaw Washington's approach to exchange diplomacy with China.

---

[64] Brady, *Making the Foreign Serve China*, xii.

If it is worth emphasizing the quantity of the previously unused documentary material available while researching this book, it is also necessary to be frank about what evidence we still lack. The Chinese Foreign Ministry archive, while now re-opened after a multi-year closure, has available only a tiny fraction of the documents that were accessible a decade ago, and none on the Sino-American relations of the 1970s. To circumvent the restrictions on using the Foreign Ministry collection, this book draws upon documents from Chinese provincial and municipal archives that have been comparatively better stocked. In recent years, even these archives have been removing material – including some that was available at the time of research for this book. Until this trend is reversed, our understanding of the Chinese government's approach to relations with the United States in the 1970s will remain partial and incomplete.[65]

This is not to say, however, that we cannot gain significant insight into this topic from Chinese archival sources. Indeed, exchange contacts are one of the few areas of China's foreign relations of the 1970s that can be examined using Chinese archival sources still available after the reclassification of the vast majority of Foreign Ministry archive material: while it is no longer possible to gain access to the sort of internal, high-level documents held at that archive, the records of local archives do provide substantial insight into interactions between Chinese and Americans on the ground during exchange visits. Moreover, many additional relevant Chinese-language primary sources are available in published form. These sources include government documents and transcripts published in primary source collections (*nianpu, wenxuan, nianbian, wenji*, etc.) and in memoirs of high-level policymakers and other actors such as the scientist Zhou Peiyuan.

Improbable Diplomats is composed of six main chapters, as well as a prologue and an epilogue. They are organized in chronological order. The prologue introduces the history of Sino-American people-to-people contacts before 1969, as well as the broader context of the PRC and US approach to exchange diplomacy during the Cold War. The prologue concludes with an examination of the context in which the National Committee and Committee on Scholarly Communication were founded in 1966. The following three chapters of the book cover the Nixon years; the fourth and fifth, Ford's presidency; and the

---

[65] All direct quotations from Chinese-language archival and other sources in the text are the author's translation, unless otherwise stated.

sixth, the period between Carter's entry to office and, just under two years later, the final agreement of normalization. An epilogue examines the impact that the normalization agreement of 1978 had on deepening Sino-American cultural and scientific exchanges into the 1980s and beyond. *Improbable Diplomats'* broadly chronological narrative underscores the central assertion of this work: that the development of exchange and high-level diplomacy were codependent, with influence flowing between these two tracks of diplomacy in different directions at different times.

Chapter 1 reveals the popular origins of the Nixon–Mao summit. It argues that people-to-people diplomacy and non-state actors made a critical contribution to the beginning of rapprochement in 1971. Private US organizations, chief among them the NCUSCR, helped change American minds about the need for engagement with the PRC, and thereafter people-to-people interactions were the first means by which direct contact between China and the United States resumed – through ping-pong diplomacy but also a raft of other 1971 visits by American scientists, students, and ideologically motivated travelers.

Ping-pong diplomacy did not end with the US team's 1971 trip to China, even if most historical accounts of the phenomenon do. A year after American and Chinese table tennis players broke the ice in Sino-American relations, the two teams faced off again – this time in the United States. This ping-pong return leg is at the heart of Chapter 2, which shows how the first exchange delegation sent by the PRC to the United States helped transform Nixon and Mao's secret diplomacy into a broader rapprochement between Chinese and US societies. That chapter further reveals how the success of the ping-pong return leg underpinned the effort by the hosts of the table tennis players – the National Committee – to convince both governments to recognize their organization and their allies at the Committee on Scholarly Communication as the foremost American conduits for managing US exchanges with China. The chapter concludes with a connected development: the creation of a third nongovernmental organization to manage Sino-American societal contacts, the National Council for United States-China Trade.

The high watermark in the Sino-American relationship during the Kissinger era came in 1973 with the creation of "liaison offices," or de facto embassies, in each capital. Chapter 3 reveals that – in cause, conception, and execution – liaison offices were a direct outgrowth of the exchange relationship. Other new milestones in that relationship were also set in 1973, not least during the visit of the largest cultural delegation yet to travel to the PRC: the Philadelphia Orchestra. However, 1973 also saw the first signs of new tensions in exchange diplomacy as lingering Sino-American disagreements about Cambodia and Taiwan, as well as turbulent Chinese domestic politics, led to confrontations in cultural contacts and during a Congressional delegation to China led by Senator Warren Magnuson.

Chapter 4 considers the tensions in exchange diplomacy felt in the wake of the Watergate scandal and Nixon's resignation and replacement by Gerald Ford. Ford lacked domestic political authority and thus was unable to find the negotiating flexibility necessary to achieve a normalization deal. The resulting deadlock in high-diplomatic negotiations was one cause of stasis and conflict over cultural exchanges in 1974 and 1975, culminating in the last-minute cancellation of a tour by a famous Chinese performing arts troupe, news that made the front pages of US newspapers. Chapter 4 also examines the more gradual accumulation of tension in exchanges arising from American resentment at tight controls on visitors to China and Chinese resentment at impolitic behavior by American guests, ranging from photographing evidence of Chinese "backwardness" to drunken brawls.

Despite these conflicts in the exchange program, Ford hoped to use exchange diplomacy as one means to realize a successful summit trip to China in 1975. Chapter 5 shows, however, that this tactic proved largely unsuccessful: Ford's primary interlocutor, Deng Xiaoping, was uninterested in expanding cultural ties before an improvement in the diplomatic relationship – even if the vice premier could not hide his interest in deeper scientific cooperation with the United States. Deng and his colleagues' growing interest in US science and technology was already well known to American scientists and, while Ford and Kissinger declined to exploit this interest toward political ends, the Committee on Scholarly Communication advocated that the United States must demand something more in return for the benefits that China was gaining from scientific exchange with the United States.

Chapter 6 analyzes how just such a demand was central to the Jimmy Carter administration's successful realization of normalization. Carter hired the Committee on Scholarly Communication's chairman and staff director, and this recruitment helps explain the seamless cooperation between the White House and that organization in the Carter era. This cooperation, Chapter 6 shows, helped achieve a simultaneous upgrading of the scientific and diplomatic relationship with China in

1978 that offered a final demonstration of the symbiotic relationship between exchange and high-level Sino-American diplomacy in the pre-normalization era.

The book's epilogue briefly considers the new era that followed the 1979 establishment of official diplomatic ties. The epilogue argues, however, that there were as many continuities as changes between pre- and post-normalization exchanges and that the legacies of the Sino-American exchange diplomacy of the 1970s continued to be felt in the decades that followed, and into our own time.

Prologue

Chinese and US Cold War Era Exchange Diplomacy before the Nixon Era

At the conclusion of his 1972 visit to China, President Nixon reflected on how his trip had helped end "22 years of hostility" between the United States and China. Nixon was of course right that the two governments had been, up until his entry to office, in a state of confrontation that began with Americans and Chinese killing one another on the battlefields of Korea and then sunk into a state of wary Cold War opposition. But the hostility between the two governments had not prevented there being a limited amount of intense contact between a small number of Americans and the People's Republic of China during this period. Indeed, some Americans, attracted to the PRC's brand of socialism and courted by its government, had not only spent months traveling in China but had found themselves living there for years, even decades.[1]

This chapter traces the history of visits and transnational contact between Americans and China before 1971, showing how this earlier contact acted as a precursor to the far more numerous and frequent – but in other ways not wholly dissimilar – exchange visits of the 1970s. The chapter also places these Sino-American contacts in two broader contexts: the PRC's overall people-to-people and exchange diplomacy before 1971, and the role of cultural exchanges in the Cold War-era

---

[1] These Americans are not the focus of this prologue or book, although some of their activities are discussed in the pages below. This is in recognition of, as Beverley Hooper argues, their very different experience to exchange and other short-term visitors to China, as well as the more developed historiography on these contacts. As Hooper reports, the long-term American and other Western residents of Mao's China saw little affinity with even compatriots on such short-term visits; they were, indeed, situated in a different category of China's foreign relations. Hooper, *Foreigners under Mao*, especially 6.

foreign relations of the United States. The chapter reviews a substantial historiography that demonstrates that the governments of both the PRC and the United States saw exchanges as a critical part of their country's relations with the outside world before 1971. This necessarily ascribed importance to Chinese and American actors beyond officials, although, as will be explored, both states – especially the PRC – sought to control and influence the individuals involved in exchange contacts. The chapter concludes with a section detailing the context in which, in the mid-1960s, the National Committee on US-China Relations and the Committee on Scholarly Communication with Mainland China (later the Committee on Scholarly Communication with the PRC) were founded.

US-PRC PEOPLE-TO-PEOPLE CONTACT, 1949–1969

Americans inside and outside of government had initially hoped that China's 1949 Communist revolution would not completely sever the cultural ties that had been built up for a century prior.[2] Those ties had been deep: as Mary Brown Bullock has shown, the American scientific and educational role in China in the first half of the twentieth century "greatly exceeded" that of any other country.[3] This was in spite of the limited involvement of the US state in these ties.[4] American institutions with a long-standing presence in China such as the Peking Union Medical College – the Rockefeller Foundation's first major overseas project when established in 1917 – hoped they could continue to operate if they worked with the new PRC regime. Harry Truman's administration did nothing to discourage such cooperation as the US government itself sought to keep the door open for contact with Mao's new regime. These initial hopes soon seemed overly optimistic, however, and the prospects for maintaining institutions seeking to promote Christian principles and the liberal arts within the PRC were already dimming by the outbreak of the Korean War in June 1950. China's entry to that war on the opposite

---

[2] Hooper, *Foreigners under Mao*, 1–2. There is not space here for an overview of all Sino-American contact before 1949. For key works that offer a sense of that complex history, and that emphasize ties between the American and Chinese people, see, for example, Chang, *Fateful Ties*; Xu, *Chinese and Americans*.

[3] Mary Brown Bullock, "American Exchanges with China, Revisited," in *Educational Exchanges: Essays on the Sino-American Experience*, ed. Joyce K. Kallgren and Denis Fred Simon (Berkeley, CA: University of California Press, 1987), 24.

[4] Frank Ninkovich, "The Rockefeller Foundation, China, and Cultural Change," *The Journal of American History* 70, no. 4 (1984): 799, 818–19.

side of the United States in October was the final death knell for cultural ties; many of the Americans who had not left the PRC by that point were quickly imprisoned, including several Fulbright fellows and American Catholic missionaries.[5]

The famous ban on all American travel to China was enacted in May 1952; thereafter, all US passports stated they were "not valid" for entry to the PRC.[6] In part a product of McCarthyism, the ban would linger long after the senator and the hysteria he fueled had passed.[7] The ban was not wholly effective, however: in October of the year it was enacted, several Americans attended a peace conference in the PRC. The US government made good on threats to take legal action against those who flouted the ban and seized the passports of at least some of the attendees.[8] Fear of US government reprisals limited even the most mundane of contact: Grace Liu, an American living in China, broke off contact with her family at home for fear that this would bring them under US government suspicion. For almost twenty years, the only contact between Liu and her family was a letter informing Liu of her mother's death in 1954.[9]

American domestic politics made any official encouragement of even the most apolitical of contacts politically dangerous. As Joyce Mao has shown, in the 1950s, American conservatives attacked Democrats for allowing a Communist victory in the Chinese Civil War that they alleged amounted to a moral betrayal of a country they claimed had been receptive to both Christianity and capitalism. For the "Asia Firsters" in what was often labeled the China lobby (later, the Taiwan lobby), containment of the PRC was not enough: they demanded the US government maintain a fanatical loyalty to Chiang Kai-shek's "Free China" regime on Taiwan and an active aspiration to end Communist rule on the mainland.[10] Nancy Bernkopf Tucker argues that Dwight D. Eisenhower, president from 1953

---

[5] Warren I. Cohen, "While China Faced East: Chinese-American Cultural Relations, 1949–71," in *Educational Exchanges: Essays on the Sino-American Experience*, ed. Joyce K. Kallgren and Denis Fred Simon (Berkeley, CA: University of California Press, 1987), 45–46; Hooper, *Foreigners under Mao*, 2.

[6] Oyen, *Diplomacy of Migration*, 240; "US Discourages Visits to Captives," *New York Times*, January 22, 1955.

[7] Hooper, *Foreigners under Mao*, 21.

[8] "City Couple's Passports Are Seized over Trip to China 'Peace' Parley," *New York Times*, November 26, 1952; Hooper, *Foreigners under Mao*, 26.

[9] Hooper, *Foreigners under Mao*, 30.

[10] Joyce Mao, *Asia First: China and the Making of Modern American Conservatism* (Chicago, IL: University of Chicago Press, 2015), 5–6, 176.

Improbable Diplomats

until 1961, quietly believed that trade ties with the PRC – and even eventual recognition of the regime – "made sense." But even a Republican
like Eisenhower was fearful enough of the conservatives in Congress to
uphold the criminalization of private travel to the PRC.[11]

This American domestic context helps explain why a temporary softening of the PRC's stance toward the United States in the mid-1950s had
limited effects. As part of a broader Chinese initiative to reduce the PRC's
international isolation, Zhou Enlai said at the 1955 Bandung Conference
that "the Chinese people are friendly to the American people" and stated
that Beijing wanted to negotiate with Washington. This stance led to the
beginning of ambassadorial-level talks, first in Geneva and then, from 1958,
in Warsaw. As historians Zhang Baijia and Jia Qingguo have shown, a key
Chinese objective for the talks was reestablishing cultural contact, although
the Eisenhower administration remained exclusively focused on the repatri-
ation of Americans detained in China and extracting a pledge from Beijing
not to use force against the Chiang regime on Taiwan. During the early
rounds of the talks, the Chinese side suggested inviting eight American journalists to travel to China and then, in 1956, invited fifteen of the foremost
US news agencies to send their journalists to the PRC on month-long visits.[12]
This proposal was warmly welcomed by American news organizations, who
pressed the State Department to allow them to accept. The US government
was unmoved, however, and threatened severe fines for any journalist bold
enough to accept Beijing's invitation. A further offer to receive American
scientists was made by China but ignored by Washington.[13]

At least three American journalists soon traveled to China anyway:
William Worthy, an African American reporter for the *Baltimore Afro
American* and CBS News, arrived in China in December 1956, followed, a
few days later, by *Look* magazine's Edmund Stevens and the photographer

---

[11] Nancy Bernkopf Tucker, "Taiwan Expendable? Nixon and Kissinger Go to China," *The Journal of American History* 92, no. 1 (2005): 112–13.

[12] Zhang is the son of Zhang Wenjin, who features in the pages ahead as a frequent inter-
locutor for Americans such as Kissinger. Zhang Baijia and Jia Qingguo, "Steering Wheel,
Shock Absorber, and Diplomatic Probe in Confrontation Sino-American Ambassadorial
Talks Seen from the Chinese Perspective," in *Re-Examining the Cold War: U.S.-China
Diplomacy, 1954–1973*, ed. Robert Ross and Jiang Changbin (Cambridge, MA: Har-
vard University Press, 2002), 178–86.

[13] Brown to Stone, April 23, 1971, "POL Chicom-U.S. 4/1/71," Subject Numeric Files,
1970–73, Political & Defense (SNF1970-73PD), Record Group 59: Records of the
Department of State (RG59), US National Archives, College Park, MD, United States
(NACP); Frazier, *The East Is Black*, 96.

Philip Harrington, who both traveled to the PRC on the back of a trip to the Soviet Union. Worthy, Stevens, and Harrington were following in the footsteps of Joseph Starobin, who had become the first American journalist to visit the PRC, in 1952. The State Department, fearing that not punishing Worthy, Stevens, and Harrington would lead to "a stream of other correspondents and probably also [visits] by missionaries, scholars, and others," considered freezing the journalists' bank accounts, but settled for invalidating their passports; Worthy's was only reinstated in 1968.[14]

Faced with the Eisenhower administration's refusal to permit people-to-people exchanges, the PRC government switched to directly appealing to Americans to travel to China.[15] It was in this context that a large delegation of American youths visited the PRC in 1957, disregarding attempts by the US government – and their parents – to prevent their trip. The State Department warned that the American teenagers and twentysomethings could be prosecuted under the Trading with the Enemy Act and promised to revoke their passports – a threat made good on in the cases of those not dissuaded. Nonetheless, 41 of the 160 American youths that traveled to the Moscow World Youth Festival from July to August 1957 continued on to China, where Premier Zhou Enlai welcomed them as "pioneers in opening the contacts between the people of the two countries."[16] The visit was, Sofia Graziani states, "one of the most publicized cases of people-to-people contact between China and the West" before 1971, even if it had little impact on Sino-American diplomatic relations.[17]

Responding to the public relations failure of trying and failing to stop a group of idealistic young Americans from visiting the PRC, the Eisenhower administration switched tack in 1957. Reversing its previous position, the US government said that twenty-four American journalists could, after all, visit China. The PRC did not immediately withdraw its suggestion of allowing American reporters in – but added the condition

---

[14] State Department director of the Office of Chinese Affairs, Ralph N. Clough, quoted in Frazier, *The East Is Black*, 73–98, 105; Johnson, "From Peace to the Panthers," 251.

[15] Zhang and Jia, "Sino-American Ambassadorial Talks," 174.

[16] "41 Defy Warning, Set Off for China," *New York Times*, August 15, 1957; "China Visitor Applies," *New York Times*, December 10, 1957; "Zhongguo renmin de pengyou bian yu quan shijie: Zhou zongli zhaodai wushi duo guo waibin" [The friends of the Chinese people can be found all over the world: Premier Zhou hosted more than 50 foreign guests], *Renmin Ribao*, October 1, 1957; Oyen, *Diplomacy of Migration*, 301.

[17] Sofia Graziani, "The Case of Youth Exchanges and Interactions between the PRC and Italy in the 1950s," *Modern Asian Studies* 51, no. 1 (2017): 206.

that any journalistic exchanges must be reciprocal, with Chinese journalists also being invited to the United States. In the face of this condition, the US government demurred, mirroring the State Department's resistance just a year earlier to reciprocal US-Soviet exchanges that would see Soviet citizens travel to the United States. At the end of 1957, Washington unilaterally downgraded US representation at the Geneva ambassadorial talks, prompting China to pull out of the negotiations in protest. By the following year, Mao's interest in exploring détente with the Americans had dissipated and in August the PRC shelled the offshore islands between Taiwan and the mainland, beginning the 1958 Taiwan Straits Crisis that saw the United States mobilize additional military forces to defend the island from prospective PRC attack.[18]

The opportunity for Sino-American exchanges negotiated between the governments had passed. In the years after 1957, the US side used the ambassadorial talks in Warsaw to repeatedly make offers of restarting exchange contacts – often the very same proposals that the PRC had previously made – but were told by Chinese interlocutors that negotiations over Taiwan had to come first.[19] The US government meanwhile explored other avenues for contact: at the 1960 Pugwash Conference on Science and World Affairs in Moscow, Jerome B. Wiesner, an engineer who had advised the Eisenhower administration and who had ties to incoming President John F. Kennedy, told Chinese scientist Zhou Peiyuan that he had been sent to the conference in order to make discreet contact with the PRC scientists there. Zhou cabled officials in Beijing, who approved tentative further contact at the conference, but Wiesner then gave a public presentation that angered Chinese attendees. Again, the opportunity passed: the PRC declined to apply for visas for the 1961 Pugwash conference in Vermont for fear that their application would be humiliatingly refused.[20] By 1963, President Kennedy was predicting that China would be a "great menace in the future to humanity ... and freedom on earth" and even approached Soviet leaders about a joint attack on the PRC's burgeoning nuclear weapons program.[21]

---

[18] Zhang and Jia, "Sino-American Ambassadorial Talks," 187–90; Oyen, *Diplomacy of Migration*, 240–41; David C. Engerman, *Know Your Enemy: The Rise and Fall of America's Soviet Experts* (New York: Oxford University Press, 2009), 87.

[19] Michael Lumbers, *Piercing the Bamboo Curtain: Tentative Bridge-Building to China during the Johnson Years* (Manchester: Manchester University Press, 2008), 226–27.

[20] Barrett, "China's 'People's Diplomacy,'" 161–65.

[21] Chang, *Fateful Ties*, 206–7.

While the PRC declined to arrange exchanges through the ambassadorial talks, Beijing continued to handpick individual Americans known to be sympathetic toward Communist China for invitations to the country, as further discussed later in this section. The radical political views of the individuals selected by Beijing led the US government, ostensibly supportive of cultural exchange with China, to attempt to frustrate the travel of most of the Americans who were invited to the PRC. The contrasting approaches of the two governments sometimes played out in invitations for a specific American: when the Chinese government invited an American surgeon, Samuel Rosen, to the country in 1964, the State Department opted to allow his travel on humanitarian grounds – only for this approval to attract Beijing's suspicion about Rosen, who was thus disinvited.[22]

During the Lyndon B. Johnson administration, which lasted from November 1963 until Nixon was inaugurated in January 1969, the US government used the Warsaw talks to propose that the United States unilaterally welcome Chinese visitors, removing the earlier requirement for reciprocity in the exchange of journalists. Johnson's government also proposed sending American doctors and public health scientists to the PRC on compassionate grounds and, in 1965, made travel to China for medical personnel permissible as a general policy. Johnson's 1968 State of the Union address made public his support for the mutual exchange of journalists with the PRC and the restarting of other cultural and educational exchanges.[23] By 1969, the State Department had waived travel restrictions for more than 300 prospective visitors to China, although only a fraction of these had been able to also gain Beijing's approval to enter the PRC.[24]

While Washington's proposals for exchanges were rebuffed by Beijing, the Chinese government hosted a combination of American long-term residents and short-term visitors – almost all staunch domestic critics of the US government. As Beverley Hooper and Anne-Marie Brady have examined in detail, many of the first Americans to spend time in the PRC were those who, for political or personal reasons or both, opted to stay after the 1949 Communist takeover. The fates of these Americans

---

[22] Oyen, *Diplomacy of Migration*, 241.
[23] Ibid., 239–42; Lumbers, *Piercing the Bamboo Curtain*, 146–48, 187–88, 220–21.
[24] National Security Study Memorandum (NSSM) 69, July 14, 1969, *FRUS, 1969–1976*, Vol. XVII, Document 18.

varied: some were imprisoned, but others became "foreign friends" who enjoyed a privileged if sequestered existence in exchange for playing an important role in Beijing's propaganda efforts.[25] Short-term visits by Americans started soon after the establishment of the PRC: Eslanda Goode Robeson, an African American anthropologist and political activist who was married to the singer and actor Paul Robeson, traveled to the PRC in December 1949 to attend the Asian Women's Federation meeting in Beijing, just two months after Mao had established the new Chinese state.[26]

The PRC government chose carefully who was selected for invitations to China and the criteria for selection were dictated by Beijing's political objectives. With the exception of the brief period between 1954 and 1957 – when Beijing welcomed the aforementioned youth delegation and offered to host mainstream American journalists – the Americans invited to the PRC before 1971 had one defining feature in common: a track record of criticizing the US government. Matthew D. Johnson argues that Beijing sought "to undermine and erode support for US global power from within, through the establishment of contacts with existing domestic critics of the US federal government." Many of these critics were African American political radicals, the visits of whom have been the focus of much recent scholarship. Johnson, Robeson Taj Frazier, and Keisha A. Brown all argue, however, that Beijing's interest in inviting Black Americans was primarily because Mao had concluded that they were effective partners against the larger enemy of US imperialism, rather than because of any intrinsic Chinese interest in the African American struggle against racism within US society.[27] African Americans proved an enthusiastic audience for Mao and the PRC's interest: as Julia Lovell has observed, the Chinese leader's ideology had a special attraction for ethnic minorities in white-dominated societies, not least because Mao himself – unlike Marx and Lenin – was not white.[28] But American visitors to the PRC were not exclusively African American: other short-term visitors were members of the Communist Party of the United States of America (CPUSA), such as

---

[25] Hooper, *Foreigners under Mao*; Brady, *Making the Foreign Serve China*.

[26] Frazier, *The East Is Black*, 35.

[27] Johnson, "From Peace to the Panthers," 236, 234, 256; Keisha A. Brown, "Blackness in Exile: W. E. B. Du Bois' Role in the Formation of Representations of Blackness as Conceptualized by the Chinese Communist Party (CCP)," *Phylon* 53, no. 2 (2016): 24; Frazier, *The East Is Black*, 6.

[28] Julia Lovell, *Maoism: A Global History* (London: The Bodley Head, 2019), 268, 276–77.

the journalist Starobin and James Jackson, a senior CPUSA official who met with Mao during a 1959 visit.[29] (The CPUSA would, however, follow the Soviets in the Sino-Soviet split and thus broke ties with the PRC in the early 1960s.)[30]

As further explored in the next section of this chapter, the PRC state's perception of an individual's level of influence in their home society was also critical to their receiving an invitation to China.[31] As Herbert Passin, an early scholar of China's exchange contacts, wrote, "The overwhelming majority [of visitors] are drawn from the most influential and articulate strata of their home countries, so that their impact value is incomparably greater than that of ordinary tourists, no matter how large their number."[32] For example, among the African American writers invited to China were towering figures such as W. E. B. Du Bois and his second wife, Shirley Graham, as well as Robert F. Williams, who helped inspire Huey Newton to found the Black Panther Party and would later be honored with a funeral eulogy from Rosa Parks.[33]

Inviting only the most influential of guests, and those known to have sympathy with the PRC, was central to Beijing's primary purpose in hosting foreign guests: influencing the image of China abroad.[34] Views of the PRC in the United States were starkly divided. For the vast majority of the population, China was seen in the mid-1960s, for example, as a grave threat to world peace and perceived by many in the racist terms of a yellow peril.[35] But for a minority of the population that held politically radical views, that decade was also a period when, as Lovell puts it, China "enjoyed perhaps its greatest [degree of] international soft power since the Enlightenment."[36] Thus, as Gordon H. Chang characterizes the duality of American public opinion on Mao's China before 1971, "Dreams

---

[29] Johnson, "From Peace to the Panthers," 251; He, *Dangdai Zhong Mei minjian jiaoliu shi*, 111.

[30] Karen Shaw Kerpen, "Voices in a Silence: American Organizations That Worked for Diplomatic Recognition of the People's Republic of China by the United States, 1945–1979" (PhD dissertation, New York University, 1981), 106.

[31] Graziani, "Youth Exchanges," 203, 207.

[32] Herbert Passin, *China's Cultural Diplomacy* (London: China Quarterly, 1962), 8.

[33] Yunxiang Gao, "W. E. B. and Shirley Graham Du Bois in Maoist China," *Du Bois Review: Social Science Research on Race* 10, no. 1 (2013): 64–65, 60–61; Johnson, "From Peace to the Panthers," 244; Chang, *Fateful Ties*, 213.

[34] Lovell, "Foreigners in Mao-Era China," 144.

[35] Chang, *Fateful Ties*, 207–8.

[36] Lovell, "Foreigners in Mao-Era China," 136.

and nightmares about revolutionary China came easily to Americans who had no direct connection with the country."[37]

Hosting foreign American guests was the most important method by which the PRC state sought to produce eye-witness accounts of post-revolution China likely to be considered reliable by at least some Americans back at home.[38] Brady puts it thus, "A visit to see new China was not meant to be an exchange of ideas: the visitors' role was to learn and admire, and if possible write favorable reports which could be used in China and the West."[39] Chinese hosts usually got what they wanted: before 1971, American guests were almost unfailingly positive about what they witnessed in the PRC – despite, we now know, some having reason to doubt that they were shown the whole picture. Du Bois said that he had "never seen a nation which so amazed me as China in 1959" after a carefully choreographed tour intended to keep the writer ignorant of both the Great Leap Forward and the Tibetan uprising that were occurring while he was in China. Johnson reports, based on Chinese evidence, that Du Bois did ask his hosts "embarrassing" questions about the rights of Tibetans and Mongols within the PRC, but any skepticism expressed while in China was absent from his account of the country. Shirley Graham Du Bois, who accompanied her husband, also told Americans of China's successful ethnic integration, absence of "signs of want," and its gender equality. William Worthy wrote positively about his 1956–1957 China trip, for example claiming that the PRC "had virtually wiped out contagious diseases … there were no people starving in China and no trucks going around picking up bodies of people who had died the night before." He did so in spite of his uneasiness about omnipresent state security in the PRC and tensions between him and his hosts about the journalist's interest in stories that would appeal to American audiences, such as the treatment of Black American prisoners of war who had opted to live in the PRC rather than return home after the Korean War ended in 1953.[40]

In the most detailed study of views of China among Black radicals, Robeson Taj Frazier makes clear that the "articulations" of Black Americans that traveled and lived in the PRC were often "extremely narrow,"

[37] Chang, *Fateful Ties*, 214.
[38] Johnson, "From Peace to the Panthers," 248–53.
[39] Brady, *Making the Foreign Serve China*, 94.
[40] Brown, "Blackness in Exile," 26–27; and Gao, "W. E. B. and Shirley Graham Du Bois in Maoist China," 70, 76; Johnson, "From Peace to the Panthers," 253–54; Frazier, *The East Is Black*, 51–60, 73–74, 97.

"romanticizing," and largely disconnected from the reality of the PRC and its relationship with even the radical Americans that Beijing favored.[41] There were many reasons for Black and other American left-leaning radicals to write positively about the PRC: ideological sympathy; a desire to write evocative published accounts, the reception of which would benefit their careers; and feelings of indebtedness to generous hosts who, in addition to providing red-carpet hospitality, also often presented guests with lavish gifts. But China's control of what visitors saw was central to influencing what they wrote: the PRC state invested much energy in shaping what American visitors experienced in China and, even if some visitors pushed against these constraints as Worthy had, guests typically left with no more than suspicions about official narratives, rather than proof that Chinese claims were misleading.[42]

Visitors were rarely transparent about the limited field of vision afforded to them while in China, however. Why were some of the most insightful critics of the US government prepared to repeat a narrative presented to them by the Beijing government, even when they had personal doubts about its veracity? One explanation is their privileging of personal experience and being on the spot. Many visitors to China, before and after 1971, argued that, given that they could not assess the extent to which what they had been allowed to witness was representative of the PRC's overall reality, they would accentuate their own direct experience in their accounts of China. As Du Bois put it, although he "did not see everything" and "may have been in part deceived," nonetheless, he averred, "The truth is there ... I saw it." This claim, however, overlooked that visitors' direct experience was precisely what the Chinese state could so effectively control.[43]

Another explanation for the uncritical accounts of leftist American visitors to China is offered by Fabio Lanza: fellow travelers were "caught in the tension between the desire to understand Chinese socialism politically and the need to explain Chinese realities academically, between friendship and investigation." (Lanza is writing about contacts in the early 1970s, but his point is relevant to early visitors of similar political persuasion, too.)[44] Later accounts by visitors and sources that were

---

[41] Frazier, *The East Is Black*, 10, 18.
[42] The best recent overview of the extent and effectiveness of this control is Lovell, "Foreigners in Mao-Era China."
[43] Hollander, *Political Pilgrims*, 353–54; Frazier, *The East Is Black*, 59–60.
[44] Lanza, *End of Concern*, 21.

unpublished at the time, such as the diary entries of the serial China visitor Edgar Snow or the Chinese records relating to the visits of Du Bois and Worthy, reveal that many visitors were perfectly capable of Lanza's "investigation" while on the ground. But these visitors, despite personal doubts, actively chose "friendship" as the mode with which to speak publicly at a time when they and the PRC state were both demonized by mainstream opinion in the United States.[45]

This self-censorship did nothing to limit the influence of visitors' accounts among those American communities that were predisposed, for reasons of shared political values and identity, to trust the authors (while also having little or no access to information about China unmediated by the PRC party state). Thus, American visitors' accounts often had profound consequences. Du Bois's account of China inspired Robert F. Williams to himself travel to China, as further discussed in Chapter 1, and was also likely one reason for Malcolm X's pledge, on the final page of his autobiography, to learn Chinese, the future's "most powerful political language."[46] Frazier argues that, in turn, Williams and other American visitors' "idealistic portrayals" of China "enabled" the Mao cult to spread beyond China's borders – including among political activists in the United States.[47] The influence of these accounts went beyond political radicals, however: Snow's 1961 account of post-revolution China, *The Other Side of the River*, which repeatedly denied the famine that followed the Great Leap Forward, was widely read and taken seriously even by centrist China scholars such as John K. Fairbank.[48]

Ultimately, however, the overall influence of US-PRC exchanges on American society before 1971 was limited. The number of Americans that traveled to China was extremely low: Johnson estimates that, other than the youths that traveled in 1957, only 19 Americans visited the PRC before 1966 (the true number is at least slightly higher: Johnson makes no mention, for example, of the Americans that traveled to the Beijing peace conference in 1952).[49] Moreover, the exclusive targeting of American political radicals already sympathetic to the PRC regime limited how much first-hand reports of visits could influence broader American opinion. As will be seen in this book, what later proved far more influential

[45] Lovell, "Foreigners in Mao-Era China," 151–52.
[46] Chang, *Fateful Ties*, 212.
[47] Frazier, *The East Is Black*, 184.
[48] Caute, *The Fellow-Travellers*, 364; Lovell, "Foreigners in Mao-Era China," 150–52.
[49] Johnson, "From Peace to the Panthers," 234.

were similarly positive reports from Americans who had previously been critics of the PRC government or who were known to be no friends of Communism.

Visits by Americans to China had other purposes beyond influencing American public opinion. Hosting Americans played a role in the PRC government's domestic policy. Frazier argues that championing African American liberation was used by the PRC state to distinguish China's "model of global power" from the two superpowers to audiences at home.[50] Visits of prominent African Americans were important to this discourse as a means by which the PRC state gave an embodied meaning to the narratives it constructed about the United States. For example, Brown argues that Du Bois's presence in China in 1959 and 1963 provided "an anchoring authenticity to CCP messages and diplomacy" toward and regarding Black Americans.[51] Moreover, cultivating American visitors also served PRC foreign policy objectives beyond Sino-American relations and was part of Beijing's efforts to position the PRC within international and transnational coalitions: the Du Boises, for example, were cultivated in part because of their stature in post-colonial African states with which Beijing struggled to develop relations in the 1950s.[52]

Contacts between the PRC and Americans were not the only Sino-American exchanges that occurred between 1949 and 1971. While the US government worked to frustrate leftist Americans from traveling to China, Washington also actively promoted exchange contacts with other parts of the Sinophone world, in particular the Republic of China on Taiwan and British colonial Hong Kong. As Zhao Qina has shown, the United States played a dominant role in Taiwan's cultural diplomacy in this period, making use of cultural ties not only to promote the image of the United States on the island but also to champion "Free China" as the guardian of traditional Chinese culture and the true representative of modern Chinese culture.[53] Funders such as the Luce Foundation and the State Department supported the exhibiting of Taiwan's collections of Chinese art in the United States. One particularly notable event was the 1961 National Gallery of Art show "Chinese Art Treasures." Featuring highlights from the Palace Museum collection that the Republic of China

---

[50] Frazier, *The East Is Black*, 11.
[51] Brown, "Blackness in Exile," 24–25, 28.
[52] Gao, "W. E. B. and Shirley Graham Du Bois in Maoist China," 67–68.
[53] Zhao Qina, "Meiguo zhengfu zai Taiwan de jiaoyu yu wenhua jiaoliu huodong (1951–1970) [US governmental educational and cultural exchange activities in Taiwan (1951–1970)]," *Ou-Mei yanjiu* 31 (March 2001): 79–127.

had so valued that it had moved the objects four times since 1933 for fear of the Japanese and later the Communists, the exhibit was, Warren Cohen writes, then "the greatest show of Chinese art ever exhibited in America."[54]

If Cold War exigencies stymied US contact with the PRC, they also influenced the converse relationship with the ROC: American scientific knowledge that supported Taiwan's economic development was shared, for example, through several hundred Fulbright fellows – mostly in the natural sciences – traveling in each direction, while American training in Taiwan equipped a new generation of American China scholars with the linguistic and other skills needed to "know thy enemy" in a program comparable to the training of American Soviet specialists during the Cold War.[55] The ROC's exchange footprint in the United States was substantial: in 1959–1960, students from Taiwan and Hong Kong – who were counted together – formed the second largest "national" group of foreign students in the United States, second in size only to Canada.[56] Other flows of people between Taiwan and the United States were also important to the diplomatic relationship. Meredith Oyen has explored the important role of "migration diplomacy" in both the ROC and US governments' approach to Sino-American relations: policies toward Chinese nationals were used by Washington to offset US unwillingness to accede to demands made by its ally on Taiwan, while the Chiang regime sought to derive legitimacy and other political benefits from individual Chinese that moved between greater China and the United States.[57] Thus, before 1971, the movement of Americans and Chinese – broadly defined – between the United States, PRC, and ROC was a deeply political question that was interactively connected to the three state's foreign relations in a multitude of ways.

THE PRC'S PEOPLE-TO-PEOPLE DIPLOMACY BEFORE 1971

If there was some important Sino-American transnational contact before 1971, the number of Americans to travel to the PRC was still an infinitesimal proportion of China's overall people-to-people contacts with

54 Cohen, "While China Faced East," 50.
55 Zhao, "Meiguo zhengfu zai Taiwan de jiaoyu yu wenhua jiaoliu huodong"; Cohen, "While China Faced East," 51, 48; Engerman, *Know Your Enemy*.
56 Kramer, "Is the World Our Campus?," 793.
57 Oyen, *Diplomacy of Migration*, 5.

the outside world. As Americans came in ones and twos, in 1955 alone China welcomed some 435 *delegations* from the non-Communist world. Foreign visitors that year totaled more than 4,760, including about 1,300 from Eastern European Socialist states. (Unlike contacts with Americans, these flows were not one-way: 5,833 Chinese in return visited 33 countries in 1955.)[58] Limited transnational contacts with Americans had a political importance to Beijing far greater than their volume might suggest. Nonetheless, the PRC's strategy toward Americans was a part of a broader strategy of employing people-to-people contracts and exchanges to serve the state's goals – particularly in foreign policy, but also in domestic policy, too.

The CCP's people-to-people diplomacy predated the foundation of the People's Republic in 1949, with Americans among those that the party had received in their Yan'an base area in the 1930s.[59] The hosting and sending of exchange delegations in the newly founded People's Republic began immediately: less than a year after the state's October 1949 founding, Chinese basketball and volleyball teams visited Hungary, Czechoslovakia, Romania, and the Soviet Union.[60] Exchange contacts were recognized as politically important from the beginning: in 1950, Beijing ordered that any Chinese institution planning to receive foreign guests must first consult the Foreign Ministry.[61]

The PRC's earliest exchange contacts were focused on the Socialist bloc, but cultural exchanges began with nonaligned states in the early 1950s, too, with the hosting of, for example, a 1953 performing arts delegation from India.[62] This reflected the post-Korean War attempt by Beijing to counter its international isolation at a time when only twenty-one states had broken relations with the Republic of China and diplomatically recognized the PRC (a trend also reflected in the simultaneous softening of Beijing's policy toward the United States discussed above).[63] Thus, during the 1950s and the first half of the 1960s, Western European countries including the United Kingdom, France, West Germany,

---

[58] Passin, *China's Cultural Diplomacy*, 2.
[59] Barrett, "China's 'People's Diplomacy,'" 141; Hooper, *Foreigners under Mao*, 13–20.
[60] Amanda Shuman, "Learning from the Soviet Big Brother: The Early Years of Sport in the People's Republic of China," in *The Whole World Was Watching: Sport in the Cold War*, ed. Christopher Young and Robert Edelman (Stanford University Press, 2019), 167.
[61] Lovell, "Foreigners in Mao-Era China," 145.
[62] Emily Wilcox, "Performing Bandung: China's Dance Diplomacy with India, Indonesia, and Burma, 1953–1962," *Inter-Asia Cultural Studies* 18, no. 4 (2017): 521.
[63] Lovell, "Foreigners in Mao-Era China," 141.

and Italy were also targeted in the PRC's exchange diplomacy. Although the depth of exchanges with Western European countries remained limited, some notable contact occurred: France, for example, was able to send students to study for extended periods in Chinese universities decades before American students were allowed to do the same. Cultural exchanges, alongside some level of trade, were developed by nongovernmental organizations but also contributed, historians such as Graziani have argued, to the decision by several European states to diplomatically recognize Beijing long before the United States: France in 1964 and Italy in 1970, for example.[64] There were similarities in the PRC's people-to-people diplomacy approach to capitalist countries and their courting of individual Americans before 1971: several Australian scientists, for example, were recruited for invitations to visit China in 1964 on the basis of recommendations from a left-leaning Englishman, Michael Lindsay, in a similar manner to how invitations to Americans were often made on the recommendation of compatriots known to the CCP.[65] (Student exchanges between China and all countries were broken off during the Cultural Revolution but began to gradually resume with European countries in the early 1970s.[66])

The political importance of exchange and people-to-people contacts made the reception of these foreign guests a matter of high importance to the Chinese state. What Paul Hollander called the PRC's states "techniques of hospitality" were honed to a fine art in the Mao era.[67] As Brady has shown, these techniques were themselves a product of the PRC's international interactions: many of the methods employed were copied from China's Soviet ally.[68] No expense was spared in this important work: fourteen hotels in Beijing alone were allegedly dedicated to receiving foreign delegations through the 1950s, a period in which Passin estimates that between 75,000 and 100,000 foreigners visited the PRC as part of the country's cultural diplomacy. Even during the famine of the late 1950s, foreign guests were treated to banquets.[69] (Beijing's generosity was a cause for concern in Washington, where the State Department worried that its own expenses-paid exchanges for foreign guests were

---

[64] Graziani, "Youth Exchanges"; Lanza, *End of Concern*, 106; Romano and Zanier, "Circumventing the Cold War."

[65] Barrett, "China's 'People's Diplomacy,'" 155; Hooper, *Foreigners under Mao*, 15.

[66] Brady, *Making the Foreign Serve China*, 182.

[67] Hollander, *Political Pilgrims*; Lovell, "Foreigners in Mao-Era China."

[68] Brady, *Making the Foreign Serve China*.

[69] Lovell, "Foreigners in Mao-Era China," 140–42; Passin, *China's Cultural Diplomacy*, 1.

proving ineffective because foreign visitors considered the US government's hospitality far more spartan than that offered by the PRC or the Soviet Union.)[70]

Lovell has documented in detail the PRC state's meticulous preparation for receiving foreign guests. She cites a former factory manager turned "reformed capitalist" who described a system that stressed how "even a small slip ... could have international repercussions." Hosts were vigilant for any such mistakes: cadres masquerading as interpreters would minute all interactions and then write "full reports of everything seen and discussed" (such reports from the 1970s are discussed in the main chapters of this book and are valuable sources for historians). Preparations were ambitious: Chinese hosts claimed to have a preprepared example of every different type of site that guests might request – a school, factory, commune, nursery, and so forth – and even children were primed to perform certain rehearsed behaviors toward guests. Luxury was standard: Simone de Beauvoir was particularly impressed with her Beijing hotel room's two brass double beds and pink silk sheets during her 1954 visit (and soon after claimed that the PRC was free of state repression). All preparations for receiving foreign guests began at the top: Zhou Enlai was once mocked by his deputy foreign minister, Zhang Wentian, for dedicating so much energy – and state funds – to receiving foreign guests, but Zhou said that the work was so important that he would, if necessary, pay for the guests' Maotai liquor himself.[71]

As Nicolai Volland has shown, cultural exchanges served both foreign policy and domestic ends for China: "the government set out to build a cultural diplomacy that would assist and complement the PRC's efforts on the high-level diplomatic fronts and would penetrate deep into the populace to instill identity politics in the people's minds." Lovell also highlights how China's receiving of foreign guests created a "spectacle to underscore at home the triumph of the revolution." Sending and receiving orchestras, writers, and drama troupes, and the participation of Chinese delegations in international competitions and festivals, were all critical to this process. As with American visitors, how foreigners saw China was also important: Lovell's reconstruction of the PRC state's mechanisms for receiving foreign guests reveals that the system, while flexible, sought to present a consistent image of a superior socialist system in China whether

---

[70] Loayza, "'A Curative and Creative Force,'" 966.
[71] Lovell, "Foreigners in Mao-Era China," 142–43, 146; Caute, *The Fellow-Travellers*, 366.

guests were from the Socialist, Third, or capitalist world. How Chinese citizens saw foreigners was also a key consideration: Austin Jersild has shown, for example, how Sino-Soviet Friendship Societies attempted to dispel the widely held view among the Chinese population that the West represented levels of wealth and power that the Soviet Union could not. There were also more practical goals in exchanges: Sino-Soviet organized student exchange began formally in 1952 and was focused on engineering and natural science subjects that would directly benefit the PRC's development. During the Cultural Revolution, the goal of exporting, rather than just showcasing, China's revolution inflected visits by foreign guests. Nonetheless, the treatment of visiting Maoists during that period was fundamentally similar to how guests had been received before 1966: carefully controlled and choreographed visits ended with the visitors praising the PRC's revolutionary achievements – and declining to subject Chinese society to the sort of criticality with which they approached their own societies in the revolutionary decade of the 1960s.[72]

The PRC made use of participation in international and transnational organizations within and beyond the socialist world to facilitate exchanges. As Graziani has analyzed, the World Festival of Youth and Students was one such venue, with the importance attached to the 1957 festival in Moscow indicated by the 1,222-member delegation sent by the PRC. There, Chinese youth interacted with counterparts from 130 countries, including 7,000 young people from the UK, France, West Germany, and Italy – as well as the Americans that traveled to the festival discussed in the previous section.[73] The Pugwash Conferences on Science and World Affairs provided China with another venue for interactions with citizens from Western countries, as well as, as Gordon Barrett shows, for demonstrating Sino-Soviet solidarity.[74]

Within the PRC's varied exchange contacts with the outside world before 1971, there were a number of precedents for the Sino-American exchanges that are examined in the body of this book. These precedents offer an important context for the interactions of the 1970s. Sports diplomacy would be critical to Beijing's pursuit of rapprochement with

---

[72] Nicolai Volland, "Translating the Socialist State: Cultural Exchange, National Identity, and the Socialist World in the Early PRC," *Twentieth-Century China* 33, no. 2 (2008): 52–53, 58; Lovell, "Foreigners in Mao-Era China," 157, 148–49; Jersild, *The Sino-Soviet Alliance*, 181; Lovell, *Maoism*, 289.
[73] Graziani, "Youth Exchanges," 203–6.
[74] Barrett, "China's 'People's Diplomacy.'"

the American people and government. The use of sports toward such important foreign policy ends was not new to Chinese foreign policy: as Wang Guanhua and Xu Guoqi have argued, sports played a critical role in the PRC's *waishi* foreign affairs strategies from the earliest years of the new state. The PRC's use of sports to serve political and foreign policy ends had been evident almost as soon as the state was founded, with Beijing dedicating scarce resources to develop teams that could win sporting competitions – but also, Premier Zhou Enlai made clear, "political influence."[75] No expense had been spared for important moments in the PRC's sporting diplomacy: the world's largest ping-pong stadium had been built for the 1961 table tennis championship in Beijing against the backdrop of the famine resulting from the Great Leap Forward.[76] Sporting exchanges had also been the means by which the PRC developed the athletic and physical ability of the Chinese people that would in turn bring the glory of success in international competition. Amanda Shuman has shown how early sporting exchanges with the Soviet Union and other Socialist states were critical to the development of the early PRC's sporting capabilities and the country's proficiency in hosting exchange delegations that had a political importance by embodying the new state's foreign relations and helping convince the Chinese citizenry of the value of following the Soviet example.[77]

Ping-pong would prove central to the Sino-American rapprochement, but the table tennis encounters between Chinese and Americans in the early 1970s were far from the first instance in which that sport had played an important role in the PRC's foreign relations. Li Yongan and Zhang Yingqiu are among the Chinese historians who argue that, from the Chinese perspective, the term "ping-pong diplomacy" does not specifically refer to the breakthrough 1971 visit by the American team to China, but instead to the centrality of table tennis to China's people-to-people contacts with other countries during the Cold War. If the visit of the American team was a big-bang shock that immediately created change, ping-pong exchanges with Japan were more like a "trickle," beginning with the PRC's involvement in a table tennis world championships hosted in Japan – not the 1971 games in Nagoya, but the 1956 tournament in

---

[75] Wang Guanhua, "'Friendship First': China's Sports Diplomacy during the Cold War," *Journal of American-East Asian Relations* 12, no. 3–4 (2003): 134–36; Xu, *Olympic Dreams.*
[76] Nicholas Griffin, *Ping-Pong Diplomacy: Ivor Montagu and the Astonishing Story behind the Game That Changed the World* (London: Simon & Schuster, 2014), 102.
[77] Shuman, "Learning from the Soviet Big Brother."

Tokyo.[78] Wang also highlights Australia, Canada, Singapore, and Malaysia as countries targeted by Beijing for ping-pong diplomacy, some before and some after the exchanges with the American team.[79]

Dance and the performing arts were another important facet of the PRC's cultural exchange program developed during the country's first two decades of existence and then deployed in Sino-American contacts of the 1970s. Emily Wilcox has shown how "dance diplomacy," and in particular studying other country's dance traditions while on cultural exchange visits, contributed to the early PRC's cultivation of its southern neighbors and China's successful efforts to gain an invitation to the Bandung Afro–Asian Conference in 1955. The specific targets of this dance diplomacy were often, Wilcox shows, determined by the immediate priorities of PRC foreign policy: a huge 246-person cultural delegation was sent to Burma in 1960–1961, just after the signing of a Sino-Burmese treaty of friendship and as the PRC military began an armed campaign against Kuomintang army holdouts in China's southern neighbor. Thus, Wilcox finds "each cultural tour coinciding either with a newly formed relationship or crucial moment of diplomatic tension" – a dynamic not dissimilar to the major successes and failures of Sino-American performing arts delegations in 1973, 1975, and 1978 that will be discussed in the chapters ahead.[80]

Scientific exchanges were also a feature of the PRC's exchange diplomacy before the Cultural Revolution. The unique scientific achievements of the PRC were one facet of Chinese society showcased to exchange visitors: in the early 1950s, Chinese hosts demonstrated acupuncture treatment to Soviet visitors on cultural exchange.[81] As previously discussed, transnational scientific networks were another arena in which Chinese scientists demonstrated the achievements of the PRC. This aroused interest abroad: the UK Royal Society sought to send individual scientists to

---

[78] Li Yongan and Zhang Yingqiu, "Pingpang waijiao de wenhua fenxi [A Cultural Analysis of Ping Pong Diplomacy]," *Tiyu wenhua dao kan*, no. 1 (2012): 140. Qian Jiang also makes a similar argument. Qian Jiang, "Zhou Enlai xu xie 'pingpang waijiao' huazhang [Zhou Enlai writes another chapter in China's ping-pong diplomacy]," *Dangshi bolan*, no. 8 (2017): 45. On Sino-Japanese ping-pong exchange, see also Wang, "Friendship First," 143–44.

[79] Wang, "'Friendship First,'" 146–47.

[80] Wilcox, "Performing Bandung."

[81] Su Jingjing, "Diplomatie de La Médecine Traditionnelle Chinoise En République Populaire de Chine: Un Atout Dans La Guerre Froide," *Monde(s)* 20, no. 2 (2021) : 141–61; Fang Xiaoping, *Barefoot Doctors and Western Medicine in China* (Rochester, NY: University of Rochester Press, 2012), 100–101.

China for cooperative research as early as the mid-1960s. The first four British scientists to travel to the PRC for such research had their 1966 trips disrupted by the early stages of the Cultural Revolution, however, which had also led to the recall of thirty of the first PRC students sent to study in the UK.[82] Where the first half of the 1960s had seen scientific exchange between China and a range of Western European countries, by 1971, the only scientific attachés left in Beijing represented France, Sweden, North Korea, and North Vietnam (although, within a year, the UK was again receiving Chinese exchange students).[83] In scientific contacts, as in all aspects of the PRC's exchange contacts with the outside world, politics was at the forefront, defining what was possible but also giving exchanges an importance as a key facet of the country's foreign relations.

US COLD WAR EXCHANGE DIPLOMACY BEFORE 1969

The PRC was not alone in placing a political value on exchanges during the Cold War era: this was the case in the exchange diplomacy of the United States during that era, too. China had played a role in the development of modern US exchange diplomacy: both Paul Kramer and Xu Guoqi cite educational exchanges with Qing China – the nineteenth-century Chinese Educational Mission and educational exchanges funded through the Boxer Indemnity – as early antecedents of the international student exchanges and migration of the twentieth century.[84] China was also, as Sam Lebovic has explored, the original site for the development of the Fulbright program after the conclusion of the Second World War.[85] Indeed, viewed over the long durée, the limited Sino-American cultural contact between 1950 and 1971 appears as an interregnum between the deep interactions before 1949 and after 1971 that were central to both countries' exchange and cultural relations with the outside world.

While both American and Chinese exchange diplomacy were forged in part in the context of the Sino-American relationship, the US approach to exchanges during the Cold War differed from that of the PRC in several ways. One way was the central role of private and nongovernmental

---

[82] Jon Agar, "'It's Springtime for Science': Renewing China-UK Scientific Relations in the 1970s," *Notes and Records of the Royal Society of London* 67, no. 1 (2013): 10.

[83] Kathlin Smith, "The Role of Scientists in Normalizing U.S.-China Relations: 1965–1979," *Annals of the New York Academy of Sciences* 866, no. 1 (1998): 116, 119; Roberts, "Bringing the Chinese Back In," 309.

[84] Kramer, "Is the World Our Campus?"; Xu, *Chinese and Americans*.

[85] Lebovic, "From War Junk to Educational Exchange."

actors in exchanges. Michael L. Krenn highlights how historians of US cultural and public diplomacy have emphasized how US exchange diplomacy has been primarily the domain of private actors – particularly before the Cold War, but often during that conflict, too. An array of American institutions from the Museum of Modern Art through the Institute of International Education to the American National Theatre and Academy were the primary drivers of their exchanges in the first half of the twentieth century but also into the Cold War – even as the US government accepted that the conflict necessitated a more activist government stance toward exchanges. Often working closely with government, and benefitting from piecemeal but often generous public funding, nongovernmental actors not only executed exchanges but also defined the content of such contacts through programming and negotiation with host countries.[86] As we have seen, there was no comparable role for private actors in the PRC's exchange diplomacy: the party state sought to monopolize control over such contacts – even if the participation of, for example, athletes and artists meant that diplomats in Beijing could not control every interaction.

The US government's historic reluctance to manage exchanges directly notwithstanding, the exigencies of the Cold War did push the US state to involve itself in exchanges and to attempt to shape the experience of exchange for private participants. This involvement is traced by Kramer in the correlation between the closeness of a bilateral relationships and the number of foreign students from that respective country in the United States. Before 1945, these two variables were unrelated, with the United States becoming, for example, a major destination for Soviet students in the 1930s despite frosty diplomatic relations. During the Cold War, however, the US government intervened to influence the number of students from foreign states studying in the United States, with close diplomatic relations being accompanied by support for educational contacts in the form of state funding, government bureaucratic support for programs, and the granting of visas – all of which were often withheld for students from countries that Washington considered hostile.[87] Matt Loayza has revealed how the State Department similarly exercised state influence through the Eisenhower-era US Leader Program. That initiative brought prominent figures from Latin America to the United States on

---

[86] Krenn, *United States Cultural Diplomacy*, see for example pp. 1–3, 7, 129–30, 133–34; Cull, "How We Got Here," 26.
[87] Kramer, "Is the World Our Campus?," 791–92.

short, expenses-paid trips intended to disabuse visitors of any negative impressions of America. Loayza argues that the state power of the United States allowed Washington to (generally) impose a certain impression of American society on the hand-picked participants in the program, even as the State Department sought to preserve a sense of authenticity in such exchanges.[88] Indeed, Krenn argues that the US government had, throughout the Cold War but also before that conflict, been simultaneously conscious of the importance of cultural diplomacy to US foreign policy and the perceived virtue of avoiding overbearing government involvement in such contacts.[89] Even when the US government did seek influence, this did not guarantee control: Deborah Cohn's study of William Faulkner as an American cultural ambassador offers a reminder that even individuals under State Department management often proved to be unpredictable and resistant to scripting cultural exchanges – and that this unpredictability could hurt or enhance the efficacy of exchanges.[90]

In his discussion of the Fulbright program, Lebovic identifies the US government's basic stated motivation behind exchange programs: the accepted belief that increased contact between peoples is the basis for peace and understanding.[91] This explanation was also often cited by both Chinese and US governments and by US non-state actors active in the Sino-American exchange program in the 1970s. However, as Lebovic, Kramer, Loayza, and Cohn all argue, the reality of exchange contacts is rarely so simple.[92] In fact, throughout the Cold War, the US government primarily intended exchange programs to serve more conventional US foreign policy interests and political goals (not dissimilarly to the PRC state's approach to similar contacts). As Loayza shows, ostensible interest in organic mutual understanding was sacrificed in favor of presenting a more controlled image that would shore up positive perceptions of the United States among pro-American elites that led friendly states or, as Cohn argues, counter anti-American sentiment abroad.[93] Another important objective in exchanges was one-way performance. The nature of American

---

[88] Loayza, "A Curative and Creative Force."
[89] Krenn, *United States Cultural Diplomacy*, 4–5.
[90] Cohn, "In between Propaganda and Escapism."
[91] Lebovic, "From War Junk to Educational Exchange," 291–92.
[92] Ibid.; Kramer, "Is the World Our Campus?"; Loayza, "A Curative and Creative Force," 954; Cohn, "In between Propaganda and Escapism."
[93] Loayza, "A Curative and Creative Force," 954; Cohn, "In between Propaganda and Escapism," 394.

society made it harder for the US government to stage the precisely choreographed exchange visits orchestrated by the PRC government. Thus, the US government sought spaces in which managed performance was possible – such as on stage. Gienow-Hecht's study of tours by American symphony orchestras shows how the US government used such exchanges for the purposes of "presence, visibility ... and effective unilateral communication" – but further argues that these goals were at the heart of the objectives of US cultural diplomacy more broadly.[94]

The limits to the US government's commitment to mutual learning were demonstrated by an absence of any concern that American participants in exchanges might gain the wrong understanding from contact with other peoples: that they might become seduced by foreign ideas and cultures. Instead, it was assumed that American participants in, for example, the Fulbright program would only come to appreciate American values more as a result of their experiences abroad.[95] One US experiment in mutual benefit through exchange was notable as an exception – and as a failure. The Volunteer to America program was, David S. Busch has shown, something akin to a "reverse Peace Corps." The program brought volunteers from Asia, Africa, and Latin America to participate in social work in the United States, reversing the typical role of Americans traveling abroad in a philanthropic role. The program, however, immediately met powerful political resistance within the United States and was ended after the participation of just 120 volunteers over four years.[96] When Americans engaged in exchange, it was assumed that they occupied the position of benefactor, not beneficiary.

The motivations and objectives of the Americans outside of government that supported exchanges "partly overlapped" with those of the US state, Kramer argues, but "there were also places where they failed to fully align." Kramer highlights how private actors in US student exchanges were unwilling to support the State Department's hopes of using exchanges for "informational" purposes – that is, transparent propagandistic aims.[97] Gienow-Hecht has argued that participants in cultural exchanges "always perform for themselves, not just for others" and that "nongovernmental actors often do not behave like they should, but

---

[94] Gienow-Hecht, "The World Is Ready to Listen."

[95] Lebovic, "From War Junk to Educational Exchange," 307–8.

[96] David S. Busch, "The Politics of International Volunteerism: The Peace Corps and Volunteers to America in the 1960s," *Diplomatic History* 42, no. 4 (2018): 669–93.

[97] Kramer, "Is the World Our Campus?," 800.

rather pursue their own political or cultural goals" through exchanges.[98] Nonetheless, Loayza's analysis shows that "Exchanges of Persons" programs were run by a combination of state and carefully selected non-state actors precisely because the government was able to identify private participants who shared many of the same values as the government wanted to see promoted, as well as a sense of responsibility for promoting those ideals to foreign audiences.[99]

In spite of the US government's interest in ensuring that exchanges transmitted a curated image of the United States, American officials also showed themselves willing to work with non-state actors who did not simply read from the State Department's script. For example, Cohn reveals that the government tolerated Faulkner's many foibles as a cultural ambassador – his unpredictability, his willingness to criticize the United States, his alcoholism – because foreign populations saw him as an authentic representation of his home country and not as a shallow propagandist. The importance of this perceived authenticity was not lost on the State Department, which observed that the cultural diplomats that proved the most effective were often those who were prepared to offer even harsh criticisms of the failures of US society.[100] Gienow-Hecht documents a similar practice in US government-sponsored orchestral tours, citing the example of the left-leaning conductor of the New York Philharmonic, Leonard Bernstein, as an independent-minded but nonetheless effective US cultural diplomat – in spite of his criticism of US foreign policy.[101] Loayza further argues that the State Department was acutely aware of criticisms of Soviet exchanges in which visitors were chaperoned and prevented from interactions with "average" Soviet citizens. Thus, the State Department based their exchange program "on the fact that America and Americans sell themselves" and provided freedom of movement to exchange visitors, hoping that this would help obscure the propagandistic purposes of the program to its target audience.[102] Lebovic argues that the Fulbright program was similarly premised on the belief that authentic interpersonal cultural exchange was more effective than one-directional cultural propaganda.[103]

---

[98] Gienow-Hecht, "The World Is Ready to Listen," 25, 18.
[99] Loayza, "A Curative and Creative Force," 949.
[100] Cohn, "In between Propaganda and Escapism," 396–97, 408.
[101] Gienow-Hecht, "The World Is Ready to Listen," 23–25.
[102] Loayza, "A Curative and Creative Force," 960, 964.
[103] Lebovic, "From War Junk to Educational Exchange," 301.

When the State Department or other Americans made an argument for authenticity in exchanges, they often did so by drawing a contrast between such an approach and the approach of Socialist states to exchanges. However, even as the US approach to exchange diplomacy in the Cold War era was often defined in relief to the Soviet and Socialist approach to exchanges, US exchange contacts with the Soviet Union also acted as a key model for cultural diplomacy with other states. As will be further discussed in the body of this book, the US-Soviet exchange program was used as a partial model for US-China exchanges after 1971, particularly for scientific contacts. This was done in part because several figures who played a critical role in US-Soviet exchanges went on to make major contributions to US-China exchanges. Philip Handler, for example, was president of the National Academy of Sciences from 1969 until 1981 and, during that period, pioneered US-Soviet scientific exchanges and, soon after, scientific contacts with the PRC. The broader program of US-Soviet exchange began much earlier, however, with meaningful exchanges occurring as early as 1958, and thus provided a ready-made model for Americans to study as US-China exchanges began from 1971.[104]

Exchanges were an important early form of contact between the United States and the Soviet Union. Although, unlike in the Sino-American case, Washington and Moscow had established official diplomatic relations in 1933, the academics involved in early post-Second World War US-Soviet exchanges were nonetheless among some of the first Americans to visit the Soviet Union since the 1930s. Their contacts received significant attention at home: many of the visitors wrote newspaper articles and gave talks and seminars on their experiences, thus rendering exchanges an important mode of American learning about the Soviet Union – as it would later be for China.[105]

Another similarity with later Sino-American scholarly contact was how, as Justine Faure has shown, US-Soviet academic exchanges became centralized under a single organization, the International Research and Exchanges Board (IREX). IREX played a similar role in Soviet-American contacts as the Committee on Scholarly Communication with the PRC later would in Sino-American exchanges. Indeed, the CSCPRC was partially modeled on the former, and both organizations were sponsored by the American Council of Learned Societies and the Social Science

---

[104] Engerman, *Know Your Enemy*, 7.
[105] Ibid., 88.

Research Council. Moreover, both received substantial federal government funding: more than 60 percent of IREX's funding for 1979, for example, came from just two federal agencies, at the same time as government support for the CSCPRC rapidly grew.[106]

Despite this financial support, US-Soviet exchanges featured what David Engerman calls a "not entirely happy relationship" between academia and government – and one that was in many ways similar to how the landscape of US exchanges with China would develop in the 1970s. On the one hand, the practical need to secure government funding initially trumped concerns about how such funding might affect academic independence. Moreover, conflicts with Soviet authorities often forced American academics to seek assistance from the State Department. Nonetheless, these demands for state assistance did not prevent American academics from resenting the State Department's participation in negotiations with the Soviets over exchanges – a dynamic similar to what would occur in the Sino-American exchanges of the 1970s.[107] In both cases, academics were also prepared to take their complaints directly to those responsible for exchanges in the other country: both IREX and the CSCPRC developed close, trusting relationships with their Soviet and Chinese counterparts, respectively, that they leveraged at times of crisis or tension in the exchange relationship.[108]

US-Soviet exchanges were distinct from the Sino-American exchanges of the 1970s in some ways, however. Perhaps the most important distinction is that humanists came to make up as much as three-quarters of the scholars sent on exchange between the United States and the Soviet Union; as we will see, a far smaller proportion of those involved in Sino-American exchange before 1979 specialized in the humanities – in spite of substantial American pressure for humanists to be allowed greater participation in exchanges.[109] Nonetheless, Faure's concluding comment on US-Soviet exchanges bears striking similarity with the dynamics that will be explored in this book: "The history of IREX … represents an intriguing example of a fully functional public-private network in the

---

[106] Justine Faure, "Working on/Working with the Soviet Bloc: IREX, Scholarly Exchanges and Détente," ed. Ludovic Tournès and Giles Scott-Smith (Oxford: Berghahn Books, 2017), 231–33.
[107] Engerman, *Know Your Enemy*, 72, 75–76, 90.
[108] Faure, "Working on/Working with the Soviet Bloc," 236.
[109] That said, initial US-Soviet exchanges focused on technical experts and the performing arts, not wholly dissimilarly to the first eight years of Sino-American contacts. Engerman, *Know Your Enemy*, 6, 86.

midst of the Cold War. As a non-governmental organization rooted in the academic world but financed by the federal government and the Ford Foundation, IREX was at the heart of sometimes harmonious, sometimes conflictual cooperation between its different funding sources."[110] This is, in short, the landscape in which both the National Committee and the Committee on Scholarly Communication were created: a Cold War context of public-private partnership to facilitate exchanges that were couched in lofty ideals but that as often served the goals of US foreign policy, that were subject to government influence but were far from entirely managed by the state.

THE 1966 FORMATION OF THE NCUSCR AND CSCPRC

As discussed, the American public was, in the 1950s and 1960s, split between a minority of people who were attracted to China – and, in some cases, were even prepared to risk imprisonment to travel there – and a majority who feared and distrusted the PRC and supported the US government's attempt to hermetically contain China. The hostility of much of the American political ruling class to contact with Beijing did not prevent some interest from within mainstream American civil society for engagement with the PRC, however. As early as 1957, the Ford Foundation – the major funder of American China studies in that decade – began setting aside money to support research trips to the PRC, a decision that proved overly optimistic but that was nonetheless indicative of a belief that contact might soon be possible.[111]

As the 1950s gave way to the 1960s, a locus of academics interested in Sino-American engagement emerged out of the embers of the foremost US nongovernmental organization concerned with Asia during the pre-Cold War era, the Institute of Pacific Relations (IPR). As Priscilla Roberts has analyzed, the IPR had, since the first years of the Cold War, faced political attack from the American right on account of the sympathies of some IPR members for communism and the Chinese Communist Party; American scholars of Asia including Fairbank, Robert W. Barnett, and William W. Lockwood struggled to obtain security clearances or even passport renewals through the 1950s because of their connections with the Institute. The IPR, in decline since the McCarthyism era, was

---

[110] Faure, "Working on/Working with the Soviet Bloc," 241.
[111] Cohen, "While China Faced East," 49.

finally dissolved in 1960. Many of those previously active in the organization quickly found a new forum for discussing US China policy in the Council on Foreign Relations. Among them were Fairbank, Edwin O. Reischauer of Harvard, Lucian Pye of MIT, and Alexander Eckstein of the University of Michigan. They were joined at the Council by leading figures from the next generation of scholars of China, including Robert Barnett's younger brother, A. Doak Barnett, and Robert A. ("Bob") Scalapino of the University of California at Berkeley.[112]

Scalapino was central in opening the scholarly and policy-oriented discussion of US-China relations held at the Council on Foreign Relations to a larger, public audience. Scalapino, a political scientist, was no stranger to Washington: in 1959, he had been tasked by the Senate Committee on Foreign Relations with conducting a study on Washington's options in its stance toward the PRC. The resulting Conlon Report argued for establishing contacts with Beijing and even recognizing Chiang Kai-shek's regime on Taiwan as the "Republic of Taiwan." These were both bold, heterodox views in the 1950s, although Scalapino simultaneously supported other aspects of US Asia policy in the 1960s such as the Vietnam War. In his efforts to engage the American public on the question of US China policy, Scalapino found a collaborator in Cecil Thomas of the Quaker organization, the American Friends Service Committee (AFSC). The Quakers had a longstanding interest in China and had sent ambulance corps to the country during the Second World War, including to tend to Red Army troops in Yan'an; after 1949, they had consistently advocated that the United States should develop a relationship with the PRC.[113]

Together Scalapino and Thomas organized a one-day conference at the University of California, Berkeley, in 1964 that attracted more than a thousand attendees, chiefly "middle-class and middle-aged," to discuss how the United States might alter its relationship with the PRC. A follow-up event on the same subject held the following year in Washington was similarly well-attended and was co-sponsored or endorsed by the AFSC, the League of Women Voters, the National Council of Churches,

---

[112] Roberts, "Bringing the Chinese Back In," 312–13.
[113] Nancy Bernkopf Tucker, *Strait Talk: United States-Taiwan Relations and the Crisis with China* (Cambridge, MA: Harvard University Press, 2009), 32; Robert A. Mang and Pamela Mang, "A History of the Origins of the National Committee on United States-China Relations" (prepared for the Christopher Reynolds Foundation, Inc., January 1976), 8–9, available at www.ncuscr.org/wp-content/uploads/2016/06/page_attachments_NCUSCR-Early-History-Mang.pdf, accessed June 24, 2022; Kerpen, "Voices in a Silence," 108–09, 115–16.

and the United Auto Workers. The Washington conference was publicly applauded by left-leaning figures such as Edgar Snow, but also attracted sixty-five Congressmen or their staff and several State Department representatives, including Robert Barnett and Marshall Green. Well covered by the press – although not in universally laudatory terms – the discussion was even taped by Voice of America for broadcast into the PRC. There was diversity in the views expressed by the thirty speakers at the conference and no consensus on how to change US policy toward China. Nonetheless, together the two large events demonstrated the public interest in debating that policy, as did the decision by the League of Women Voters to select China as their annual study issue for 1966.[114]

Meanwhile, calls for an open discussion of how the United States might improve relations with the PRC were beginning to be heard from politicians, too. In 1964, Democratic Senator J. William Fulbright and Clare Boothe Luce, a prominent former Republic member of the House of Representatives and ambassador to Italy, both made such an appeal, with their suggestions met by 12,000 letters sent to Fulbright in response – overwhelmingly in favor of his suggestion.[115] Soon thereafter, President Johnson attempted to assuage liberal politicians, academics, and journalists who were critical of his Vietnam policy and favored an end to containing Beijing by unilaterally lifting the ban on travel to China for academics and journalists – although this had little tangible effect in the short term because of China's Cultural Revolution introspection.[116] Then, in 1966, Senate hearings led by Foreign Relations Committee chair Fulbright heard Doak Barnett, Scalapino, Eckstein, Fairbank, and others argue that the United States must develop some kind of relationship with the PRC, both at a governmental and a societal level, in a position summed up by Barnett as "containment without isolation."[117]

Scalapino and Barnett were, at the very same time as Fulbright's hearings, finalizing plans for the establishment of a new organization through which these debates could be further encouraged: the National Committee on US-China Relations. After the Berkeley and Washington conferences of 1964 and 1965, Scalapino had written to around a hundred

---

[114] Mang and Mang, "The Origins of the NCUSCR," 8–17; Kerpen, "Voices in a Silence," 126–28.

[115] Mang and Mang, "The Origins of the NCUSCR," 1–2.

[116] Lumbers, *Piercing the Bamboo Curtain*, 147; Goh, *Constructing the U.S. Rapprochement with China*, 56–57.

[117] Roberts, "Bringing the Chinese Back In," 312–13.

individuals inviting their participation in a prospective committee; within two months, sixty had signed on. The National Committee was publicly announced on June 9, 1966, with Scalapino as its first chair and the AFSC's Thomas as Executive Director. Early members were drawn not only from academia, but also businesses, organized labor, and church groups.[118] A founder of the American Civil Liberties Union, Roger Baldwin, joined, as did Socialist Party member (and six-time presidential candidate) Norman Thomas – but so too did former Kennedy administration officials Betty Lall, James Thomson, and Roger Hilsman. There was a conscious effort to represent leaders from the Black community – A. Philip Randolph and Bayard Rustin, two of the leading organizers of the 1963 March on Washington, joined – and the former president of the League of Women Voters, Anna Strauss, also signed on.[119]

The organization was founded in the lingering shadow of McCarthyism. The core founding figures of the organization were mostly too young to have themselves been targeted by the purges, but they had witnessed their teachers and mentors be subjected to the censures of the early 1950s and had spent the rest of that decade and the early 1960s carefully avoiding any statements that might lead to them, too, being accused of disloyal sympathy toward the PRC.[120] The National Committee initially decided to exclude any individuals "too prominently battle scarred from the McCarthy era," as one internal history put it, although both John S. Service and O. Edmund Clubb, prominent State Department victims of McCarthy's attacks, would join the organization.[121]

Memories of McCarthyism also influenced the early political stance of the National Committee. Scalapino later described his motivation for launching the organization as "shifting the issue of U.S.-China relations from shrill polemics to in-depth, less emotional dialogue." Scalapino sought to avoid both "left and right extremists," but it was right-wing hawks that the NCUSCR's early leadership blamed for steadfastly resisting any level of American interaction with the PRC.[122] Hoping to erect some defense against the same forces that had attacked the Institute of Pacific Relations and China scholars in the 1950s, the NCUSCR claimed to be nonpartisan and declined to take specific policy positions.

[118] Mang and Mang, "The Origins of the NCUSCR," 21–23, 27.
[119] Kerpen, "Voices in a Silence," 142–46, 152–53.
[120] Roberts, "Bringing the Chinese Back In," 312.
[121] Mang and Mang, "The Origins of the NCUSCR," 28; Chang, *Fateful Ties*, 218; NCUSCR Annual Report, 1979, NCUSCROC.
[122] *Notes from the National Committee (NFTNC)*, Vol. 30, No. 2, Fall/Winter 2001.

The organization's own internal history admits that most of the founding members favored a policy that would lead to normalization of US diplomatic ties with the PRC, but formally lobbying for normalization was never made an official policy of the organization. This stance was intended to allow the Committee to claim objectivity when encouraging debate of US China policy and to cast a wider net when recruiting members. Nonetheless, the NCUSCR was clearly set against the status quo of US China policy under Johnson. As Thomas put it, the "Committee would need to have a forward thrust in the direction of a new China policy even if it did not immediately say what that policy should be ... it should be willing to voice serious misgivings about present policy and suggest lines of approach for a new policy." The NCUSCR did, however, strictly eschew any position on other key foreign policy issues of the day: there were divergences in opinions on the Vietnam War even within the inner core of the Committee's leadership, for example, and the organization strictly limited the remit of the discussions it promoted to US China policy.[123]

The NCUSCR's formation was in part a reflection of changing American public opinion on China: by the mid-1960s, prominent figures from academia and other sectors were prepared – albeit with some trepidation – to support an initiative that questioned the official policy of containing the PRC. However, the National Committee was also established to further persuade other Americans of the value of contact with Beijing – that is, to change public opinion. Indeed, most Americans were not in favor of a softening of US China policy: in 1964, a majority of the American public still considered China as the greatest threat to world peace, and even as the NCUSCR was being founded two years later, the Committee of One Million that constituted the heart of the China lobby and vigorously opposed any seating of the PRC at the United Nations (UN) still counted over one hundred members of Congress among its ranks.[124] As ordinary Americans began to learn of Mao's Cultural Revolution, 1967 would see an "overwhelmingly hostile" public reaction to the US government's relaxation of the sale of pharmaceuticals and medical supplies to China. A poll from that year found that 71 percent of Americans still saw China as a threat to world peace.[125]

---

[123] Mang and Mang, "The Origins of the NCUSCR," 25, 28; Kerpen, "Voices in a Silence," 128.

[124] Mang and Mang, "The Origins of the NCUSCR," 29, 3; Chang, *Fateful Ties*, 207.

[125] Lumbers, *Piercing the Bamboo Curtain*, 224, 187–89.

The National Committee had to work hard, then, to convince fellow Americans of the need for engagement with the PRC. To do so, the organization organized some 180 forums, seminars, and events to discuss US-China relations between its 1966 founding and 1972.[126] National Committee figures also enjoyed high-level access during the last years of the Johnson presidency. Doak Barnett, Pye, and Reischauer met with President Johnson in February 1968 to provide tangible proposals for how Johnson could improve relations with Beijing, with the NCUSCR men suggesting further liberalizing restrictions on American travel and trade with China and modifying the US stance on seating the PRC at the United Nations.[127] The National Committee's early activities were funded largely with private foundation money: the Ford Foundation, which had funded so much of American cultural and educational activities toward the Sinophone world since 1949, joined with the Rockefeller Brothers Fund and the Sloan Foundation to provide $275,000 in start-up funds.[128]

While the National Committee emerged in the context of a growing public debate on US China policy, the Committee on Scholarly Communication was the product of quieter discussions. As early as 1963, the National Academy of Sciences had resolved to establish an organization that would seek to resume scientific contact with China at a time when American scientists watched with envy as their Western European counterparts were successfully collaborating with Chinese scientists. By 1964, money from the Carnegie Corporation and the Hazen Foundation had been secured to fund such an initiative, with the donors encouraged by the Johnson administration's softening stance on societal contacts with the PRC. The Joint Committee on Contemporary China, a shared initiative between the American Council of Learned Societies and the Social Science Research Council, was making similar, coeval plans for scientific engagement with the PRC and agreed in 1965 to merge their efforts with those of the National Academy. Other possible homes for the organization were considered, including within the Pugwash conferences network, but ultimately the National Academy was selected, in part in recognition of its experience sponsoring Soviet-American bilateral scientific exchanges.[129]

---

[126] Norton Wheeler, *The Role of American NGOs in China's Modernization: Invited Influence* (London: Routledge, 2013), 28–29.

[127] Lumbers, *Piercing the Bamboo Curtain*, 221.

[128] Cohen, "While China Faced East," 54; Kerpen, "Voices in a Silence," 154.

[129] NAS paper, "Committee on Scholarly Communication with Mainland China," June 1966, "1966" folder, CSCPRCP, NAS; Smith, "Role of Scientists," 115–17; Cohen, "While China Faced East," 53–54.

The following year, the Committee on Scholarly Communication with Mainland China was created under the joint auspices of the National Academy, the ACLS, and the SSRC (in 1971, the organization would be renamed the Committee on Scholarly Communication with the People's Republic of China). Reflecting the US tendency to frame exchanges as a source of mutual understanding as discussed in the previous section of this chapter, the Committee's founding documents placed the initiative in the context of an (imagined) tradition in which "scholarly communication will assist men and nations better to understand each other and to live in peace."[130] Irrespective of the veracity of this lofty statement, it is important that we take this claim seriously – because those involved in the Committee on Scholarly Communication did. As Richard Suttmeier and Denis Simon have argued, we can only fully comprehend the motivations of American scientists for developing a relationship with the PRC if we recognize their almost-inextinguishable optimism for the benefits of transnational scientific interaction.[131] Fourteen scholars originally sat on the Committee, which formally met for the first time in October 1966 – just as China's Cultural Revolution intensified.[132]

While the NCUSCR was initially concerned with fostering public discussion of US-China relations and only later became interested in directly facilitating Sino-American exchanges, the Committee on Scholarly Communication was, from its inception, focused on encouraging exchanges. Unlike the National Committee, the Committee on Scholarly Communication did not aspire to public prominence (although the group would later have an important role disseminating information about scientific contacts with China into the US scientific community). Indeed, the Committee on Scholarly Communication sought to "shun publicity" and some of the scientists involved only agreed to participate in the organization if it steered clear of any position on US government policy toward China.[133]

---

[130] NAS paper, "Committee on Scholarly Communication with Mainland China," June 1966, "1966" folder, CSCPRCP, NAS; Cohen, "While China Faced East," 53–54.

[131] Richard Suttmeier and Denis Simon, "Conflict and Cooperation in the Development of U.S.–China Relations in Science and Technology: Empirical Observations and Theoretical Implications," in *The Global Politics of Science and Technology*, ed. Maxmillan Mayer, Mariana Carpes, and Ruth Knoblich, vol. 2 (Berlin: Springer, 2014), 143–59.

[132] Smith, "Role of Scientists," 118.

[133] NAS paper, "Committee on Scholarly Communication with Mainland China," June 1966, "1966" folder, CSCPRCP, NAS; Bodde to Seitz, June 29, 1966, "1966," CSCPRCP, NAS.

The extreme anti-intellectualism and rabid anti-Americanism of the early phases of the Cultural Revolution initially rendered the Committee's hoped-for Sino-American scientific exchange impossible, however.[134] By 1967, the Committee had concluded that the best chance it had to open contact with China's scientists in the short term was an expected "exodus [of] scholars" rendered "refugees" by the PRC's internal political tumult.[135] Thus, the late 1960s saw the Committee on Scholarly Communication lapse into dormancy, with the organization only being reactivated in January 1971 when the dampening of political radicalism in China prompted renewed attempts to establish contact with scientists in the PRC by, for example, asking European scientific academies to pass messages to their equivalents in Beijing.[136]

The late 1960s also saw the founding of another American nongovernmental organization that would later organize two important early exchanges to the PRC, covered in Chapters 1 and 2. Driven by a comparable sense of the need to provide alternative information about Asia to the American public and government that lay behind the founding of the National Committee, a group of students and scholars studying Asia – the early core of the group met while based in Taiwan – established the Committee of Concerned Asian Scholars in 1968. Like the National Committee, CCAS's first mission was to influence public discourse on Asia and the US government's Asia policy. However, CCAS was explicitly founded in opposition to the "rational," "moderate" opinions on this subject expressed by many of the leading figures in the National Committee – Scalapino, Barnett, Pye, and Reischauer. (This notwithstanding, the two organizations were not without some overlap: Fairbank had ties to the National Committee but also played a role in the founding of CCAS, perhaps even first suggesting the organization's name.)[137]

The Committee of Concerned Asian Scholars was distinct from the NCUSCR in other ways, too: its core demographic was graduate students and younger academic faculty, in contrast to the middle-aged, established scholars that made up the core academic constituency of the National

---

[134] Jin Ge, "Zai Waijiaobu 'duoquan' qianhou [Before and After the Seizure of Power in the Foreign Ministry]," in *Zhou Enlai de Zuihou Suiyue, 1966–1976* [Zhou Enlai's Final Years, 1966–1976], ed. An Jianshe (Beijing: Zhongyang wenxian chubanshe, 1995), 237–77.

[135] Waterman to Burkhardt, April 11, 1967, "1967" folder, CSCPRCP, NAS.

[136] Smith, "Role of Scientists," 121.

[137] Lanza, *End of Concern*, 29–31, 48, 208; Letter to the Editors from John K. Fairbank, February 1, 1973, "Committee of Concerned Asian Scholars," Box 119, John K. Fairbank papers (JKFP), Harvard University Archives, Cambridge, MA (HUA).

Committee. CCAS was also an open organization: anyone who agreed to sign the group's charter and paid a $5 membership fee could join. In contrast, membership of the National Committee was by invitation only and in the 1960s numbered only in the hundreds.[138] As we will see in the next chapter, it would be the Committee of Concerned Asian Scholars that would be the first of these three committees to oversee an exchange visit with China, when a group of students affiliated with the organization traveled to the PRC in June 1971. However, ultimately CCAS would thereafter only send one further delegation to China, whereas both the National Committee and Committee on Scholarly Communication would come to play a central role in the Sino-American exchanges of the 1970s.

CONCLUSION

As Warren Cohen has argued, the exchange contacts that the United States had with China in the 1970s were in part a product of the 1960s and 1950s: even if actual contact had been limited to those by leftist Americans described early in this chapter, the "almost incredible buildup of resources and desire for exchange with China in the 1950s and 1960s" ensured that, once the possibility of broader contact with the PRC become possible starting in 1971, many Americans were both prepared and hungry to realize that possibility.[139] Indeed, as Michael Lumbers argues in his study of US China policy during the Johnson presidency, when we place the remarkable breakthrough of the Nixon era in a longer context, it is clear that, on the US side at least, many of the conditions for Sino-American rapprochement were in place before Nixon entered office. Chinese journalists had even been invited to cover the presidential election that saw Nixon elected (although this invitation, like so many earlier unilateral suggestions for exchange, had been ignored by Beijing).[140] Thus, while the 1970s saw many remarkable breakthroughs in Sino-American exchange diplomacy, these changes occurred in a context shaped by a landscape created in the 1960s and before, both in the PRC and in the United States. Likewise, Sino-American exchange was by no means the first time that exchange diplomacy had played a critical role in either Chinese or US foreign policy: as this prologue has explored, this had been the case throughout the Cold War era, if not before.

---

[138] He, *Dangdai Zhong Mei minjian jiaoliu shi*, 116.
[139] Cohen, "While China Faced East," 55.
[140] Lumbers, *Piercing the Bamboo Curtain*, 1–3, 226.

I

By Popular Demand

A "land of milk and honey," at once "fertile, productive, happy," with lychees hanging from the trees – this was the first impression of China as recalled by one of the first American visitors to the country in the 1970s. Susan Shirk would go on to become deputy assistant secretary of state, helping oversee US China policy under President Bill Clinton. In June 1971, she was still a young graduate student – one of fifteen who made up the first ever delegation of graduate students studying China to travel to the People's Republic. This was an unprecedented opportunity: the group had been researching China from within the British colony of Hong Kong and, like a generation of American scholars of China before them, could hardly have hoped to experience the People's Republic in the flesh.[1]

The circumstances of Shirk's visit to China reveal the tensions evident in Sino-American people-to-people contacts before President Nixon's February 1972 summit visit. Shirk and her fellow graduate students were members of the Committee of Concerned Asian Scholars, the organization founded in 1968 to protest US involvement in the Vietnam War and the government's policy of containing China (see the Prologue). Their request to visit the PRC had been accepted while so many more had been ignored because of their record of criticizing Nixon's stance toward China. And yet their visit was one that helped realize the sea change in relations between the United States and China achieved in 1971 – and would most likely not have happened had it not been for the secret communications between the two governments that predated their trip.

[1] Author interview with Susan Shirk, Beijing, China, December 17, 2017.

Sino-American people-to-people contacts and high-level diplomacy were thus mutually dependent before the Nixon–Mao summit. In 1971, transnational contacts proved a (sometimes) effective backchannel for communication between the two sets of leaders, while also offering proof to a nervous Nixon of American popular support for ending the containment of the PRC. Indeed, between 1969 and 1971, the initiative for a new US China policy often came from beyond the White House, whether through public lobbying by prominent academics or through visits to China that cast ordinary Americans such as Shirk as unofficial diplomats.[2] Even once early exchanges like Shirk's visit had helped build the burgeoning Sino-American diplomatic ties that resulted in the Nixon–Mao summit, Beijing continued to invite Americans who had been historically critical of the Nixon administration's domestic and foreign policies – a cause for alarm within the US government in 1972 and a demonstration of the limits of US governmental control over the relationship between Chinese and American societies.

A CHANGING CONSENSUS

As discussed in the Prologue, both the Chinese and US governments had intermittently made unilateral proposals for beginning exchange contacts between their two societies during their long, wary truce following the Korean War. Upon entering office, Nixon and Kissinger soon ordered that the long-standing suggestion of restarting government-endorsed exchanges be reiterated to the Chinese government, a proposal that elicited no immediate response from Beijing.[3] During his first year in office, Nixon was, however, lukewarm about encouraging broader people-to-people contacts with the PRC, just as he rejected any immediate departures elsewhere in US China policy.[4] One State Department suggestion for restarting such contacts – that the government remove all remaining official restrictions on travel to the country – was declined by the president in March 1969.[5]

---

[2] Paul Pickowicz, another then-graduate student who traveled alongside Shirk, noted in his diary on June 22, 1971, "We are unlikely diplomats (having never considered these sort of implications at the outset of our venture) – yet diplomats we are now." Paul Pickowicz, *A Sensational Encounter with High Socialist China* (Hong Kong: City University of Hong Kong Press, 2019), 25.

[3] Elliot Richardson to Kissinger, undated, *FRUS, 1969–1976*, Vol. XVII, Document 19.

[4] Lorenz M. Lüthi, "Restoring Chaos to History: Sino-Soviet-American Relations, 1969," *The China Quarterly* 210 (June 2012): 381; Talley, *Forgotten Vanguard*, 25.

[5] Richardson to Kissinger, *FRUS, 1969–1976*, Vol. XVII, Document 19.

In practice, these restrictions were hardly in effect anyway. Nixon was to later make great fanfare about his decision to ultimately remove the ban on travel to China, realized through a gradual easing of restrictions from July 1969 and an eventual ending of all restrictions in March 1971. "I called the signals myself," the president told Senator Carl T. Curtis in November 1971. Historians have also given Nixon credit: Chris Tudda identifies Nixon's easing of trade and travel restrictions as the means by which the president encouraged Mao's own reciprocal signaling through people-to-people contacts, including, ultimately, the invitation for the US table tennis team to tour China.[6] The State Department's internal communications make clear, however, that Nixon's lifting of the travel ban was a change in nominal policy only: even before the first removal of restrictions in 1969, the government had been validating the passports of "virtually anyone" wishing to travel to China for anything more consequential than tourism. (The famous prohibition on travel to "Mainland China" contained in American passports did include the caveat that such travel was permitted – if "specifically validated ... by the Department of State.") More than 300 prospective visitors, including congressmen, journalists, academics, and medical scientists, had received US official authorization to visit the PRC since 1957. Only a fraction of these had been able to visit China – but this was due to Beijing's refusal to grant them entry, not because of any restrictions from their own government in Washington. As explored in the Prologue, the real barrier to greater people-to-people contact before 1971 was the stark contrast in *who* the two governments wanted to travel between their countries: Washington waived its restrictions on travel to the PRC for all but its most implacable domestic political critics – the only Americans to which a revolutionary PRC state extended invitations.[7] Meanwhile, Nixon would admit in April 1971 that the relaxation of restrictions on trade with China was "mostly symbolic": no one expected any great increase in commercial interactions before the Sino-American political relationship changed substantially.[8]

During and after his time in office, Nixon presented the decision to go from containing to engaging the PRC as the product of closed-door discussions in the West Wing and daring decision-making on his part. As Nancy Bernkopf Tucker argues, both men were able, by jealously

---

[6] Tudda, *Cold War Turning Point*, viii, 205.
[7] NSSM 69, July 14, 1969, *FRUS, 1969–1976*, Vol. XVII, Document 18; Pickowicz, *A Sensational Encounter*, 8.
[8] Talley, *Forgotten Vanguard*, 28.

controlling the historical record, to shape early historical narratives about their China initiative – to create "a myth" that they were the "only individuals who could have realized" this change. Historians have been more critical about Nixon's claim that this was a bold and novel policy departure that originated from the White House: Tucker, Margaret MacMillan, and Evelyn Goh have been among those who have argued that, in MacMillan's words, Nixon deserves the credit – "but not all of it."[9] Yang Kuisong and Xia Yafeng report that Mao himself subscribed to the view that Nixon single-handedly drove the change in US China policy, with the chairman believing in 1970 that the US president "had dared to adopt the policy of rapprochement with China" and that doing so was "defying the political climate and sentiment in his country."[10]

However, an examination of historical sources from beyond the government record shows clearly that the removal of restrictions on trade and travel with China – the first steps toward rapprochement – was, far from an audacious shot in the dark, a change that had, since the late 1960s, been loudly advocated by influential American voices outside of government.[11] One venue at which this advocacy took place was a "national convocation" on China policy held in New York by the National Committee on US-China Relations two months into Nixon's term. The convocation, the then-largest event organized by the three-year-old National Committee, featured thirty-four speakers and attracted 2,500 attendees, representing fifty major corporations and twenty-four universities, as well as 200 journalists. The Hilton hotel, where it was hosted, claimed that they had never held an event with more press coverage.[12]

Similar to previous National Committee events, the convocation was carefully tailored for an audience drawn from the centrist American public and policymaking circles. Thirty-four speakers included America's most esteemed scholar of China, John Fairbank; Senator Jacob K.

[9] Tucker, "Taiwan Expendable?," 109, 112; MacMillan, *Seize the Hour*, 5; Goh, *Constructing the U.S. Rapprochement with China*; Tyler, *A Great Wall*, 58–59.

[10] Yang and Xia, "Vacillating between Revolution and Détente," 404; Huang Hua, *Memoirs*, 219–23.

[11] As the previous discussion of the historiography suggests, this has been recognized if not explored by historians. Xu Guoqi says that the NCUSCR had "quietly laid the groundwork for a reexamination of the U.S. China policy." I conclude this advocacy was more loud than quiet. Xu, *Chinese and Americans*, 247. See also Tucker, *Strait Talk*, 31–32.

[12] "The China Talkers and the Absentees," *Washington Post*, March 23, 1969; NCUSCR Program Summary, 1968–1969, NCUSCROC; Kerpen, "Voices in a Silence," 170.

Javits; John D. Rockefeller III; Pulitzer Prize-winning journalist Harrison Salisbury; and the conservative commentator William A. Rusher. Virulent anti-Communist conservatives such as "the unofficial dean of the Taiwan lobby" Congressman Walter Judd and Maoist sympathizers like Felix Greene were equally shunned, while a State Department representative was invited to offer the government's perspective – and to ensure that the officials in Foggy Bottom received a firsthand account of the event.[13]

In the convocation's dinner address, Senator Ted Kennedy called for what the *Washington Post* described as the "customary bag of liberals' demands for exchanges, [and] ending bars on travel and nonstrategic trade" as a precursor to more fundamental shifts in US China policy – although not at the expense of a continuing relationship with the ROC government on Taiwan. Fairbank agreed that "the best thing" the Nixon administration could do was to adopt Senator Kennedy's proposals, while the former US ambassador to Japan Edwin O. Reischauer argued that there also needed to be a fundamental shift in how Americans were educated about China, away from "culture-bound" and "fundamentally racist" assumptions fit only for a "19th-century world." The conservative Rusher offered some dissent, defending US containment of China, but the vast majority of opinions voiced and the huge public turnout for the event together offered "evidence ... that American public opinion on China has outrun American policy," the *Post* concluded. This was further demonstrated by a Gallup poll from two months prior that recorded that most Americans favored the United States "going along" with the PRC being seated at the UN if this was voted for by other countries.[14]

The convocation confirmed the National Committee as the most prominent American public organization concerned with US-China relations. The group was not alone, however, in advocating change in Washington's China policy: Kazushi Minami has shown how the League of Women Voters had, since 1965, increasingly taken an interest in China, organizing a number of conferences from 1966 that, while not on the

[13] "The China Talkers and the Absentees," *Washington Post*; NCUSCR Program Summary, 1968–1969, NCUSCROC; Talley, *Forgotten Vanguard*, 41.

[14] "Sinologists Praise Kennedy Initiative," *Washington Post*, March 22, 1969; "The China Talkers and the Absentees," *Washington Post*; David D. Perlmutter, *Picturing China in the American Press: The Visual Portrayal of Sino-American Relations in Time Magazine, 1949–1973* (Lanham, MD: Lexington Books, 2007), 189.

scale of the NCUSCR's national convocation, nonetheless attracted hundreds of attendees. After 1969, the League dropped its previously neutral stance on US China policy and instead channeled the changing views of its 160,000 strong membership to actively advocate for the United States opening exchange contacts with the PRC and ultimately normalizing relations with Beijing.[15] Meanwhile, the Committee of Concerned Asian Scholars hosted conventions in Philadelphia in 1968 and Boston in 1969 at which the radical left-wing academics involved in the organization denounced the US government's approach to the PRC in more strident terms than employed by the speakers at the NCUSCR's national convocation.[16] The shifting public discourse on China was a death knell for what had previously been the foremost nongovernment voice on China policy in the 1950s and early 1960s: the Committee of One Million. In the week of the NCUSCR's convocation, the ever-more-incredibly named organization closed its offices in New York and arranged for phone calls to be redirected to its director's personal telephone, while its chief money raiser packed up shop and moved to London.[17]

Herbert Levin, a National Security Council (NSC) staff member for East Asian affairs from 1970 to 1971, recalled in an oral history interview that "at that time the scholars took the lead" in shaping public discourse on China. Within the White House, Kissinger was, Levin claimed, glad that nongovernmental organizations such as the National Committee were, through their judicious appeal to the political center, helping to "split the domestic conservative opposition" to an official approach to China that Washington felt they could not yet openly make.[18] Kissinger was happy to take a back seat as the NCUSCR advocated engagement with the PRC in part because Nixon had made clear that, while he wanted Kissinger to "plant [the] idea" in academic communities that the president was interested in rapprochement, he had also warned him in 1969 that "this should be done privately and under no circumstances get into the public prints from this direction."[19]

15 Kazushi Minami, "'How Could I Not Love You?': Transnational Feminism and US-Chinese Relations during the Cold War," *Journal of Women's History* 31, no. 4 (2019): 14–17.
16 Lanza, *End of Concern*, 31–33.
17 "The China Talkers and the Absentees," *Washington Post*; Tucker, *Strait Talk*, 37.
18 The National Security Council Project Oral History Roundtables: China Policy and the National Security Council, interview by Ivo Daalder and I. M. Destler, April 11, 1999, 9.
19 Tudda, *Cold War Turning Point*, 8.

In addition to this role shaping public discourse on China, leading members of the NCUSCR had direct input into Nixon's incipient China policy through consultations. The most notable of these was an April 1969 day-long West Wing meeting between five prominent academics and Kissinger, attended by Nixon for an hour. Three of those at the meeting – Lucian Pye, Doak Barnett, and Edwin Reischauer – were board members of the National Committee, with Barnett then the chairman of the organization.[20] These meetings took place at the same time as internal government studies of China policy were putting forward many of the same arguments articulated by these academics, and while US allies were also urging Washington to take concrete steps to open a dialogue with Beijing.[21] Thus, Barnett was far from alone in suggesting to Kissinger in October 1969 that the United States remove American warships from the Taiwan Straits, relax trade restrictions, and establish a new communication channel with the Chinese beside the Warsaw talks. Nonetheless, Barnett's encouragement surely helped and, a month after he made these suggestions to Kissinger, patrols of the Taiwan Straits ended; three months later, trade in the areas advocated in the letter was permitted; a year later, the United States established a backchannel with the PRC through Pakistan.[22]

The origins of Nixon's early initiatives toward China are complex, with many ideas for "bridge building" dating back at least as far as the Lyndon Johnson era (see the Prologue).[23] Together, however, the public and private dialogue between American academics and policymakers in 1969 demonstrates that Nixon and Kissinger should be credited more with the execution than the invention of the moves that began rapprochement and that, even before the earliest signaling to Beijing, voices from outside of the White House and the State Department had contributed to policymaking toward the PRC.[24] As in the case of other innovative Nixon

[20] Barnett to Roehrich, February 5, 1981 [*sic*], "Kissinger, 1968–81," Box 106, A. Doak Barnett papers (ADBP), Rare Book and Manuscript Library, Columbia University, New York, United States (RBMLCU).
[21] Lüthi, "Restoring Chaos to History," 395.
[22] Barnett to Nixon, October 9, 1969, "Kissinger, 1968–81," Box 106, ADBP, RBMLCU.
[23] Lumbers, *Piercing the Bamboo Curtain*; Oyen, *Diplomacy of Migration*, 242.
[24] For just one example, see Reischauer to Kissinger, January 6, 1969, "Nixon, 1968–71," Box 106, ADBP, RBMLCU. Kissinger himself would later admit that "[f]or both sides necessity dictated that a rapprochement occur, and the attempt had to be made no matter who governed in either country." Henry Kissinger, *Diplomacy* (New York: Simon & Schuster, 1994), 729.

policies – the establishment of the Environmental Protection Agency, the extension of Medicare, the introduction of Title IX legislation against sex discrimination – the president's genius was perceptively reading the shifting political ground of the 1960s and then enacting policy change that appeared bold in form but that the president was confident would have popular support across the political spectrum.

MIXED MESSAGES

While the Nixon White House weighed the suggestions of Ted Kennedy and senior NCUSCR members as a means to indicate to Beijing its interest in dialogue, Washington also sought to read Chinese intentions through the PRC's attitude to private American citizens. One early instance was the freeing of two American yachtsmen arrested in Chinese waters in December 1969. The US government was formally told of their release and Washington correctly guessed that this indicated that the action had been on the direct orders of Premier Zhou and Chairman Mao. Zhou and Mao had taken this step as a positive response to the US ambassador to Poland, Walter Stoessel, conveying to Chinese diplomats in Warsaw Nixon's desire to resume talks and in recognition of the easing of the US trade embargo on the PRC.[25]

The State Department also sought to gage Beijing's attitude to the United States by speaking to Americans who had been in direct contact with the Chinese leadership. It was to this end that Harry E. T. Thayer, a senior State Department officer who had served in Hong Kong and Taipei, interviewed one of the very few Americans who had been permitted entry to the People's Republic: Robert F. Williams. The Black civil rights activist had come to fame in the 1950s after leading a successful public campaign to free two young Black boys – aged seven and nine – imprisoned for rape after being kissed on the cheek by a white girl of similar age. Williams had been forced to seek refuge in Cuba in 1961

---

[25] The Chinese government had also earlier shown clemency toward another pair of American yachtsmen in July 1969. Zhonggong zhongyang wenxian yanjiushi [CCP Central Committee Document Research Office] (ZGZYWXYJS), ed., *Mao Zedong nianpu, 1949–1976* [Mao Zedong Chronicle, 1949–1976], vol. 6 (Beijing: Zhongyang wenxian chubanshe, 2013), 274; ZGZYWXYJS, ed., *Zhou Enlai nianpu, 1949–1976* [Zhou Enlai Chronicle, 1949–1976], vol. 3 (Beijing: Zhongyang wenxian chubanshe, 1997), 336–37; Cline to Rogers, December 9, 1969, "POL Chicom-U.S. 7/1/70," SNF1970–73PD, RG59, NACP; Lüthi, "Restoring Chaos to History," 395; MacMillan, *Seize the Hour*, 167.

after the FBI launched a manhunt for him based on a framed-up kidnapping charge for sheltering a white couple in his home when they came under threat from a mob. Inspired by reading accounts of W. E. B. Du Bois's 1959 visit to China, Williams had himself traveled to the country, first for short visits in 1963 and 1964 and then, in 1965, for a longer relocation that only ended with his return to the United States in 1969. While in China, he had enjoyed close access to the PRC leadership (as well as a highly privileged, luxurious existence): Williams's correspondence with Mao dated back to 1962 and he claimed responsibility for the chairman's endorsement of Martin Luther King and the US nonviolent civil rights movement; previously, the *People's Daily* had referred to King as an Uncle Tom, a "traitor," and a "spokesman for the Nazi Los Angeles Police Chief, William Parker." Williams had spent more than two hours with Premier Zhou immediately before he departed China, which followed Nixon personally sending word that Williams would not be arrested upon his return.[26] (Williams' affection for China would continue until his death: he would be buried in 1996 in a Chinese-style Mao suit earlier presented to him by the chairman himself.)[27]

Thayer was personally unsure of the reliability of Williams's comments – in a thorough eight-page analysis, he described their four-hour conversation as "impressionistic" – but he nonetheless passed on to his superiors at the State Department Williams's claims that the Chinese felt "insulted" by the selective nature of the scaling back of travel and trade restrictions and how this cast the leadership as "beggars" to other governments in the Third World and left-leaning radicals in Beijing; this information may have contributed to the US government's abandonment of the remaining restrictions on travel over the following year.[28] In his book on contacts between Black radicals and China, Frazier wonders what consequences there were to Williams's conversation with Thayer. Williams had won the Chinese leadership's attention in the early 1960s through his advocacy of African American violence against the US government. Now, however, he "seemed wholly sincere in his desire to 'work for peace,'" and Thayer suggested that the government consider him as

[26] Lovell, *Maoism*, 280–81; Frazier, *The East Is Black*, 136–37, 140, 185, 198; Johnson, "From Peace to the Panthers," 242–46; Gao, "W. E. B. and Shirley Graham Du Bois in Maoist China," 77–79; "On the Platform with Mao Tse-tung: China Through the Eyes of a Black American Dissident," *New York Times*, February 20, 1971, 27.

[27] Chang, *Fateful Ties*, 212–13.

[28] Report on conversation, Thayer and Williams, January 12, 1970, SNF1970–73PD, RG59, NACP.

a "possible channel" of direct communication with the Chinese leadership, even if he suggested "caution" in doing so. There is no evidence that Thayer or anyone else from the US government subsequently asked Williams to pass messages to the PRC leadership.[29]

Despite the US government's renewed interest in Sino-American people-to-people interactions, few Americans traveled to China in 1970. Perhaps reflecting their resentment at the partial travel ban reported by Williams, Beijing welcomed only a lone American visitor – John S. Strong – in the four months following Washington's relaxation of its travel restrictions in March 1970.[30] Strong had been born in China in 1948 and was the grandnephew of the late American Marxist Anna Louise Strong, who had lived in China for much of the People's Republic's existence and had died in Beijing the same month that travel restrictions were loosened, being buried in the Babaoshan Revolutionary Martyrs' Cemetery. Anna Louise Strong had spent decades communicating the CCP's message to the outside world: she had written one of the first English-language accounts of the party in the form of the bestselling 1928 book *China's Millions: Revolution in Central China, 1927*, followed by a 1959 celebration of the CCP's transformation of Tibet, *When Serfs Stood up in Tibet*, and then the regular "Letters from China" that was published from 1962 until her death.[31] It had been in an interview with her in 1946 that Mao had first coined the term "paper tiger."[32] The invitation of her nephew was in a similar mode, then, to those few Americans who had been invited to the PRC in the 1960s: he had been granted a visa in recognition of his family's political views.

Meanwhile, Beijing gave little away in its response to Nixon's efforts to restart Sino-American trade. The PRC was in fact quietly increasing its purchases of a range of US goods, from vegetable oil to advanced electronics. They were doing so, however, in ways that concealed their involvement, buying under the table in Hong Kong or through Japanese or European suppliers, and refusing to acknowledge that American products were reaching China. Indeed, the mainland authorities warned

---

[29] Ibid.; Frazier, *The East Is Black*, 195–98.
[30] American Consul Hong Kong (ACHK) to Department of State (DOS), July 21, 1970, SNF1970–73PD, RG59, NACP.
[31] Premier Zhou had personally visited Strong the day before she passed away, thanking her for all she had done for the Chinese people over her lifetime. ZGZYWXYJS, *Zhou Enlai nianpu, 1949–1976*, 3:358–59; "Anna Louise Strong," *China Daily*, August 9, 2005.
[32] ZGZYWXYJS, ed., *Mao Zedong waijiao wenxuan* [Selected Works of Mao Zedong on Diplomacy] (Beijing: Zhongyang wenxian chubanshe, 1994), 60–61.

Hong Kong distributors of PRC-manufactured goods that if they were publicly found dealing with US firms they would be harshly sanctioned by Beijing.[33] Thus, while Beijing was prepared to occasionally release an imprisoned American or two, Chinese leaders opted to limit their signaling to their own chosen initiatives, rather than publicly embrace the openings offered by Washington.

Frustration at Beijing's subversion of US initiatives toward people-to-people contact encouraged Kissinger and Nixon to seek a secret high-level backchannel with the PRC leadership. However, while the White House used both the Warsaw talks and the Romanian and Pakistani leadership to communicate that the United States was prepared to negotiate political questions, Washington did not abandon their previous position that people-to-people exchanges were an important avenue of opportunity for Sino-American contact and should resume.[34] At the February 20, 1970 ambassadorial meeting in Warsaw – the 136th, and, as it turned out, last – the Americans directly responded to Chinese reluctance to allow exchanges, arguing that the United States and China "can and should" move forward on bilateral issues while "simultaneously" discussing Taiwan.[35] This was the first articulation of what was to become the US negotiating position toward exchanges until the 1978 normalization agreement: that exchange contacts were a parallel track in the Sino-American relationship that should move forward alongside diplomatic negotiations, rather than after major political agreements – in particular, normalization – as Beijing often demanded. It was also the basis of the emerging broader US position that any visit by an American official representative to China – suggested by the Chinese in this meeting – could not be exclusively to discuss Taiwan and must also include talks on issues such as renewing exchanges and trade.[36] In time, both of these strategies would bring success, but there were limited hints of this before the drama of ping-pong diplomacy.

---

[33] ACHK to DOS, July 21, 1970, "POL Chicom-U.S. 7/1/70," SNF1970–73PD, RG59, NACP.

[34] Mircea Munteanu, "Communication Breakdown? Romania and the Sino-American Rapprochement," *Diplomatic History* 33, no. 4 (2009): 615–31; F. S. Aijazuddin, *From a Head, through a Head, to a Head: The Secret Channel between the US and China through Pakistan* (Oxford: Oxford University Press, 2000); Tudda, *Cold War Turning Point*, 22–34; Lüthi, "Restoring Chaos to History," 389–90.

[35] February 20, 1970 talks, in "A Résumé of the Warsaw Talks, 1955–1970," October 12, 1971, "POL Chicom-U.S. 4/1/71," SNF1970–73PD, RG59, NACP.

[36] Tudda, *Cold War Turning Point*, 46–49, 56–58.

THE MISREAD EDGAR SNOW MESSAGE

Before that breakthrough, however, there was one final signal sent through a people-to-people channel that has subsequently become widely remarked upon but also misunderstood. Kissinger claimed in his memoirs that "the inscrutable" Mao's decision to publicize a meeting between himself and the American journalist Edgar Snow with a picture of the pair alone atop Tiananmen Gate was "so oblique that our crude Occidental minds completely missed the point."[37] Certainly, Snow's interactions with Mao were intended to be a signal from the Chinese: the Christmas Day edition of *The People's Daily* not only included the picture of Mao with Snow but also the chairman's statement that, "People from all over the world, including the American people, are our friends."[38] Mao called the meeting and its publicity a "trial balloon" to test US interest in opening contacts with the PRC.[39]

Snow had long been, as Fairbank wrote, one of the "chief means through whom Mao and Chou tried to reach Americans." Ever since the publication of his world-bestselling *Red Star Over China* in 1937, Snow was the window through which many Americans encountered and made sense of the Chinese Communists. He had returned to China in 1960 and again in 1964 through 1965 before the final visit of his life beginning in 1970.[40] During Snow's 1970 to 1971 trip, Premier Zhou confided in Snow that the journalist's visit was also a means by which he and Mao could gain some insider understanding of the US government's intentions, just as the State Department had done with Robert F. Williams (although, in fact, Snow and the US government had long been frostily estranged). Snow was extensively quizzed by the premier against that frequent backdrop to Chinese foreign relations initiatives – a table tennis match, on this occasion between visiting North Koreans and their Chinese hosts.[41]

---

[37] Kissinger, *White House Years*, 698–99.

[38] "Mao Zedong zhuxi huijian Meiguo youhao renshi Aidejia Sinuo" [Chairman Mao Zedong Meets with American Friend Edgar Snow], *Renmin Ribao*, December 25, 1970.

[39] ZGZYWXYJS, *Mao Zedong waijiao wenxuan*, 592–94.

[40] Zhou Enlai's surname was romanized as Chou in the older Wade Giles system widely used at Fairbank's time of writing. John K. Fairbank, "To China and Back," *New York Review of Books*, October 19, 1972; Edgar Snow, *The Long Revolution* (New York: Random House, 1972).

[41] Huang, *Memoirs*, 212–16; Ji Chaozhu, *The Man on Mao's Right: From Harvard Yard to Tiananmen Square, My Life Inside China's Foreign Ministry* (New York: Random House, 2008), 242; Tudda, *Cold War Turning Point*, 58.

Kissinger alleges that he was ignorant of the Snow signal until several months after it took place – by which time "we had had communications from Chou En-lai sufficiently explicit for our less supple minds to grasp" – and Harding is one of several distinguished scholars who repeats the idea that the State Department did not report on the meeting until April 1971.[42] This, however, is contradicted by at least three long memoranda circulated within that department in late December 1970 and early January 1971. These memoranda analyzed in detail the possible implications of both the content and symbolism of Mao's meeting with Snow. As they had over Williams's testimony and the release of American yachtsmen, government analysts diligently attempted to understand the meaning of changing Chinese behavior toward American citizens. Tudda claims that the arrival of two of these three memoranda on New Year's Eve meant that Secretary of State William Rogers missed them. This does, not, however, explain how a third memorandum, entitled "Did Chou tell Edgar Snow anything new about Taiwan?" and signed off by senior US government China watcher William Gleysteen, could have fallen under the radar: it arrived January 4.[43] (It is possible that only Kissinger was out of the loop: Nixon stated in his own memoirs that the White House, "learned of Mao's statement [to Snow] within a few days after he made it.")[44]

A simple reason that Mao's most important message to Snow – that Nixon himself would be welcome to come to China – was missed by Kissinger is that the journalist initially kept it to himself. Mao had revealed to Snow that he was planning to break the PRC's long-standing practice of inviting only American leftists to the country. Frankly admitting that, "One of our policies now is to prevent Americans from coming to China," Mao stated that, in the future, "Left, center, right – let them all come."[45] Snow's earlier talks with Zhou in November included other suggestions that Beijing was open to talks with the United States (albeit specifically to discuss US withdrawal from Taiwan) and accounts of these

[42] Kissinger, *White House Years*, 702–03; Harding, *Fragile Relationship*, 39, 394; Brady, *Making the Foreign Serve China*, 177–79.

[43] ACHK to DOS, December 31, 1970, "POL 1 Chicom 6/1/70," SNF1970–73PD, RG59, NACP; ACHK to Rogers, "POL 2 Chicom 9/1/70," SNF1970–73PD, RG59, NACP; Bureau of Intelligence and Research (INR), "Did Chou Tell Edgar Snow Anything New about Taiwan?," January 4, 1971, "POL Chicom-U.S. 1/1/71," SNF1970–73PD, RG59, NACP; Tudda, *Cold War Turning Point*, 62.

[44] Richard M. Nixon, *The Memoirs of Richard Nixon*, vol. 2 (New York: Warner Books, 1979), 11.

[45] ZGZYWXYJS, *Mao Zedong waijiao wenxuan*, 592–94.

discussions were immediately published abroad and included in the State Department's analysis.[46] Snow's long account of his talks with Mao, however, was rejected by *The New York Times* and took four months to appear in *Life* magazine. Chen Jian suggests that this delay was in part because, fearing the domestic consequences of Mao's criticism of Cultural Revolution excesses in the interview, the Chinese state initially prevented Snow from publishing a full account.[47] Mao had indeed told Snow to keep at least some of their conversation between them: he revealed to the journalist much of the content of Nixon's backchannel communications to Beijing, before saying, "We haven't published it, keep it secret!"[48] Mao should further shoulder some of the blame for mistakenly believing that Snow worked for the CIA or State Department.[49] In fact, either as a result of the Chinese insistence on secrecy or because of Snow's resentment from years of suspicion from American officialdom – Snow had been driven to move to Switzerland to avoid the challenges he had faced in the United States – the journalist did not even reveal the chairman's invite to Nixon when he was eventually, belatedly interviewed by the CIA in Geneva.[50] Even when, later in 1971, Nixon personally wrote a letter of thanks to Snow after the July announcement of the presidential visit to China, Snow ignored his letter, seeing Nixon's initiative as too long overdue to be worthy of his approval.[51]

Tyler and MacMillan both suggest that a critical reason for this missed connection was the government's lingering suspicions of left-wing Sinophiles such as Snow, a claim based in part on Kissinger's memoirs.[52] This prejudice unquestionably existed, as seen in the caution with which the radical Williams had been treated by Thayer. Yet, the State Department nonetheless recognized that the journalist must be taken seriously,

[46] Jin Chongji, *Zhou Enlai zhuan* [Zhou Enlai Biography], ed. ZGZYWXYJS, vol. 2 (Beijing: Zhongyang wenxian chubanshe, 2008), 1845–46; ACHK to DOS, December 31, 1970, "POL 1 Chicom 6/1/70," SNF1970–73PD, RG59, NACP.

[47] Chen, *Mao's China*, 257.

[48] ZGZYWXYJS, *Mao Zedong waijiao wenxuan*, 593.

[49] Brady, *Making the Foreign Serve China*, 177; Tyler, *A Great Wall*, 83; Xu, *Olympic Dreams*, 124; Lovell, "Foreigners in Mao-Era China," 151.

[50] That Snow was interviewed by the CIA is reported by Tyler, based on correspondence with Snow's late wife, Lois. Tyler, *A Great Wall*, 86. Robert Keatley also repeated the claim that Snow was interviewed by the CIA in an interview the author conducted with him. Keatley met Snow before he himself traveled to the PRC later in 1971. Author interview with Robert Keatley, Washington, DC, United States, September 2, 2015.

[51] Huang, *Memoirs*, 217.

[52] Tyler, *A Great Wall*, 86; MacMillan, *Seize the Hour*, 172; Kissinger, *Diplomacy*, 725–26.

as "Peking considers Snow an important vehicle for carrying Chinese views ... to the West" – just as Thayer had made time to travel to Detroit to meet Williams.[53] What is a more likely explanation is that the *known* content of Snow's contacts with the Chinese was hardly news to the US government. Undisclosed to the public though this was at the time, the February 20, 1970 meeting in Warsaw had included a PRC suggestion that the United States send a senior minister or presidential envoy to China.[54] Snow was only one of the multiple channels through which the Chinese suggested starting such a dialogue, and, whether Rogers saw the memoranda about the journalist or not, he (not to mention Kissinger) would already have been aware that the Chinese had recommended the resumption of higher level talks.

The four-month delay in the release of Mao's suggestion of Nixon personally coming to China was, then, a partially missed signal, but Kissinger overstated how ignorant Washington was of the importance of Snow's interactions in Beijing – and completely misidentified why the most critical aspect of Mao's message – Nixon's invitation – did not reach the White House. In any case, Mao and his colleagues were also using Snow for another purpose: as a signal to the Chinese and American *people* that the diplomatic hostility between Beijing and Washington was easing.[55] Judged by this criterion, Beijing's signaling was more effective: Snow's *Life* article, when it eventually came out, further stoked American public interest in China in the same month as ping-pong diplomacy, while the historian Chen Jian recalls that, as an eighteen-year-old educated youth in Shanghai, he and his friends had all recognized that Mao's meeting with Snow – and its abundant press coverage within China – was significant, even as they remained unsure as to its precise meaning.[56] Meanwhile, grassroots CCP branches throughout the country were given the minutes of the Mao–Snow interview, beginning to prepare the party rank-and-file for the changes in Sino-American relations that were to come.[57] The most dramatic of these occurred just a few months later, in April 1971.

[53] ACHK to DOS, December 31, 1970, "POL 1 Chicom 6/1/70," SNF1970–73PD, RG59, NACP.

[54] ZGZYWXYJS, *Zhou Enlai nianpu, 1949–1976*, 3:348; "A Résumé of the Warsaw Talks, 1955–1970," October 12, 1971, "POL Chicom-U.S. 4/1/71," SNF1970–73PD, RG59, NACP.

[55] Huang, *Memoirs*, 212–16.

[56] Chen, *Mao's China and the Cold War*, 255–56.

[57] Xiong Xianghui, *Wo de qingbao yu waijiao shengya* [My Career in Intelligence and Diplomacy] (Beijing: Zhonggong dangshi chubanshe, 1999), 198.

THE PING-PONG BREAKTHROUGH

The sensational tour of China by the American ping-pong team that took place between April 12 and 24, 1971, is the most documented event in Sino-American exchange contact in history. As soon as the possibility of the visit became clear, American news organizations clamored to secure coverage: one of the team, the Guyanese-born George Braithwaite (Figure 1.1), ended up traveling around the PRC with cameras around his neck from four different news organizations, including *Ebony*.[58] The players left China via Hong Kong, where some six hundred reporters had gathered to cover the conclusion of the tour.[59] The visit has hardly received less attention from historians. It is the centerpiece of Nicholas Griffin's popular 2014 book and features prominently in Xu Guoqi's account of the role of sports in twentieth-century Chinese diplomacy. The tour has also been the focus of much Chinese-language scholarship, including Qian Jiang's dedicated study *Xiaoqiu zhuandong daqiu* [Little Ball Moves Big Ball]. It is, therefore, unnecessary to provide here another detailed account of the specifics of the trip. Instead, the following section seeks to make two important points regarding the visit that connect with the larger arguments of this book. First, Chinese sources are used to document the close involvement of the highest leaders in Beijing – Zhou and Mao – in the ping-pong initiative, something absent from earlier American accounts of the event. More broadly, this section provides a different perspective on the visit: as an opening episode in the Sino-American cultural exchange program. As the coming pages will show, the ping-pong diplomacy of 1971, while remarkable, was far from the last time that a cultural exchange – even a ping-pong exchange – would significantly influence the diplomatic relationship between China and the United States.[60]

By late 1970, the signaling employed by each government, as well as the Warsaw talks and the backchannel messages sent through Romania and Pakistan, had confirmed to both sets of leaders that a rapprochement was possible. At this point, Beijing decided to shift its focus away from high-level backchannels and to instead take a decisive step in the people-to-people channel. Mao had ordered that China pull out of the

---

[58] Griffin, *Ping-Pong Diplomacy*, 207.

[59] Xu, *Olympic Dreams*, 138.

[60] Griffin, *Ping-Pong Diplomacy*; Xu, *Olympic Dreams*; Qian Jiang, *Xiaoqiu zhuandong daqiu: "Pingpang waijiao" muhou* [Little Ball Moves Big Ball: Behind the Scenes of Ping-Pong Diplomacy] (Beijing: Dongfang chubanshe, 1997).

FIGURE 1.1 Premier Zhou Enlai greets George Braithwaite, a member of the
US table tennis team, in Beijing's Great Hall of the People. Courtesy of the
University of Hong Kong Libraries

Warsaw talks in June 1970 in protest at the March coup by the US-backed
Cambodian general Lol Nol against the neutralist Prince Sihanouk and
Beijing had then also suspended the Pakistani backchannel in February
1971 in further protest against the US military intervention in Cambodia.[61]
While the Chinese objected to Nixon's escalation in Indochina, Chinese
leaders still believed that US power was necessary to counter the imminent
Soviet threat. They had continued to signal their interest in rapprochement through their treatment of private American citizens: James Walsh,
an American Catholic bishop who had been arrested in 1958 for spying,
was released on July 10, 1970, a month after the initial suspension of talks
due to the bombing of Cambodia.[62] With those talks suspended, Mao and
Zhou turned to the only remaining channel of communication available
to them – people-to-people contacts – to kick-start rapprochement.

---

[61] ZGZYWXYJS, *Zhou Enlai nianpu, 1949–1976*, 3:373; ZGZYWXYJS, *Mao Zedong
waijiao wenxuan*, 584; MacMillan, *Seize the Hour*, 169; Gong, "Chinese Decision Making," 338–39.
[62] 'Wo zhuanzheng jiguan chuli waiguo fanren' [Foreign Prisoners Processed by Organs of
our Dictatorship], *Renmin Ribao*, July 11, 1970.

We now know that Mao and Zhou were deeply and personally involved in the seemingly spontaneous contact between the American and Chinese table tennis teams at the world championships in Nagoya, Japan in March and April 1971. Mao had ordered in February 1971 that the Foreign Ministry admit Americans to China in the near future: noting that 830 Americans had applied for visas since Nixon had entered office, Mao said that about thirty Americans should be allowed to come before the end of the year and again stated, as he had to Snow that, "effective rightist figures" should be allowed to come.[63] Chinese sources further reveal that, even before the PRC team had traveled to Japan, Zhou had briefed party officials that the American team might be invited to China soon. Mao and Zhou's participation in the decision for the Chinese team to travel and be involved in their first international sporting competition since the launch of the Cultural Revolution has now been well documented: it took Zhou's intervention to overcome Cultural Revolution prejudice that international sporting competitions were tantamount to collusion with imperialists and reactionaries, and even a late final instruction from the chairman himself to quell fears from within the Chinese Foreign Ministry about the political risks of PRC players attending a high-profile tournament at which Americans would be present. Mao instructed the team that they should be prepared for death in their daring journey to Nagoya – but added that it would be better if they did not die.[64]

Once both teams were at the championships in Nagoya, pleasantries were exchanged between some of the Chinese and Americans in the practice hall, while an American player sat next to a member of the Chinese team's delegation at a banquet and mentioned his aspiration for the US team to visit China, as other country's teams had been invited to do when they met the Chinese at the Nagoya tournament – comments quickly noted by Wang Zhaoyun, the deputy head of the delegation and an experienced diplomat.[65] United States Table Tennis

---

[63] ZGZYWXYJS, ed., *Jianguo yilai Mao Zedong wengao* [Mao Zedong's Manuscripts since the Founding of the PRC], vol. 13 (Beijing: Zhongyang wenxian chubanshe, 1987), 211.

[64] ZGZYWXYJS, *Zhou Enlai nianpu, 1949–1976*, 3:449–51; Jin, *Zhou Enlai zhuan*, 2:1847–50; Qian, *Xiaoqiu zhuandong daqiu*, 127–28; Li Gong, *Kuayue honggou: 1969–1979 nian Zhong Mei guanxi de yanbian* [Bridging the Divide: The Evolution of Sino-American Relations from 1969 to 1979] (Zhengzhou: Henan renmin chubanshe, 1994), 77; Ma Jisen, *The Cultural Revolution in the Foreign Ministry of China* (Hong Kong: Chinese University Press, 2004), 328–29; Xu, *Olympic Dreams*, 128–29.

[65] Eckstein, "Table Tennis Project" [handwritten notes], April 20, 1972, "Athletic Exchanges – Table Tennis (Ping-Pong) – History of Table Tennis Exchange," Box 3, Alexander Eckstein Papers (AEP), Bentley Historical Library, University of Michigan,

Association (USTTA) President Graham Steenhoven pointedly observed to Song Zhong, general secretary of the All-China Sports Federation, that Nixon had lifted the ban on Americans traveling to China just two weeks earlier. Later, Steenhoven made explicit why he had done so: the Americans were "absolutely envious" of other teams invited to China while in Nagoya, ultimately including teams from Canada, the United Kingdom, Nigeria, and Colombia.[66] A Chinese account of the tournament records six friendly approaches from the US team and American journalists before the Chinese responded.[67] Mao was being personally kept abreast of these developments and asked the Chinese team to telephone in reports several times a day.[68]

The famous breakthrough followed when Glenn Cowan (Figure 1.2) boarded the Chinese team bus and was greeted by the senior Chinese player Zhuang Zedong, who presented him with a silk-screen depiction of the Huangshan mountains. The next day, Cowan reciprocated, gifting Zhuang a red, white, and blue shirt emblazoned with the three-pronged peace sign and the lyrics to the Beatles song "Let It Be." The invitation for the American team to visit China after the championships came shortly thereafter – despite further vacillation in Beijing over whether apolitical ping-pong players should precede further American leftist visitors, overcome when Mao had his head nurse telephone the Foreign Ministry at midnight on the night before the world championships wrapped up.[69] Appropriately enough given Mao's dire warning to the Chinese team, when the American delegation heard of their invitation, some worried that they might themselves die on their trip to China.[70] Two members of the team that had traveled to Nagoya declined the invitation to go on to China, including the best American player, Dal Joon Lee, a Korean-born American who still held the PRC responsible for his family's suffering during the Korean War.[71]

Ann Arbor, MI, United States (BHL); Zhaohui Hong and Yi Sun, "The Butterfly Effect and the Making of 'Ping-Pong Diplomacy,'" *Journal of Contemporary China* 9, no. 25 (2000): 435.
[66] Gong, *Kuayue honggou*, 78; Xu, *Chinese and Americans*, 241; Qian, *Xiaoqiu zhuandong daqiu*, 237.
[67] Ma, *The Cultural Revolution in the Foreign Ministry*, 329.
[68] Gong, *Kuayue honggou*, 78; Huang, *Memoirs*, 223.
[69] Gong, *Kuayue honggou*, 79–80; Qian, *Xiaoqiu zhuandong daqiu*, 198–99; Ma, *The Cultural Revolution in the Foreign Ministry*, 329–30; Xu, *Olympic Dreams*, 133–34.
[70] Hong and Sun, "The Butterfly Effect," 440.
[71] Griffin, *Ping-Pong Diplomacy*, 198.

FIGURE 1.2 US table tennis player Glenn Cowan in Beijing. Cowan's long hair, colorful clothes, and breezy friendliness was a source of amused fascination for Chinese locals. Courtesy of the University of Hong Kong Libraries

The close involvement of the Chinese leaders in the initiative continued into the Americans' stay in China. Zhou drafted in some of China's top foreign policymakers to help oversee the visit, including Huang Hua, then vice minister of foreign affairs and soon to be China's permanent representative to the United Nations. Zhou told Huang that of the six table tennis teams invited to China following the Nagoya championships, the Americans were the most important and that their trip must be prioritized over all other work.[72] Zhou personally organized the team's itinerary – he wanted them to "get a good look at the new China" – including specially opening the then-closed Forbidden City for the visitors. The premier even munificently ordered that the Americans should be allowed to win a few of the matches against their Chinese opponents.[73] This was

[72] Qian, *Xiaoqiu zhuandong daqiu*, 236.
[73] Dunde Chen, *Mao Zedong Nikesong zai 1972* [Mao Zedong and Nixon in 1972] (Beijing: Kunlun chubanshe, 1988), 124; Qian, *Xiaoqiu zhuandong daqiu*, 236, 267–68.

but one example of the "friendship first, competition second" approach the PRC had pioneered in its sporting diplomacy through the Cold War: China would ensure its opponents were given face, but the PRC's athletes must do so from a position of athletic strength.[74] Further reflecting this long-standing policy, the premier personally examined the remarks with which Chinese television commentators introduced the matches, ensuring they stressed friendship between the Chinese and American people.[75] The micromanagement extended to Zhou ensuring the Chinese program for the matches included an instruction – in bold typeface – that the American team should be applauded.[76] This may have been necessary: when another team of table tennis players from a former enemy visited China – the Japanese team sent to the 1961 world championships in Beijing – they received no applause from Chinese crowds, who instead cheered whoever was on the other side of the net – that is, until Chinese officials intervened behind the scenes.[77]

Zhou met with the US team, telling them of his hope that both the Chinese and American people would soon be able to pay friendly visits to the other, to applause from the players (Figure 1.3).[78] The premier even indulged questions from Cowan about his feelings about "hippie" culture in the United States: Zhou took the opportunity for what may have been a sideways comment on Chinese domestic politics, applauding young people finding their own truth – but then adding that building consensus was also important and that the young did not always express themselves in ways that were "mature."[79]

The White House was far less involved in the ping-pong initiative than were top Chinese leaders – and was remarkably uncertain as to how the trip would be received. Kissinger later praised the initiative of William Cunningham, a staff member at the US embassy in Tokyo for encouraging the team to accept the Chinese invitation – even though his only basis for doing so was Nixon's comment that the United States was open to athletic exchanges with China, made during one of the president's foreign

---

[74] Wang, "Friendship First."

[75] Song Shixiong, *Zishu: Wo de tiyu shijie yu ying ping chunqiu* [Autobiography of Song Shixiong: My Sports World and Days on Screen] (Beijing: Zuojia chuban she, 1997).

[76] Xu, *Olympic Dreams*, 137.

[77] Wang, "Friendship First," 142.

[78] Tudda, *Cold War Turning Point*, 66.

[79] ZGZYWXYJS, ed., *Zhou Enlai waijiao wenxuan* [Selected Works of Zhou Enlai on Diplomacy] (Beijing: Zhongyang wenxian chubanshe, 1990), 473.

FIGURE 1.3 US table tennis player Olga Soltesz alongside Chinese ping-pong opponent Zhu Naizhen in Shanghai. Soltesz and Zhu struck up a friendship during the 1971 ping-pong visit – despite neither speaking the other's language. Courtesy of the University of Hong Kong Libraries

policy reports to Congress.[80] Nixon did then personally endorse the team traveling to the PRC – but on the proviso that the US government have no further direct involvement in what still seemed a risky venture.[81] In the wake of this endorsement, Kissinger waited anxiously for the American public response, concerned that allowing the ping-pong players to travel to the PRC might lead to anger at the White House.[82] He ordered US government personnel in Hong Kong and Japan to stay well away from the American players after they left China and traveled home via Tokyo.[83] Kissinger believed that the Chinese invitation, while a positive step, also contained a veiled warning that, if Beijing's overtures to the White House were rebuffed, the Chinese government would step up

---

[80] Kissinger, *White House Years*, 709; Griffin, *Ping-Pong Diplomacy*, 201–02.
[81] Ruth Eckstein, "Ping Pong Diplomacy: A View from Behind the Scenes," *Journal of American-East Asian Relations* 2, no. 3 (1993): 327.
[82] Hong and Sun, "The Butterfly Effect," 441.
[83] Griffin, *Ping-Pong Diplomacy*, 226.

its efforts go under the heads of US leaders and directly appeal to the American people, as Hanoi was doing by stoking the anti-Vietnam War movement.[84] The Nixon tapes reveal that the president, while thrilled by the Chinese invitation to the team, still planned to remain "quiet and enigmatic about further moves" toward Beijing while the players were in China.[85] Nixon's response to the team's trip was so closely held that his own vice president, Spiro Agnew, publicly criticized the favorable American press coverage of the visit – angering Nixon so much that he considered removing Agnew from his re-election ticket.[86] Nixon and Kissinger need not have worried about the American public response: a Gallup poll conducted a few weeks after the ping-pong visit revealed a marked improvement in American impressions of the PRC and greater desire for engagement with Beijing – precisely the outcome the president would have hoped for.[87]

Amidst the rapturous American public reaction to the ping-pong visit, Nixon shed some of his inhibitions and offered a positive response to Beijing's action. On April 14, the day that Zhou personally welcomed the team to China, the US president announced the further relaxation of the restrictions on travel and trade between the two societies, promising to expedite visas for groups of Chinese visitors and permitting trade in an array of new goods.[88] The timing of the announcement was brought forward after Beijing's invitation to the American table tennis team.[89] The president also encouraged the Democratic Senator Mike Mansfield to accept an offer of travel to China extended via Prince Norodom Sihanouk of Cambodia, then in refuge in Beijing, that had been sent while the ping-pong team was in the PRC.[90] The White House was thus continuing to make eager use of all channels of indirect communication with Beijing to respond to the ping-pong initiative – until, soon after the table tennis visit successfully concluded, on April 27,

---

[84] Kissinger, *White House Years*, 710.
[85] Tudda, *Cold War Turning Point*, 67, 180.
[86] Xu, *Olympic Dreams*, 143.
[87] Hong and Sun, "The Butterfly Effect," 429–48.
[88] National Security Decision Memorandum 105, April 13, 1971, *FRUS, 1969–1976*, Vol. XVII, Document 116.
[89] Kissinger, *White House Years*, 712.
[90] Mansfield's visit ultimately took place in April 1972, having been deliberately delayed by the White House once Nixon expected to himself go to China. Don Oberdorfer, *Senator Mansfield: The Extraordinary Life of a Great American Statesman and Diplomat* (Washington, DC: Smithsonian Books, 2003), 393–96.

the White House received Zhou's unexpected invitation for Kissinger to visit China.[91]

Though ignorant of Kissinger's invitation, the National Committee on US-China Relations had also rushed to welcome the ping-pong team's visit to China and to use the visit as the basis for beginning exchange contacts. The organization worked quickly to facilitate an invitation to the Chinese to send their own table tennis team for a return ping-pong exchange in the United States. The American team had decided even before they entered the PRC that they wished to invite their hosts to the United States and had hastily sought a sponsor with the resources and expertise to host what promised to be the highest-profile tabletennis event to ever be hosted on American soil. Officials at the US embassy in Tokyo had told Steenhoven that, although the departments of State and Justice agreed to the issuing of visas to a prospective visiting Chinese team, the funding for any return tour must come from a private organization. The USTTA was a private group but had nothing like the funds necessary to underwrite the visit: the American players were amateur athletes with day jobs, and the team collectively ranked twenty-third in the world (the Chinese men, in contrast, won gold at Nagoya; the women, silver). In line with other sporting delegations of political importance hosted by the PRC, the Chinese government had covered all the costs of the American team's visit to China – with the American players even raising the question of covering the expenses of changing their return flight date before they agreed to embark.[92] Fay Willey, a *Newsweek* journalist, heard of the predicament facing Steenhoven from the magazine's Tokyo bureau and urgently contacted Douglas Murray, vice president of the National Committee. With less than twenty four hours until the team's entry to China, Murray was able to quickly secure the NCUSCR board's backing and the organization's executive director, B. Preston Schoyer, cabled Steenhoven in Hong Kong to offer the organization's services co-hosting and funding the return ping-pong visit if the Chinese accepted the invitation.[93] Steenhoven, who had a day job at Chrysler,

[91] Jin, *Zhou Enlai zhuan*, 2:1850; Zhou to Nixon, April 21, 1971, *FRUS, 1969–1976*, Vol. XVII, Document 118.

[92] Shuman, "Learning from the Soviet Big Brother," 169.

[93] Willey to Arne [J de Keijzer], June 9, 1971, and Schoyer to American Table Tennis Team, April 8, 1971, "USTTA – Kaminsky – 1972," Box 15, National Archive on Sino-American Relations (NASAR), BHL; Qian, *Xiaoqiu zhuandong daqiu*, 243; Murray to Steenhoven, April 15, 1971, "Athletic Exchanges – Table Tennis (Ping-Pong) – Miscellanea," Box 4,

later told the National Committee that, had the organization not got in touch, his invitation to the Chinese would not have been offered; deputy head of the team, J. Rufford Harrison, described the team as "completely reliant" on the NCUSCR.[94] The National Committee's offer was in retrospect both a recognition and a cause of the organization's prominence: Willey contacted the NCUSCR because of the profile and resources it had accrued since its founding in 1966, but the group's central role in future Sino-American exchanges grew out of its experience hosting the Chinese table tennis team.

The Chinese players agreed to travel to the United States but did not commit to a date. Beijing was ready for the invitation: Zhou had spoken within the Foreign Ministry of the possibility of China's table tennis team traveling to the United States as early as 11 March, nearly a month before the Americans arrived. The premier argued that, as China's ping-pong players had already traveled to West Germany and to Japan before the establishment of diplomatic relations with Bonn or Tokyo, the lack of official ties with Washington should not prevent a ping-pong tour of the United States.[95] The return visit would ultimately be delayed until April 1972 – partially as a result of Beijing wanting to avoid sending their team while a rival ping-pong team from Taiwan was touring the United States (although Zhou also used the delay to encourage the team to practice their English before their US tour).[96] Nonetheless, China's acceptance of the invitation was a significant step in the resumption of people-to-people contact after the hiatus at the height of the Cultural Revolution.

Meanwhile, American journalistic travel to China resumed as a corollary of the first ping-pong visit: a trio of US journalists accompanied the team, the first American reporters to visit the PRC on behalf of politically centrist publications, as distinct from earlier visits by radical, left-leaning journalists and writers such as Edgar Snow, Anna Louise Strong, William Worthy, and W. E. B. Du Bois (see the Prologue). Beijing's earlier preference for journalists known to be sympathetic toward the PRC was being diluted, but still lingered: among the three journalists was John Roderick, an Associated Press reporter who had spent six months in the CCP base in Yan'an in the 1940s and who was personally known to Mao and

---

AEP, BHL; author interviews with Douglas Murray, New York, United States, September 9, 2015, and Jan Berris, New York, United States, August 15, 2015, and June 19, 2019.

[94] Xu, *Olympic Dreams*, 150; Griffin, *Ping-Pong Diplomacy*, 215.

[95] Xu, *Olympic Dreams*, 127–28.

[96] Qian, "Zhou Enlai xu xie 'pingpang waijiao' huazhang," 47.

Zhou.[97] In the month that followed, Robert Keatley of the *Wall Street Journal* and Tillman Durdin of the *New York Times* also both traveled to China individually, with Durdin returning to the country from which he famously reported on the Sino-Japanese War – including with some of the first reports of the 1937 Nanjing massacre. (Keatley's visit had an unexpected significance: his then-wife, Anne Keatley, traveled with him. Anne was a staff member of the CSCPRC and used her presence at a meeting between her then-husband and Zhou to present a letter from her employer proposing that China work with the CSCPRC on scientific exchanges. Zhou did not immediately respond to the letter, but later recalled that meeting as the moment that he became aware of the CSCPRC and its interest in exchanges with China.[98]) The first exchange delegation of American journalists would be sent by the American Society of Newspaper Editors in October 1972, with the Chinese sending a reciprocal delegation to the United States in May 1973 (Chapter 3).[99]

Ping-pong diplomacy was also closely covered by PRC state media – including on television. This was not the first time that Chinese audiences would have experienced positive news coverage of Americans: the politically radical American "foreign friends" that visited or lived in China had often been featured in Chinese media. Sidney Rittenberg, one of the foremost Americans living in China, had even had his speeches broadcast throughout China during the Cultural Revolution (although this influence had prompted jealous enemies, including Jiang Qing, to have Rittenberg imprisoned, where he languished even while his country's table tennis team toured China).[100] The televising of the American team's visit similarly contained a clear political message. Internal Chinese documents discussing the coverage of the team's visit to Shanghai explained to local cadres – surely as surprised as Americans at the Chinese central government's sudden invitation to a US national sports team – that the PRC distinguished between the American people, toward whom China was friendly, and the US government that set the country's hostile policy toward the PRC (the document quoted both Mao and Zhuang Zedong in stressing this distinction). If the ping-pong visit was still internally framed

[97] Hong and Sun, "The Butterfly Effect," 442; ZGZYWXYJS, *Zhou Enlai waijiao wenxuan*, 469–75; Griffin, *Ping-Pong Diplomacy*, 213.
[98] NFTNC, Vol. 1, No. 3, Summer 1971; Anne Keatley to Handler, July 21, 1971, "1971 – General," CSCPRCP, NAS; author interview with Robert Keatley.
[99] *NFTNC*, Vol. 5, No. 2, July 1975.
[100] Brady, *Making the Foreign Serve China*, 155, 163–65.

in terms similar to those of earlier visits by the radical American political activists discussed in the Prologue, there were nonetheless surely some among the Chinese who witnessed the ping-pong tour – whether on television or by other means – and wondered if the event might not indicate some change the PRC leadership's stance toward the US government, as well as its people.[101]

When Nixon himself traveled to Beijing in February 1972, Mao looked back on the extensive American efforts to restart Sino-American contact through people-to-people contacts: "if one counts the time since you put forward your suggestion at Warsaw it is less than two years. Our side also is bureaucratic in dealing with matters. For example, you wanted some exchange of persons on a personal level, things like that; also trade. But rather than deciding that we stuck with our stand that without settling major issues there is nothing to do with smaller issues. I myself persisted in that position. Later on I saw you were right, and we played table tennis." The chairman's words were a fitting epithet on the initial failure and ultimate success of the American and then Chinese initiatives to restart Sino-American relations via exchange diplomacy.[102]

THE FIRST AMERICAN SCIENTIFIC VISITS TO THE PEOPLE'S REPUBLIC

In May, the same month that the American journalists Keatley and Durdin toured China, scientific exchanges began with the visit of Arthur Galston and Ethan Signer to the PRC – the first American scientists to visit China since the outbreak of the Korean War.[103] The invitation of Galston and Signer ahead of any of their American scientific colleagues showed how Beijing's earlier preference for critics of the US government was lingering: Galston had become vocally critical of US foreign policy after discovering that his doctoral research on soybean fertilizers had, without his

---

[101] "Shanghai renmin guangbo diantai! Shanghai dianshitai!" [Shanghai People's Broadcasting Station! Shanghai TV!], April 16, 1971, Folder B92-2-1485-7, SHMA.

[102] ZGZYWXYJS, *Mao Zedong waijiao wenxuan*, 595; Memcon: Mao, Nixon, et al., February 21, 1972, FRUS, *1969–1976*, Vol. XVII, Document 194.

[103] The American physician George Hatem lived in China throughout the Mao period and wrote and spoke about the country. Galston and Signer were, however, the first American research scientists to visit the country and the first to do so on a visit framed as a scientific exchange. Sigrid Schmalzer, "Speaking about China, Learning from China: Amateur China Experts in 1970s America," *Journal of American-East Asian Relations* 16, no. 4 (Winter 2009): 339; Hooper, *Foreigners under Mao*, 25.

knowledge or consent, been used as the basis for the development of the notorious defoliant Agent Orange, while Signer was an active member of the left-leaning, anti-Vietnam War organization Science for the People.[104] Although Signer believed that Zhou Enlai had, during a two-and-a-half-hour meeting, indicated that future invitations would also be dictated by the politics of the guests, Galston admitted to the Committee on Scholarly Communication that Chinese leaders had, in fact, made clear that they planned to host American scientists with a broad range of political persuasions, rather than limiting invitations to politically active leftists. Galston also reported to the CSCPRC on his return that the PRC would soon begin sending medical and natural science delegations to the United States. "Another three years and you may be tired of Chinese visitors," Chinese leaders had joked.[105]

Galston was deeply impressed by what he witnessed in China. The Cultural Revolution – still officially proceeding in 1971, though in a less chaotic phase than in the late 1960s – had included a strong emphasis on the practical application of science to the immediate needs of those in society, particularly those most in need of its benefits. Basic and theoretical scientific research had been eschewed, with scientists pushed out of their laboratories and down into the countryside.[106] In his reflections on the trip published soon after his visit, Galston praised many of "the innovations of the Cultural Revolution." At a time of increasing awareness of environmental degradation in the United States – it had been less than a decade since the publication of Rachel Carson's landmark book *Silent Spring* – Galston applauded the Chinese as the world's best recyclers – citing, for example, their production of monosodium glutamate (better known as MSG) from sweet potatoes – and claimed that their applied science had led to the production of chemical growth enhancers for broad beans that exactly paralleled the cytokinins used in the United

---

[104] Arthur Galston, *Daily Life in People's China* (New York: Crowell, 1973), 1–3; Schmalzer, "Speaking about China," 316; Li Mingde, "Zhong Mei keji jiaoliu yu hezuo de lishi huigu [A Historical Review of Sino-American Science and Technology Exchanges and Cooperation]," *Meiguo yanjiu*, no. 2 (1997): 144–47; He, *Dangdai Zhong Mei minjian jiaoliu shi*, 131. The PRC's initial favoring of American left-wing scientists, and the tendency of these scientists to praise Cultural Revolution science, was reflected in contacts between the PRC and British scientists, too. See Agar, "It's Springtime for Science," 11.

[105] Schmalzer, "Speaking about China," 313, 319; Meeting between Galston and CSCPRC members, June 9, 1971, "1971 – General," CSCPRCP, NAS.

[106] ZGZYWXYJS, ed., *Zhou Enlai xuanji* [Selected Works of Zhou Enlai], vol. 2 (Beijing: Renmin chubanshe, 1984), 473.

States. These had, Galson claimed, "arisen independently on the basis of farmers' lore, rather than from the laboratory."[107]

There was acute American public interest in what the two scientists had seen: as soon as they got back on US soil, they were guided to a room packed with reporters, and in the weeks that followed the *New York Times* published an array of articles on their visit, with two on the front page. Galston, who had become the chair of Yale's botany department after training at Cornell and Caltech, elaborated on these articles with a book-length account of the trip that was published in 1973. He also claimed to have given some one hundred talks in the first year after his trip, to high-school and college students, political and church groups, among others; he later told historian Sigrid Schmalzer that his "life as a scientist was wrecked for a year."[108]

Soon, other visitors – particularly those with no scientific training – would echo Galston's praise of Chinese applied science. Audrey Topping was the Canadian-born American wife of the journalist Seymour Topping and one of the *New York Times* journalists who had covered Galston and Signer's visit. She picked up another of the threads of Galston's account of Chinese science when, based on her own personal experiences in China later that year, she celebrated the PRC's use of acupuncture. The PRC had been showcasing acupuncture as a uniquely Chinese treatment since the 1950s – the treatment had been praised by Soviet cultural exchange visitors as early as 1951 – and now it was a prominent feature in early American visits to China (in spite of the relatively low number of Chinese medicine doctors proficient in the technique before the 1970s).[109] Commenting on PRC claims that they were now able to perform surgery on patients anesthetized only with acupuncture, Topping proclaimed, "It was true – the only anesthetic we saw used was acupuncture needles." Topping even went as far as repeating, with no critical commentary, the claim that acupuncture was also responsible for restoring some hearing capacity to 90 percent of the deaf patients treated with the technique. Topping described acupuncture as "an ancient Chinese medical practice" that has

---

[107] Galston, *Daily Life in People's China*, 53, 49.

[108] The *New York Times* articles feature on the newspaper's front page were "U. S. Biologists in China Tell of Scientific Gains," May 24, 1971 and "Peking Aiming Research at China's Special Needs," June 7, 1971. Galston, *Daily Life in People's China*; Schmalzer, "Speaking about China," 320.

[109] Su, "Diplomatie de La Médecine Traditionnelle Chinoise En République Populaire de Chine"; Fang, *Barefoot Doctors and Western Medicine in China*, 100–101.

been enhanced by the addition of Mao Zedong Thought: a miracle of Chinese revolutionary science. In the years to come, acupuncture would soon become a craze among an American public looking for an ancient panacea to treat the malaise wrought by high-modern living in the United States: Galston, the first American to report on the treatment, even began declining invitations to speak on the subject if the hosts were not also prepared to listen to his views on China and its people more broadly, and Susan Shirk also grew annoyed that acupuncture was the first thing that interviewers would ask her about when discussing her 1971 trip.[110]

In contrast to the popular enthusiasm for China's revolutionary science, many elite American scientists showed immediate skepticism toward Galston's claims. Philip Handler, the distinguished president of the National Academy of Sciences who had in 1970 pioneered cooperation with the Soviets in space research, commented that Galston "appears to be extending himself in order to find aspects of Chinese science of which he can speak with approbation and admiration." Handler believed that, contrary to Galston's judgments, the Chinese use of makeshift gibberellin hormones would lead to "disaster," as they had in the United States, and that the use of human excrement as fertilizer was hardly the "great accomplishment" that Galston claimed.[111] Handler's most scathing criticism was for Galston's celebration of acupuncture. Handler concluded that, while "fascinating," the use of the treatment as an anesthesia for surgery was "of dubious clinical merit" and as a technique to treat deafmutes was "outrageous and clearly unsuccessful." In an early comment that anticipated his later stance on the relative value of scientific exchange with China, Handler concluded his judgment of Galston's account: "On balance, it is clear that the Chinese have far more to learn from Western science than vice versa. Let us by all means foster communications – but

---

[110] Audrey Topping, "Return to Changing China," *National Geographic Magazine*, December 1971; Schmalzer, "Speaking about China," 320; author interview with Shirk. He Hui also highlights Topping's analysis of China as uncritical and part of the so-called "China fever" of the early 1970s. He, *Dangdai Zhong Mei minjian jiaoliu shi*, 125–27. For later Chinese admissions about the efficacy of acupuncture anesthesia, see Paul U. Unschuld, *Medicine in China: A History of Ideas* (Berkeley, CA: University of California Press, 1985), 360–66.

[111] Schmalzer highlights how Chinese farmers did in fact make enthusiastic use of chemical fertilizers – on those limited occasions when such fertilizers were available. Chinese demand for chemical fertilizer was sufficient that in 1973, a contract was signed with the US Kellogg Corporation to build ten large ammonia factories in China to produce fertilizer. Sigrid Schmalzer, *Red Revolution, Green Revolution: Scientific Farming in Socialist China* (Chicago, IL: University of Chicago Press, 2016), 7, 12.

let us do it in full knowledge of the relative technological sophistication of the two societies."[112]

Galston later reported in an oral history interview that his medical colleagues at Yale had also been dismissive of his accounts of the use of acupuncture, growing "contemptuous or even angry and insistent that [he] was either lying or had been 'duped'." And, indeed, Galston had been deceived in many of his interactions in China: eight years later, he would discover that Loo Shih-Wei, an old colleague and friend who Galston had named on his visa application, had only finally been allowed to return from the countryside after the Cultural Revolution in order to receive Galston in Shanghai in a "Potemkin village" apartment that he had been forced by the Chinese authorities to pretend was his own. When Loo traveled to the United States in 1979 on an exchange of botanists that Galston had helped organize, a sobbing Loo explained that his "stolid" and "emotionless and distant" behavior toward Galston during his 1971 trip was a result of trauma from his suffering during the Cultural Revolution for being a Western-trained scientist interested in theoretical problems "not directly connected to the needs of the Chinese people."[113]

FELLOW TRAVELERS FAVORED

Revelations about the tightly controlled nature of scientific exchanges were still many years off in 1971, however, and, in the meantime, Americans grew excited by the prospect of following Signer and Galston to China. The possibility for doing so seemed all the greater when, on July 15, 1971, Nixon made his sensational public announcement that Kissinger had conducted a secret visit to the PRC and that the president himself would follow early the next year. In practical terms, Kissinger's first visit to China had little direct impact on developing exchanges. The trip was brief, and, in the interests of secrecy, Kissinger was accompanied by only a skeleton staff. His talks with Zhou were focused on discussing

---

[112] Among Americans, it was not only elite scientists that doubted aspects of Cultural Revolution science: the physician George Hatem, whose loyalty to Beijing was indicated when he became perhaps the first foreigner ever granted PRC citizenship, was privately angered by the use of, for example, chicken blood injections for a multitude of diseases. Hooper, *Foreigners under Mao*, 25. Handler to Todd, June 23, 1971, "1971" folder, CSCPRCP, NAS; Ethan Signer and Arthur W. Galston, "Education and Science in China," *Science*, January 7, 1972, 18; Galston, *Daily Life in People's China*, 182–85.
[113] Schmalzer, "Speaking about China," 320; Arthur Galston, "Shih-Wei Loo Remembered," *Plant Science Bulletin* 45, no. 2 (Summer 1999).

shared geostrategic interests and drawing up arrangements for a second Kissinger trip and the subsequent Nixon–Mao summit. There were too few Americans in the party for counterpart talks between mid-ranking officials of the sort that would soon become the key channel for governmental negotiation of cultural and scientific exchanges. All the same, during his talks with Zhou, Kissinger applauded the American visits to China that had taken place since 1971 and made clear that he saw these as buttressing the high-level dialogue he and the premier had begun.[114]

If Kissinger welcomed people-to-people exchanges in the abstract, he and his staff were worried that they lacked the means to influence the ground game of these contacts. An internal government memorandum sent in May had explicitly suggested that it "should ... be U.S. policy to try to move our [exchange] contacts more into a governmental plane or to involve the government in some appropriate way in people-to-people contacts."[115] The political dangers posed to the government by exchanges wholly outside their influence were underlined by Beijing's continuing preference for inviting political radicals to China. In spite of Mao's February 1971 proclamation that China should welcome rightists as well as leftists, the majority of the limited number of Americans that made it to China in that year were drawn from left-wing groups highly critical of the US government.[116] Delegations from the Black Panthers and the Black Worker's Congress had taken prominent Black radicals Huey Newton, Elaine Brown, and James Forman to China, and the PRC had also invited the Puerto Rican nationalist group the Young Lords, which had been drawing inspiration from Maoism since the 1960s.[117] 1971 also saw the Marxist William H. Hinton return to China after a long absence from the country that had been effectively imposed by the US government: the State Department had confiscated his passport in 1953 in retribution for his research in rural Shanxi on Communist land reform, later published – after a decade-long legal dispute with the US government over his research notes – as Hinton's globally bestselling 1966 book *Fanshen*.[118] His passport had not been returned until 1968.[119]

[114] Memcon: Zhou, Kissinger, et al., July 11, 1971, *FRUS, 1969–1976*, Vol. XVII, Document 143.

[115] Response to NSSM 124, May 27, 1971, *FRUS, 1969–1976*, Vol. XVII, Document 129.

[116] ZGZYWXYJS, *Mao Zedong waijiao wenxuan*, 592–94.

[117] NFTNC, Vol. 2, No. 1, November 1971; He, *Dangdai Zhong Mei minjian jiaoliu shi*, 112.

[118] Hooper, *Foreigners under Mao*, 31; Lovell, *Maoism*, 277–78; William H. Hinton, *Fanshen: A Documentary of Revolution in a Chinese Village* (New York: Monthly Review Press, 1966).

[119] Kerpen, "Voices in a Silence," 104.

As part of their efforts to begin rapprochement, the US government had removed their objections to Hinton returning to China, as well as permitting other "foreign friends" to travel between the two countries: Joe Hatem visited his brother George, who had been resident in the PRC since 1949, while Sidney Shapiro, a naturalized citizen of the PRC since 1963, became the first of the handful of American long-term residents in the PRC to return to the United States to visit relatives.[120]

In addition to these personal avenues for arranging ad hoc exchanges, 1971 also saw the emergence of an organizational route into China for fellow travelers in the form of the US-China Peoples Friendship Association. Friendship associations were a long-standing mechanism employed by the PRC in their relations with Western countries: organizations similar to the USCPFA had been founded in the UK, France, and Italy in the 1950s and acted as a conduit of, for example, youth delegations to the PRC.[121] The US Friendship Association was initially a decentralized cooperative of self-governing local chapters, the first of which was founded in 1970; a national-level organization was not set up until 1974, by which time there were already some forty local constituent groups.[122] The USCPFA began arranging travel to China for its members from 1971. Susan Warren was a founding chair of a Friendship Association chapter, and this helped her return to China that year, visiting the country where she had sought refuge after being hauled before the House Un-American Activities Committee in 1957 and 1959 for editing *The Far East Reporter*, a New York-published Maoist magazine founded by the 1939 Yan'an visitor, Maud Russell, that regularly featured articles by American leftists resident in the PRC.[123] The influence of figures such as Warren contributed to the pro-Beijing political stance of the Friendship Association, as did the participation of earlier leftist visitors to China who had, as we have seen, been selected for their sympathy with the PRC regime, including Shirley Graham Du Bois and the Pan-Africanist Vicki

[120] Hooper, *Foreigners under Mao*, 31.

[121] Graziani, "Youth Exchanges," 202.

[122] Douglas P. Murray, "Exchanges with the People's Republic of China: Symbols and Substance," *The Annals of the American Academy of Political and Social Science* 424, no. 1 (1976): 36.

[123] Transcript of oral history interview with Susan Warren, April 17, 1976, "Warren, Susan" folder, Box 9, Series 1, Oral History of the American Left collection, Tamiment Library and Robert F. Wagner Labor Archive, New York University, New York, United States (TLWLANYU); *NFTNC*, Vol. 2, No. 1, November 1971; Hooper, *Foreigners under Mao*, 31.

Garvin, who had lived in China from 1964 until 1970.[124] The Friendship Association attracted Maoist sympathizers, some of whom claimed that totalitarianism in China was a "myth" and lambasted the US government for its continuing ties to the "the fascist Chiang Regime" on Taiwan "province" (while also applauding steps taken by Washington toward rapprochement with Beijing).[125]

Politics also lay behind Susan Shirk's aforementioned invitation to what Shirk called a "land of milk and honey." The young MIT graduate student traveled to China in June 1971 alongside Paul Pickowicz, David Lampton, and twelve other Committee of Concerned Asian Scholars-affiliated graduate students. CCAS had, by its own account, "consistently sought to challenge the Cold War myth about China" and had campaigned for the seating of the PRC at the United Nations – ultimately realized three months after their trip. Founded "in opposition to the senior 'blue ribbon experts' who have served as advisors to the United States government" on US policy toward China and Vietnam, CCAS had come out in favor of Sino-American normalization long before Nixon and Kissinger began publicly working toward that end. Fortune favored the bold: a speculative letter sent by the students from Hong Kong to the Chinese People's Association for Friendship with Foreign Countries had been rewarded with the first invitation for a delegation of American university students of China to visit the PRC since the country's establishment in 1949.[126]

For a group founded in part "to develop a true understanding of the People's Republic of China," the visit was enormously exciting.[127] Their month in the PRC provided the young scholars with their first opportunity for direct encounters with the Chinese people they had spent years studying with little hope of direct encounter. They reveled in being "encouraged to wander off on our own," speaking the Chinese they had studied with locals over tomato picking and impromptu basketball games (when they could understand their accents and dialects),

[124] Minami, "How Could I Not Love You?," 18–19.
[125] "Statement of Principles and Activities," USCPFA, November 17, 1974, Folder 24, Box 17, David Sullivan US Maoism collection (DSUSMC), TLWLANYU; "National Office Report – 1/77–4/77," Folder 7, Box 1, USCPFAR, NYPLAMD.
[126] Author interview with Shirk; "Press Release: American Scholars Visit China," June 23, 1971, "Feuerwerker, Albert" folder, Box 5, NASAR, BHL; Pickowicz, *A Sensational Encounter*, 1–10.
[127] "Press Release: American Scholars Visit China," June 23, 1971, "Feuerwerker, Albert" folder, Box 5, NASAR, BHL.

FIGURE 1.4 Chinese physicist Zhou Peiyuan meets with the 1971 Committee of Concerned Asian Scholars delegation of students during a visit to Peking University. Courtesy of Paul Pickowicz Collection, UC San Diego Library

as well as shooting enough home-movie footage to make a one-hour-long documentary upon their return home. Shirk recalls that she "felt like Queen Elizabeth," such was the friendliness of their hosts – and the speed with which the students were whisked from place to place. Kissinger's secret visit took place while the students were in China and, shortly after his departure, Zhou Enlai gave up some four hours of his time to discuss changing Sino-American relations with the visitors. (This was yet another example of signaling through the people-to-people channel: Zhou had the students tape-record the meeting and release the transcript once back home.) High-level access was accompanied by the chance to visit (selected) model units (Figure 1.4). Shirk was able to ask one peasant in northern China whether he enjoyed personal and civil freedom under the CCP: "Yes, now we have the right to love. We are free to work full-time, to have a secure home, to earn enough food." If the opportunities the visitors were given were exciting, the group was also conscious of the choreography of the trip (Figure 1.5). Pickowicz recalls that "enormous ... thought" had gone into the "messages ... communication." "The staging was meticulous. The script was detailed.

FIGURE 1.5 Tea is served during a "short briefing" to the Committee of
Concerned Asian Scholars 1971 delegation. Courtesy of Paul Pickowicz
Collection, UC San Diego Library

And we were the audience."[128] Impressions among the students were not
uniform, however: Richard Bernstein later recalled that the first twenty-
four hours in China was enough to change him from a Maoist sympa-
thizer to "a lifelong anti-communist and devotee of liberal democracy,"
such was his distaste for the "pervasive odor of orthodoxy" and ideological conformity (Figure 1.6). He recalls being a "Menshevik minority"
among the CCAS delegation.[129]

The CCAS visit sparked something of a sensation when the visitors returned to the United States. Nixon's scheduled visit to China
had been announced while the students were in the PRC and now the
American press and public were desperate to hear from anyone that
had firsthand experience of the mysterious People's Republic (the level
of American ignorance of China is suggested by the students explaining

[128] Committee of Concerned Asian Scholars, *China! Inside the People's Republic* (New
York: Bantam Books, 1972), 1, 6, 33; Hanchao Lu, "Versatility, Interdisciplinarity, and
Academic Collaboration: Paul Pickowicz's Insights on Chinese Studies," *The Chinese
Historical Review* 27, no. 1 (January 2020): 53–54; Pickowicz, *A Sensational Encoun-
ter*, 27, 41, 52, 63–65, 129–32; author interview with Shirk.
[129] "A Bridge to a Love for Democracy," *New York Times*, December 29, 2010.

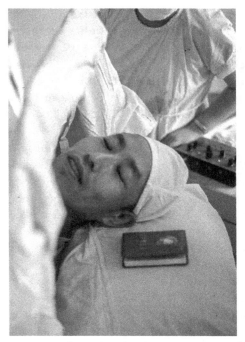

FIGURE 1.6 Surgery is performed with Mao quotations in close proximity during the Committee of Concerned Asian Scholars delegation's visit to Beijing Medical College, Hospital No. 3, on July 16, 1971. Courtesy of Paul Pickowicz Collection, UC San Diego Library

what a Chinese dumpling is in their account of the visit). The fresh-faced students quickly became "academic celebrities" and faced a cascade of media interviews. They also found themselves on the oppo-site side of their own classrooms at MIT, Stanford, and Wisconsin, giving their eyewitness accounts of a China that their esteemed aca-demic mentors had previously taught them only through books and outdated accounts. This lecture circuit was followed by the publication of a bestselling book-length trip report with a simple, effusive title: *China! Inside the People's Republic.* (The book was rushed out to be released before Nixon's trip; its hurried preparation was achieved in part by having much of the text written by CCAS members that had not been on the China trip.) The students' China visit had brought them fame unlike any had known before; for many of them, it would be the beginning of distinguished careers as recognized experts on the country.[130] They would not be the last Americans to quickly rise in prominence within the field of China studies because of their good fortune in securing scarce invitations to the PRC while many more senior professional scholars were passed over.[131] The visit also led some within CCAS to believe that, as the possibility of exchanges with China was realized, the organization might be able to leverage their trip to become, as Fabio Lanza writes, "the central conduit for exchanges with China."[132]

The US government was given its best opportunity yet to establish its influence over the exchange program and to address Beijing's favoring of leftist visitors like the members of CCAS and the Friendship Association when Kissinger made his second visit to China, beginning on October 20, 1971. In his talks with Chinese leaders, Kissinger took a personal interest in selling the benefits of expanding the program of exchanges to Zhou, stressing that Washington "considered progress in these fields [of cultural and scientific exchanges] not as a substitute for fundamental agreements but rather to give impetus to them." Kissinger also argued that greater people-to-people contact "would keep off balance those who wished to see the new U.S.-China dialogue fail."[133] This was a sincere concern of the White House: in the summer of 1971, the president still considered the right-wing pro-Taiwan China lobby "a considerable group" and worried they might "descend on me like a pack of little jackals" over changes to the White House's China policy.[134]

Although Kissinger reported to Nixon that the Chinese had only "unenthusiastically" agreed to a reference to promoting exchanges in the draft communiqué to be made public after the Nixon summit, the full record of his second visit suggests that important progress was made on that front.[135] The head of the Asian Communist Affairs desk at State, Alfred L. Jenkins, had spent hours discussing exchanges, both in the abstract and in practical detail, with leading Chinese foreign affairs advisor Xiong Xianghui, who had shown himself enthusiastically

---

[130] Pickowicz, *A Sensational Encounter*, 127–34; He, *Dangdai Zhong Mei minjian jiaoliu shi*, 127. Author interview with Shirk; author interview with Paul Pickowicz, by telephone, November 11, 2020; Committee of Concerned Asian Scholars, *China!*, for the "dumplings" reference, see 54. See also Lanza, *End of Concern*.

[131] Schmalzer, "Speaking about China," 313.

[132] Lanza, *End of Concern*, 102.

[133] Kissinger to Nixon, November 1971, *FRUS, 1969–1976*, Vol. XVII, Document 164.

[134] Tudda, *Cold War Turning Point*, 74.

[135] Kissinger to Nixon, November 1971, *FRUS, 1969–1976*, Vol. XVII, Document 164.

interested in the twenty-five specific exchange delegations proposed by Jenkins.[136] Wei Shiyan also concludes, based on the Chinese record, that the Jenkins–Xiong negotiations were a success.[137] PRC leaders had, however, refused to discuss arms control and "airily dismissed the subject of trade," the latter stance reflecting a May 1971 Chinese politburo decision not to allow significant trade before progress in negotiations over Taiwan was made.[138] Xiong also rebuffed Jenkins request that exchanges be conducted on a "semi-official" basis through "a government-to-government arrangement." Xiong insisted that exchanges continue on an ostensibly people-to-people basis – although Beijing in fact had no plans to cease their own close involvement in such contacts.[139]

The Chinese side had their own points to raise regarding exchanges. One sore spot was the recent tour of the United States by a table tennis team from Chiang Kai-shek's Republic of China regime to Taiwan. The group – all purportedly Christians – had been invited by the evangelical Presbyterian and virulent anti-Communist Carl McIntire and had arrived in the United States in August for a two-month tour.[140] Zhou claimed that the visit had delayed Beijing's plan to send its own team for the return leg of the ping-pong exchange planned by the National Committee on US-China Relations and Xiong argued that the issuing of visas to the ROC visitors made the US government culpable for the tour going ahead, overriding NSC member John Holdridge's objections that the visit had been arranged by the same domestic enemies of rapprochement of which Jenkins had previously spoken. (Later, during the Nixon summit visit, Marshall Green of the State Department admitted

---

[136] Memcons: Xiong, Jenkins, Holdridge, et al., October 21, 1971, and Xiong, Jenkins, and Holdridge, October 22, 1971, *FRUS, 1969–1976*, Vol. E-13, Documents 39 and 43; Xiong, *Wo de qingbao yu waijiao shengya*, 449–50.

[137] Wei Shiyan, "Jixinge di er ci fang Hua [Kissinger's Second Visit to China]," in *Xin Zhongguo waijiao fengyun* [Winds and Clouds in New China's Diplomacy], ed. Waijiaobu waijiaoshi bianjishi [Foreign Ministry Editorial Office on Diplomatic History], vol. 3 (Beijing: Shijie zhishi chubanshe, 1990), 65.

[138] Memcon: Kissinger and Zhou, October 20, 1971, Remote Access Collection Program (RACP): NLC-26-17-7-2-5, Jimmy Carter Library (JCL), Atlanta, GA, United States; Yafeng Xia, "China's Elite Politics and Sino-American Rapprochement, January 1969–February 1972," *Journal of Cold War Studies* 8, no. 4 (October 2006): 17–21.

[139] Memcon: Xiong, Jenkins, Holdridge, et al., October 21, 1971, *FRUS, 1969–1976*, Vol. E-13, Document 39.

[140] "Free Chinese Table Tennis Team to Visit Peru, U.S.," *News from China*, July 23, 1971, Folder 288, Box 30, Series 9, RG4, NCUSCR records, RAC.

to Xiong that the US government's provision of visas had been an "error."[141])

Kissinger – ultimately incorrectly – concluded from the argument that the continued presence of a Republic of China embassy in Washington would not only prevent any visit to the United States by a Chinese leader but also the expansion of exchanges and trade before normalization brought an end to the formal US relationship with Taipei. Kissinger was right that this was a sensitive subject for the PRC, particularly in the wake of the Republic of China's ejection from the UN in October 1971: while a victory for Beijing, Premier Zhou and the PRC leadership believed that this victory might stoke a nascent Taiwanese independence movement that was anathema to the PRC.[142] Beijing's sensitivity on the issue of Taiwan was one reason that the Committee on Scholarly Communication had so far failed to gain Chinese attention: Galston reported to the organization that the ties between the National Academy of Sciences and Academia Sinica on Taiwan explained why the Chinese had favored another American scientific group, the Federation of American Scientists (FAS), for initial scientific contacts (although another good reason why the FAS had quickly established a relationship with Beijing was that Galston had recommended the organization to his hosts).[143]

The Federation of American Scientists was also preferable to Beijing on account of its greater distance from the American government and due to its political pedigree. Set up by scientists who had been involved in the Manhattan Project to lobby for nuclear disarmament, the group's criticisms of US government policy had been praised by Chinese state media since the 1950s.[144] The Federation lacked privileges such as tax exemption that were afforded to the National Academy because of its

[141] Kissinger to Nixon, November 1971, *FRUS, 1969–1976*, Vol. XVII, Document 164; Memcon: Ji, Green, et al., February 22, 1972, *FRUS, 1969–1976*, Vol. E-13, Document 91.

[142] ZGZYWXYJS, *Zhou Enlai nianpu, 1949–1976*, 3:494.

[143] Meeting between Galston and CSCPRC members, June 9, 1971, "1971 – General," CSCPRCP, NAS; Schmalzer, "Speaking about China," 324–25.

[144] "Meiguo Kexuejia Lianhehui zai huikan shang fabiao shengming zhengshi Mei zhengfu changqi yilai zhunbei jinxing xijunzhan" [Federation of American Scientists Issue Statement Offering Proof that the US Government has Long Been Preparing for Biological Warfare], *Renmin Ribao*, April 9, 1952.

stature.[145] The proximity between the Academy and the state was not lost on the PRC government. The Chinese American physicist and Nobel laureate Chen Ning Yang visited the PRC in July and August 1971, meeting with Chinese leaders including Mao and Zhou. Upon his return, Yang told NAS Foreign Secretary Harrison Brown that his hosts had ruled out government-to-government scientific exchanges and that they saw the Academy as a government agency.[146] Then, during Kissinger's October visit, Chinese interlocutors had asked pointed questions about the level of government funding the Academy received.[147] In November, Chinese leaders told the visiting American physician Victor Sidel that a relationship with an institution that Beijing saw as more official than not would have to wait until after normalization.[148]

As 1971 drew to a close, Beijing's preference for left-leaning organizations as facilitators of exchanges remained, in spite of Kissinger and his colleagues' efforts during the October visit. The Committee of Concerned Asian Scholars that had sponsored Shirk's trip to China was in late 1971 organizing a second trip for thirty of its members – twice as many as had traveled on the first delegation – while the Committee for a New China Policy, an academic pressure group founded in 1968 by academic Daniel Tretiak to push for immediate recognition of the PRC and an end to US assistance to Taiwan, was putting together a delegation that ultimately traveled in January 1972. The continued Chinese interest in American leftists was not an exclusive preference: Beijing was aware that the US Table Tennis Association was working with the National Committee on plans for receiving the Chinese ping-pong players, while an early ally of the National Committee – the Quaker group the American Friends Service Committee – had also been welcomed to China in the autumn and was planning a future trip by a larger group.[149] As discussed in the Prologue, fellow travelers had been targeted for invitations to China in

---

[145] Audra J. Wolfe, *Freedom's Laboratory: The Cold War Struggle for the Soul of Science* (Baltimore, MD: Johns Hopkins University Press, 2018), 95.

[146] Yang is also known by other romanizations of his name, including Chen-ning Yang and, as written in Pinyin, Yang Zhenning. Smith, "Role of Scientists," 122.

[147] Memcon: Xiong, Holdridge, and Jenkins, *FRUS, 1969–1976*, Vol. E-13, Document 43.

[148] "Scientists Vie for Peking Trip," *Washington Post*, November 18, 1971; Su Jingjing and Zhang Daqing, "Xin Zhongguo shouci fu Mei yixue daibiaotuan zhi tanjiu [An Exploration of New China's First Medical Delegation to the United States]," *Zhongguo keji shi zazhi* 32, no. 3 (2011): 396.

[149] *NFTNC*, Vol. 2, No. 1, November 1971, and Vol. 2, No. 2, February 1972; Kerpen, "Voices in a Silence," 161–62.

the 1950s and 1960s in part in the belief that transnational political links could help ferment domestic revolution in the United States. This revolutionary ambition had been abandoned by the Chinese politburo in May 1971.[150] Now, invitations were issued as a reward for those Americans most vocally channeling Beijing's calls for the United States government to recognize the PRC regime. Meanwhile, China held out the possibility of exchange visits overseen by the government – or even with private groups considered by Beijing to be semi-official – for after progress had been made toward that end.

NEGOTIATING EXCHANGES AT THE NIXON–MAO SUMMIT

Nixon's February 1972 summit visit to China was an event of extraordinary scale and significance. Chinese documents from the local level offer a reminder of the extent of the preparations for the president's visit. A November 1971 memorandum from the Beijing Municipal Transportation Bureau complained of the challenges of sourcing some 270 automobiles to transport the vast entourage that would accompany Nixon: the entire Beijing municipal government's stock was not sufficient, and some cars had to be brought in from the city of Tianjin, nearly a hundred miles away. The task was made more difficult by the – presumably, politically motivated – requirement that all cars used in the visit be of Chinese manufacture.[151] Nixon would conclude his visit in Shanghai, where plans were simultaneously being made to temporarily supplement the pool of 125 local government drivers with another eighty that could be relied upon – both behind the wheel and ideologically. The president's visit was a red-carpet event of the highest order; indeed, the Shanghai local government found itself some 2,300 meters short of the velvet, velveteen, silk, and brocade needed for his elaborate reception. Some 382,500 yuan was going to be expended to prepare the city's government facilities for the reception – the equivalent of the average yearly income of nearly 1,300 Chinese citizens.[152] These

[150] Yang and Xia, "Vacillating between Revolution and Détente," 405.
[151] Revolutionary Leading Group of Beijing Municipal Transportation Bureau, "Guanyu wei yingjie Nikesong xu zengjia cheliang de biaoshi baogao" [Report on the Need to Increase the Number of Cars for Nixon's Reception], November 29, 1971, Folder 117-2–354, Beijing Municipal Archives, China (BJMA).
[152] Municipal Revolutionary Committee Office Machine Management Group, "Guanyu jiedai Nikesong zhunbei gongzuo zhong xuyao jiejue de ji ge wenti de qingshi baogao" [Report on Issues to be Solved in Preparation for Receiving Nixon], December 9, 1971, Folder B123-8–503, Shanghai Municipal Archive, China (SHMA).

were hardly wasted efforts, however: hundreds of American reporters would accompany the president in perhaps the greatest media showcase of the People's Republic to a foreign audience since the country's founding. The pomp mattered most to the guest of honor: Nixon said that the sight of being "received by a million Chinese people" would have "a hundred times the effect" of any official communiqué agreed between the governments.[153]

The Nixon–Mao summit also had profound consequences for the burgeoning relationship between the people of the two countries. The visit occurred as the trickle of exchange visitors in each direction began to rapidly intensify: before the president's trip, only about ten American scientists had visited the PRC since Galston and Signer's first, May 1971 trip; by the end of 1972, around 100 had made the trip.[154] Moreover, the concurrent presence in the PRC of practically every US official that influenced the country's China policy provided an opportunity for extensive face-to-face negotiations with Chinese counterparts – including over exchanges. The American priority in the negotiations over people-to-people contacts was to take up where Kissinger had left off in October 1971 and convince Beijing to invite more Americans who would build support for rapprochement among the mainstream public, rather than courting the White House's domestic enemies. The US side tabled exchanges as a key point of negotiation at the summit even before the president's arrival: during a final January 1972 preparatory trip, General Alexander Haig, Kissinger's deputy, argued that, in light of the "major problem" of US domestic opposition to rapprochement, Nixon was concerned that the summit "succeed in both fact and in appearance." Haig thus asked that there "might be some strengthening of the positive aspects of the Joint Communiqué" set to be issued during Nixon's trip, to include "something that would give an immediate sense of accomplishment as a result of the visit, such as increased scientific or cultural exchanges."[155]

Negotiations over exchanges continued in the talks between Secretary of State Rogers and his Chinese interlocutors during Nixon's trip. These have been largely remembered as the kids' table discussions of the summit, a sideshow to give Rogers face while the president and Kissinger discussed the real matters of importance with Mao and Zhou.[156] The

---

[153] Tudda, *Cold War Turning Point*, 128, 124.
[154] Smith, "Role of Scientists," 122.
[155] Memcon: Zhou and Haig, January 3, 1972, *FRUS, 1969–1976*, Vol. XVII, Document 183.
[156] Tudda, *Cold War Turning Point*, xiv.

calculated exclusion of the secretary of state from the meeting with Mao was, of course, a major slight. However, the record of the counterpart talks suggests that much of the summit's substantive negotiations happened at Rogers's table. While Nixon and Kissinger talked with the chairman in philosophical terms and crafted a new discourse of strategic cooperation with Zhou, Rogers negotiated agreements for greater exchanges and trade that were the only tangible announcements included in the Shanghai Communiqué that capped Nixon's visit: no other aspect of that milestone document led directly to changes in Sino-American interaction, even if the expansive rhetoric of the agreement publicly confirmed Beijing and Washington's strategic marriage of convenience.[157]

Indeed, in the run up to the summit, Edward David, Nixon's top science advisor, offered a similar analysis of the role exchanges played at the summit: the White House "wanted to offer the Chinese something more than the geopolitical repositioning that would occur – something more tangible, more concrete." "Science cooperation [will] show the Chinese we are serious about some kind of enduring engagement," David told one of his aides, who worked with the CSCPRC's Anne Keatley to produce "some forty different initiatives" to suggest to the Chinese during the summit.[158] In the wake of the Nixon–Mao summit, Zhou told his colleagues that one benefit of the agreements made during Nixon's visit was an increase in access to the advanced scientific knowledge and technology of the United States – access that would come primarily through scientific exchanges.[159] Agreements on exchanges were also of much interest to Americans who wondered if they might be able to soon follow in Nixon's footsteps: the traveling American press corps that accompanied the president plied him with questions about the possibility of tourist visas and were excited when Nixon seemed to hint they might soon be granted (in the event, individual tourist visas would not be issued in large numbers for another half decade).[160]

---

[157] Lorenz Lüthi and Gordon H. Chang have also recently argued that the Nixon visit lacked substance. Lorenz M. Lüthi, *Cold Wars: Asia, the Middle East, Europe* (Cambridge: University Press, 2020), 134; Chang, *Fateful Ties*, 228. For a discussion of the discursive purpose of these and other Sino-American summit meetings, see Goh, *Constructing the U.S. Rapprochement with China*.

[158] Gerson S. Sher, *From Pugwash to Putin: A Critical History of US-Soviet Scientific Cooperation* (Bloomington, IN: Indiana University Press, 2019), 22.

[159] ZGZYWXYJS, *Zhou Enlai nianpu, 1949–1976*, 3:515.

[160] MacMillan, *Seize the Hour*, 277.

Foreign Minister Ji Pengfei was more forthcoming than he and his colleagues had been during Kissinger's October 1971 visit. Ji expressed interest in an array of sporting exchanges, including basketball, tennis, badminton, and gymnastics delegations, and said that a group of Chinese doctors were interested in becoming the first scientific delegation to the United States. Ji told Rogers that exchanges would grow faster than trade before diplomatic normalization but conceded that China and the United States could "carry out a very limited amount" of trade "on a non-governmental basis" before normalization, revising Beijing's previous reluctance to endorse any level of commercial exchange.[161] Ji also added a significant addendum to the principle that all exchanges must be on a nongovernmental, people-to-people basis, now saying that both governments "should assist in the process of improving people-to-people contacts." Rogers eagerly welcomed this change, and the US side lobbied the Chinese to consider some form of mutual permanent presence in each other's capital to provide just such government assistance with exchanges and trade. This idea was not taken up by the Chinese at this stage – but would later be accepted in the form of the establishment of liaison offices in 1973 (Chapter 3).

On the final day of the visit, Rogers sought to bolster US governmental influence over exchanges via a different route. Ji had previously asked for a recommendation for the best American group to coordinate exchanges and now Rogers explicitly sponsored the National Committee on US-China Relations. The NCUSCR had been recommended for this role to Kissinger before the visit by his closest aide, Winston Lord, as well as in lobbying from outside the White House by former NCUSCR chairman Doak Barnett. Ji was hesitant to accept Rogers's suggestion, responding that Beijing was concerned that "other friendly organizations will be unhappy" if the PRC agreed to work directly with the National Committee. Rogers said it would be "fine" if Beijing preferred another group, but Jenkins persisted, arguing that the exchange program needed a "central organization to help on the mechanics of visits" – both the second ping-pong trip and other exchanges – or else a government body would be required. Convincing the Chinese to accept Rogers's recommendation of the NCUSCR as the primary US conduit for cultural exchanges would soon become an important goal for the government.[162]

---

[161] Memcon: Ji, Rogers, et al., February 22, 1972, *FRUS, 1969–1976*, Vol. E-13, Document 91.

[162] Memcon: Ji, Rogers, et al., February 28, 1972, *FRUS, 1969–1976*, Vol. E-13, Document 107; Lord to Kissinger, undated, "China trade/exchanges – February 2, 1972–74

Nixon's visit also saw agreement for one particular cultural exchange that would soon capture American popular attention. As one of his gifts for his hosts, Nixon presented the Chinese with a prime example of American fauna: a pair of rare white musk oxen, named Milton and Mathilda.[163] The Chinese internal report on the animals suggests appreciation for the diplomatic and scientific value of the gift – though the report does also comment that the particular musk oxen presented were not in optimal health. Whether because of the stresses of their travel to China or some other reason, they were missing patches of their fur, and weighed only 102 kilograms; Chinese care would quadruple that weight in four months. The musk oxen joined a menagerie of other animals presented to China as diplomatic gifts, which by 1974 included Japanese flamingos and penguins, Romanian bears, Canadian beavers, and British deer.[164] The noble American musk oxen were rather outshone, however, by the gift the Chinese presented in return: two giant pandas. Ling-Ling and Hsing-Hsing would travel to the US National Zoo in May. An internal Chinese report proudly commented that Theodore Reed, the director of the Zoo, told a visiting Chinese cadre, "Before the giant pandas arrived, the white tigers were the zoo's most valuable animal. Now that the Chinese have sent the giant pandas, the pandas have become the most valuable animals."[165] First Lady Pat Nixon reportedly had an equally positive, if less sober, reaction to the gift: when Zhou Enlai took a break between smoking Panda brand cigarettes at the opening banquet of the Nixon summit to point at the packet and tell her, "We will give you two," she allegedly screamed with joy.[166]

CONCLUSION

People-to-people contacts were central to the early moves in Sino-American rapprochement and the realization of the Nixon–Mao

July, 1973," Box 93, Kissinger Files – Country Files – Far East (HAKCFFE), Richard Nixon Library, Yorba Linda, CA (RNL); Barnett to Kissinger, August 21, 1971, "Kissinger, 1968–81" folder, Box 106, ADBP, RBMLCU.

[163] MacMillan, *Seize the Hour*, 236.
[164] Beijing Zoo, "Guanyu guoji liwu dongwu de jiankang zhuangkuang baogao" [Report on the Condition of Animals Sent as Gifts by Foreign Countries], April 28, 1974, Folder 98-2-378, BJMA.
[165] Committee of Beijing Municipal Bureau of Landscape Architecture, "Guanyu Meiguo song gei Beijing dongwuyuan de liang zhang bailaohu huapian de qingkuang bao" [A Report on the Two Paintings of White Tigers Given to the Beijing Zoo by the United States], May 22, 1974, Folder 98-2-378, BJMA.
[166] MacMillan, *Seize the Hour*, 147.

summit. In lieu of other means of communication, both Washington and Beijing had sought to indicate their interest in dialogue through their approach to the other country's citizens, whether through lifting the long-standing US embargo on travel and commerce between the two countries or through the pomp with which Beijing received Edgar Snow. If these early messages had been garbled by decades of mistrust, there was nothing ambiguous about the ping-pong breakthrough of April 1971 that preempted Kissinger and then Nixon's first visits to China. People-to-people contacts also provided the earliest substantive agreements between the two sides: the Shanghai Communiqué pledges to begin exchange visits and restart trade were the only public evidence of the changed Sino-American relationship beyond the pageantry of Nixon's trip, at a time when the US press was critical of how Kissinger and the president kept practically every detail of their negotiations with Chinese leaders to themselves.

American actors beyond the US government made an important contribution to the changes in the Sino-American relationship before the Nixon–Mao summit. These changes were not, as they have often been portrayed, simply the result of secretive communications from heads of state to heads of state. In fact, many of the signals Nixon used to show his interest in negotiations with the Chinese were first advocated by people outside of the White House and State Department, both in private briefings and in public forums. Moreover, by traveling to China in April 1971, the American ping-pong team – without any instruction from their government – achieved in a week what the White House's backchannels and subtle posturing had failed to in two and a half years, finally moving Sino-American contacts beyond cryptic signaling and into face-to-face engagement.

Soon thereafter, PRC leaders opened direct talks with Kissinger. This tentative diplomatic dialogue was buttressed by people-to-people visits: 1971 saw American scientists, journalists, and political activists travel to China, as well as the delegation of graduate students in which Susan Shirk first traveled to China. Many of the Americans that traveled to the PRC were not endorsed (much less selected) by Washington. Indeed, most were, like Shirk's colleagues in the Committee of Concerned Asian Scholars, vocal domestic critics of the Nixon administration. This did not prevent their trips from contributing to the thaw between the two countries, however. As Shirk's traveling companion and fellow-CCAS member Paul Pickowicz later recalled: "when we started the trip, we saw ourselves as engaging in people-to-people diplomacy, but we never imagined that our trip would end on such a surprising and seriously diplomatic note," with the students answering questions at the Hong Kong Foreign Correspondents Club about the Chinese government's changing policy toward the United States.[167] Still, the political leanings of the Americans invited to China irked the White House, and 1972 would see Washington push hard to convince Beijing to begin exchange contacts with nongovernmental organizations that were prepared to cooperate with, rather than lambast, the Nixon administration.

[167] Pickowicz, *A Sensational Encounter*, 134.

2

Ping-Pong Diplomacy's Return Leg and After

"We have received the two letters you sent us on behalf of the American Council of Learned Societies," the note began.

We the Chinese people are very dubious about your purpose and intention of you sending the two letters to us .... The aggressive ambitions and schemes of the United States can never be concealed before the devil-finding mirror of Mao Tsetung thought. Here we would solemnly warn you that if you dare to play any schemes or tricks, we will certainly smash your dog head. Long live down with U.S. imperialism! Long live Mao Tsetung Thought![1]

Frederick Burkhardt, a senior member of the Committee on Scholarly Communication and the chairman of the American Council of Learned Societies, received this note in response to a letter he had sent to Guo Moruo. Guo was the distinguished head of the Chinese Academy of Sciences who had, alongside his vast corpus of original work, also translated Goethe, Tolstoy, and Upton Sinclair into Chinese. But it was a self-described Red Guard Team, not Guo, that had responded to Burkhardt's letter. The content of the correspondence would have been alarming at any time but it was particularly concerning as the note arrived in July 1972 – just as the CSCPRC was seeking to persuade the Chinese Academy of Sciences to begin exchanges and scientific cooperation with the American scientific establishment, in addition to the left-leaning scientists

---

[1] "Red Guard Team in Academy of Sciences, Peking" to "Mr. Burkheart" [*sic*], July 25, 1972, "China Exchange, Miscellaneous," Part II: Box 308, American Council of Learned Societies records (ACLSR), Manuscript Division, Library of Congress, Washington, DC, United States (LOCMD).

previously favored by Beijing. The belligerent rebuttal sent to Burkhardt suggested how hard this might prove.

Burkhardt and his colleagues at the ACLS and CSCPRC knew that the stakes were high for forging a partnership with their Chinese counterparts – and doing so quickly. Americans inside and outside of government were acutely aware that, as the volume of exchange contacts with China rapidly increased in the wake of Nixon's February 1972 summit, the precedents set would shape interactions for years to come. Indeed, this chapter will show how a structure for Sino-American exchange contacts was established in the year and a half following Nixon's visit – one that would remain largely unchanged until the final normalization agreement of 1978. Negotiations covered principles, but at least as important was how such principles were practically applied to the high-profile exchanges of 1972, particularly the return leg of ping-pong diplomacy in April of that year. That visit was cohosted by the National Committee on US-China Relations and the tour's success underpinned the National Committee's bid to establish itself as the foremost American group for overseeing cultural exchanges with the PRC. The NCUSCR's gambit was challenged, however, by leftist Americans unwilling to cede their earlier dominance in Sino-American people-to-people contacts and resistant to the elite and centrist NCUSCR and CSCPRC becoming the leading mediators between American society and China. Given the importance of exchanges to the Sino-American relationship, this intra-American dispute attracted the White House's attention, with the US government becoming a powerful ally of the NCUSCR and CSCPRC in their efforts to convince Beijing to recognize the two organizations as the primary US clearing houses for Sino-American cultural and scientific exchanges, as well as playing a role in the 1973 establishment of a third nongovernmental organization to promote commercial exchanges with China – the National Council for United States-China Trade.

GOVERNMENT STRATEGIES TOWARD
SINO-AMERICAN EXCHANGES

The threat to "smash your dog head" suggested that, even in the wake of the Nixon–Mao summit, many in China were still at best ambivalent about contact with the United States. The PRC leadership internally presented the secret talks with top American leaders as a clever manipulation of repentant arch imperialists: Vice Foreign Minister Fu Hao proudly told cadres in Hunan that "Nixon came flying a white flag." Such a narrative attempted to square Mao's bold initiative with two decades of vilification of the United States as China's foremost ideological enemy. In doing so, it helped create an uneasy tension in China's ties with the United States in the late Mao era: anti-Americanism lingered, even as contact quickly deepened.[2]

The American public seemed less equivocal about the new relationship with China. The visits of the US ping-pong team, and then of Kissinger and Nixon, had sparked a whirlwind romance between Americans and China. In 1972, many Americans thought of the PRC not primarily in ideological Cold War terms but instead in the manner that Americans had been thinking of China since their country's clippers had first began a roaring trade in ginseng, sandalwood, and tea that had made the fortunes of the Forbes, Cabot, and Peabody families in the eighteenth and nineteenth centuries.[3] The February 1972 cover of *The Ladies Home Journal* showed Pat Nixon in a dress of "opulent chinoiserie for grand evenings" that, the *New York Times* commented, "evokes China's imperial past [with] ornate design, rich fabric, and … large sleeves" reminiscent of the court dress of the Qing dynasty. American clothes designers were frustrated that they were not yet able to buy items directly from China; in the meantime, they created their own fabrics with "oriental flair." Meanwhile, *Playboy* featured the literary epitome of old China meets new – seven poems penned by Mao himself – and *Ingenue*, a fashion magazine for American teenagers, provided advice on how to capture the "essence of Chinese beauty": "make-up techniques to convey the impression of Oriental eyes, round face and a flatter nose." Shoppers could even visit the "China Passage" section of Bloomingdale's and purchase items of wicker ware, rattan, straw, and bamboo – or a porcelain neck warmer in the shape of a cat for the not insignificant sum of $17.50.[4]

The Nixon administration sought to further cultivate American popular interest in China through the expansion of exchange visits and trade that had been endorsed by the PRC leadership during the Nixon summit visit. A month after the president's trip, his foreign policy advisors sought to draw up a coherent strategy toward Sino-American exchanges in the form of National Security Study Memorandum (NSSM) 148.[5] Kissinger

---

[2] "Zhonggong Shanghai shi caimao wu qigan xiao weiyuanhui shi ganbu dahui taolun qingkuang huibao (san)" [3rd Report on the Discussion at the Municipal Cadre Meeting of the Shanghai Municipal Finance and Trade Committee], January 7, 1972, Folder A98-2-703, SHMA; Ma, *The Cultural Revolution in the Foreign Ministry*, 332.

[3] Chang, *Fateful Ties*, 20–22.

[4] "China: It's the Latest American Thing," *New York Times*, February 16, 1972.

[5] NSSM 148, March 9, 1972, *FRUS, 1969–1976*, Vol. XVII, Document 209.

chaired a meeting to discuss the study, as well as the accompanying NSSM 149 on US-China trade. "The President has a personal interest in this," he told his staff, "and what is most important is that we don't defeat our other, larger purposes in developing contacts with the Chinese" – the strategic and political value of the relationship. Beijing had refused to allow Washington to directly oversee exchange visits, but the government still hoped to influence contacts initiated by nongovernmental organizations. Kissinger wanted to challenge the long-standing practice of the PRC giving invitations to individual Americans or hand-picked groups and, to do so, he ordered the identification of nongovernmental "umbrella organizations" that could then be conduits for structured exchanges. Which organizations were chosen was critical: "with an umbrella organization, we must have control, or there will be an emphasis on those groups sympathetic to the new left."[6]

Kissinger already had one umbrella organization in mind. At the March meeting, Kissinger reaffirmed that the administration should continue to endorse the NCUSCR to the Chinese. He agreed to a proposal from John Richardson Jr. that other reliable organizations should be found to manage contacts beyond cultural exchanges. Richardson, hired by Nixon as assistant secretary of state for educational and cultural affairs, was a long-standing believer in using cultural contact toward Cold War ends: before his nomination by Nixon, he had spent eight years as president of the National Committee for a Free Europe, a front organization of the Central Intelligence Agency (CIA) that had been founded by Allen Dulles to use "psychological warfare" to counter Soviet influence in Europe. In the March discussion with Kissinger, Richardson added that the government needed to ensure that the National Committee on US-China Relations's programming served government objectives: "Our interest now is to try to structure the program of the National Committee," which would be achieved in part by "indirectly" channeling government funds to the organization.[7]

NSSM 148 included as one of the objectives of the exchange program "to develop favorable attitudes toward the United States among PRC elite groups." Nixon had earlier considered Chinese public opinion (as well as, of course, audiences at home) when writing the banquet toast he gave in China, which was printed unedited in the pages of

---

[6] Memcon: Senior Review Group meeting on NSSM 148 and NSSM 149, "China Trade/ Exchanges – February 2, 1972–4 July, 1973," Box 93, HAKCFFE, RNL.
[7] Ibid.

The People's Daily. Exchanges were one of the few other means through which Americans could hope to communicate with the Chinese populace without total medication from the Beijing government – although this contact was far from free of PRC state involvement. The US government worried that the PRC government would simultaneously seek to exploit the opportunity provided by access to the American people, using exchanges to undercut American public support for the government's relationship with Taipei and to promote popular sympathy for Chinese foreign policy goals. Beijing had, of course, long been doing so through its active contacts with radical left-wing American organizations and other critics of the US government.[8] This practice had not ceased with the Nixon visit: while Kissinger discussed NSSM 148, the Chinese Medical Association was hosting Charles Flato, an American Communist and sometime Soviet spy, who had been invited to the PRC to study the country's health-care system with the explicit expectation that he would return home and hail Chinese achievement in the American press.[9]

Flato's invitation notwithstanding, changes in China's strategy toward relations with American society would soon provide some reassurance to the US government. As Brady has shown, the Chinese leadership was already reversing course in the propaganda messages it was sending to both foreign and domestic audiences. At home, the government was promoting the slogan *"yang wei Zhong yong"* (洋为中用), or "make the foreign serve China", a 1956 Mao quotation that had echoes of nineteenth-century Chinese reformers' call to "use Western learning for practical uses." The propagation of this slogan in CCP mouthpieces was an indication of, and a justification for, rapprochement with the United States and had also been employed by Mao in his 1970 discussions with Edgar Snow in which the chairman had stated his interest in centrists and rightists, as well as leftists, visiting China.[10]

---

[8] Holdridge and Hormats to Kissinger, undated, *FRUS, 1969–1976*, Vol. XVII, Document 217; Nixon to Kissinger, March 9, 1972, "China – General, February 27–March 31, 1972," Box 1036, NSC – For the President's Files – China/Vietnam Negotiations, RNL.

[9] International Department of the CCP Central Committee, "Jiedai Meiguo yixue zuojia Feilatu fang Hua jihua" [Plan to Host American Medical Writer Flato on a Visit to China], March 17, 1972, Folder 135-2-338, BJMA.

[10] ZGZYWXYJS, *Mao Zedong waijiao wenxuan*, 592–94; Brady, *Making the Foreign Serve China*, 1, 180. By 1974, *yang wei Zhong yong* was being referenced even in Chinese agricultural policy: one document cited "Chairman Mao's teaching" of the mantra to justify importing of forty tons of peanut seeds from the United States. Ministry of Agriculture, "Guanyu fenpei Meiguo huasheng zhongzi de han" [Letter Regarding the Distribution of US Peanut Seeds], July 9, 1974, Folder 92-3-256, BJMA.

Brady argues that, simultaneously, Beijing was abandoning its support for radical American organizations, instead opting to work with those elite American groups closest to power. She concludes that, "In the long run, CCP decision makers cared little about the left-wing movement in the United States."[11] Yang Kuisong and Xia Yafeng echo this view, arguing that, in Mao's pursuit of Sino-American rapprochement, the chairman gave "no thought to the feeling of those revolutionary parties [in the United States or elsewhere] that had been faithfully following China's policy of anti-imperialism and anti-revisionism."[12] In the 1960s, the radicalization of PRC foreign policy had seen Beijing switch its patronage from American peace activists to those prepared to use violence to challenge the US government. Now, Mao's desire for rapprochement with the United States led the PRC to develop ties with Americans from across the political spectrum.[13] In doing so, the PRC (consciously or otherwise) followed the earlier example of their Soviet big brothers: Soviet programs for "the cultivation of more or less 'friendly' people in America" had also initially "targeted presumably sympathetic people," Austin Jersild reports. But this had "led to relatively pointless discussions with obscure American leftists," including some of the same broad categories of "disaffected leftists, alienated intellectuals, and African Americans" targeted by the Chinese. More successful were "outreach" attempts to "broader society" from the later 1950s – so much so that, already by the end of that decade, Soviet-American cultural contacts were "actually more cordial and warm" than comparable Sino-Soviet interactions.[14]

While Brady's argument for this shift in the focus of the PRC's exchange contacts bears out when considering the 1970s as a whole, we should not ignore the preference Beijing continued to show for contacts with left-wing organizations and individuals even in the early years of rapprochement. The March 1972 invitation for Flato cited his "progressive stance" and his experience of political persecution in the McCarthy era in explaining why he had been selected for an invitation to the country, to give just one immediate example.[15] As we will see, fellow travelers, Communists, and radical left-wing Americans would continue to enjoy access to China until Mao's death, even as the PRC government followed

---

[11] Brady, *Making the Foreign Serve China*, 178.
[12] Yang and Xia, "Vacillating between Revolution and Détente," 399.
[13] Johnson, "From Peace to the Panthers," 248.
[14] Jersild, *The Sino-Soviet Alliance*, 178.
[15] International Department of the CCP Central Committee, "Jiedai Meiguo yixue zuojia Feilatu fang Hua jihua," March 17, 1972, Folder 135.2.338, BJMA.

Mao's orders and also invited American visitors from across the political spectrum.[16] Nor did the Nixon–Mao summit bring an immediate end to radical America's fascination with China: even if some radical Americans like the Black Panther Eldridge Cleaver bemoaned Beijing's relationship with the Nixon government, Frazier argues that many others continued to draw inspiration from Maoism and the PRC.[17]

PING-PONG DIPLOMACY'S RETURN LEG

The month following the discussion of NSSM 148, the US government had its first, best opportunity to put into practice its framework for managing exchange contacts in the form of the most high-profile exchange visit since ping-pong diplomacy – the return leg of that matchup. The reigning world champion table tennis team arrived in Detroit on April 12 for a hotly anticipated twelve-day tour starring Zhuang Zedong, billed as the greatest ping-pong player of all time by the *New York Times* (Figure 2.1).[18] Tickets were highly sought after: it took only a week to sell out the 11,214 tickets for the games played in Detroit's Cobo Hall, which attracted audiences far larger than had ever previously watched table tennis in the United States.[19]

The Chinese team was the first official delegation of visitors from the PRC to the United States and their trip was of great significance to the burgeoning Sino-American rapprochement. Historian Xu Guoqi argues that, "From a long-term perspective, all agreed that a Chinese visit to the United States was even more important than the American team's visit to China."[20] The US government believed the success or failure of the trip would be seen as indicative of the progress of Nixon's overall China initiative and that the visit "has grave implications for the future of

---

[16] As late as 1978, for example, the Chinese were inviting a delegation of left-wing students from among the radical organization, the October League. Office of the Communist Youth League Shanghai Committee, "Guanyu Meiguo geming xuesheng (Shi Yue Tongmeng) daibiaotuan zai Hu huodong qingkuang" [Report on the American Revolutionary Student (October League) Delegation's Activities in Shanghai], August 18, 1978, Folder C21-3-104, SHMA.

[17] Frazier, *The East Is Black*, 200–01.

[18] That Mao and Zhuang share a homonymic forename in English is a coincidence; their forenames are written differently and are pronounced with slightly differential tonal inflection in Chinese. NCUSCR Annual Report, 1971–1972, NCUSCROC.

[19] "L.I. Table Tennis Draws Criticism," *New York Times*, April 2, 1972.

[20] Xu, *Chinese and Americans*, 248; Xu, *Olympic Dreams*, 148–62.

FIGURE 2.1 Three-times table tennis world champion Zhuang Zedong shakes hands with American dancer and choreographer Judith Jamison. Courtesy of Jan Berris

Sino-American relations." Internal White House communications stated that everything must be done to ensure the tour proceeds "flawlessly" for fear that any "untoward incident could have major international repercussions."[21] The visit had such a high profile as to have implications for US diplomacy with the Soviet Union. Hopes for the tour's success notwithstanding, the White House insisted that the visit must be wrapped up at least a month before Nixon's upcoming visit to the Soviet Union for fear that such a prominent public advertisement of Sino-American rapprochement immediately prior to the Brezhnev summit would poison the mood in Moscow.[22]

Beijing similarly accorded great significance to ping-pong diplomacy's return leg: Zhou was closely involved in the planning of the trip and personally selected the players sent to the United States.[23] This preparation was necessary because, for the Chinese players involved, the return leg was just as much of a venture into the unknown as the 1971 trip to China had been for the American table tennis team. Zhuang Zedong

[21] Scali and Solomon to Haig, March 23, 1972, "China Trade/Exchanges – February 2, 1972–4 July, 1973," Box 93, HAKCFFE, RNL.
[22] Scali to Kissinger, March 10, 1972, "China Trade/Exchanges – February 2, 1972–4 July, 1973," Box 93, HAKCFFE, RNL.
[23] ZGZYWXYJS, *Zhou Enlai nianpu, 1949–1976*, 3: 515–16.

was selected to lead the delegation and among his concerns for the trip was that a visit to Hollywood might put the Chinese players in danger of scandal. What if, like Soviet premier Nikita Khrushchev, they were embarrassingly accosted by scantily clad women? (The visiting team were ultimately surprised to find their hosts in Hollywood smartly and elegantly dressed, and highly civilized.)[24]

The tour was the most complex and significant event yet overseen by the NCUSCR and preparation had begun almost immediately after the first leg of the ping-pong exchanges in April 1971. Sporting advice was taken: in the interests of fairness, neither a Chinese nor an American ball was used in the matches, but instead one manufactured in Japan.[25] The provenance of the ball probably had little impact on the outcomes of the matches: with former and current world champions among their distinguished ranks, the Chinese were far superior players and won all but two of the matches.[26] Suspicions about equipment tampering were not completely unfounded, however: it is now known that Chinese ping-pong players did develop irregular bats that produced unusual spin in order to ensure their dominance of the sport during the Cold War.[27] This attention to detail was indicative of the importance of the sporting aspect of the tour, at least for the American players and organizers. For the US team, playing with the Chinese – not only in the scheduled matches but also in practice sessions and in clinics offered by the visitors – was an enviable opportunity to improve their game.[28] "If we could travel with them for six months, everybody would get five or six points better," reflected thirty-year-old Errol Resek, after becoming one of the American players to successfully beat a Chinese opponent during the tour when he defeated Chen Baoching 23–21, 16–21, 21–14. Resek's victory may well have been the result of munificence on the part of the Chinese: another of the American players, Alice Green, a twenty-year-old Columbia junior, reflected, "Sometimes the Chinese don't try to fool you or hit through you with power. Exhibition play, with long rallies, helps promote the sport."[29] The PRC had been throwing politically important sporting matches for

---

[24] Li and Minggong, *Tiyu zhizi*, 327; Qian, "Zhou Enlai xu xie 'pingpang waijiao' huazhang."

[25] "L.I. Table Tennis Draws Criticism," *New York Times*.

[26] Eckstein, "Ping Pong Diplomacy," 333.

[27] Wang, "Friendship First," 152.

[28] Eckstein, "Ping Pong Diplomacy," 340.

[29] "Chinese Go Easy on U.S., Win in Table Tennis, 4-1," *New York Times*, April 21, 1972.

decades: in one instance in Jakarta in 1963, the head of the State Physical Culture and Sports Commission, revolutionary hero Marshal He Long, sent word mid-match to a Chinese badminton player to stop winning a men's single final being watched by millions of Indonesians.[30]

The logistics of the tour went far beyond staging the matches, however. Funding was a major concern: although supportive of the visit, the State Department had judged that it was politically impossible – and anyway undesirable – to directly fund an ostensibly people-to-people visit.[31] Fortunately, the guaranteed publicity of the event – and the prospect of winning favor with the government that controlled the mythical China market – ensured the enthusiasm of corporate America: the National Committee secured more than 125 commercial sponsors for the visit.[32] Pan American Airways lent a plane to ferry the team across the United States, while American Express seconded two of their senior staff to plan how to accommodate the thirty-four strong retinue of Chinese players and coaches, interpreters, journalists, and officials. The advertising giant McCann-Erickson produced a TV documentary of the event, while an author and a literary agent were brought in to retell the dramatic narrative of the tour through a book. Other companies that made notable donations included Kodak, Continental Airlines, and all three Detroit automobile giants: Ford, Chrysler, and General Motors.[33] Donations were rewarded with stops on the tour: the team visited Chrysler's factory and traveled to Memphis – which had almost no local table tennis players – to pay a call on the headquarters of another sponsor, Holiday Inn.[34]

When the subject of how the National Committee would reimburse American Express and Pan Am came up, both companies waved the matter away. The airline was not after cash. Instead, they wanted to renew their relationship with the Chinese government; Pan Am had been involved in the establishment of the Chinese National Aviation Corporation in the

---

[30] Wang, "Friendship First," 144–5.

[31] Willey to Arne [de Keijzer], June 9, 1971, "USTTA – Kaminsky – 1972," Box 15, NASAR, BHL.

[32] Griffin, *Ping-Pong Diplomacy*, 241.

[33] Schoyer to the ping-pong trip organizing committee, June 21, 1971, and "The First Visit of Citizens of the PRC to the United States – A Summary Progress Report," November 1971, "National Committee – General Correspondence – 1969-71," Box 130, ADBP, RBMLCU.

[34] Qian, "Zhou Enlai xu xie 'pingpang waijiao' huazhang," 47; Griffin, *Ping-Pong Diplomacy*, 252–53.

1930s and continued to hold an internationally recognized license to land in China – although the license had little practical use without Beijing's cooperation. Ingratiating their company with the Chinese government might win the airline a shot at again running flights into the mainland – and that was payment enough.[35] Likewise, American Express responded to questions about compensation by simply saying that they would rather like a Beijing office, someday. Indeed, the company had already begun marketing a twenty-two-day organized tour of China, costing a tidy $1,850. The package attracted much public interest – until it became clear that the Chinese government was still unwilling to issue visas to American tourists. Both companies' investments ultimately bore fruit: in March 1976, American Express was invited by Beijing to send a delegation of its senior-most executives to China to discuss business opportunities, while in April 1979, Pan Am Chairman William T. Seawell led the first US airline delegation to the PRC.[36]

The NCUSCR conceived of the ping-pong return trip as a showcase of American diversity. When the players eventually arrived in Detroit, National Committee Chairman Eckstein welcomed them on the airport tarmac with a speech that stressed that, "[although] our cities, towns and villages appear quite similar ... underneath ... there is enormous variety and complexity imposed by the facts of geography and history and the differing ethnic backgrounds of our people."[37] To showcase that diversity, the Committee arranged an eclectic itinerary for the visitors, including trips to a Detroit auto plant, colonial Williamsburg, a majority-African American church in Memphis, the newly arrived Chinese pandas in Washington zoo – and Disneyland.[38] Some of the sightseeing was intended to appeal to Chinese curiosity, but the NCUSCR also used the tour as a chance to exhibit American industrial modernity, with the team being shown manufacturing facilities not only for cars but also soybeans, gramophones, and iron.[39] This turned

[35] Schoyer to Makely, June 29, 1971, Folder 289, Box 30, Series 9, RG4, NCUSCR records, RAC.
[36] Schoyer to the ping-pong trip organizing committee, June 21, 1971, Box 130, ADBP, RBMLCU; "China: It's the Latest American Thing," *New York Times*; NFTNC, Vol. 6, No. 1, April 1976; "Chronology of U.S.-China Relations (March 29, 1979–June 5, 1979)," Folder 6, Box 14, USCPFAR, NYPLAMD.
[37] Eckstein, "Airport Welcome," April 12, 1972, "Athletic Exchanges – Table Tennis (Ping-Pong) – Miscellanea," Box 4, AEP, BHL.
[38] NCUSCR Annual Report, 1971–72, NCUSCROC.
[39] "Wo pingpangqiu daibiaotuan dao Mengfeisi canguan fangwen" [Our Table Tennis Delegation Visited Memphis], *Renmin Ribao*, April 25, 1972.

out to accord with Chinese interests, at least as reported by the Chinese state press: Zhuang Zedong told Detroit workers that the team "salute the American working class [and] have come to learn from you."[40]

Just as important as the representation of the United States shown to the visitors was the impression given to the American public of the Chinese team. Everything was done to ensure that the trip had the maximum possible public impact. The NCUSCR resisted lucrative bids for exclusive television coverage, opting instead to have the tour covered across all networks.[41] Alongside their schedule of matches, the table tennis players were kept busy with goodwill visits to an elementary school and a children's hospital, sightseeing in Harlem, and a ballet performance at the New York City Center theater that would host a tour of Chinese acrobats the following year.[42] When the security of the tour was being discussed between the National Committee and the US government, the former pushed hard for protection for the players that, while "adequate," was not so stifling "as to [prevent] the Chinese visitors a relaxed and free view of the people of the country." This logic applied in the other direction, too: the NCUSCR was reticent to have any barrier that would impede public engagement with the visiting Chinese.[43]

To guarantee the tour's smooth running, the White House insisted on a direct role in the preparation and execution of the visit. The NCUSCR accepted this, on the condition that the "integrity" of the visit as a "nongovernmental, people-to-people exchange" was not unduly infringed. This was, of course, a compromise latent with tension. The National Committee insisted that they and the US Table Tennis Association remain the primary organizers of the event, while nonetheless ceding certain duties to the government – most notably the security of the visitors – and assuring the White House that they would "ensure that the visit leads to improved relations between the peoples of China and the United States" and that they were well aware of the foreign policy implications of the visit.[44]

---

[40] "Friendship Log: Chinese Table Tennis Delegation in USA," *Peking Review*, May 12, 1972.

[41] "The First Visit of Citizens of the PRC to the United States – A Summary Progress Report," November 1971, "National Committee – General Correspondence – 1969–71," Box 130, ADBP, RBMLCU.

[42] "Zhong Mei pingpangqiu yundongyuan zai Niuyue juxing youyisai" [Chinese and American Table Tennis Players Play Friendly Matches in New York], *Renmin Ribao*; "Wo pingpangqiu daibiaotuan dao Mengfeisi canguan fangwen," *Renmin Ribao*; "Chinese Go Easy on U.S.," *New York Times*.

[43] Gilmore to Scali, April 5, 1972, "Athletic Exchanges – Table Tennis (Ping-Pong) – Planning: August 1971–June 1972," Box 4, AEP, BHL.

[44] Ibid.

Nixon had been anxious that the visit take place as soon as possible following the first leg of the exchange and had even toyed with the idea of having the Chinese players play a table tennis match on the White House tennis court.[45] The president personally appointed John A. Scali as his representative during the visit, hoping this would assure Premier Zhou that the White House was cognizant of the importance of the event. Scali had been a noted ABC journalist who had, at the height of the Cuban Missile Crisis, secretly acted as a White House go chement:unlike Link and his fell-between with a KGB colonel. Nixon had made him a special assistant on foreign policy in 1971, and in that role, Scali had, within days of the arrival of the American table tennis players in China, encouraged Nixon to "capitalize" on ping-pong diplomacy.[46] Later that same month – and a year before the return leg took place – the president called Scali to ask him to "handle" the visit. Nixon "stressed that this Chinese visit was not just another exchange, but should be treated as something special" and that the Chinese guests must be treated "exactly the same" as the American players had during their high-profile tour in the PRC. Nixon asked Scali to make sure that "all arrangements be handled very subtly" and warned Scali off being "too visible." In a separate conversation with Kissinger that same day, Nixon said that he did not want the visit "handled by USIA [the United States Information Agency] or State." Scali's involvement ensured Nixon's influence over the initiative, without making the visit a government-run exchange.[47]

Chinese government involvement in the return leg was similarly significant but concealed. Beijing maintained, as they had with earlier delegations of Americans to China, that the exchange was conducted on a people-to-people basis. Zhou had made Zhuang Zedong the leader of the delegation in part to preserve this pretense. But the premier had also assured a nervous Zhuang that he would have "two effective deputies": Qian Dayong and Li Menghua. Li was the deputy director of the PRC National Sports Commission and would go on to become the president of China's Olympic Committee. Qian was even more influential. He traveled on the ping-pong tour in his capacity as a member of the Council of the All-China Sports Federation. But he was also the

---

[45] Xu, *Olympic Dreams*, 152, 159.
[46] Xu, *Chinese and Americans*, 244.
[47] Telcon: Scali and Nixon, April 21, 1971, Kristin L. Ahlberg, ed., *Foreign Relations of the United States, 1917–1972*, vol. VIII, Public Diplomacy, 1969–1972 (Washington, DC: United States Government Printing Office, 2018), Document 130.

deputy director of Western European, North American, and Austral-asian Affairs at the Foreign Ministry, a role that had led to his presence at the table of Kissinger and Zhou's negotiations before the Nixon–Mao summit.[48] In addition, China's mission to the United Nations was also closely involved in the planning of the tour, with four members of the office traveling with the Chinese team throughout the exchange, including First Secretary Gao Liang.[49]

Scali's most significant contribution to the tour was arranging the government security that protected the delegation, paid for with federal funds appropriated by Congress. Scali had lobbied hard to have Secret Service men accompany the team, but ultimately had to make do with twenty State Department and CIA security personnel – armed, and backed up by a police helicopter.[50] Although Scali railed at this apparent snub to the importance of the tour – the Secret Service protected visiting heads of state, and in his mind the ping-pong players were of equal status – National Committee staff member Jan Berris nonetheless later reflected that the highly trained and experienced government security personnel that were involved in the tour had made an immeasurable contribution to the success of the visit, not only by protecting the Chinese team but also through the calm assuredness with which they helped execute the on-the-ground logistics of the tour – much welcomed by the comparatively inexperienced National Committee.[51] Other security precautions taken had included a background check on all American personnel involved in the tour.[52]

The need for security to protect the visit was real. Latent Chinese fears of a violent American society were stoked when, before the visit, the aforementioned anti-Communist, self-styled Christian fundamentalist Carl McIntire threatened to trail the group and protest at the team's every stop (he did), as well as hinting that he would repeat his previous trick of inviting a Taiwanese ping-pong team to tour the United States at the same time as the PRC team in the hopes that Beijing would again postpone their team's tour. The Chinese government repeatedly directly asked their

[48] Qian, "Zhou Enlai xu xie 'pingpang waijiao' huazhang," 47.

[49] Eckstein, "Ping Pong Diplomacy," 329–30.

[50] Scali to Haig, April 3, 1972, "China Trade/Exchanges – February 2, 1972–July 4, 1973," Box 93, HAKCFFE, RNL; "Chinese Ping-Pong Players vs. the Press: Love All," *New York Times Magazine*, May 14, 1972.

[51] Author interview with Berris, August 15, 2015.

[52] Eckstein to Schoyer, August 11, 1971, "Athletic Exchanges – Table Tennis (Ping-Pong) – Publicity," Box 4, AEP, BHL.

American counterparts to ensure the PRC team's safety, eventually prompting Kissinger to promise Huang Hua, Beijing's UN ambassador, that the American government would do "everything behind-the-scenes" to ensure their safety.[53] Kissinger's assurances were apparently not enough to dissuade the Chinese from sending undercover armed security among their accompanying journalists: at one point, a purported Xinhua News Agency reporter took his coat off and revealed a pair of revolvers.[54]

During the very first exhibition match, at Detroit's Cobo Hall, protestors unfurled a banner that read "Send us our POWs not Ping-Pong players," threw hundreds of anti-Communist leaflets, and, in a particularly gruesome moment, hurled dead rats at the Chinese – one reportedly clothed in a red coat emblazoned with Kissinger's name.[55] Another banner held by McIntire's protestors read "Mao killed more Christians than Hitler killed Jews."[56] Demonstrations at a game just outside Washington were especially fierce as Tricia Nixon was in attendance, galvanizing anti-Vietnam student protestors just days after the bombing of Haiphong. The University of Maryland's Cole Field House was packed with 12,000 spectators, up from the 400 or so that usually turned out for the US national table tennis team's home matches. When Nixon's daughter entered the stadium, the protestors unveiled a banner reading "Tricia watches ping-pong while her daddy bombs Haiphong." The students had a simpler chant for the secretary of state, also in attendance: "Rogers is a murderer." Alongside this intra-American dispute was another between ethnic Chinese: 200 supporters of Chiang Kai-shek's Kuomintang regime on Taiwan had purchased a bloc of tickets directly above where the PRC team was sitting, and from that vantage point goaded the visitors to take the opportunity of being on American soil to defect, while also adding less empathetic comments such as "The Republic of China is Free China" and "Kill Chairman Mao."[57]

[53] Watson to Kissinger, March 20, 1972, and Memcon: Huang and Kissinger, April 12, 1972, *FRUS, 1969–1976*, Vol. XVII, Documents 214 and 220; Xu, *Olympic Dreams*, 157; Huang, *Memoirs*, 236.
[54] Griffin, *Ping-Pong Diplomacy*, 244.
[55] Griffin, 245; Eckstein, "Ping Pong Diplomacy," 333.
[56] Xu, *Olympic Dreams*, 157.
[57] "Woguo pingpangqiu daibiaotuan zai Huashengdun jinxing youhao fangwen" [Chinese Table Tennis Delegation Conducts a Friendly Visit to Washington, DC], *Renmin Ribao*, April 20, 1972; "Chinese Ping-Pong Players vs. the Press," *New York Times Magazine*; Jan Carol Berris, "The Evolution of Sino-American Exchanges: A View from the National Committee," in *Educational Exchanges: Essays on the Sino-American Experience*, ed. Joyce K. Kallgren and Denis Fred Simon (Berkeley, CA: University of California Press, 1987), 83; Griffin, *Ping-Pong Diplomacy*, 249; Eckstein, "Ping Pong Diplomacy," 335–36.

The flag of Chiang's Republic of China was spotted on multiple occasions during the tour, while Americans showed themselves unable to get out of the habit of writing or saying the name of the regime on Taiwan to refer to the PRC or causing offence by referring to the PRC as Red or Communist China. References to Chiang's ROC regime were much to the displeasure of the Chinese team, who boycotted invitations to everywhere from an elementary school to the Kennedy Center to the *New York Times* offices on account of references to Taiwan.[58] The visitors also told a Chinese American translator that the University of Michigan was a "bad institution" because it was harboring Peng Ming-min, who was despised by governments in both Beijing and Taipei for his advocacy of Taiwanese independence, and because a previous university president had advocated Chinese exclusion immigration policies in the nineteenth century. The fellowship the university had awarded to Robert F. Williams after his 1971 return from China (Chapter 1) helped persuade the Chinese to keep to their appointments in Ann Arbor.[59]

The Chinese team took the opportunity of Secretary of State Rogers' presence at the Maryland game to comment that the protests had rather soured the atmosphere of friendship. Rogers was unapologetic. "Our country is one of great freedom," he told Li Menghua. Li referenced one of the protestors in the audience who was holding a particularly offensive sign – the Chinese account omits its precise contents – and Rogers told him with a shrug, "So long as he does not infringe on your personal freedom, there is nothing I can do. The moment he violates the personal freedom of any member of the delegation, however, I can immediately have him arrested." (Li did notice, however, that the specific protestor did seem to have disappeared from the audience sometime later – whether on Rogers' orders or of his own volition.)[60]

The most effective protest during the tour, though, was not one of these cacophonous disruptions but instead a silence. The team's White House visit was the most politically important moment in the exchange and had been planned meticulously. But, as the final preparations were being made at past midnight the night before the team was due on Pennsylvania Avenue, the president of the NCUSCR, Carl Stover, was locked in argument with four of the six American interpreters employed by the National Committee to accompany the tour after they had declared that

[58] Eckstein, "Ping Pong Diplomacy," 332, 336, 338–39.
[59] Xu, *Olympic Dreams*, 157, 160; Eckstein, "Ping Pong Diplomacy," 333.
[60] Li and Zhou, *Tiyu zhizi*, 327–28.

they would not enter the White House in protest at Nixon's bombing of Hanoi and Haiphong just days earlier. Feelings ran high on all sides – USTTA President Steenhoven wanted the interpreters to be fired on the spot – and the absenting interpreters had not taken their decision lightly. Perry Link, then a twenty-seven-year-old graduate student at Harvard, opened up to a *New York Times* reporter accompanying the tour about his doubts about joining the protest: "I found myself really worrying that I had taken advantage of my position ... that we may have embarrassed our Chinese friends." But, Link had concluded, he had been right to refuse to participate, because "in fact I represented a majority of American opinion on the war." Indeed, once tempers had cooled and the remainder of the tour had been completed, even Steenhoven accepted that the interpreters had acted according to their principles – a very American action that might set an example to the Chinese guests, he condescendingly concluded.[61] Link need not have worried that the Chinese would be offended: one of the visiting PRC officials told another of the boycotting translators, the China-born naturalized American Vee-Ling Edwards, that the PRC was keen to invite the translators to China to show the PRC's appreciation for their contribution to the exchange, a promise made good a year later.[62]

The Chinese team's White House visit almost did not happen at all. As the bombs fell on North Vietnam, Zhou Enlai called an emergency meeting of the most senior leadership in the Foreign Ministry on April 18. Together, the diplomats concluded that Beijing had no choice but to order the ping-pong players to tell their American hosts that, in light of the bombing, they could not meet Nixon. As he had at two key moments in the first leg of ping-pong diplomacy, however, Mao intervened to prevent what would have been the most devastating protest of the tour. The chairman reminded Zhou that the players were on a people-to-people visit to the United States and that the Beijing government should not, therefore, be sending orders (or, at least, those particular orders). Besides, Mao said, the American team had met Zhou; it was only proper that the Chinese team meet Nixon. Once again, the apparent people-to-people

---

[61] Eckstein to Gilmore, Delano, and Stover, April 20, 1972, "Athletic Exchanges – Table Tennis (Ping-Pong) – Planning: August 1971–June 1972," Box 4, AEP, BHL; "Chinese Ping-Pong Players vs. the Press," *New York Times Magazine.*

[62] Griffin, *Ping-Pong Diplomacy,* 250; Kin-ming Liu, *My First Trip to China: Scholars, Diplomats, and Journalists Reflect on Their First Encounters with China* (Hong Kong: East Slope Publishing Limited, 2012), 50; Eckstein, "Ping Pong Diplomacy," 337.

nature of important aspects of Beijing's diplomacy toward the United
States allowed Mao to skirt contradictions in Sino-American rapprochement: unlike Link and his fellow translators, the Chinese players smiled
and shook Nixon's hand.[63]

Not all the Chinese Americans who turned out to see the touring team
were protestors. By far, the majority of those who greeted the ping-pong
players were supporters. While some were able to secure tickets to the
matches, most of the overseas Chinese who witnessed the exchange had
to content themselves with waving banners and the PRC flag to greet the
Chinese team's tour bus. Other Chinese visitors to the United States at
the time of the return ping-pong exchange reported to Beijing that they
found overseas Chinese in the country "yearning for the motherland"
and "proud of the growing power" of the PRC, as recognized in Beijing's
1971 entry to the UN.[64] If the ping-pong players were perturbed by raucous protestors, they were also visibly moved by the pride of these overseas Chinese. It was hard for them not to be, given the lengths gone to by
their supporters: in just one example, a welcoming crowd stayed out until
past midnight just to greet the team as they arrived at their Washington
hotel. For much of the visit, State Department security kept the team well
removed from crowds – supporters and protestors alike. But at the team's
final stop in Los Angeles, a throng of several hundred supporters were
close enough to sing the Chinese revolutionary anthem "The East is Red"
within earshot of the players. That was enough to prompt the delegation
to finally defy their minders and insist on personally thanking the throng
of supporters with handshakes and embraces.[65]

It was not only Chinese Americans who made extraordinary efforts
to welcome the team. The single longest stop of the tour was in New
York, the home of both the National Committee and of the only official
Chinese government representation in the United States – Ambassador
Huang Hua's mission at the United Nations. The UN headquarters was

---

[63] Qian, "Zhou Enlai xu xie 'pingpang waijiao' huazhang," 48; ZGZYWXYJS, *Zhou Enlai nianpu, 1949–1976,* 3: 520.
[64] Beijing Revolutionary Committee, "Guanyu husong da xiongmao qu Meiguo qingkuang de baogao" [Report on Escorting Giant Pandas to the United States], May 6, 1972, Folder 98–2–89, BJMA.
[65] "Wei cujin Zhong Mei renmin de liaojie he youyi, dui Meiguo jinxing huifang: wo ping-pangqiu daibiaotuan daoda Meiguo Ditelu" [To Promote Understanding and Friendship between the Chinese and American People, They Pay a Return Visit to the United States: Our Table Tennis Team Arrives in Detroit], *Renmin Ribao,* April 14, 1972; "Friend-ship Log," *Peking Review*; "Chinese Ping-Pong Players vs. the Press," *New York Times Magazine.*

one of the stops during the team's stay, with Huang hosting a 600-person reception for the team. Huang also watched matches between his compatriots and a UN team, captained by an American but composed of players of various nationalities employed at the multilateral institutions' headquarters. That match had originally been slated to be played in the august setting of the General Assembly hall, but this was ultimately deemed an honor too far for table tennis players – even world champions – and instead the marginally less austere Trusteeship Council chamber was used.[66] The less hallowed but equally storied – and far larger – Nassau Coliseum in Long Island was the site for the team's next match, at which 8,518 spectators braved heavy rain.[67] A more intimate setting was provided by some NCUSCR members, who hosted small groups of the players at private dinners in their family homes.[68]

The protests that were a feature of the tour were proof that both governments' concerns of the security risks faced by the players were genuine. This real danger also, however, provided an opening for the US government to influence what sights were shown to the Chinese visitors – decisions that were ostensibly the exclusive purview of the NCUSCR. In one instance, under encouragement from Kissinger's right-hand man, Winston Lord, Scali sanitized the team's visit to Detroit by cancelling a scheduled visit to a hospital with a heroin clinic that was located "in the ghetto area," in spite of protests from what he called the "liberal wing" of the National Committee. Although Scali ostensibly did so "on security grounds alone," the government's internal communication over the decision makes clear that the White House was primarily concerned that the National Committee was offering too honest a depiction of the problems of American society.[69] This was a frequent concern in US cultural diplomacy of this era, leading, for example, to the US government Information Agency censoring a film it had itself commissioned on the 1965 Los Angeles Watts riots to remove scenes showing "neglect, discrimination,

[66] "Huang Hua wei wo pingpangqiu daibiaotuan juxing zhaodai hui" [Huang Hua Held a Reception for our Table Tennis Delegation], *Renmin Ribao*, April 23, 1972; "China's Table Tennis Team Visits City, Plays at U.N.," *New York Times*, April 20, 1972; Qian, "Zhou Enlai xu xie 'pingpang waijiao' huazhang," 48.

[67] "Zhong Mei pingpangqiu yundongyuan zai Niuyue juxing youyisai" [Chinese and American Table Tennis Players Play Friendly Matches in New York], *Renmin Ribao*; "Huang Hua wei wo pingpangqiu daibiaotuan juxing zhaodai hui," *Renmin Ribao*; "Chinese Go Easy on U.S.," *New York Times*.

[68] Eckstein, "Ping Pong Diplomacy," 340.

[69] Lord to Kissinger, April 13, 1972, "China Trade/Exchanges – February 2, 1972–July 4, 1973," Box 93, HAKCFFE, RNL.

hopelessness, frustration" and to the powerful political resistance to the "reverse Peace Corps" Volunteers to America program of 1967 to 1971 on the grounds that it might "enable foreign volunteers to reveal the shortcomings of the United States."[70]

Notwithstanding protests by Americans and Chinese, the return ping-pong exchange was ultimately a success. Lord gladly reported to Kissinger that there had been "tremendous publicity in the local papers, all of it good."[71] Both governments were grateful that the Chinese team returned home safe and encouraged by the warm reception that had been given by the majority of the American public. In an open letter to the *New York Times*, National Committee Chairman Eckstein publicly admitted that the tour had not been free of controversy but said that it was nonetheless "remarkable" how well the Chinese guests had been received, given that "only a few years ago many Americans considered citizens of the People's Republic of China their enemies."[72]

Beijing had been acutely anxious about how the team would be treated by the American public and had considered the visit a test case to determine whether to send further delegations to the United States. The reception given to Chinese visitors was a focal point of internal PRC government reporting on these early trips. While the ping-pong players were touring the country, another group of Chinese cadres was in Washington, DC, to deliver two other Chinese celebrities who would soon become the most famous and loved representatives of the PRC in the United States: Ling-Ling and Hsing-Hsing, the two giant pandas promised to Pat Nixon by Premier Zhou Enlai. The Chinese cadres accompanying the pandas – personally briefed by Zhou before their departure – took the opportunity of traveling to the United States to analyze the American public mood. "Judging by the American people we were in contact with, the vast majority of the American people are willing to be friendly with the Chinese people," the cadres reported. They admitted that many years of "deceptive propaganda" had embedded misperceptions of the PRC but believed direct contact could help overcome this barrier. Young Americans seemed particularly receptive. Students asked the Chinese visitors to sign photographs, while, at a family dinner at the home of the director

[70] Krenn, *United States Cultural Diplomacy*, 138–9; Busch, "The Politics of International Volunteerism," 672.

[71] Lord to Kissinger, April 13, 1972, "China Trade/Exchanges – February 2, 1972–4 July, 1973," Box 93, HAKCFFE, RNL.

[72] Eckstein, "Ping Pong Diplomacy," *New York Times*, August 20, 1972.

of the Smithsonian's National Museum of Natural History, Richard Sumner Cowan, the cadres answered curious questions about Chinese schooling and what jobs a Chinese Communist citizen could look forward to after graduation. Early visits such as this and the ping-pong tour helped build confidence in Beijing that Chinese cultural contact with the United States could overcome lingering suspicion of the PRC among the American populace.[73]

Zhou Enlai was deeply satisfied with the outcome of the ping-pong tour, inviting the entire delegation to his home for a celebratory meal.[74] On the back of the ping-pong trip's success, Chinese officials confirmed their interest in expanding exchanges and suggested to the NCUSCR that the organization send a delegation of its leadership to China.[75] Beijing also quickly proposed dates for the first PRC scientific exchange delegation to traveling to the United States: a group of Chinese doctors who were sent in what Beijing considered the reciprocal return visit for Galston and Signer's 1971 visit to the PRC.[76] Meanwhile, the National Committee was relieved to have successfully managed the visit, with Eckstein noting (privately, this time) that it was a "miracle of some kind" that the trip had gone as well as it did, given that the Chinese had provided only four-weeks' notice of their arrival date and that the NCUSCR had never before hosted an exchange delegation, let alone one of the size, prominence, and significance of the return ping-pong trip. When reflecting on how their inexperienced and relatively small organization had pulled off such a feat, Eckstein and his colleagues were in no doubt that a significant factor in the visit's success had been government involvement. Indeed, Eckstein personally thanked Kissinger for arranging this assistance – even as he and his colleagues recovered from the experience of working with Scali.[77] For his part, Scali had found the National Committee competent and easy to work with – far more so than USTTA President Steenhoven, with whom both Scali and the NCUSCR had become exasperated by the

---

[73] Beijing Revolutionary Committee, "Guanyu husong da xiongmao qu Meiguo qingkuang de baogao," May 6, 1972, Folder 98–2–89, BJMA.

[74] Li and Zhou, *Tiyu zhizi*, 328.

[75] Eckstein, "Table Tennis Project" [handwritten notes], April 20, 1972, "Athletic Exchanges – Table Tennis (Ping-Pong) – History of Table Tennis Exchange," Box 3, AEP, BHL.

[76] Su and Zhang, "Xin zhongguo shouci fu Mei yixue daibiaotuan," 396.

[77] Eckstein to Kissinger, June 13, 1972, "National Committee – General Correspondence – 1972," Box 130, ADBP, RBMLCU; author interview with Berris, August 15, 2015; Xu, *Olympic Dreams*, 154.

tour's end.[78] (Steenhoven may not have been a natural choice for cultural diplomacy with the Chinese visitors: in a pre-trip briefing, he had supplemented to a list of possible cross-cultural faux pas – beckoning with palm face up, for example – a suggestion of his own: "Don't call them Chinamen." Stunned silence followed.)[79]

An important legacy of the visit, then, was an intensification of mutual trust between the National Committee and the government. This helped allay the fears expressed by Kissinger the month before the ping-pong players arrived that an exchange program outside of the government's control might threaten US foreign policy interests. Instead, it seemed that in the NCUSCR, the government had found the "umbrella group" it was looking for. It would not be long after the conclusion of the visit that the US government and the NCUSCR agreed to a closer ongoing collaboration – and the beginning of government funding for the National Committee's exchange program. However, if Scali's occasional meddling in the ping-pong visit had provoked misgivings from some within the NCUSCR, a more permanent government role in financing and overseeing exchanges would evoke stiffer resistance.

STRUCTURING US EXCHANGES WITH CHINA

On April 27, 1972, just three days after the ping-pong tour formally concluded, while the Chinese team were still relaxing in Napa Valley before their return home, the NCUSCR held its third roundtable meeting on exchanges. The meeting came on the back of not only the first official delegation of PRC citizens to the United States but also as the number of individual Americans to visit China since April 1971 reached into the hundreds. It would go on to exceed a thousand by July 1972. Twenty-four individuals attended, representing the National Committee, the CSCPRC, the International Research and Exchanges Board (IREX) – which oversaw 90 percent of academic exchanges with the Soviet Union – and the US Advisory Commission on International Education and Cultural Affairs – a government body that advised the State Department. Between them, they agreed that, in the wake of the successful ping-pong exchange, the NCUSCR and CSCPRC should together propose to

---

[78] Lord to Kissinger, April 13, 1972, "China Trade/Exchanges – February 2, 1972–July 4, 1973," Box 93, HAKCFFE, RNL.
[79] "Chinese Ping-Pong Players vs. the Press," *New York Times Magazine*.

the US and Chinese governments a structure for the US side of managing cultural and scientific exchanges with China.[80]

The position paper that was the vehicle for this proposal was to become the foundation of the NCUSCR and CSCPRC's shared strategy toward exchanges until normalization in 1979 and was a manifesto for the two organizations assuming the leading role in overseeing US exchanges with China, ahead of all other private organizations. The final NCUSCR–CSCPRC paper was sent to Kissinger and the State Department in early June, at a critical moment in the development of exchanges: after the first visit of a Chinese exchange delegation to the United States but before the back and forth of reciprocal visits had been regularized – and just as Beijing was beginning to shift the focus of its contacts with Americans from leftists to a more diverse constituency. The NCUSCR and the CSCPRC knew, just as Kissinger and the government did, that "the future pattern of exchange relations will be strongly influenced by the principles and arrangements governing [these] early visits."[81]

The NCUSCR and CSCPRC did not seek a monopoly over exchanges, and they argued that the US government should do nothing to prevent any group or individual having contact with China – as Washington had done for so much of the Cold War (Prologue). This notwithstanding, the proposal argued that the leading organizations in managing exchanges must be "responsible and non-political" and should have the "confidence of the U.S. Government," while at the same time retaining independence from official oversight. For its part, the government should facilitate exchanges by offering partial funding to exchange organizations and by using its influence with Beijing to underline American nongovernmental expectations of a reciprocal exchange relationship. This would entail US organizations being assured the right to select which Americans would travel to China, rather than Beijing continuing to invite individual Americans selected by the PRC after personal background checks to evaluate their political leanings.[82]

[80] NFTNC, Vol. 2, No. 3, July 1972; Committee of Concerned Asian Scholars (CCAS) Newsletter, January 1973. A copy of this small-circulation newsletter is located at "Committee of Concerned Asian Scholars," Box 119, JKFP, HUA; Faure, "Working on/ Working with the Soviet Bloc."

[81] Handler, Burkhardt, and Tyler, to Kissinger, June 7, 1972, "1972 – Exchange Program – Proposed," CSCPRCP, NAS.

[82] Ibid; He, *Dangdai Zhong Mei minjian jiaoliu shi*, 126; Lovell, "Foreigners in Mao-Era China," 146.

The NCUSCR pointed to its "invaluable" experience in the ping-pong exchange when arguing for why they should oversee future exchanges, as well as highlighting how the National Committee had, since 1966, "contributed in a major way to creating the climate of public opinion that made possible [the] reassessment of U.S. policy toward China." The case for the CSCPRC sharing this role was much weaker. Although Beijing had retreated from its previous refusal to deal with the National Academy of Sciences – the planned delegation of Chinese doctors was to be hosted by the Academy's Institute of Medicine – the CSCPRC itself had still failed to initiate any effectual communication with the Chinese.[83] By contrast, the Federation of American Scientists were, at the time that the position paper was being drafted, enjoying a state banquet hosted by Chinese Academy of Sciences President Guo Moruo during a four-week tour of the country.[84] That the position paper proposed that the CSCPRC nonetheless jointly manage future exchanges makes clear that the paper was not a codification of how the exchange program had evolved in the fifteen months after the first leg of ping-pong diplomacy but instead an ambitious attempt by the two Committees to define the future landscape of US exchanges with China on their terms.

The US government enthusiastically received the position paper. Kissinger called the paper an "outstanding job" and welcomed the model for government-private cooperation suggested by the NCUSCR and CSCPRC.[85] Richardson at State said that the paper "will be immensely helpful to us in future planning" and told National Committee chair Eckstein that "your general philosophical approach to the matter of developing U.S.-PRC exchanges ... is very similar to ours." Richardson also informed the two organizations that "there is no question ... but that we shall be trying to establish the role of the responsible private American organizations in forthcoming exchanges" and that he believed the Chinese were moving toward accepting the proposed central role of both the NCUSCR and, more slowly, the CSCPRC.[86]

[83] Handler, Burkhardt, and Tyler to Kissinger, June 7, 1972, "1972 – Exchange Program – Proposed," CSCPRCP, NAS.

[84] "Guo Moruo, Yu Liqun, Zhu Kezhen, Wu Youxun huijian bing yanqing Meiguo Kexuejia Xiehui daibiaotuan" [Guo Moruo, Yu Liqun, Zhu Kezhen, and Wu Youxun Met and Hosted a Delegation from the Federation of American Scientists], *Renmin Ribao*, June 2, 1972.

[85] Kissinger to Handler, Burkhardt, and Tyler, July 10, 1972, "NCUSCR, General Correspondence, 1972," Box 130, ADBP, RBMLCU.

[86] John Richardson to Eckstein, July 11, 1972, "NCUSCR: Cultural exchanges, 1971–1973," Box 4, AEP, BHL; John Richardson to Handler, Burkhardt, and Tyler, June 16, 1972, "1972 – Exchange Program – Proposed," CSCPRCP, NAS.

Why did both the NCUSCR and the US government accept a central role for the Committee on Scholarly Communication in exchanges even before that organization had developed a relationship with Beijing? For the National Committee's part, this division of labor freed the organization to focus on the intimidating task of hosting further cultural exchanges of the scale of the ping-pong return tour. The NCUSCR also believed that no single organization should oversee US exchanges with China in case that group's relationship with Beijing broke down – a failsafe that proved prescient when just such a situation occurred two years later (Chapter 3). But the NCUSCR and US government's enthusiasm for the CSCPRC sharing the management of exchanges was also a reflection of political and social inclinations and connections. There were many close personal relationships that bridged the senior leadership of the two organizations, and between the leadership of both organizations and the government: Doak Barnett, Eckstein, Fairbank, Ezra Vogel, and Chalmers Johnson were all closely involved in both Committees, with many of these men also enjoying influence in corridors of powers in Washington.[87] Moreover, the broader makeup of the CSCPRC was very similar to the National Committee: both were groups made up of socially elite, establishment figures, often from academia, interested in engagement with the PRC but with little ideological sympathy toward that country's government.[88] Membership in the NCUSCR was by invitation only, and every one of its members – 289 individuals, as of 1972 – had been carefully selected and screened based on the influence they could bring to the National Committee in American society (as well as, in many cases, their ability to raise private funds from companies and other donors).[89] The Committee on Scholarly Communication likewise sought to carefully cultivate a nationwide network of the most influential scientists and academics: selection for CSCPRC funding was focused on the "standing" and "scholarly excellence" of the applicant and nomination to its leadership was reserved for some of the most august scientists in their fields.[90]

---

[87] *CCAS Newsletter*, January 1973, "Committee of Concerned Asian Scholars," Box 119, JKFP, HUA.

[88] John Richardson to Eckstein, July 11, 1972, "NCUSCR: Cultural exchanges, 1971–1973," Box 4, AEP, BHL.

[89] NCUSCR Annual Report, 1971–72, NCUSCROC.

[90] Keatley to CSCPRC members, August 29, 1972, "1972 – General," CSCPRCP, NAS; Brown to Handler, February 8, 1972, "1972 – General," CSCPRCP, NAS.

Critical to the US government was the makeup of the organizations – in particular, their centrist political identity – and their enthusiasm for building rapprochement in a manner similar to how Washington envisaged ties. The visit of twenty Black Panthers to China in March 1972, the second Committee of Concerned Asian Scholars delegation of the same, and an invitation to Edgar Snow's widow Lois to return to China to bury her late husband's ashes were reminders that, if the government did not sponsor the NCUSCR–CSCPRC proposal, exchanges would remain outside of even indirect influence and provide a political platform for leftists who were critical of the US government's foreign and domestic policies.[91] Thus, the recommendations that the NCUSCR and CSCPRC had written into their proposal were rapidly incorporated into government policy, almost without modification: ahead of Kissinger's next visit to Beijing in June, National Security Council senior staff member Richard Solomon argued that Kissinger work with his Chinese interlocutors to regularize exchanges as proposed in the position paper and to work directly with the NCUSCR and the CSCPRC. The precise wording of Solomon's recommendation closely mirrored that of the position paper: the government was effectively adding its authority to the plans drawn up by the two Committees.[92]

The proposals in the position paper were central to the extensive negotiations over exchanges during Kissinger's visit. Both sides reflected positively on recent milestones: the Chinese table tennis team's visit; a first congressional delegation to China; and the imminent visit of Chinese doctors to the United States. Sino-American trade had finally restarted and would amount to $92.5 million in 1972, up from a total of just $5 million the year before.[93] Jenkins and Holdridge advocated for "the establishment of some sort of explicit and responsible mechanism for proposing, agreeing upon, and managing these exchange programs [that] would simplify the problem [of managing exchanges] and perhaps prevent something from going awry in the future." Jenkins added that there were "at least two organizations with the experience and resources to be helpful perhaps primarily behind the scenes": the NCUSCR and the CSCPRC.[94]

---

[91] Snow travelled in 1973; the burial was at Peking University. Holdridge to Kissinger, August 28, 1972, *FRUS, 1969–1976*, Vol. XVII, Document 248; *NFTNC*, Vol. 2, No. 3, July 1972.

[92] Solomon to Kissinger, June 9, 1972, *FRUS, 1969–1976*, Vol. XVII, Document 229.

[93] Ibid.; Talley, *Forgotten Vanguard*, 7.

[94] Memcons: Jenkins, Holdridge, Solomon, and Zhang, June 21 and 22, 1972, *FRUS, 1969–1976*, Vol. E-13, Documents 142 and 144.

Jenkins's counterpart, Zhang Wenjin, gave a mixed response. On the one hand, Zhang moved away from Beijing's previous position that all exchanges should be ostensibly free of government influence and conducted exclusively on a people-to-people basis. The Chinese government had, in practical terms, already begun working with Washington on the ping-pong return exchange and now accepted a "double track basis" whereby both governments and nonstate organizations would be involved in managing exchanges. The two governments should, Zhang agreed, consult to "insure [sic] the success of the visits" and give "encouragement and assistance to the non-governmental institutions" involved in exchanges. However, Zhang also said only that the PRC had "taken note of such organizations" as the NCUSCR and the CSCPRC and that Beijing would let the US government "know whether we can have direct or indirect contacts with these organizations you have mentioned."[95]

In the wake of Beijing's lukewarm reaction to the US endorsement of the two Committees, the White House turned to pressuring other Americans to recognize the need for the NCUSCR and CSCPRC to take the lead in exchanges. A week after Kissinger's return to the United States, Winston Lord met with Jeremy Stone, a leading American scientist-activist who would later help convince Mikhail Gorbachev to commit the Soviet Union to nuclear disarmament.[96] Stone had just returned from China as leader of the Federation of American Scientists delegation hosted by Guo Moruo and the Scientific and Technical Association of the PRC.[97] In the face of Lord's pressure, he agreed to cooperate with the Committee on Scholarly Communication. Nonetheless, Stone also warned that, although the Chinese had clearly understood Washington's preference for the CSCPRC, Beijing was still resistant to dealing with the National Academy of Sciences and its subsidiaries because of the contacts between the Academy and Taiwan, something that was also repeated to CSCPRC member Fairbank while he was in China in August.[98] Meanwhile, the Foreign Secretary of the UK's Royal Society, which was also struggling to expand contacts with China, had been told by a Chinese counterpart "to oust Taiwan from international scientific

[95] Ibid.
[96] Evangelista, "Transnational Organizations and the Cold War," 419.
[97] He, *Dangdai Zhong Mei minjian jiaoliu shi*, 136.
[98] Lord to Kissinger, June 29, 1972, "China Trade/Exchanges – February 2, 1972–July 4, 1973," Box 93, HAKCFFE, RNL; Keatley to CSCPRC members, August 29, 1972, "1972 – General," CSCPRCP, NAS.

organizations whether intergovernmental or not" if they wanted greater scientific exchange with the PRC.[99] A month after Lord met Stone, fellow CSCPRC member Burkhardt received his incendiary letter from the Beijing Red Guards in which they told him they would "smash your dog head" if he continued his efforts to build academic links with the Chinese Academy of Sciences.[100]

Holdridge considered Stone and the Federation of American Scientists reliable enough – the historian of science Zuoyue Wang has characterized the group as centrist and politically liberal – but complained to Kissinger that the Chinese favoring of the FAS was "effectively undercutting" the CSCPRC and that FAS lacked the "staff, funds and experience" to guarantee a successful exchange. A Chinese proposal for sending a delegation of journalists to be hosted by the more radically left-wing America-China Relations Society was even less acceptable: "Manton is definitely not one in whom we could have confidence," Holdridge wrote.[101] Alleged to be "trying to become the official Chinese beachhead in America," Manton's organization was a mouthpiece of Beijing's more radical foreign policy pronouncements and had been a rival and vocal critic of the National Committee since the NCUSCR first rose to public prominence in the late 1960s. Manton had visited China when the PRC was still focusing on cultivating American leftists besotted with the idea of the Chinese revolution. His America-China Relations Society counted among its more prominent members Han Suyin, the famed Chinese-Belgian author of the bestselling *A Many-Splendored Thing* who had hailed the Cultural Revolution and the Chinese "remaking of man" and who later admitted to "lying through my teeth (with a smile)" about the signs of famine she personally witnessed in the PRC during the Great Leap Forward.[102]

[99] Agar, "It's Springtime for Science," 12–13.
[100] "Red Guard Team in Academy of Sciences, Peking" to "Mr. Burkheart" [*sic*], July 25, 1972, "China Exchange, Miscellaneous," Part II: Box 308, ACLSR, LOCMD.
[101] Holdridge to Kissinger, August 28, 1972, *FRUS, 1969–1976*, Vol. XVII, Document 248; Zuoyue Wang, "Controlled Exchanges: Public-Private Hybridity, Transnational Networking, and Knowledge Circulation in US-China Scientific Discourse on Nuclear Arms Control," in *How Knowledge Moves: Writing the Transnational History of Science and Technology*, ed. John Krige (Chicago, IL: University of Chicago Press, 2019), 376, 384.
[102] De Keijzer to Schoyer, undated (circa mid-1971), Folder 284, Box 30, Series 9, RG4, NCUSCR records, RAC; "Large Assortment of China Trade Entrepreneurs," *Washington Post*, October 15, 1972; "Han Suyin obituary," *Guardian*, November 4, 2012; Han Suyin, *My House Has Two Doors* (London: Triad, Grafton Books, 1980), 373.

Beginning in late August, the US government upped the ante, making both requested State Department security and Rockefeller Brothers Fund support for the FAS-sponsored visit of Chinese scientists conditional on the CSCPRC being made co-hosts. Kissinger made plans to directly confront Huang Hua in Paris about the threats made to Burkhardt's "dog head" but was saved the trouble when Huang wrote to Burkhardt claiming that the vitriolic letter had been a "pure fake" and "written with ulterior political motives." Huang explained that Burkhardt's initial correspondence to the Chinese Academy of Sciences had been intercepted by the "so-called 'red guard team of Academy of Sciences'" [sic] and offered to act as a personal go-between for Burkhardt with the Chinese Academy.[103]

Beijing soon accepted the CSCPRC as co-hosts of the delegation of Chinese doctors due in October and also welcomed the Committee on Scholarly Communication being made co-hosts, alongside the Federation of American Scientists, of the visit of another delegation of Chinese scientists scheduled for November. The importance of these first Chinese scientific delegations – and thus of the CSCPRC's involvement in hosting the visits – was indicated when Zhou Enlai personally met with the doctors on the eve of their departure.[104] Huang explicitly told Kissinger that the decision to include the Committee as cohosts of the two delegations had been made because "the U.S. side has recommended the U.S. Committee on Scholarly Communication with the PRC as an organization for regular reception of visiting Chinese science and scholarly delegations." A grateful Kissinger promised to ensure that now that the CSCPRC were co-hosting, the government would make the "maximum effort" in contributing to security and other logistical arrangements (the Chinese doctors were apparently ultimately protected by the Secret Service detail denied to the ping-pong delegation).[105] On the same day, Nixon agreed to personally receive the delegation, in order to "demonstrat[e] to the Chinese that such high-level treatment and interest in their visits here is possible, when they are willing to deal with our preferred institution for

---

[103] Holdridge to Kissinger, August 28, 1972, *FRUS, 1969–1976*, Vol. XVII, Document 248; Huang to Burkhardt, September 7, 1972; Huang to Burkhardt, September 24, 1972, and Holdridge to Burkhardt, September 11, 1972, all at "China Exchange, Miscellaneous," Part II: Box 308, ACLSR, LOCMD.

[104] ZGZYWXYJS, *Zhou Enlai nianpu, 1949–1976*, 3: 557.

[105] Memcon: Huang and Kissinger, September 19, 1972, *FRUS, 1969–1976*, Vol. XVII, Document 253; Su and Zhang, "Xin zhongguo shouci fu Mei yixue daibiaotuan," 397, 402.

scientific-technical exchanges."[106] Nixon and Kissinger beamed as they welcomed the Chinese doctors on October 14.[107]

Beijing's acceptance of the CSCPRC was a significant victory for the two Committees and for the US government, but there was other resistance to the emerging partnership between the US state and the NCUSCR and CSCPRC. Such resistance came not least from within the National Committee itself. The debate over the organization's relationship with the US state first played out over the issue of government funding. A government offer to fund the National Committee was first made by Richardson at the NCUSCR's annual members' meeting in 1972.[108] Committee Chairman Eckstein had previously worked for State but even he cautioned his colleagues to "move very cautiously on the State Department fund," for fear that government support would hurt the Committee's ability to fundraise from charitable foundations and the private sector – the Committee's main sources of funding to date – and deter Beijing from working with the NCUSCR.[109] The National Committee urgently needed new funds, however. For all its success as a public spectacle, the Chinese ping-pong team's US visit had been a financial disaster, with the decision not to sell exclusive broadcasting rights and to keep ticket prices artificially low – as little as a dollar for a seat – leading to the NCUSCR making back only half of the quarter of a million dollars they had spent.[110] Eckstein initially had the National Committee push hard for greater private foundation funding rather than accept government support, but when these appeals failed, and when the NCUSCR learned that Beijing had softened its stance on US governmental support for exchanges, the organization's board bowed to circumstance and agreed to accept the State Department's money.[111] It was a decision from which the National Committee would not soon turn back: in the 1972–73 financial year, the organization would receive $76,600 from the government; five years

---

[106] David to Nixon, September 19, 1972, "China Trade/Exchanges – February 2, 1972–July 4, 1973," Box 93, HAKCFFE, RNL.

[107] Su and Zhang, "Xin zhongguo shouci fu Mei yixue daibiaotuan," 395.

[108] Lockwood to Eckstein, May 17, 1972, "NCUSCR: Cultural exchanges, 1971–1973," Box 4, AEP, BHL.

[109] Emphasis in the original. Eckstein to Case, May 25, 1972, "National Committee – General Correspondence – 1972," Box 130, ADBP, RBMLCU.

[110] Schoyer to Boggan, December 5, 1972, Folder 288, Box 30, Series 9, RG4, NCUSCR records, RAC; Schoyer to Joint Committee [organizing the ping-pong visit], August 16, 1971, Folder 289, Box 30, Series 9, RG4, NCUSCR records, RAC.

[111] Barnett to The Files, June 26, 1972, and Barnett to Pye and Eckstein, July 31, 1972, "NCUSCR, 1972," Box 130, ADBP, RBMLCU.

later, yearly government funding for the group had risen as high as $290,000, some 55 percent of the organization's revenue.[112]

Others within the National Committee objected to the concurrent change in focus of the organization away from public education toward facilitating exchanges. Many NCUSCR members still saw the organization as a broad church of volunteers interested in encouraging discussion of American engagement with China, not as a professionalized organization dedicated to facilitating exchanges that would, in a different context, be the responsibility of the State Department. The Princeton academic William W. Lockwood, who had helped lead the Institute of Pacific Relations in the 1930s and 1940s, was just one of the dissenting voices within the board of the NCUSCR. Lockwood commented that he "was dismayed by ... suggest[ions] that our educational job was done" with the achievement of the Nixon–Mao summit. "Such judgments may partly reflect the euphoric mood that prevails today in regard to our China relations – a mood that probably won't last very long."[113] Objections by Lockwood and others forced the core of the National Committee leadership – Eckstein, Barnett, Murray and a handful of others – to make minor changes to the position paper before it was approved at a November board meeting. Plans to manage exchanges through a well-sized standing committee of both NCUSCR members and nominees from outside the group were dropped; instead, that role was given to a small in-house subcommittee – although the importance of that committee was indicated when Eckstein resigned as National Committee chair to lead it.[114] This was a turning point for the National Committee. Its core leadership had pushed for changes that would ensure the NCUSCR became an organization dedicated to exchanges; three years later, the group would transfer its public education arm to the Asia Society and dedicate all its efforts to managing exchanges (until 1987, when such activities again became part of the Committee's programming).[115]

While the National Committee internally debated the organization's future direction, the rival Committee of Concerned Asian Scholars published a long and well-informed attack that alleged that the NCUSCR and

[112] NCUSCR Annual Reports, 1972–73 and 1977–78, NCUSCROC.
[113] Lockwood to Eckstein, May 17, 1972, "NCUSCR: Cultural Exchanges, 1971–1973," Box 4, AEP, BHL.
[114] Record of the 1st meeting of NCUSCR ad hoc committee on exchanges, September 26, 1972, "NCUSCR: Exchanges with the PRC, General: 1972–1974," Box 3, AEP, BHL.
[115] Wheeler, *American NGOs in China's Modernization*, 30.

CSCPRC were pushing "to have the U.S. government designate them as the two major conduits for such [exchange] activities" and were proposing to work only with "appropriate" other exchange organizations that met their own preferences of professionalization and political persuasion. The NCUSCR and CSCPRC "have moved quietly in small committees over the summer and fall of 1972 to set themselves up as the major semi-official conduits for exchanges without wide consultation with other organizations, especially those which are younger, more radical, and less powerful." They had done so highly effectually, the CCAS critics pointed out: "So far, they have not hesitated to sponsor or co-sponsor every major Chinese group coming to the U.S." The exposé issued by the Committee of Concerned Asian Scholars was not only intended for an American audience. The group also directly complained to the PRC state-run China International Travel Service. CCAS named names: they pointed the finger for seeking to monopolize exchanges at leading members of the NCUSCR and CSCPRC, including Barnett, Eckstein, Vogel, Scalapino, Fairbank, Chalmers Johnson, and Albert Feuerwerker.[116]

There was substance to CCAS's allegations, but the tone of their complaints also reflected frustrations felt within the radical group about its own direction. In the wake of the Nixon–Mao summit, the group had lost the collective purpose that had made it a powerful force when the Vietnam War raged and Washington seemed so obdurate about engaging with China. Instead, as Lanza has shown, CCAS had succumbed to internal jealousies and infighting over planned exchange delegations from and to China. CCAS members jockeyed for places on any future trip to the PRC, while there was internal disagreement about whether the group should honor a 1971 invitation for a return delegation of Chinese students that might now help Nixon's reelection prospects and would force CCAS into at least begrudging cooperation with the US government. Soon thereafter, CCAS abandoned plans for a third delegation to China and to host the Chinese student delegation, with an internal CCAS committee concluding that the visit "could ... be just as well handled by other groups," leading the group to approach that old collaborator of the National Committee – the Quaker American Friends Service Committee – to host. Thus, another reason for the National Committee's

---

[116] "A Statement on U.S. China Exchanges," made by CCAS and printed in CCAS Newsletter, January 1973, "Committee of Concerned Asian Scholars," Box 119, JKFP, HUA; Lanza, *End of Concern*, 138–39, 229.

growing dominance of cultural exchanges with China from 1972 was that leftist groups like CCAS that had earlier been favored by Beijing ceded the realm of exchanges in the wake of China's rapprochement with the arch imperialist Nixon. There was irony here: as we have seen, CCAS had made an important contribution to reopening Sino-American people-to-people contact – but by doing so, they had helped midwife a relationship between the US president they hated and the PRC government they admired. Disenchantment and disaffection were the results.[117]

OPENING THE DOOR TO TRADE

As Nixon took the oath of office that began his second term on January 20, 1973, Sino-American relations were buoyant. The Paris Peace Accords that presaged US withdrawal from Vietnam would be signed a week later and welcomed by Beijing, in part because Nixon and Kissinger had told Premier Zhou that US withdrawal from Taiwan was linked to the end of the Vietnam conflict.[118] Cultural and scientific exchanges between the two sides were accelerating. The first PRC scientific delegations to the United States had been successful: thirteen doctors from the Chinese Medical Association had, over some twenty days in October, visited American medical institutions, hospitals, and medical schools in New York, Boston, Kansas City, Chicago, San Francisco, and Washington, DC. As he had with other landmark exchanges, Premier Zhou had personally selected the delegation's members and then met with them before departure, telling them that, "There is no doubt that this event is not purely an academic exchange; it is also an important diplomatic mission." Chinese historians of medicine Su Jingjing and Zhang Daqing argue that the trip had another significance: to help an underdeveloped Chinese medical community obtain valuable information from more advanced American colleagues, for example regarding cardiovascular disease and cancer. At the same time, however, the delegation's composition also reflected the PRC's medical innovations, with specialists on acupuncture and herbal pharmacology and the delegation presenting a mannequin with acupuncture points to the National Institutes of Health. The delegation head, Wu Weiran, had previously employed acupuncture techniques to relieve pain after performing an appendectomy on *New*

---

[117] Lanza, *End of Concern*, 111–25; NFTNC, Vol. 2, No. 1, November 1971.
[118] Gong, "Chinese Decision Making," 356.

York Times reporter James Reston while the journalist had been in China covering Kissinger's July 1971 visit (local anesthetic injections had also been used before the operation). Reston and Wu were reunited during the visit, with the journalist joining Wu and the delegation for a dinner at the home of John R. Hogness, the president of the National Academy's Institute of Medicine. When Wu met Nixon, the president alerted the gathered press that it was Wu who had operated on their colleague with such skill.[119]

The success of the Committee on Scholarly Communication's co-hosting of Chinese doctors and a further delegation of scientists in November had persuaded Beijing to agree to the organization single-handedly overseeing the visit of an American medical delegation to China in June 1973.[120] This was the CSCPRC's first involvement in American travel to China, coming after a hundred American scholars had already traveled to the PRC in the two years prior under various different banners.[121] The PRC was also considering other forms of scientific exchange: the Chinese Psychological Society planned to accept a US invitation to attend the 1973 annual meeting of the American Psychological Association in Montreal, for example.[122]

Meanwhile, the National Committee had hosted its second exchange, an event that rivalled the ping-pong trip for glamour. The Shenyang Acrobatic Troupe (Figure 2.2) was a storied group that dated back to 1951 and was particularly daring in their high-altitude trapeze acts. In 1971, the troupe had won a national-level competition between troupes from six provinces and municipalities that had led to the group being sent to conduct "acrobatic diplomacy" with South American countries and North Korea before their 1972 tour of the United States.[123] The acrobats

[119] Su and Zhang, "Xin zhongguo shouci fu Mei yixue daibiaotuan," 395–99; ZGZY-WXYJS, *Zhou Enlai nianpu, 1949–1976*, 3: 557; James Reston, "Now, About My Operation in Peking," *New York Times*, July 26, 1971.

[120] "Wo kexuejia daibiaotuan fangwen Meiguo hou huiguo" [Our Delegation of Scientists Returned Home after a Visit to the United States], *Renmin Ribao*, December 19, 1972.

[121] "You pengzi yuanfang lai—Zhongguo kexuejia daibiaotuan fangwen Meiguo ceji" [There are Friends Coming from Afar – Highlights from the Visit by Chinese Scientists to the United States], *Renmin Ribao*, January 9, 1973.

[122] Shanghai Normal University Revolutionary Committee, "Guanyu Meiguo Xinli Xuehui yaoqing wo xiao pai daibiao canjia gai hui di bashiyi jie nian hui yishi de qingshi baogao" [Request for Guidance on Invitation from the American Psychological Association for our University to Attend their 81st Annual Meeting], May 2, 1973, Folder B244-3-551, SHMA.

[123] Wang Jiyu, "Shenyang zaji tuan: wushi nian licheng [50 Years of the Shenyang Acrobatic Troupe]," *Zaji yu moshu*, no. 05 (2001): 19–21.

FIGURE 2.2 The Shenyang Acrobatic Troupe of China, whose tour of the United States beginning in December 1972 was the second cultural exchange delegation sent to the country by the PRC, after the table tennis visitors of the same year. Courtesy of the Shenyang Acrobatic Troupe of China.

arrived in December and then performed eighteen sold-out shows beginning with an opening-night performance at the Chicago Lyric Opera House described by one critic as "thrilling, delightful, charming, artful, amazing and joyful." A capacity audience of 3,000 spectators gave the Chinese performers a standing ovation and five curtain calls worth of cheers and applause for what *Newsweek* claimed was "closer to ballet than acrobatics."[124]

In total, 50,000 spectators saw the Shenyang troupe perform over the course of their US tour, with thousands more watching a special color television broadcast on ABC.[125] In addition to their mesmerizing performances on stage, the acrobats won respect for their behavior between shows. They played baseball and frisbee – a new American craze – and gave impromptu performances to bedridden Americans in hospital; they

[124] "Shenyang zajituan zai Zhijiage juxing fang Mei shouci yanchu" [Shenyang Acrobatic Troupe Gives First Performance in Chicago during Visit to the United States], *Renmin Ribao*, December 21, 1972; "China's Acrobatic Diplomats," *Newsweek*, January 1, 1973; *NFTNC*, Vol. 3, No. 2, February 1973.
[125] "Wo Shenyang zajituan jieshu zai Meiguo de fangwen yanchu" [Our Shenyang acrobatic troupe ended its performance in the United States], *Renmin Ribao*, January 15, 1973; NCUSCR Annual Report, 1972–73, NCUSCROC.

raced around the Indianapolis 500 racetrack and even swapped their
props for brooms to sweep their stage themselves when American stage-
hands refused to work overtime.[126] Post-performance sightseeing was
also a chance for the National Committee to again showcase the productive underpinnings of US modernity, as they had to the ping-pong
players: one stop took the troupe to a farm in Lebanon, Indiana, where
the Chinese guests marveled at how just four American farmers managed
more than 1,200 acres of land. This sight-seeing had important consequences: the acrobats were accompanied, as all major delegations were,
by political escorts, and this showcase of American mechanized agriculture prompted these officials to ask if a group of Chinese agricultural
scientists could follow in the wake of the acrobats. Soon, agriculture
was to become one of the most productive areas of scientific cooperation
between the two countries.[127] One manifestation of this were substantial
Chinese imports of American "improved varieties" of crops – typically
called high-yield variants in English – such as soybeans, that was occurring by 1974 if not before.[128] The political importance of only the fourth
PRC exchange delegation to the United States had been indicated by a
welcoming address given by Senator Adlai Stevenson and by a trip to the
White House. On Capitol Hill, the acrobats were met by Speaker of the
House Carl Albert and sat down to a luncheon with recent China visitors
Senators Mike Mansfield and Hugh Scott.[129]

Less dramatic but still of much significance was the concurrent visit
of NCUSCR board members to the PRC. The top brass of the organization traveled: National Committee founder Scalapino, the former Chair-
men Eckstein and Barnett, former acting Chairman Pye, and Executive

---

[126] "Zhong Mei renmin youhao chaoliu buke zudang" [The Current Friendly Trend
between China and the United States is Unstoppable], *Renmin Ribao*, January 17, 1973;
NFTNC, Vol. 3, No. 2, February 1973; "China's Acrobatic Diplomats," *Newsweek*.

[127] *NFTNC*, Vol. 3, No. 2, February 1973; Kissinger to Nixon, July 4, 1973, "China Trade/
Exchanges – February 2, 1972–July 4, 1973," Box 93, HAKCFFE, RNL; Press and
Keatley to Zhou Peiyuan, January 23, 1976, "1976 – Exchange Agreement – Negotiations," CSCPRCP, NAS; ZGZYWXYJS, ed., *Deng Xiaoping sixiang nianbian* [Chroni-
cle of Deng Xiaoping Thought] (Beijing: Zhongyang wenxian chubanshe, 2011), 97.

[128] Ministry of Agriculture, "Guanyu fenpei Meiguo dadou zhongzi de tongzhi" [Notice
on the Distribution of US Soybean Seeds], February 22, 1974, Folder 92-3-256,
BJMA. On the PRC's use of high-yield varieties, see Schmalzer, *Red Revolution, Green
Revolution*, 9–10.

[129] "Wo Shenyang zajituan jieshu zai Meiguo de fangwen yanchu," *Renmin Ribao*;
"Zhongguo Shenyang zajituan daoda Meiguo Zhijiage" [Chinese Shenyang Acrobatic
Troupe Arrives in Chicago], *Renmin Ribao*, December 18, 1972.

Director B. Preston Schoyer were all on the trip, as was influential board and executive committee member Michel Oksenberg, who later became Jimmy Carter's top China advisor.[130] The delegation spent three hours with Chinese vice foreign minister, Qiao Guanhua, as well as having multiple meetings with the National Committee's counterpart organizations: the hosts of the visit, the Chinese People's Institute of Foreign Affairs, as well as the Chinese People's Association for Friendship with Foreign Countries, the All-China Sports Federation, and the China Council for the Promotion of International Trade (CCPIT). The NCUSCR leadership concluded from the trip that, "Both the extraordinarily warm reception and the substance of the discussions made the visit a remarkably fruitful and successful experience."[131]

Several members of the National Committee leadership were returning to a country they had once known well but had not set foot in since the 1940s. The Shanghai-born Barnett wrote in the *New York Times* after the visit of the "prevailing mood ... of political relaxation" and the "return to normalcy" after the height of the Cultural Revolution, as well as of the relative freedom to "wander ... freely, widely and unaccompanied" extended to the delegation and the importance attached to exchange contacts by the Chinese. Barnett, whose academic work included analysis of the Chinese economy, also concluded, however, that the PRC government had "only begun ... transforming the material base" of the country, and that, in some areas, the PRC was less technologically and economically modern than the pre-revolution China that Barnett had known so well. Electric lighting, for example, was used very sparingly, which gave the country "a dim and dreary look at night," and there were vast droves of cyclists – because of an almost complete absence of other forms of public transport.[132]

A suggestion discussed with the NCUSCR during this trip rapidly led to a significant new development in the landscape of the exchange program. Beijing remarked approvingly on expanding Sino-American trade

---

[130] Alexander Eckstein, "China Trip Notes," undated, "Eckstein, Alexander" folder, Box 5, NASAR, BHL.

[131] "Qiao Guanhua huijian 'Mei Zhong Guanxi Quanguo Weiyuanhui' xuezhe fang Hua daibiaotuan" [Qiao Guanhua Meets with NCUSCR Delegation], *Renmin Ribao*, December 24, 1972; Program Report, November 1972–May 1973, "Annual Meeting, NCUSCR, 1973," Box 131, ADBP, RBMLCU.

[132] A. Doak Barnett, "There Are Warts There, Too: More Thoughts out of China," *New York Times*, April 8, 1973, 1–2, 5–6.

but was also conscious that American products were selling twice as fast in the PRC as Chinese exports were in the United States. An official from the China Council for the Promotion of International Trade had asked the National Committee in August 1972 if the organization might be able to help reduce this imbalance by organizing a trade exhibition to promote Chinese wares to American buyers. This was a favored tactic of the PRC in this period: during the following year, China would hold commercial exhibits or participate in trade fairs in some twenty-five countries. In response to the CCPIT suggestion, the National Committee had drawn up initial plans for a trade exhibition to be discussed during the organization's December 1972 board visit to China.[133]

Unbeknownst to the NCUSCR, these efforts were coeval with other private and governmental American interest in promoting greater trade with a China reopen for business: the PRC registered a 30.2 percent year-on-year increase in foreign trade in 1972 and then a sharp 74.2 percent increase in 1973 (75 percent of this trade was now with capitalist countries, too).[134] In late 1972, Thornton Wilson, the Boeing CEO who had recently sold China ten 707 airliners for a reported $150 million, and Eugene Theroux, a commercial lawyer who had accompanied Representatives Gerald Ford and Hale Boggs during the first delegation to the PRC from the House of Representatives, were among a group of likeminded businessmen who approached the Nixon administration for support in establishing an organization that would promote trade with China.[135]

Internally, the Nixon administration had discussed the formation of such a group just a month after the president's February 1972 visit to China. From these earliest discussions, Kissinger had been clear that he wanted the government to take the lead in forming such a group, rather than allowing the initiative to be driven solely by the private sector.[136] In October, Kissinger instructed the Department of Commerce to encourage

---

[133] Kissinger to USLO, February 14, 1974, "China Trade and Exchanges – July 5, 1973–February 28, 1974," Box 93, HAKCFFE, RNL; NCUSCR Annual Report, 1972–73, NCUSCROC; Ma, *The Cultural Revolution in the Foreign Ministry*, 338.

[134] Ma, 337.

[135] Eugene Theroux, "The Founding of the Council," *The China Business Review* 20, no. 4 (1993); author interview with Eugene Theroux, Washington, DC, United States, September 21, 2015.

[136] Holdridge and Hormats to Kissinger, undated, *FRUS, 1969–1976*, Vol. XVII, Document 217.

Wilson and Theroux's scheme – but to shape it, too. The government agreed to give its support to the creation of a private trade council – if the group accepted official guidelines for its format and function. One of the five guidelines explicitly stated that, "given the highly politicized nature of China's foreign trade" the council "will maintain a close relationship with interested government agencies."[137] By January 1973, Kissinger's aides reported that, "To control [private] pressures, and sustain USG[overnment] influence over the evolution of Sino-U.S. trade, we have taken steps – with your approval – to form the National Council for Sino-American Trade."[138]

The US government's desire to oversee the creation of the National Council for United States-China Trade was not intended to completely curtail the independence of the group, however. Instead, as with the NCUSCR and CSCPRC, the council would be afforded significant operational independence within the (in this case, explicit) ground rules established by its government backers. The National Committee and the Committee on Scholarly Communication were specifically made the model for the proposed trade organization: Holdridge told Kissinger that the new group would operate "on the same pattern of 'people-to-people' contacts that we have evolved with the Chinese in the culture and scientific exchange areas."[139] In another parallel between the planned trade council and the two existing exchange groups, the government felt comfortable allowing the National Council for United States-China Trade to operate independently in recognition of who would be running the group: blue-ribbon American business elites who the White House knew could be trusted to seek expanded trade opportunities with the Chinese as a corollary to the US government's diplomatic relationship with Beijing.[140]

Discreet support for the Council from Washington suited Chinese preferences, too. When Kissinger had previously raised the matter of trade, Beijing had consistently downplayed the prospects for commercial exchange. By contrast, it had been an official from the China Council for the Promotion of International Trade that had suggested to the NCUSCR

[137] Lynn to Kissinger, October 1, 1972, "China Trade/Exchanges – February 2, 1972–July 4, 1973," Box 93, HAKCFFE, RNL.
[138] Holdridge to Kissinger, January 3, 1973, "Visit to the PRC – Feb 1973 – Briefing Book," Box 98, HAKCFFE, RNL.
[139] Ibid.
[140] Theroux, "The Founding of the Council;" author interview with Theroux.

a trade exhibition in the United States and, in June 1973, Zhou discussed in detail how to simplify and increase trade with the first vice chairman of the National Council for United States-China Trade, David Rockefeller – at a time when Washington officials were failing to pin down Chinese officials on lingering political barriers to trade such as disputed property claims and frozen assets left over from the imposition of the US commercial embargo of the PRC after the outbreak of the Korean War.[141] Beijing's resistance to discussing trade through governmental channels encouraged the White House's decision to support a private trade council.[142]

When the NCUSCR learned of the separate efforts to create a trade council, the group voluntarily scaled back its own plans for promoting commercial exchange and threw its organizational resources behind the new trade council, seconding a member of staff to work with the new organization in the run up to its formal establishment on May 31, 1973.[143] The National Committee did not completely cease advising American businessmen – such consultations helped solicit valued corporate donations – but in general adopted the same close working relationship with the new trade council that it had already cultivated with the CSCPRC, seeking collaborations with the new group and promoting its activities, rather than competing for clients or audience.[144]

As the plans for the establishment of the trade council were being finalized, the Chinese government looked to the US market with anticipation. The Guangdong provincial government completed a study of Sino-American trade in March 1973, in connection to the famous Canton Trade Fair that was held in the province twice a year and to which Americans had been invited beginning in April of the previous year. The study documented the "China fever" that had overtaken the US market. American department stores had, the study claimed, set up special departments or even entire shops dedicated to Chinese merchandise,

---

[141] ZGZYWXYJS, *Zhou Enlai nianpu, 1949–1976*, 3: 601–02; David Rockefeller, *Memoirs* (New York: Random House, 2002), 249; William Burr, "'Casting a Shadow' Over Trade: The Problem of Private Claims and Blocked Assets in U.S.-China Relations, 1972–1975," *Diplomatic History* 33, no. 2 (April 2009): 315–49.

[142] Holdridge to Kissinger, January 18, 1973, "Visit to the PRC – Feb 1973 – Briefing Book," HAKCFFE, RNL.

[143] The organization continues to exist to this day, having changed its name to the US-China Business Council. Program Report, November 1972–May 1973, "Annual Meeting, NCUSCR, 1973," Box 131, ADBP, RBMLCU.

[144] Minutes of 23rd meeting of NCUSCR board, October 29, 1973, Folder 73, Box 6, Series 1, DPMP, RAC.

while American businessmen were capitalizing on the interest in Chinese goods by raising the prices of products from the country. (These price hikes were attributed in part to the demand for Chinese goods among the American people but, the study claimed, "also reflect the speculative nature of American businessmen and fluctuations in the US market brought on by changing fashions.") The study went on to provide practical guidance on how the PRC might successfully market its products to the United States, ranging from an overview of the role of wholesalers, agents, and retailers in the US supply chain to how American consumers' preference for convenience led them to favor easy to wash, non-iron tablecloths. Guangdong was the region of China that had historically been most involved in trade with Western nations (and that would soon be again). Nonetheless, the report shows how at least some within the PRC were thinking concretely about how to immediately increase sales to American consumers.[145]

The National Council for United States-China Trade's May 1973 launch meeting thus came at an opportune moment. The Council would prove an immediate success: representatives from 500 American businesses attended the trade council's inaugural conference and early recruits to the Council included powerhouses such as Chase Manhattan Bank, General Electric, Westinghouse, and Monsanto. This intense American interest in the Chinese market came at a time when bilateral trade remained less than the sales of the JCPenney department store chain alone. It was the prospect of future trade that animated the new trade council's membership body, not the scale of current transactions; American businessmen were again slack-jawed about cracking the mythical China market.[146] The NCUSCR had already experienced this unbridled hunger for doing business with China: Pan Am, American Express, and Holiday Inn had all provided generous sponsorship of the ping-pong return exchange long before China allowed US flights into the country, credit card transactions, or foreign-owned hotels.[147] The then-NCUSCR staff member Jan Berris

---

[145] Reference materials of Guangdong Foreign Trade Work Conference, "Meiguo shichang gaikuang he dui maoyi ying zhuyi de wenti" [Overview of the US Market and Issues That Should be Paid Attention to in Trade], March 19, 1973, Document 342-2-122-101-103, Guangdong Provincial Archives (GDPA), PRC.

[146] Theroux, "The Founding of the Council;" author interview with Theroux; Talley, *Forgotten Vanguard*, 3.

[147] Schoyer to the Joint Committee [organizing the ping-pong visit], June 21, 1971, "National Committee – General Correspondence – 1969–71," Box 130, ADBP, RBMLCU.

later recalled that, in the heady days of early US-PRC trade, a Holiday Inn executive manically accosted a visiting Chinese official during an early exchange trip, telling the startled visitor that his company wanted to open a hotel in every Chinese city – a proposition that seemed ridiculous then, but appears prescient now.[148] During the first China Council for the Promotion of International Trade delegation sent to the United States in 1975, eager American executives would offer to provide their own private planes to fly the Chinese to cities not on their seven-city itinerary if they would then meet with their company – a generous offer gently refused by a delegation overwhelmed by American interest.[149]

Beijing signaled its approval of the creation of the trade council by having senior diplomat Han Xu attend the launch.[150] The significance of Han's presence was not lost on the businessmen: taking his appearance as an indication that the new trade council might have the ear of the Chinese government, most firms paid the substantial dues for Council membership there and then.[151] Han may well have been encouraged by the enthusiasm of the businessmen for trading with his country; he was also, however, angered by a speech by the ranking US official present at the event, State Department Undersecretary for Economic Affairs William Casey. Casey spoke of expanding trade with Chinese on both sides of the Taiwan straits and drew a parallel between his audience and a forthcoming Republic of China trade mission to the United States. As soon as he learned of Casey's comments, Kissinger cabled an apology to Han, assuring him that the remarks had not been cleared with his superiors.[152] The quarrel, however fleeting, was a reminder of the political sensitivities present in commercial contacts with China – and of why Kissinger and his aides had wanted to keep the trade council closely under government watch.

CONCLUSION

In the year that followed the Nixon–Mao summit, exchanges continued to be at the heart of rebuilding a broad Sino-American relationship

---

[148] Author interview with Berris, August 15, 2015.

[149] Phillips to NCUSCT member firms, July 7, 1975, "National Committee on US-China Trade, 1974–93," Box 131, ADBP.

[150] Solomon to Kissinger, June 1, 1973, "China Exchanges, May 16–June 13, 1973," Director's Files of Winston Lord (DFWL), RG59, NACP.

[151] Theroux, "The Founding of the Council"; author interview with Theroux.

[152] Solomon to Kissinger, June 1, 1973, "China Exchanges, May 16–June 13, 1973," DFWL, RG59, NACP.

between both peoples and governments. The success of the visit of the Chinese table tennis team to the United States – the first official delegation of PRC citizens to the United States – confirmed that reacquainting these two long-estranged societies would be possible and popular. Both the NCUSCR and the government concluded from their collaboration overseeing that exchange that their public-private partnership was a model that could work, while the Chinese government was similarly impressed with the National Committee and soon invited the organization's board to Beijing to discuss future cooperation. The NCUSCR quickly sought to confirm its centrality in exchanges in the form of the joint position paper authored with the CSCPRC. In the Committee on Scholarly Communication's case, however, the position paper was not simply capitalizing on earlier success: Beijing's lingering preference for American exchange organizers on the political left in 1972 and Chinese leaders' perception of the National Academy of Sciences as an arm of government had stymied the CSCPRC's efforts to begin exchange with Chinese scientists. There was irony in the Committee on Scholarly Communication's response: although in fact a nongovernmental organization, the CSCPRC's elite standing and its pledge to act in a politically reliable manner – that is, support Washington's China policy – allowed the Committee to leverage US government influence with Beijing to force its way into Sino-American scientific exchanges. Soon after, the creation of the National Council for United States-China Trade – a move foreseen and shaped by the government but arising from private initiative – completed the process of creating a framework for exchanges that were managed by private US organizations but in collaboration with both governments.

3

New Liaisons

Two months before Nixon resigned the presidency in August 1974, Kissinger delivered a speech to a dinner jointly hosted by the National Committee on US-China Relations, the Committee on Scholarly Communication with the PRC, and the National Council for United States-China Trade. The secretary of state could not help but be defensive. The Watergate scandal had sapped the vitality of the Nixon administration, and the enervation had spread even to Nixon's boldest foreign policy initiative: rapprochement with China. "Despite periodic accounts of supposed ups and downs in our bilateral relations," Kissinger averred, "there should be no doubt in anyone's mind that, from the United States' point of view, we remain firmly on course." Kissinger was complimentary about his hosts. As a result of their combined work, the secretary of state said, "some of our country's most talented and influential men and women have achieved a far greater understanding of the people of China and their goals. Through this process of understanding, immeasurable strength has been added to the fundamental tenet of our policy: ... the normalization of relations with China."[1]

There was truth in what Kissinger said. Nixon's truncated second term had seen a swift expansion in the cultural, scholarly, and commercial exchanges overseen by these three organizations, vastly increasing the number of Chinese and Americans who had participated in the new

[1] Kissinger's speech to NCUSCR, CSCPRC, and NCUSCT dinner, June 3, 1974, "Spring 1974 Board Meeting," Box 131, ADBP, RBMLCU. The speech made the Chinese state-run press: "Jixinge guowuqing tan Mei Zhong guanxi" [Secretary Kissinger Discusses US-China Relations], *Renmin Ribao*, June 8, 1974.

relationship and who supported the initiative – although this American support was not necessarily because of some deep understanding of the Chinese people, as Kissinger suggested. These exchanges had indeed also directly contributed to progress toward normalization. As this chapter will show, having underpinned early breakthroughs in the rapprochement, the exchange relationship was central to the most concrete achievement in Nixon's China policy: the establishment of "liaison offices" – de facto embassies – in Beijing and Washington in May 1973. This achievement, the closest that either Nixon or Kissinger would come to realizing normalization, was, in conception and realization, deeply connected to exchanges: mooted in Beijing's talks with the National Committee, the offices were designed to facilitate exchanges and trade, and did – including the most important exchange visit to China since the breakthrough ping-pong visit in the form of the Philadelphia Orchestra's September 1973 tour of China.

Nonetheless, despite this progress, it was not true that the US government was "firmly on course" in its relations with Beijing by July 1974 – and this downturn had been connected with "ups and downs" in exchange contacts. One moment of conflict – a disastrous congressional delegation led by Senator Warren Magnuson – even prompted Chinese leaders to disinvite Kissinger from a planned visit of his own, marking the beginning of the end of his smooth relationship with Chinese interlocutors during his time in office. Thus, where the breakthroughs in Sino-American relations of Nixon's first term had been the result of intertwined initiatives in exchange and high-level diplomacy, so, too, were the more checkered contacts between the two governments and peoples during the president's second term more than simply a consequence of negotiations between Kissinger and his Chinese interlocutors.[2]

THE ORIGINS OF THE LIAISON OFFICES IN EXCHANGES

As detailed in the previous two chapters, Kissinger had always been in two minds about encouraging Sino-American exchange ties that were wholly free of governmental influence. Chinese insistence (as well as the reasoning of his aides) had ultimately forced the national security advisor to accept that early contacts between the American and Chinese peoples would have to be on an unofficial basis on the US side. Nonetheless,

[2] Ibid.

Kissinger and his advisors had believed that, as rapprochement deepened, the most important of these contacts could be brought under formal governmental control, with the State Department and White House coming to negotiate the most significant exchanges directly with Beijing. By January 1973, Holdridge was becoming increasingly frustrated that this has not yet happened. While there was "substantial movement" in nongovernmental contacts, there had been "largely inaction" in negotiating officially sponsored exchanges: the Chinese continued to ignore Washington's requests to directly coordinate sporting and cultural exchanges and to arrange a hoped-for trip by a delegation of US state governors.[3]

The US government, then, had no choice but to continue to pin its hopes for an exchange program that would serve its political objectives on the three nongovernmental organizations with which it held sway: the NCUSCR, the CSCPRC, and the emerging National Council for United-States-China Trade. It was in the context of the continuing centrality of these private groups that the idea of creating liaison offices in Beijing and Washington resurfaced in late 1972. First mentioned during internal US government discussions as early as 1969, the possibility of Sino-American diplomatic representation in the two country's capitals that was permanent but less formal than an embassy had been debated by the Chinese politburo in 1971.[4] The US government had first raised the idea with their Chinese interlocutors in bilateral talks during Kissinger's first, secret visit to Beijing in November of that year; the Chinese had initially responded that such a significant political step was premature.[5] The possibility of an ongoing American presence in Beijing resurfaced when, during the National Committee's board visit to China in December 1972, the Chinese mentioned to the group their practice of establishing unofficial trade offices with countries with which they did not (yet) have official diplomatic relations. The NCUSCR's leaders quietly communicated the Chinese suggestion to officials in Washington, thus prompting a renewed push by the US government to establish an ongoing diplomatic presence in the two capitals in 1973.[6]

---

[3] Holdridge to Kissinger, January 18, 1973, "Visit to the PRC – February 1973 – Briefing Book," Box 98, HAKCFFE, RNL.

[4] Xia, "China's Elite Politics and Sino-American Rapprochement", 18–19.

[5] Kissinger to Nixon, November 1971, *FRUS, 1969–1976*, Vol. XVII, Document 164.

[6] Holdridge to Kissinger, January 18, 1973, "Visit to the PRC – February 1973 – Briefing Book," Box 98, HAKCFFE, RNL.

This representation was conceived primarily to facilitate exchanges and trade. Internally, the National Security Council – channeling Kissinger's preference for secretive contacts – hoped that permanent representation might be in the form of an "official presence of low visibility." This might take the form of US government employees working from within the embassy of an ally, such as the United Kingdom. Such an arrangement could have been similar to how the United States and the PRC had had the UK and India, respectively, provide third-party support to Americans in the PRC and Chinese in the United States in the 1950s. But Holdridge told Kissinger that Beijing had framed the liaison offices as a means to support societal contacts – hence their decision to resurrect the proposal in talks with the National Committee. Given this, Holdridge recommended to his boss that Washington should base their case for the establishment of the offices around the growing exchanges and trade between the two societies. Indeed, proof that the US government expected the offices to exist primarily to facilitate such contact was found in Holdridge's proposed staffing arrangement: a combination of State Department specialists on cultural and economic affairs alongside representatives from the NCU-SCR, CSCPRC, and NCUSCT.[7]

Kissinger perceived that the Chinese rationale of facilitating nongovernmental contact was only a pretense to deepen the governmental relationship. He said as much to Premier Zhou during his February 1973 visit to Beijing: "we should also maintain the fiction that [each liaison office] is also dealing with the Commerce Department and with cultural groups. But certainly we would envision that the chief of your liaison office would have the right to contact the State Department, and that this would be his normal contact for routine business." To Kissinger, if exchanges and trade provided public justification for liaison offices, their true function was to allow continuous high-level diplomacy that had, to date, only been possible through occasional China trips, backchannel communication, and indirect routes like the PRC representation at the United Nations in New York. Zhou, however, presented the offices differently, skirting Kissinger's talk of governmental contacts and stating, "But of course through the [Chinese] Foreign Ministry we will arrange for your liaison office to have communications with the Foreign Trade Ministry, cultural organizations and also people's organizations—organizations similar to what you have as the National Committee on Chinese-U.S. Relations [sic] and the

---

[7] Ibid.; Oyen, *Diplomacy of Migration*, 207–11.

scientific organizations." For the Chinese premier, facilitating trade and cultural and scientific contact was no mere pretense.[8]

If Kissinger's reference to "the fiction" of such contacts harked back to the secretive diplomacy he and Nixon had conducted with Zhou and Mao before 1971, Zhou's comments reflected the reality that the US-China relationship was by 1973 as much based on contact between the American and Chinese people as it was talks between their highest leaders. Cold War geostrategy had not ceased to be important: the success of Kissinger's February 1973 visit was in part due to Mao's short-lived interest in forming a "horizontal line" with the United States and its Asian allies to "commonly deal with a bastard" – the Soviet Union (although, by the end of the year, Mao had changed tack substantially and accused the United States of capitulation to Moscow).[9] Nonetheless, by 1973, the original geopolitical motivation for Sino-American rapprochement could not alone provide momentum to negotiations. Both the PRC and the United States had benefitted from their strategic realignment: the rapprochement had immediately shaken Moscow into a more committed détente with Washington, and to a frosty peace with Beijing after the war scare of 1969.[10] But, as the Nixon–Mao summit receded into the past, it became necessary to put meat on the bones of this positional realignment: an ongoing diplomatic relationship between the two sides demanded more than biannual connivances.

Institutionalizing the rapprochement with Beijing seemed increasingly urgent. In 1973, Zhou was seventy-five years old, and Mao had become an octogenarian. US leaders did not yet know that Zhou was dying of cancer, learning of this the following year from Senator Henry "Scoop" Jackson after a congressional delegation to China.[11] Nonetheless, the US government was already worried that rapprochement might well die with those two men. Immediately before Kissinger's February 1973 summit trip, Marshall Green, the State Department's most senior Asia expert,

---

[8] Memcon: Zhou, Kissinger, et al., February 17, 1973, David P. Nickles, ed., *Foreign Relations of the United States, 1969–1976*, Vol. XVIII, China, 1973–1976 (Washington, DC: United States Government Printing Office, 2007), Document 10.

[9] Memcon: Mao, Kissinger, et al., February 17–18, 1973, *FRUS, 1969–1976*, Vol. XVIII, Document 12; Kazushi Minami, "Re-Examining the End of Mao's Revolution: China's Changing Statecraft and Sino-American Relations, 1973–1978," *Cold War History* 16, no. 4 (January 2016): 362–63.

[10] Yang Kuisong, "The Sino-Soviet Border Clash of 1969: From Zhenbao Island to Sino-American Rapprochement," *Cold War History* 1, no. 1 (2000): 21–52.

[11] Bruce to Kissinger, July 5, 1974, "China Exchanges, April 1–August 8, 1974," HAK-CFFE, RNL.

wrote to Kissinger that, "The greater our success in institutionalizing the relationship through a broad range of formal and informal agreement and contacts, the greater the chances that it will survive intact through the succession period."[12] Kissinger himself added his approval to this logic in a memorandum to Nixon the following month.[13]

Chinese approval for this institutionalization came from the very top. During Kissinger's February visit, Mao was more explicit than Zhou, telling their guest that the longevity of the Sino-American relationship depended on increasing exchanges and trade. Mao argued that if his people learned the English language and interacted with Americans, they would continue to support rapprochement, regardless of who led their countries. Zhou subsequently told Kissinger that Mao had thus personally approved institutionalizing the relationship through the creation of liaison offices – implying that Mao, too, saw the offices as the means by which to facilitate deeper interaction between the Chinese and American people.[14] Internally, the Chinese Foreign Ministry told CCP members that establishing a liaison office in Washington would be "conducive to expanding China's influence among the American people."[15] In keeping with this goal and Mao's comments, during Kissinger's February visit, the Chinese also approved an extensive program of exchanges to be overseen by the NCUSCR and CSCPRC over the coming year: Beijing agreed to receive six delegations, including the Philadelphia Orchestra and teams of basketball players and swimmers, and to send eight delegations of their own, ranging from computer scientists and high-energy physicists to gymnasts and an exhibition of prized archaeological finds. This raft of contacts would more than double the number of exchanges yet overseen by the two organizations.[16] As Holdridge had hoped, there was a clear connection between this future exchange activity and the establishment of the liaison offices needed to facilitate such contacts. The visit's final communiqué announced: "The two sides agreed that the time was appropriate for accelerating the normalization of relations. ... They agreed on a concrete program of expanding trade as well as science, cultural and other exchanges. To facilitate this process and to improve communications, it

---

[12] Green to Nixon, February 2, 1973, "POL – Chicom – 15-1 – 3/10/73," RG59, NACP.
[13] Kissinger to Nixon, March 2, 1973, "HAK China Trip – February 1973 – Memcons & Reports (Originals) [TS, 2/2]," Box 98, HAKCFFE, RNL.
[14] Kissinger to Nixon, February 24, 1973, "HAK China Trip – February 1973 – Memcons & Reports," Box 98, HAKCFFE, RNL.
[15] Gong, "Chinese Decision Making," 358.
[16] Keatley to CSCPRC members, March 5, 1973, "1973 – General," CSCPRCP, NAS.

was agreed that in the near future each side will establish a liaison office in the capital of the other."[17]

This was a critical moment in the transition from isolation to normalization in the Sino-American relationship. Kissinger was not completely mistaken in seeing this as an agreement to deepen government-to-government interchange: the communiqué stated that the liaison offices would also "improve communications" between the two sides and, to Washington's surprise, the Chinese agreed to the offices being staffed wholly by government employees with diplomatic immunity. Seeking to maximize the political capital gained from this forward step, Nixon appointed the most senior diplomat he had – David K. E. Bruce – to head the new liaison office in Beijing. Bruce had served as US ambassador in Paris and then in Bonn and London – the only American to ever serve as ambassador to France, Germany, and the United Kingdom. Mao reciprocated by naming the similarly well-heeled Huang Zhen. Huang had obtained high military rank in the Chinese Civil War and accompanied Zhou Enlai to the Bandung Conference of 1955 before becoming vice foreign minister of the PRC. Huang had served as ambassador to Hungary and Indonesia and then, from 1964, to France. While in Paris, he had been involved in early Sino-American diplomacy, arranging Edgar Snow's 1970 invitation to China and acting as Kissinger's interlocutor on four occasions and General Vernon Walters's forty-five times as part of the secret Paris channel between the governments. Before Huang departed Beijing, Mao asked him, "Do you think your transfer from the position of ambassador to France to head of the liaison office in the United States is a promotion or demotion?" Huang smiled but did not answer. "The liaison office is of greater significance than the embassy," Mao told him, "You have been promoted." The appointment of ambassadors of the stature of Bruce and Huang would ensure that the liaison offices could facilitate dialogue at a high political level.[18]

The existing historiography has recognized the significance of the establishment of these de facto embassies: never before had the PRC agreed to open a diplomatic mission in a capital where the ROC still maintained an embassy.[19] Historians have seen this agreement much as Kissinger did: as

---

[17] Joint US-PRC communiqué issued on establishment of liaison office, February 22, 1973, "1973 – General," CSCPRCP, NAS.

[18] Geng Biao, Ji Pengfei, Wang Youping, Han Nianlong, "Huainian lao zhanyou Huang Zhen tongzhi" [Remembering our Old Comrade Huang Zhen], *Renmin Ribao*, May 31, 1990; Memcon: Nixon and Bruce, May 3, 1973, *FRUS, 1969–1976*, Vol. XVIII, Document 30; Gong, "Chinese Decision Making," 357.

[19] Tucker, *Strait Talk*, 63.

primarily the product of momentum in government-to-government contacts, a prize offered by Beijing for the diplomatic progress of 1971 and 1972.[20] However, this overlooks how this important way-station between initial rapprochement and the final normalization deal was in fact directly and deeply connected to growing exchange contacts: the idea first resurfaced in Chinese talks with the National Committee, Zhou had framed the offices as clearing houses for trade and exchanges, and the US government had planned to have NCUSCR, CSCPRC, and NCUSCT personnel help staff the offices. Mao had elevated the formality of the offices but, as we will see, once established, both the Beijing and Washington offices nonetheless spent the majority of their time dealing with societal contacts.[21] When Senator Warren Magnuson's congressional delegation visited China in July, they found that "in its principal task of liaison with the Chinese on commercial and cultural exchange matters, the [US Liaison Office] was functioning at full tilt and doing a first-rate job."[22] The establishment of liaison offices, then, was a major political achievement in the Sino-American relationship that came about as a result of exchange contacts and in order to deepen such links: the two tracks of high-level and exchange diplomacy were, in early 1973, clearly and productively connected.

AS CLOSE AS LIPS AND TEETH?

Both the NCUSCR and CSCPRC naturally welcomed the prospect of more frequent exchange visits. In 1973, both Committees sought to use the gathering momentum in exchange for contacts to expand and professionalize as organizations and to offer greater opportunities to their constituents in American society. Concurrently, however, the establishment of liaison offices and the Chinese direct negotiation of a package of exchange proposals during Kissinger's February visit reignited concerns among both the NCUSCR and CSCPRC that the US government might

---

[20] See, for example, Goh, *Constructing the U.S. Rapprochement with China*, 226; Tyler, *A Great Wall*, 152–54; Barbara Barnouin and Yu Changgen, *Chinese Foreign Policy during the Cultural Revolution* (London: Kegan Paul International, 1998), 111.

[21] This is made clear in the memoir of Bruce's successor as head of the US Liaison Office, George H. W. Bush. George H. W. Bush, *The China Diary of George H. W. Bush: The Making of a Global President*, ed. Jeffrey Engel (Princeton, NJ: Princeton University Press, 2008).

[22] Warren G. Magnuson, *China Report: Report of a Special Congressional Delegation* (Washington, DC: United States Government Printing Office, 1973), 13.

seek to make them supplicants in a government-led exchange program that could become private and unofficial only in name.

The Committee on Scholarly Communication's role in receiving two scientific delegations in the autumn of 1972 marked the beginning of a prominent role for the organization in exchanges. A Chinese official on one of the 1972 delegations had promised that "many Chinese scholars" would soon travel to the United States and Beijing invited the CSCPRC to send its leadership to China in May 1973 to negotiate this future collaboration.[23] To accommodate the exchange activity promised by the Chinese official, in February 1973, the Committee on Scholarly Communication sought out $150,000 in new funding – expecting a third to come directly from the State Department, and two-thirds from the National Science Foundation – to expand its small staff. The Committee had, for the moment, only one full-time staff member, with Committee members themselves providing more intermittent labor.[24] Anne Keatley had grown up in rural Florida wanting to be a scientist. But the science and math classes she took in her public high school included only one other girl and, when she graduated, her dream career was not among those listed as available for women. Instead, her first long-term job after college had been as a Pan Am air steward based in Asia. Her salary from the unenviable assignment of flying American troops between Saigon and Hong Kong on R&R trips – she would ferry the same young, hungover, faces back to the War after two weeks in the colony – was enough to pay for her to spend two years at the Yale in Hong Kong Chinese language program. Keatley's Chinese abilities were the reason that, in January 1970, Alexander Haig had interviewed her for the job of Kissinger's secretary. The White House "begged me to take the job," she later recalled, but instead she harked back to her childhood dream and accepted an offer from the National Academy of Sciences. That same year, she married the journalist Robert Keatley and, in 1971, had met Zhou Enlai during her husband's trip to China (Chapter 1) – where she had first introduced the premier to the Committee on Scholarly Communication.[25]

[23] Todd to Harris, February 5, 1973, "1973 – General," CSCPRCP, NAS.

[24] Ibid. Keatley was aided by an administrative assistant and a secretary. By October 1974, the CSCPRC had grown to nine full-time staff members. "Proposal for Partial Support of the CSCPRC," October 1974, "1974 – Request for funds," CSCPRCP, NAS.

[25] Author interview with Anne Solomon (previously Anne Keatley), New York, United States, June 25, 2018.

While Keatley oversaw the expansion of the CSCPRC, the National Committee was making personnel changes of its own that reflected growing ambition: in May, the organization named its first president from beyond academia, appointing Charles W. Yost, an experienced and well-connected diplomat who had served as Nixon's first ambassador to the UN and had held three ambassadorships under Eisenhower. If Yost's appointment reflected the National Committee's reorientation from public education to exchange diplomacy, the appointment of a former ambassador did not prevent the NCUSCR's leadership from worrying about the direct involvement of both governments in negotiating exchanges during Kissinger's February 1973 visit. Eckstein – still the NCUSCR's lead on exchanges – referred to a "dilemma ... in the relationship between the National Committee and the U.S. government" created when the White House agreed to accept Beijing's preformulated agenda for exchanges without consulting the NCUSCR or CSCPRC (Keatley was similarly concerned). The National Committee had made suggestions for specific delegations during their December 1972 board visit to China, but these had been transformed into a set agenda for cultural and scientific exchanges without either of the Committees being given a say about their willingness to organize and fund the trips.[26]

The NCUSCR and CSCPRC acted quickly to reassert their independent role in the exchange program – but sought to do so without sabotaging their working relationship with both governments. The critical question for the two organizations was who would determine what culture and science would be exchanged during visits. This would be determined above all by the topical focus of each delegation, and by which individuals were included in the trips. The two groups wanted their government to negotiate with Beijing only the volume of exchanges and then to leave the nongovernmental organizations to work out which Americans would travel on the visits and what Chinese delegations they were willing to host.[27] This was of fundamental importance to the viability of both Committees. For the Committee on Scholarly Communication, the scientific subjects chosen for delegations would determine the value of exchanges to the US scientific community: some American scientists would gain a great deal from a visit to China, while others would learn almost nothing. For the

---

[26] Minutes of annual members meeting of NCUSCR, May 16, 1973, "23rd Meeting – Board of Directors – October 29, 1973" [*sic*], Box 131, ADBP, RBMLCU; Keatley to CSCPRC members, March 5, 1973, "1973 – General," CSCPRCP, NAS.
[27] Ibid.

National Committee, topics of sporting or artistic exchanges dictated the size of American audiences – and thus ticket sales, media coverage, and fundraising potential, all of which were critical to the organization as it emerged from the table tennis exchange-induced budget crisis.[28]

The concerns of the NCUSCR and CSCPRC might have seemed compatible with the White House's stance: that the government cared only about the volume of exchanges – a public indication of the strength of rapprochement – not their content. In fact, however, official indifference to the content of exchanges was alarming to the NCUSCR and CSCPRC: US diplomats had been delighted that the Chinese had offered as many exchanges as they did and were thus disinclined to push their interlocutors on the content of the program. The government would rather lump the two Committees with unwanted exchanges than risk the Chinese striking delegations off the list altogether.[29]

In the wake of Kissinger's February visit, the NCUSCR made clear that it would not accept the government's calculus: the organization declined to sponsor – that is, fund and take full responsibility for – the delegations of American basketball players and swimmers and divers to China, agreeing only to provide more hands-off assistance. The National Committee threatened to do likewise with any other exchanges that were agreed by the governments without the organization's prior agreement.[30] Likewise, the Committee on Scholarly Communication's leadership made its own support of the seven agreed scientific exchanges conditional on being invited to Beijing to talk directly with the Chinese about what "fields of special interest to American scholars" should be made the subject of future exchange. The State Department was initially cold to the pushback from the NCUSCR and CSCPRC. Richardson at State made clear that Washington did not plan to stop negotiating the content of exchanges – and implied that the government had already shown considerable favor toward the two groups in the past.[31]

The Committee on Scholarly Communication simultaneously set out their terms to their Chinese counterparts. In a May 9 proposal sent to the Scientific and Technical Association of the PRC, the Committee made clear that the CSCPRC's cooperation in hosting exchanges was "on the

[28] Murray to Eckstein, August 16, 1974, "Exchange Proposals for 1975," Box 131, ADBP.
[29] Keatley to CSCPRC members, March 5, 1973, "1973 – General," CSCPRCP, NAS.
[30] Minutes of annual members meeting of NCUSCR, May 16, 1973, "23rd Meeting – Board of Directors – October 29, 1973" [sic], Box 131, ADBP, RBMLCU.
[31] Keatley to CSCPRC members, March 5, 1973, "1973 – General," CSCPRCP, NAS.

condition that there be established a general reciprocal arrangement allowing the CSCPRC to sponsor groups to visit China" – that is, the Committee should be free to propose exchange delegations on subjects of their own choosing. This hit on an issue that would remain a source of tension in academic exchanges until 1979. The Committee on Scholarly Communication leadership used their May to June 1973 visit to China to point out – as tactfully as possible – that, while Chinese natural scientists would benefit enormously from visiting the high-tech facilities in the United States, the Americans that would gain most from access to China were not physical scientists but instead social scientists and humanities scholars who were desperate to gather new data through access to the Chinese population and to the country's unique art, culture, and historical artifacts in situ. This was particularly the case as Chinese commitment to showcasing the revolutionary science to American visitors had hardly waned since Galston and Signer's first visit: Beijing would soon propose hosting delegations that would study Chinese acupuncture anesthesia and herbal pharmacology, for example. Where natural science exchanges were to take place, the CSCPRC pushed for these to be on topics in which both the United States and the PRC both had advanced research – for example, physics – such that the exchange could advance cumulative shared scientific understanding.[32]

The content of scientific exchanges was the one matter of substance that Zhou himself was involved in negotiating during the Committee on Scholarly Communication's summer visit. The organization's top brass had traveled, including the Committee's chair, biochemist Emil Smith, ACLS President Burkhardt, and SSRC President Eleanor Sheldon. The Chinese premier made clear to the visitors that China was not yet ready to receive American social scientists. Wu Youxun, a physicist and senior Chinese Academy of Sciences official, described social science in the PRC as in a period of "struggle, criticism and transformation."[33] The CSCPRC trip indeed provided evidence for Zhou's claim: Ezra Vogel, already a

---

[32] Emphasis in the original. "Report on Exchange Discussions," May 15–June 15, 1973, "1973 – International Relations – Visits: Com Visit on Scholarly Exchanges," CSCPRCP, NAS; "Meiguo kexuejia daibiaotuan likai Guangzhou huiguo" [US Scientific Delegation Leaves Guangzhou to Return Home], *Renmin Ribao*, June 16, 1973; Keatley to CSCPRC members, March 5, 1973, "1973 – General," CSCPRCP, NAS.

[33] He, *Dangdai Zhong Mei minjian jiaoliu shi*, 137; "Report on Exchange Discussions," 15 May–15 June 1973, "1973 – International Relations – Visits: Com Visit on Scholarly Exchanges," CSCPRCP, NAS; author interview with Eleanor Sheldon, New York, United States, January 17, 2020.

prominent analyst of China after the publication of his 1969 book *Canton Under Communism*, was a member of the nineteen-person delegation, and one of four social scientists among the thirty-odd members of the delegation. After a Chinese social scientist was not included in the welcoming delegation at one of the five cities visited, Vogel asked their Chinese guide "if this meant that natural science was considered more important." He was assured otherwise, and a social scientist was duly included in the next welcoming committee. "But," Vogel later recalled, "the poor man was so afraid of making an error" – of a political, not academic variety – "that every time I asked a question he quickly changed the subject to talk about the weather." When the CSCPRC delegation visited social scientists working at the Nationalities Institute, Vogel thought it "painfully obvious that the researchers had not been given a chance to do field work for many years."[34] The NSC's Richard Solomon was in China a month after the CSCPRC, accompanying Senator Magnuson. A political scientist by training, Solomon reported to Kissinger after the trip that "there is nothing resembling social science" at Chinese universities and reflected that the "most depressing aspect of our trip was exposure to elderly, foreign-trained intellectuals who have been reduced to self-abasing, anxious hollow shells of men."[35]

There were limits, then, on the content and scope of Sino-American scientific exchanges that even Premier Zhou could not immediately alter, however, hard the CSCPRC pushed. This notwithstanding, the organization's China visit went some way to resolving the tensions over exchange negotiations created by Kissinger's February visit: the very fact of direct talks with the Beijing government had allayed CSCPRC fears that the organization would have no involvement in the process of formulating the exchange program it was expected to facilitate. The Committee's Chinese hosts had been receptive to the organization deciding the topic of delegations sent to the PRC and to the content of scientific exchanges being negotiated outside of formal government channels.[36] Reflecting on the visit, the organization internally reaffirmed that, "The CSCPRC is not, and does not intend to operate as, a branch of the federal administration."[37]

[34] Liu, *My First Trip to China*, 191–92.
[35] Solomon to Kissinger, July 18, 1973, "China Exchanges, July 10–October 31, 1973," DFWL, RG59, NACP.
[36] "Report on Exchange Discussions," May 15–June 15, 1973, "1973 – International Relations – Visits: Com Visit on Scholarly Exchanges," CSCPRCP, NAS.
[37] "Report on the CSCPRC visit to China, May 15–June 15, 1973," "Feuerwerker, Albert" folder, Box 5, NASAR, BHL.

The CSCPRC's Beijing negotiations appear to have benefitted the National Committee, too: by September, the organization's counterpart – the Chinese People's Institute of Foreign Affairs – had assured National Committee Vice President Murray that the CPIFA would work directly with the NCUSCR when planning exchanges and that the National Committee could now expect to conduct most of its communication with the Chinese government through the new PRC Liaison Office (PRCLO) in Washington, obviating the need to communicate through the White House.[38] The effectiveness of the Committee on Scholarly Communication's direct approach to negotiating with Beijing was demonstrated, too, by concern shown by its own government: the CSCPRC and NCUSCR were called to a meeting at the State Department in July at which Solomon made "an effort to keep the participants sensitized to the larger interest that is being served by exchange programs, and to discourage any uncoordinated approaches to the PRC Liaison Office."[39] The White House would have rested easier if the CSCPRC had dutifully accepted whatever scientific cooperation was agreed between the two governments; that the organization did not is a reminder that they could, and did, dissent from official foreign policy when the interests of American scientists – and their own organization – demanded they do so.

THE CONTRADICTIONS OF CONGRESSIONAL DELEGATIONS

The manner in which the program of exchanges for 1973 had been agreed had, then, revealed a latent tension between, on the one hand, the NCUSCR and CSCPRC and, on the other, the Nixon administration. This section covers a more immediate source of conflict: between the administration and other American actors over congressional delegations to China. Congressional delegations were the only Sino-American exchange contacts that were considered "official" by the two governments, on account of their being each individually negotiated between the two capitals. These visits were considered part of the exchange program despite being one-directional: no Chinese equivalents of American congressmen or senators visited the United States before 1979, although some Chinese high- and mid-ranking officials were sent in groups hosted by the NCUSCR in 1977 and 1978 (Chapter 6). The first congressional

---

[38] Murray to The Record, September 28, 1973, "23rd Meeting – Board of Directors – October 29, 1973," Box 131, ADBP, RBMLCU.

[39] Solomon to Kissinger, July 30, 1973, *FRUS, 1969–1976*, Vol. XVIII, Document 45.

delegations had occurred in 1972: first, the leaders of the Senate – Mansfield and Scott – visited in April and, then, those of the House of Representatives – Ford and Boggs – did in June. These visits were significant moments in rapprochement: all four men had left China deeply impressed by the country and had subsequently acted as influential advocates for Washington's new relationship with Beijing. The impact of this advocacy was enhanced by the distance between the visitors and the executive branch: Mansfield and Boggs were senior Democrats and owed nothing to Nixon; Scott and Ford's endorsements helped build support on Capitol Hill for an initiative launched out of the White House.[40]

Nonetheless, these early congressional visits had also shown that such trips could hurt as well as help the diplomatic relationship. Ford had angered Zhou by publicly repeating the premier's revelation that the Chinese now supported the US security treaty with Japan and the continuing presence of US troops in East Asia as a means to limit Soviet influence in the region. Mansfield was a consummate diplomat, originally considered by Nixon as a candidate for the first secret visit to China. But even Mansfield had stepped on toes while in China when he inadvertently insulted the Beijing-based, deposed Cambodian leader, Norodom Sihanouk, by referring to him as provisional head of state while in exile – when both the former king and the Chinese government considered him the actual Cambodian head of state.[41]

In this way, the first two congressional visits had revealed a tension in the purpose of such trips. These visits were intended by both governments as a form of public diplomacy that would expand the support base of rapprochement in Washington. Hence Zhou confiding in Ford about Beijing's change in heart about a strong American presence in the region: the premier was presenting the PRC as a cooperative partner in US global efforts to resist the Soviets, rather than as the implacable enemy of American power in Asia that China had been seen as in the 1960s. The tension inherent in Beijing's gambit was revealed, however, when Ford went public with these comments – a decision resented by the Chinese premier at a time when the PRC was still trying to balance

---

[40] Mike Mansfield and Hugh Scott, *Journey to the New China: April–May 1972* (Washington, DC: United States Government Printing Office, 1972); Hale Boggs and Gerald Ford, *Impressions of the New China: Joint Report to the United States House of Representatives* (Washington, DC: United States Government Printing Office, 1972).

[41] Memcon: Zhou, Kissinger, et al., February 17, 1973, *FRUS, 1969–1976*, Vol. XVIII, Document 10.

its geopolitical tilt toward the United States with its long-standing relationships with North Vietnam and other states set against American
power in Asia. Ford was less inclined than Kissinger and Nixon to
assure fellow Americans of Beijing's benign intentions without revealing the specifics of the pledges they had made. Mansfield's poorly chosen words about Sihanouk also led Zhou to question the senator's
credentials for diplomacy. "Mansfield looks very earnest but perhaps
he is not very mature politically," Zhou commented. Kissinger agreed:
"Yes ... and we don't want him involved in political negotiations ... he
has no standing with us on political problems." Perennially disinclined
to have anyone other than himself talk shop with the Chinese, Kissinger
worked to ensure that congressional delegations, while important to
the public presentation of rapprochement, should not be an arena for
diplomatic negotiation.[42]

This approach was further reflected in Kissinger's preparation for the
third congressional trip to the PRC, by Senator Magnuson in July 1973.
Magnuson had a keen interest in China, dating back at least as far as his
sponsorship of the Magnuson Act of 1943 that finally ended the hated
Chinese Exclusion laws that had racially discriminated against Chinese
migrants for some sixty years. This had won the then-congressman great
favor within China that had lingered into the Communist era. By 1973,
Magnuson had reason to be grateful to the PRC, too: his home state of
Washington was at the forefront of developing US trade with the country. The total value of Sino-American trade would climb to some $825
million in that year, including $759 million in Chinese purchases – a
more than eightfold increase on the year prior. Washington state was
home to both Boeing – behind the largest single American sale to the
PRC to date – and many of the farmers that had begun to sell hundreds of
millions of dollars of wheat to China, the largest category of US exports
to the PRC.[43] Washington state's newfound trade with China, while
expanding, was not without friction, however. A Chinese internal report
on grain imported from the United States in 1973 complained of the low
quality of the wheat and corn that was sold to the PRC – considered the
worst of all that the country imported, and inferior to Australian, Canadian, and Argentinian supplies – and suggested that the United States
was dumping low-quality grain on the Chinese market that American

---

[42] Ibid.
[43] Talley, *Forgotten Vanguard*, 7; Magnuson, *China Report*, 6; Chang, *Fateful Ties*, 228.

producers could not find buyers for anywhere else – but that they needed to sell because of the "US national economic crisis."[44]

Magnuson's delegation was focused on trade. It included four senators and as many congressmen – but Kissinger ensured that none of them were briefed on the current state of high-level negotiations on trade or any other substantive issue before arriving in China, hoping that this would ensure that they did not stray where he did not want them. The national security advisor even moved to prevent newly appointed US Liaison Office (USLO) chief Bruce passing information to Kissinger's own staffer, Richard Solomon, while he was accompanying the delegation, wary that the information might then find its way to the rest of the group.[45] Kissinger and Bruce, mindful of the experience of the Ford delegation, had also put pressure on Magnuson and his entourage not to reveal the contents of their discussions with the Chinese to the press.[46]

Kissinger's attempts to prevent the possibility of controversy during the visit proved woefully inadequate – and perhaps misguided. Alfred Jenkins had been on Kissinger's first, secret visit to China and was now one of the senior-most American officials serving at the US Liaison Office in Beijing. He reported to Kissinger that Magnuson had, throughout the trip, shown "unbelievable insensitivity" and described an "avalanche of gaucheries and worse" from the senator before summarizing that Magnuson "proved to be impressively accomplished at downright inventive ineptitude."[47] Jenkins complained that several of the politicians in Magnuson's delegation had also shown an "evident built-in feeling of American superiority" – a sideways reference to cultural chauvinism, if not downright racism – but singled out Magnuson for having "bragged" to other Chinese officials that "Zhou Enlai put his ministers at my disposal." That comment was so insensitive that Magnuson's translator had declined to render it in Chinese; unfortunately, some of the Chinese

---

[44] "Shanghai shi waimaoju geweiyuanhui: Guanyu jinkou Meiguo mianhua, liangshi de qingkuang he cunzai de wenti baogao" [Shanghai Foreign Trade Bureau Report on the Situation and Existing Problems Connected to Importing US Cotton and Grain], February 4, 1974, Folder B248-2-690, SHMA.

[45] Kissinger to Bruce, July 3, 1973, "China Exchange [*sic*] – June 14–July 9, 1973," Box 95, HAKCFFE, RNL.

[46] Bruce to Kissinger, July 6, 1973, "China Exchanges, June 14–July 9, 1973," DFWL, RG59, NACP.

[47] Jenkins and Holdridge to Kissinger, July 20, 1973, and Jenkins to Kissinger, undated, "China Exchanges, July 10–October 31, 1973," DFWL, RG59, NACP.

at the table understood English.[48] Another of Magnuson's unfortunate moments was when he asked the Chinese Vice Foreign Minister Zhang Wenjin how Chiang Kai-shek had fled to Taiwan during the Chinese Civil War. "Was it by boat?" "No," responded Zhang, "it was by American airplanes."[49] Meanwhile, Magnuson's wife told Mao's grandniece, Vice Foreign Minister Wang Hairong, that the best ambassadors the United States could send to China would be washing machines and electric irons "to ease the burden of your people."[50]

Magnuson's constant improprieties were perhaps in part the product of the senator's frustration at the limited political importance afforded to his delegation. As might have been expected given Zhou's reflections on the previous two congressional delegations, Chinese leaders were careful to limit the level of political recognition of Magnuson's delegation in order to convey that they did not plan to involve the senator and his colleagues in the high-level diplomatic negotiations conducted with White House envoys. Magnuson complained of the rank of the officials that greeted him at the airport and that only one journalist accompanied them, as well as at being lodged in the Peking Hotel and not a government guest house. But, above all, the senator protested not being given an appointment with the premier. Magnuson had complained, Bruce reported from Beijing, that his time was "wasted in idle sight-seeing instead of discussions in matters of substance" and that this suggested that Chinese officials did not recognize the importance of the legislative arm of the US government.[51]

Reflecting the focus of the delegation on commercial ties, Magnuson's discussions with Chinese Minister of Foreign Trade Li Qiang were extensive.[52] In the joint report that he and his traveling companions sent to Congress upon their return, Magnuson highlighted trade as an area of agreement during the trip: where, in 1972, the Chinese had told Representatives Ford and Boggs of multiple barriers to deeper trade – Taiwan,

[48] Jenkins to Kissinger, undated, "China Exchanges, July 10–October 31, 1973," DFWL, RG59, NACP.

[49] Bruce to Kissinger, July 8, 1973, "China Exchanges, June 14–July 9, 1973," DFWL, RG59, NACP.

[50] Solomon to Kissinger, July 18, 1973, "China Exchanges, July 10–October 31, 1973," DFWL, RG59, NACP.

[51] Bruce to Kissinger, July 8, 1973, "China Exchanges, June 14–July 9, 1973," DFWL, RG59, NACP.

[52] "Li Qiang huijian Meiguo Guohui Yiyuan tuan" [Li Qiang Meets with the US Congressional Delegation], *Renmin Ribao*, July 6, 1973.

Vietnam, unresolved claims and assets from the 1950 trade embargo of the PRC – now their hosts declined to link progress in diplomatic relations with the flow of goods or people, instead talking up the possibility of exchanges of both. Indeed, the PRC had recently purchased three chemical plants from US companies such as Pullman-Kellogg, and as many as ten from foreign subsidiaries of US companies. The visiting Americans were taken to see textile mills at work in the ancient capital city of Xi'an – soon to be familiar to many Americans as the home of the Terracotta Warriors – and the vast cotton fields that fed them. Guides touted the achievements of China's socialist science, claiming that innovations in fertilizers and irrigation had enabled as many as five harvests a year. The tour of the textile mills was perhaps intended as a nudge to the Americans: if the quality of US exports did not improve, China had its own supplies to rely upon.[53]

Conversations with American businessmen at the Canton Trade Fair had focused the attention of Chinese trade officials on the importance of Most Favored Nation (MFN) status for exports to the US market, prompting Chinese officials to raise this issue with the visiting American politicians. Magnuson's delegation argued that MFN was, for the time being, probably not as important as producing goods that fit American expectations of "quality and style" – something that Chinese exporters had themselves puzzled over (Chapter 2). But the Chinese emphasis on the discriminatory nature of not being most favored suggested their concern was about status as well as trade volumes.[54]

Despite these productive discussions over trade, Magnuson remained unsatisfied. He berated Vice Foreign Minister Qiao Guanhua so thoroughly about his not being granted a meeting with Zhou – telling him that his trip would be "useless" if he did not see the premier – that eventually his hosts relented and granted the senator an audience with the man who was, unbeknownst to Magnuson, undergoing censure from Mao on account of the Foreign Ministry's analysis of US-Soviet relations.[55]

[53] Magnuson, *China Report*, 3–6; "U.S. Party in China Tours Factory City," *New York Times*, July 10, 1973; Richard Baum, *China Watcher: Confessions of a Peking Tom* (Seattle: University of Washington Press, 2010), 61. On the claims and assets dispute that impeded early trade, see Burr, "'Casting a Shadow' Over Trade."

[54] Magnuson, *China Report*, 6–8.

[55] "Zhou zongli huijian Meiguo Guohui Yiyuan tuan" [Premier Zhou Met with the US Congressional Delegation], *Renmin Ribao*, July 7, 1973; ZGZYWXYJS, *Zhou Enlai nianpu, 1949–1976*, 3:603–05; Frederick Teiwes and Warren Sun, *The End of the Maoist Era: Chinese Politics during the Twilight of the Cultural Revolution, 1972–1976* (Armonk, NY: ME Sharpe, 2007), 89–91.

The meeting was a disaster: in the most damaging moment of the trip, Magnuson patronizingly told Zhou that the premier should be patient about the US bombing of Cambodia while Congress worked to tie the hands of the White House. Zhou pointed out that it was hard for him to tell Sihanouk – who the premier was hosting a dinner for later that same day – to remain serene when bombs are falling on his country. Zhou finally lost his temper – almost unheard of when the premier was receiving American guests – when asked when he would visit the United States. "Frankly ... I cannot come because Chiang Kai-shek has a representative there," he snapped. To make matters worse, Magnuson relayed much of their conversation to the US press that same evening.[56]

The contradictions at the heart of the developing congressional exchange program were evident in the discussion between Magnuson and Zhou. The Chinese premier complained that Magnuson had traveled to see China, not negotiate over Cambodia. But of course to Magnuson this was untrue. He had entered the Senate in 1944 and, after his successful campaign to pass the Chinese Exclusion Repeal Act, had then risked the fire of McCarthyism to advocate engagement with the newly established People's Republic. On finally coming to the PRC, he had not, then, expected a junket. Magnuson's comments to Zhou were patronizing in tone but meant in good faith: given Beijing's vocal opposition to US involvement in Southeast Asia, Magnuson expected praise for Congress's (ultimately successful) efforts to force Nixon's extrication from the conflict. Zhou and Kissinger wanted senior American politicians of the stature of Mansfield, Ford, and Magnuson to visit the PRC to build political support for Nixon's bold but still controversial reopening of contacts with Beijing. And yet neither Kissinger nor Zhou was prepared to grant these prominent politicians the negotiating power they expected given their stature. Magnuson had shown that American senators were not content to act as mute symbols of Sino-American friendship while in China.

This tension also reflected the ongoing struggle between the branches of government during the Nixon administration's foreign policy. There was something in Magnuson's complaints that the Chinese reluctance to sufficiently recognize his delegation's importance represented an under-appreciation of Congress's power. Magnuson had steamrolled

---

[56] Solomon to Kissinger, July 18, 1973, "China Exchanges, July 10–October 31, 1973," DFWL, RG59, NACP.

Zhou on this by championing Congress's role in ending the war in South-east Asia and by telling the premier that China could only win Most Favored Nation trading status by dealing with Congress directly.[57] None-theless, in his previous conversations with Kissinger – which included a comment that the "Congressmen [that have visited China] are quite similar ... [t]hey talked a lot" – Zhou had revealed that he, like Kissinger, had a level of disdain for US politicians outside the White House.[58] Indeed, Solomon had previously suggested that the Magnuson trip might be a good opportunity to better appraise the Chinese of the function and significance of that body.[59] However, as the fiasco of Magnuson's visit unfolded, the Chinese asked only one particular question about Congress: how an individual such as the senator had risen to such a senior rank. Jenkins reflected that he believed "one of the chief results of the trip was to reconfirm the Chinese belief in the superiority of their own system of government."[60]

If the visit had been a failure in interpersonal diplomacy, Zhou and his colleagues were likely comparatively satisfied when they read the senator's report to the Congress. That report mixed alarm at, and respect for, the PRC's achievements. On the one hand, Magnuson wrote that his delegation, "could not but be struck by the total subordination of the individual to goals determined by the state and the dedicated acceptance of that situation by the citizenry." The senator had been taken aback, for example, when even Chinese children responded to that favorite American question of what they would like to do with their lives by repeating the same mantra of their parents: "serve the people." Nonetheless, Magnuson recognized that Chinese methods appeared to be getting results: the delegation was "tremendously impressed with the government's and people's seriousness of purpose, and with their great achievements in many fields."[61]

Before Beijing learned of this report, however, there was a more immediate reaction from the PRC. Just two days after Magnuson's delegation departed China, Kissinger received a message from Zhou that condemned the US bombing of Cambodia in such incendiary language

---

[57] Ibid.
[58] Memcon: Zhou, Kissinger, et al., February 17, 1973, *FRUS, 1969–1976*, Vol. XVIII, Document 10.
[59] Solomon to Kissinger, June 9, 1972, *FRUS, 1969–1976*, Vol. XVII, Document 229.
[60] Jenkins to Kissinger, undated, "China Exchanges, July 10–October 31, 1973," DFWL, RG59, NACP.
[61] Magnuson, *China Report*, 11, 3.

that Washington felt compelled to postpone Kissinger's forthcoming visit to China. The national security advisor would not travel to Beijing for another five months; as Kissinger's trips were typically twice-yearly, the July visit had effectively been cancelled. Solomon, Jenkins, and Holdridge certainly thought it was no accident that the cancellation had occurred so soon after the Magnuson visit. Kissinger told his advisors that this was a "stupid point" and that Zhou's decision to go hell-for-leather in his message must reflect something more fundamental.[62] As ever, Nixon's national security advisor believed that Zhou and Mao were motivated only by changes in the geostrategic situation and that they were unmoved by the day-to-day Sino-American interactions outside of the highest-level dialogue. Undoubtedly, Zhou's note was more than simply a reaction to Magnuson's behavior: Soviet leader Leonid Brezhnev's June visit to Washington to sign the Prevention of Nuclear War Agreement, a seeming renewal of official US ties with Taiwan, and Zhou's ongoing political censure in Beijing all provided further context.[63] Nonetheless, the timing of the premier's letter and its focus on Cambodia – an issue previously skirted by the Chinese in their dialogue with Kissinger – suggests that Magnuson's trip might have been the straw that broke the camel's back.

FABULOUS PHILADELPHIANS
AND CULTURAL EXCHANGE IN 1973

In September 1973, the Philadelphia Orchestra traveled to China in what was the largest American cultural delegation yet sent to the PRC. The visit capped ten remarkable months in cultural exchanges. The equally prominent Shenyang acrobatics tour of the United States and the National Committee's first board delegation to China had been followed by Chinese delegations of gymnasts and journalists and American delegations of educators and athletes. In 1973 alone, the NCUSCR was involved in sending six delegations of Americans to China and hosting three delegations of Chinese visitors to the United States. These visits provided 229 Americans and 129 Chinese a chance to experience the other country

---

[62] Memcon: Kissinger, Scowcroft, Lord, Solomon et al., July 19, 1973, "China Exchanges, July 10–October 31, 1973," DFWL, RG59, NACP.

[63] ZGZYWXYJS, *Zhou Enlai nianpu, 1949–1976*, 3:601; Teiwes and Sun, *End of the Maoist Era*, 87–92; Pete Millwood, "(Mis)Perceptions of Domestic Politics in the U.S.-China Rapprochement, 1969–1978," *Diplomatic History* 43, no. 5 (November 2019): 890–915; Minami, "Re-Examining the End of Mao's Revolution," 362–63.

and to learn how fellow journalists, musicians, athletes, and educators worked and lived in a very different society. As this section will show, the reactions of both Chinese and Americans to the other country combined fascination and interest with ignorance and puzzlement.

The delegation of Chinese journalists was cohosted by the National Committee and the American Society of Newspaper Editors and was the return exchange of the delegation sent by the latter organization to China in October 1972. The group was made up of twenty-one Chinese journalists, who covered some 8,000 miles of the United States on a month-long visit from May to June 1973, crisscrossing eight states and ten cities.[64] An account from Wang Xi, one of the Chinese participants in the tour, was published in Beijing's foreign propaganda mouthpiece, *The Peking Review*, later that year. Propagandistic as it was, Wang's account still offers some insight into the Chinese experience of an exchange visit to the United States. American visitors to China often complained about the whistle-stop nature of their tours; Wang's reporting suggested this was not confined to visits to China. "My memories are crowded with New York's cotton exchange—I have only a vague idea of how it operates—with San Francisco's Golden Gate Bridge—I don't remember how long it is—with farming in the United States—about which I know next to nothing—and many other things."[65]

The questions that Wang reports being asked by Americans reveal some of the contemporary fascinations of the US public – or at least those to which a Chinese propaganda mouthpiece was glad to draw attention to. Wang reports that he and his colleagues were quizzed on the status of women in China, on acupuncture anesthesia, and political reeducation in the PRC. Wang reported with pride that Chinese antiques were omnipresent in American homes (where, in contrast, they were absent from most Chinese homes, just a few years after the Cultural Revolution campaign to destroy China's Four Olds). Similarly to other accounts by Chinese visitors to the United States and Americans to China, some of Wang's strongest memories were moments where the strictures of the exchange gave way to interactions seemingly mundane but more spontaneous. One such encounter took place in Denver, where a ranch owner invited a dozen friends over for a lunch with the visiting Chinese journalists. The invitees included two booksellers who were making a tidy trade

---

[64] "Wo xinwen daibiaotuan dida Niuyue" [Our Delegation of Journalists Arrives in New York], *Renmin Ribao*, May 19, 1973.
[65] "From Manhattan to Honolulu – A Trip through the USA," *Peking Review*, September 7, 1973.

by selling books on Buddhism and Daoism. Wang was puzzled, but the two men explained that they and others found in Daoism an escape from the rat race of American society.[66]

Some of Wang's account is more reminiscent of long-standing Chinese propaganda about the United States. "Narcotic addiction in the United States is like a contagious disease," he reported. "Many grade-school youngsters are taking marijuana and even heroin," he claimed. Wang does not make clear what evidence of this he had – other than that he asked Americans at every turn why such a problem existed. Likewise, a visit to Berkeley is concluded with the familiar comment that even American taxi drivers had master's degrees – this, in spite of "the radio and television ... feed[ing] the young with tales of the poor becoming rich." The American dream, Wang concludes, was a "lottery" – no, a "kind of drug, it's opium." Wang concluded that – in light of these social ills – American "serious-minded young people" looked expectantly to China as a "completely different type of society" in which they had "great interest."[67]

The same tropes of PRC propaganda that dominate Wang's account were also evident – albeit more subtly – in internal Chinese reports on what American visitors had to say about China. Certainly, as discussed already, there is no denying that American visitors often fell over themselves in their praise of the PRC, particularly in their comments to their Chinese hosts. Nonetheless, the PRC's internal reporting on exchange delegations seems to have amplified even this praise, with cadres reporting to their superiors the most positive comments about China, as well as any criticism of the country's ideological foes and competitors.[68]

The internal narrative of breathless praise for the PRC by foreign guests was demonstrated, for example, during the CSCPRC-sponsored November 1973 visit of a delegation of American child psychologists that included luminaries such as Urie Bronfenbrenner, a cofounder of the Head Start program, and Jerome Kagan, who did much to establish the field of developmental psychology in the United States.[69] Of the dozens of pages of analysis written by their Chinese hosts, much was dedicated to reporting the group's praise for the PRC. One member of the delegation

[66] Ibid.
[67] Ibid.
[68] Lovell also analyzes this insight into the internal workings of the PRC propaganda state. See especially Lovell, "Foreigners in Mao-Era China," 148, 156.
[69] Reception Team [for American Delegation on Child Development and Education], "Meiguo you'er jiaoyu daibiaotuan mingdan" [Name List of American Early Childhood Education Delegation], November 1973, Folder 153–6– 42, BJMA.

called Beijing "the cleanest city in the world," while another claimed that the PRC "meticulously preserves" its "beautiful ancient architecture ... and does not destroy such relics as some people claim" – a statement made in the context of the blinkered view afforded to American visitors, but one that is noteworthy for further suggesting, as Wang's comment on antiques had, that already by 1973 some PRC cadres were looking to whitewash the vandalism of the Cultural Revolution in officially authorized discourse. The Chinese author of the report also gladly reported favorable comparisons made between the PRC and the United States: Yale's William Kessen, the leader of the delegation who would go on to produce an influential book based on the visit, *Childhood in China*, stated that Chinese children had greater self-confidence than their American peers. Kagan, meanwhile, said that the PRC's early childhood education was superior to that of the United States and that Americans simply would not believe what the delegation had been shown if he told them. Kagan concluded his comparison by remarking: "American children know only how to scream." Interestingly, however, the one section of the Chinese reports on the delegation that was singled out for comment by superiors was that criticizing the PRC: the visitors observed that Chinese nurseries were dull and that activities for the children too regimented; the American suggestion that teachers at Chinese nurseries could learn something from their colleagues at kindergartens was noted.[70]

It is far from impossible to believe that the psychologists did indeed offer such praise of the PRC, given what American visitors had said publicly two months earlier, during the Philadelphia Orchestra's tour. The most notable member of the 130-strong musical delegation was Hungarian-American music director Eugene Ormandy who, alongside many of those he conducted, described the visit as the "highlight of their career" (Figures 3.1 and 3.2).[71] One of the orchestra's managers described an "instant love affair" between visitors and hosts.[72] The size

---

[70] Reception Team [for American Delegation on Child Development and Education], "Jiedai Meiguo you'er jiaoyu daibiaotuan – qingkuang jianbao – di yi qi" [Receiving an American Delegation on Child Development and Education – First Report], November 18, 1973; "Di er qi" [Second report], November 22, 1973, and "Di san qi" [Third report], November 23, 1973, all at Folder 153-6-42, BJMA; William Kessen, ed., *Childhood in China* (New Haven: Yale University Press, 1975).

[71] Bruce to Kissinger, September 20, 1973, "China Trade/Exchanges – February 2, 1972–4 July, 1973," Box 93, HAKCFFE, RNL.

[72] Sue Ellen Barber, "Music and Politics: The Philadelphia Orchestra in the People's Republic of China" (master's thesis, University of Michigan, 1977), 70.

FIGURE 3.1 Philadelphia Orchestra music director Eugene Ormandy (center) visits the Great Wall during the orchestra's September 1973 tour of China. Photo courtesy of The Philadelphia Orchestra.

and prominence of the delegation ensured the exchange had a particular political importance: Nixon, who had had the orchestra play his inauguration, had been personally involved in suggesting to the Chinese government that the fabulous Philadelphians become the first American orchestra to ever tour China. Ormandy was equally keen on this suggestion – he had himself lobbied the White House to put a word in with the authorities in the PRC – and Nixon had called the conductor to pass on the news that Beijing had agreed to host the orchestra.[73] USLO chief Bruce concluded that the orchestra's six concerts in Shanghai and Beijing between September 12 and 23 had been a "resounding success," with Kissinger calling the tour "triumphal." Chinese hosts were seemingly "equally pleased."[74]

---

[73] Jennifer R. Lin and Sharon Mullally, *Beethoven in Beijing*, Documentary (History Making Productions, 2020).

[74] "Meiguo Feicheng Jiaoxiangyuetuan zai Jing yanchu" [The Philadelphia Orchestra Performs in Beijing], *Renmin Ribao*, September 17, 1973; NCUSCR Annual Report, 1972–73, NCUSCROC; Bruce to Kissinger, September 20, 1973, "China Trade/ Exchanges – February 2, 1972–4 July, 1973," Box 93, HAKCFFE, RNL; Kissinger to Ormandy, October 26, 1973, Folder 126, Box 16, Series 3, RG4, NCUSCR records, RAC.

FIGURE 3.2 Ormandy leads a rehearsal with the Central Philharmonic Society of China. Photo courtesy of The Philadelphia Orchestra.

One particular host had been especially excited to hear the orchestra: Jiang Qing was often frosty toward American visitors but effusively welcomed the Philadelphians. Mao's wife did so not least because their visit provided her the chance to hear Western music that she herself admired but that she had nonetheless been instrumental in prohibiting as part of Cultural Revolution attempts to revolutionize – and Sinicize – the performing arts. Jiang went to great lengths to have the visitors perform one piece: Beethoven's *Symphony No. 6*, the "Pastoral Symphony" that was probably best known to American audiences for its inclusion in the 1940 Walt Disney blockbuster *Fantasia* (but to Chinese ears evoked the CCP's rural revolution, or so one US official told Ormandy). Jiang had US officials in Beijing instruct Ormandy to include the work in the orchestra's performance, only for the conductor to respond, "I hate that symphony" – and point out that the orchestra had not brought the scores for the Sixth with them. No problem: the Chinese had military couriers fetch seventy scores from Shanghai and deliver them to the orchestra in Beijing the next day. The scores were handwritten, with notations in German and not a few mistakes, and the 106 performers had only one chance to rehearse the symphony before performing in front of China's top leaders. There were some off notes, but Madame Mao clapped every movement, such was her delight (something for which she would later be criticized for in the pages of the *People's Daily*). The Chinese audience for the orchestra's performance of Beethoven went far beyond Jiang, however: Tan Dun, who later won an Oscar for scoring Ang Lee's 2000 film *Crouching Tiger, Hidden Dragon*, first heard the German composer's music through rural village loudspeakers that announced that the Philadelphians were in China.[75]

If the orchestra's visit provided Jiang an opportunity to hear her beloved Beethoven symphony, it also gave the visiting Americans the chance to hear – and, in some cases, study and perform – two distinct Chinese musical traditions. Jessica Gienow-Hecht has analyzed how symphony orchestra tours were popular with Cold War governments in part because of the universal cannon of music they performed. It was not the case, however, that the only music performed during the Philadelphia Orchestra's tour were "universal" works such as Beethoven's symphonies.[76] Instead, the orchestra's hosts used the visit to showcase both traditional Chinese music and the more recent innovations that Jiang had overseen: revolutionary model operas such as *The White Haired Girl* and the *Red Detachment of Women*. Among the orchestra, opinions on China's traditional music were mixed. Some described the performances as "grating," "drony," and "alien." One member of the orchestra described the Chinese music tradition in teleological terms: "The music is in a primitive state of development in comparison with what we hear people playing [such as] violin concertos and complicated things," he concluded. The majority of the visiting musicians, though, had far more positive opinions. Multiple members of the orchestra purchased traditional Chinese musical instruments such as the dizi or Chinese bamboo flute. Many of these ultimately became souvenirs, but the orchestra's principal flutist Murray Panitz undertook lessons on the instrument while in China and gained sufficient proficiency to perform the bamboo flute parts of *The Yellow River Concerto* in a concert back in the United States.[77]

---

[75] "Roll over, Beethoven: 1973 Orchestra Visit to China Dodges Crisis," *The Philadelphia Inquirer*, November 18, 2016; MacMillan, *Seize the Hour*, 319; Lin and Mullally, *Beethoven in Beijing*; "Beethoven in Beijing," *The Philadelphia Inquirer*, December 15, 2020.

[76] Gienow-Hecht, "The World Is Ready to Listen," 23, 27.

[77] Quotations are from oral histories conducted with the participants quoted in Barber, "Music and Politics."

Panitz's study of the dizi was an echo of earlier practices in Chinese cultural exchange in which exchange tours sought to learn something of the musical culture of host countries. In the case of Chinese delegations, this approach of "foreground[ing] mutual learning over self-presentation" was, Emily Wilcox has revealed, ordered by Zhou Enlai himself. Zhou had, in the 1950s, overruled individual Chinese dancers' preference for perfecting their ballet skills with an instruction to instead learn the dance cultures of the countries they would visit so as to cultivate friendship ties with potential allies of the newly founded Chinese state. Panitz was not the first to pursue this dynamic in reverse: Soviet and Burmese dancers had earlier learned Chinese dance that they then performed on cultural exchanges with the PRC.[78] The Chinese attempt to demonstrate cultural sensitivity could have the opposite effect, however: Thomas Gold, who translated for a number of Chinese exchange delegations that visited the United States in the 1970s, once witnessed the Dongfanghong dance troupe perform in blackface and brown tights.[79]

There was more consensus among the Philadelphia Orchestra's members about Chinese revolutionary music: there was an overwhelming sense of alarm at the political and ideological power of the form. One participant drew an analogy between the role of this music in Chinese society and that of an orchestra accompanying a film: "You don't see an orchestra in the movie, the public doesn't notice, but the orchestra grabs ahold of the public by its music, and the music can manipulate the feelings of the people who have yet to absorb the philosophy or projected statement in language and words. When the Chinese use music to portray the political thing [*sic*], that adds credibility to the philosophy. ... It's a very powerful thing, using music as part of ideology, because people ... have to sing, people have to have a tune to whistle."[80]

Despite the foreboding with which they viewed China's revolutionary musical tradition, the Americans were humbled by their experiences in the PRC and departed with greater respect for the country. "The official word before we left [the United States] implied somehow that China was backward," one participant recalled. "Take powdered coffee, we were urged, and take toilet paper. ... So the briefings went and they unwittingly created an attitude of casualness and hauteur."[81] Another member

---

[78] Wilcox, "Performing Bandung."

[79] Correspondence with Thomas Gold, by email, December 15, 2021.

[80] Quotations are from oral histories conducted with the participants quoted in Barber, "Music and Politics."

[81] Barber; Lin and Mullally, *Beethoven in Beijing*.

of the orchestra likewise believed the trip had inverted their sense of using cultural exchange as what Gienow-Hecht calls "performing the nation" – that is, the controlled, one-way demonstration of the traveling orchestra's national self-confidence.[82] The orchestra member recalled:

I think when we went over there we felt, "Oh boy, we're going to go to yet another country and show them what a great orchestra should sound like. We're going over there and teach them [*sic*] about America and our way of life and how music should be played. We're going to sell the States and the Philadelphia Orchestra." So we sat there on the stage and we gave it to them and sat back and expected than to say, "Wow, how great you are." They didn't tell us we weren't good, but they were there to show us about them. And they did. It was an experience for us to go to a place with the usual hard-on to play Philadelphia Orchestra games and to come out of there and say, holy s--- [*sic*] look what we did. We learned something for a change. And we came out of there with a completely turned around attitude about what our purpose was to go there. We went there to learn; we didn't know it until we came home.[83]

This sense of mutual exchange of culture was felt particularly in perhaps the highlight of the performances for the American visitors: a collaboration with the Chinese pianist Yin Chengzong. Yin would later migrate to the United States and play in many of the world's leading orchestras, including under Ormandy in Philadelphia. In 1973, however, he was still working closely with Jiang Qing and other radicals as they sought to remake Chinese culture; Yin had written the piano accompaniment to one of the Cultural Revolution's Eight Model Operas, *The Legend of the Red Lantern*. During the Philadelphia Orchestra's 1973 visit, Yin performed his *Yellow River Piano Concerto* with the orchestra during three of the performances – another of the few pieces of music permitted during the Cultural Revolution, and originally directed by Jiang – and also tried his hand at the classic western folk song "Home on the Range."[84] The National Committee's Murray reported that "everyone" had been "immensely impressed" by Yin, a "world class pianist." *New York Times* critic Harold Schonberg – the first music critic to win a Pulitzer and a specialist on pianists – described Yin as the finest new talent he had seen in five years. So impressed were the Americans that the US Liaison Office and some of the Philadelphia Orchestra wanted to make plans, right there and then, for Yin to tour the United States.[85]

---

[82] Gienow-Hecht, "The World Is Ready to Listen," 18.
[83] Barber, "Music and Politics."
[84] "Meiguo Feicheng Jiaoxiangyuetuan zai Jing yanchu," *Renmin Ribao*.
[85] Murray to The Record, September 28, 1973, "23rd Meeting – Board of Directors – October 29, 1973," Box 131, ADBP, RBMLCU.

Prospects for that and other visits seemed bright, and the orchestra's visit to China proved that, with the NCUSCR's assistance, the United States could put on high-profile exchanges as effectively in the PRC as they had back at home.[86]

A "HAZY, VAGUE AND MISGUIDED POLICY": KISSINGER'S TAIWAN DELUSION AND THE NCUSCR'S CRISIS

Kissinger's next visit to China after the effective cancellation of his July 1973 trip took place in November of that year, soon after Nixon had made him secretary of state following William Roger's September resignation. On the back of the success of the Philadelphia Orchestra's China tour, Kissinger's visit had seen agreement for a further expansion of cultural and scholarly exchanges: twenty facilitated exchanges were penciled in for 1974, more than had taken place in the more than two years that had passed since 1971's ping-pong diplomacy.[87] This was but one area of satisfaction for Kissinger, who immediately concluded that the visit had been "a positive success on all planes." The secretary of state believed Zhou was genuinely considering his proposal of greater Sino-American security cooperation through the establishment of a hotline between the two capitals and Chinese access to US satellite intelligence. "The most significant development of the visit," Kissinger told Nixon, however, "is the breakthrough proposed by Chou on Taiwan that requires only that the 'principle' of one China be respected as we normalize relations." Kissinger also pondered Mao's allusions to Moscow reestablishing diplomatic relations with the United States in the 1930s even though a number of Baltic states within the Soviet Union continued to have ambassadors in Washington. Was the chairman suggesting a possible parallel situation in Sino-American diplomacy?[88]

---

[86] The NCUSCR was not formally a sponsor of the tour – they did not directly fund it – but did provide significant advice to the Orchestra's own staff, both before and during the visit. Crucially, the group had also acted as liaison between the Orchestra and the PRC Mission to the UN. Murray to the Record, September 28, 1973, Folder 126, Box 16, Series 3, RG4, NCUSCR records, RAC.

[87] Minutes of 24th meeting of NCUSCR executive committee, January 8, 1974, Folder 73, Box 6, Series 1, DPMP, RAC.

[88] Kissinger to Nixon, November 19, 1973, *FRUS, 1969–1976*, Vol. XVIII, Document 62. In fact, the Soviet Union had already established diplomatic ties with these Baltic States, which further complicates establishing the meaning of Mao's allusion. Kissinger argues in his memoirs that Mao got his facts wrong but did intend to suggest a possible alternative solution to the Taiwan question. Kissinger, *Years of Upheaval*, 691–2.

Kissinger would spend much of the next two years attempting to craft a compromise for a normalization deal based on the alleged flexibility shown by Zhou and Mao during the November 1973 visit. Historians have also closely examined the negotiations during the visit – in particular because, as we will see, the visit was soon followed by a precipitous downturn in almost all aspects of Sino-American relations. Was this downturn in spite of the visit? Or because of it? Both Harry Harding and Robert Ross have seen in Zhou's statements the same subtle differences on Taiwan that Kissinger noticed and thus conclude that the visit might have been followed by further progress toward normalization.[89] The Chinese record of the visit, however, suggests a different conclusion. Where Kissinger believed discussions over mutual resistance of the Soviets had again confirmed shared thinking, Chinese accounts reveal that Mao commented a few months after Kissinger's trip that, in three hours with the American, the chairman had only one thing to say to him: "watch out, the polar bear is after the United States!"[90] Similarly, the Chinese record presents Mao's statements on Taiwan as unambiguous and states that the chairman declined to engage in horse-trading on the subject not because Taiwan was unimportant but because he had no interest in Kissinger's novel formulations of how to resolve the differences between the two sides over Taiwan. Mao perhaps learned more from the discussion than did Kissinger: after the secretary of state left China, the chairman worried that Kissinger's vagueness on Taiwan suggested that the United States would now waver from its previous promise to wind up its relationship with Taipei after the end of the Vietnam War.[91] Frederick Teiwes and Warren Sun thus argue that Mao had not, as Kissinger believed, wavered from the so-called "Japanese formula" – US withdrawal of military personnel and diplomatic recognition from Taipei, as well as Washington's abrogation of its Mutual Defense Treaty with the Kuomintang regime. Gao Wenqian has further argued that Zhou would likewise never have deviated from this line without Mao's express consent (although the chairman's subsequent censure of his premier for discussing with Kissinger the possibility of peaceful reunification with

---

[89] Harding, *Fragile Relationship*, 51; Ross, *Negotiating Cooperation*, 74.

[90] Pang Xianzhi and Jin Chongji, *Mao Zedong zhuan, 1949–1976* [Mao Zedong Biography, 1949–1976], ed. ZGZYWXYJS, vol. 2 (Beijing: Zhongyang wenxian chubanshe, 2003), 1670.

[91] Pang and Jin, 2:1669; ZGZYWXYJS, *Mao Zedong nianpu, 1949–1976*, 6:503–504.

Taiwan suggests that he, too, may have thought Zhou had given away too much).[92]

Whether his Chinese interlocutors had – perhaps inadvertently – given Kissinger reason to hope they might be flexible over Taiwan or not, the secretary of state appears to have sincerely believed they had. Kissinger's aides in Washington encouraged what Nancy Bernkopf Tucker called the secretary of state's "complacency" on Taiwan.[93] From January 1974, they sent Kissinger plans for seeking a normalization deal that would allow Beijing to "plausibly maintain that we are adhering to the principle of one China" but that would in fact see the United States continue to have an official or quasiofficial relationship with Taipei.[94] They would still be pushing such ideas in the final days of the Nixon era.[95] Maintaining such a relationship with Taiwan was seen as necessary to maintain the domestic and international reputation of the administration at a time when the fallout from Watergate had enervated Nixon's authority at home and the end of Washington's support for South Vietnam made unthinkable any deal that appeared to abandon a long-standing US ally in Asia. ROC ambassador James Shen quipped that American withdrawal from Vietnam would provide Taiwan "a breathing space" because "selling one ally down the river was quite enough for one year." Indeed, by 1974, Washington's relationship with Taipei seemed, if anything, to be strengthening: an experienced diplomat, Leonard Unger, was named as the next ambassador to the Republic of China in February, two new ROC consulates were opened in the United States in 1973 – bringing the total to twelve – and the United States was supporting Taiwan's building of an F-5E fighter plane assembly plant – all actions protested by Zhou during Kissinger's November visit.[96]

With Kissinger showing himself deaf to Beijing's protestations in their direct negotiations, the Chinese sought other means to communicate

[92] Teiwes and Sun, *End of the Maoist Era*, 125–28; Gao Wenqian, *Zhou Enlai: The Last Perfect Revolutionary: A Biography*, trans. Peter Rand and Lawrence Sullivan (New York: Public Affairs, 2007), 241; Millwood, "(Mis)Perceptions of Domestic Politics in the U.S.-China Rapprochement," 901–02.

[93] Tucker, *Strait Talk*, 64.

[94] Hummel and Lord to Kissinger, January 28, 1974, "China Exchanges, November 1, 1973–March 31, 1974," Box 96, HAKCFFE, RNL.

[95] Lord and Solomon, "People's Republic of China," August 15, 1974, "China Exchanges, August 9–December 31, 1974," DFWL, RG59, NACP

[96] Memcon: Zhou and Kissinger, November 11, 1973, and Memcon: Zhou and Kissinger, November 12, 1973, *FRUS, 1969–1976*, Vol. XVIII, Documents 56 and 57; Tucker, *Strait Talk*, 61–66, 34.

their anger at the White House's withdrawal from the promises made over Taiwan in 1971 and 1972. One of these was the cultural exchange program overseen by the National Committee. Following the Philadelphia Orchestra visit, the Chinese pulled back from the promises of frequent cultural exchanges made during Kissinger's November 1973 visit. The PRC declined to receive any NCUSCR-sponsored delegations before Nixon's resignation, and sent only one delegation of their own to be hosted by the National Committee, a troupe of wushu performers that combined the previously agreed martial arts and dance troupes (but that was nonetheless a welcome success amid this downturn; see Chapter 4).[97] In a March 1974 meeting at the PRC Liaison Office, Ji Chaozhu gave Doak Barnett an ostensible explanation for Beijing's sudden change of heart: a recent NCUSCR newsletter had advertised a Taiwanese opera delegation that was traveling to the United States. He claimed this showed that the group held an ambiguous stance on Taiwan's political status and charged that the National Committee was promoting exchanges with not one China, but two. Ji told Barnett, "I do want to emphasize that some things affect exchanges adversely ... for many years our positions were basically different on the question of Taiwan ... But this changed with the Shanghai Communiqué. We agreed then to operate ... on the principle that Taiwan is a part of China. We insist on maintaining the principle."[98]

The Chinese protest at the National Committee's stance toward Taiwan came as a surprise to the organization. As discussed in the Prologue, the NCUSCR had, since its inception, adopted a studied silence and ambivalence on whether it was appropriate for the United States to maintain contacts simultaneously with the two rival Chinese regimes in Beijing and Taipei. Although the organization had carefully avoided advocating an end to US contacts with Taiwan – loudly called for by rival organizations such as the US-China Peoples Friendship Association – the National Committee had also been one of the first and most prominent proponents of engagement with Beijing and had led the charge against the influence of the Taiwan lobby in American political circles in the 1960s. In his complaints to Barnett and in a meeting with the

---

[97] NFTNC, Vol. 4, No. 4, October 1974; "Wo wushu daibiaotuan di Tanxiangshan dui Meiguo jinxing youhao fangwen" [Our Wushu Delegation Arrived in Honolulu for a Friendly Visit to the United States], *Renmin Ribao*, June 24, 1974.
[98] Memcon: Barnett and Ji, March 14, 1974, "PRC Liaison Office, 1971–77," Box 107, ADBP, RBMLCU.

State Department, Ji admitted that the Chinese had at first tolerated the NCUSCR avoiding an explicit stance on the US relationship with Taiwan but claimed that, as exchanges were now maturing, the group's ambiguous stance on American contacts with the island had become a barrier to cooperation.[99]

It seems, however, far more likely that it was not any change in the status of the NCUSCR or of the exchange relationship but instead the continuation, even expansion, of the US government's links with the island that explained Beijing's sudden freezing out of the National Committee: the PRC was punishing the NCUSCR in order to register its discontent with the organization's backers in the State Department and the White House. Two months after the March meeting between Ji and Barnett, the PRC Foreign Minister Qiao Guanhua further underlined this connection when he told a visiting American delegation that there could be no further development of exchanges or trade until the Taiwan issue had been resolved.[100]

Beijing simultaneously sought to curtail other exchanges that were connected to the White House. During Kissinger's November 1973 visit, his hosts had agreed to the US request that they receive a delegation of state governors. In 1974, though, they stonewalled Washington on when the trip would take place, saying the time was not ripe for an exchange that was "semi-official," involving as it did elect American representatives. Kissinger remained "puzzled and concerned by this."[101] When an official exchange did later take place in the form of Senator Mike Mansfield's December 1974 return visit to China, the Chinese used the opportunity to lay out their extensive list of grievances regarding Taiwan – which by then also included hundreds of millions of dollars of new US government-backed loans to Taiwan, including for the construction of nuclear power plants that might one day contribute to the Chiang government's ambitions to develop nuclear weapons. The senator dutifully reproduced this ledger of complaints not only in his report to the Senate but also in a private report to President Ford in which he referred to Taiwan as "the key" to any effective policy toward China and called

[99] Ibid.

[100] NSC to Kissinger, May 23, 1974, "China Exchanges, April 1–August 8, 1974," DFWL, RG59, NACP.

[101] Kissinger to USLO, January 25, 1974, "China Trade and Exchanges – July 5, 1973–February 28, 1974," Box 93, HAKCFFE, RNL.

for "greater candor than has been the case to date" in discussing the US relationship with the island.[102]

That the motivation for targeting the NCUSCR and semiofficial exchanges was to protest US government foreign policy was underlined by the contrasting similar experience of the Committee on Scholarly Communication in 1974. Unlike the National Committee, the CSCPRC had no shortage of work. In the year following the Philadelphia Orchestra visit, the CSCPRC had sent seven delegations to China and received the same number.[103] In spite of their previous reluctance to deal with the organization because of the National Academy of Science's scientific contacts with Taiwan, the Chinese now claimed that they were favoring the organization over the National Committee *because* of its stance on Taiwan. Ji's PRCLO colleague, Zhang Zhixiang, told a CSCPRC staffer, "we very much appreciate the name of your Committee." Referring to the "direct" reference to the mainland regime in the CSCPRC's name, Zhang continued that it was "unlike other organizations who have a somewhat hazy, vague and misguided policy on the so-called two China question. You know we cannot deal with such organizations."[104] Zhang's claim was another of Beijing's many hints that Taiwan was of foremost importance in their contacts with the United States – but is hardly a sufficient explanation for the striking contrast between the frequency of cultural and scientific exchanges in 1974. As will be further demonstrated in the following two chapters, another important factor was the fact that Beijing had its own reasons to maintain scientific exchanges: such contacts were a valuable, cost-free conduit of American knowledge into China.

Kissinger and his aides were – as the Chinese government hoped that they would be – deeply alarmed by the precipitous downturn in cultural exchanges and semiofficial visits of politicians. Doggedly refusing to believe that Taiwan could be the root of Chinese anger given the apparent calmness of Mao and Zhou on the subject during his November visit, Kissinger instead looked to Chinese domestic politics to explain Beijing's targeting of certain exchange contacts. There is no denying that aspects of the exchange program were politically controversial in Mao's China.

[102] Mansfield, *China*, 23; Mansfield to Ford, January 6, 1975, "China – Three Years Later," "Mansfield Report on China Trip" folder, DFWL, RG59, NACP; ZGZYWXYJS, *Zhou Enlai nianpu, 1949–1976*, 3:684–85.
[103] Funding proposal to Charles F. Kettering Foundation, October 1974, "1974 – Request for Funds," CSCPRCP, NAS.
[104] Berris to The Record, March 27, 1974, "General Correspondence, 1974," Box 131, ADBP, RBMLCU.

Exchanges involved granting access to Chinese society to the former
arch enemy of the revolution and tested the flexibility of cadres who
had long been inculcated with the need to doggedly resist America and
Americans.[105] There even appeared to be resistance to cultural contacts
from one high-level leader: in the summer of 1973, Mao ordered his
wife, Jiang Qing, to attend a Sino-American basketball match featuring
a visiting American team of All-Stars and amateur champions. Jiang's
attendance was read by the US officials as proof of consensus in Beijing on cultural exchanges, but in retrospect, Mao's intervention suggests
that Jiang was otherwise reluctant to play a part in receiving visiting
American exchange delegations.[106] Later that year, renewed domestic
strife played out in China in the form of the Criticize Lin Biao, Criticize
Confucius (*pi Lin pi Kong*) campaign that Teiwes and Sun call a "second
Cultural Revolution."[107] This campaign soon began impacting cultural
contacts with the outside world: by February, France, West Germany,
and Algeria had all been forced to cancel cultural exchange delegations
to China. Meanwhile, two French language teachers had been hounded
by a mob and the local militia after being accused of taking purportedly
denigrating photographs of local Chinese at work (a harbinger of similar
accusations soon to be levelled against American visitors, as discussed in
the next chapter).[108]

Kissinger and his aides were not wholly wrong to see Chinese internal divisions as contributing to the downturn in Sino-American cultural
exchanges, then. These disruptions also, however, provided the US government with a convenient catch-all explanation for Beijing's targeting
of high-profile Sino-American cultural exchange contacts that did not
require hard thinking about how the White House's foreign policy was
angering Chinese leaders. Through the spring, Solomon used Beijing's
domestic upheaval to explain disruptions in both diplomatic and cultural
exchanges, while still claiming that "our friends" Zhou and Mao were

---

[105] For one example of how the rapprochement was portrayed to the Chinese populace, see
"Zhonggong Shanghai shi caimao wu qigan xiao weiyuanhui shi ganbu dahui taolun
qingkuang huibao (san)," January 7, 1972, Folder A98-2-703, SHMA.

[106] "Woguo lanqiu xiehui juxing yishi huanying Meiguo nannu lanqiu dui" [China Bas-
ketball Association Holds Ceremony to Welcome the US Men and Women Basketball
Teams], *Renmin Ribao*, June 20, 1973; Pang and Jin, *Mao Zedong zhuan*, 2:1655;
USLO (Bruce) to Kissinger, June 20, 1973, "China Exchanges, June 14–July 9, 1973,"
DFWL, RG59, NACP.

[107] Teiwes and Sun, *End of the Maoist Era*, 111.

[108] USLO (Jenkins) to Kissinger, February 5, 1974, "China – Liaison Offices," Box 99,
HAKCFFE, RNL.

still inclined to show flexibility on Taiwan, even if they faced domestic pressures.[109] In fact, what little flexibility Zhou had shown in November 1973 had made him the target of scathing criticism by Mao, who had forced his premier to make numerous self-criticisms – eventually prompting Zhou to offer to resign his position. The chairman had refused Zhou's resignations, but he would never permit his premier to negotiate with Kissinger again.[110] On the back of this, an increasingly unwell Zhou used a brief meeting with visiting Senator Henry Jackson in the final month of Nixon's term to again pass on the message that the only point of conflict between the United States and the PRC was the issue of Taiwan.[111] As the next chapter will show, Kissinger would avoid facing up to this reality long into the Ford administration. As Tucker has argued, Kissinger, who had after his first Beijing trip claimed that the Chinese were only using Taiwan as a bargaining chip, "never grasped the real importance of Taiwan to Beijing" and thus was able to delude himself about how "relaxed" the Chinese were toward the issue.[112]

Moreover, the continuation of scientific contacts during Nixon's second term further demonstrates that some exchanges could continue irrespective of the domestic controversy they caused within the PRC. Zhang Chunqiao and Yao Wenyuan – two of the individuals later condemned as the Gang of Four – had criticized invitations for American scientists to visit China, only for Mao to indicate his personal support for scientific exchanges when he received the visiting Chinese American physicist Chen Ning Yang in 1973. The direction of Chinese scientific development beyond the Cultural Revolution was no more settled than were the country's cultural policies: just the year prior, the personal approval of Zhou Enlai and even Mao himself had been required for a request lobbied for by a coalition of Chinese scientists that included one of the country's leading physicists, Zhou Peiyuan, to restart basic and theoretical scientific research, which had ceased at the height of the Cultural Revolution and continued to be criticized by leftist Chinese leaders.[113]

[109] USLO to Kissinger, January 28, 1974, "China Trade and Exchanges – July 5, 1973–February 28, 1974," Box 93, HAKCFFE, RNL; Hummel, Lord, and Solomon to Kissinger, May 24, 1974, "China Exchanges, April 1–August 8, 1974," Box 96, HAKCFFE, RNL.

[110] Millwood, "(Mis)Perceptions of Domestic Politics in the U.S.-China Rapprochement," 902.

[111] ZGZYWXYJS, Zhou Enlai nianpu, 1949–1976, 3:672.

[112] Tucker, "Taiwan Expendable?," 123–24.

[113] Zhou, *Zhou Peiyuan wenji*, 59–60, 64–65; ZGZYWXYJS, *Zhou Enlai xuanji*, 2:473; Teiwes and Sun, *End of the Maoist Era*, 58–59.

That Sino-American scientific exchange continued in spite of these debates highlights that domestic disagreement is not a sufficient explanation for the downturn in cultural exchange.

The drastic decrease in cultural exchanges threatened the National Committee with irrelevance and insolvency.[114] The US government attempted to help its favored organizer of Sino-American cultural exchange, supplementing its annual support for the NCUSCR with an extra $50,000 to ensure that the Committee's single confirmed exchange for 1974 – the wushu troupe that arrived in June – was a success, money that covered a third of the total cost of the visit.[115] This was, however, palliative care unless Beijing agreed to repair its relations with the National Committee. Thus, where a cultural exchange – the first ping-pong visit – had helped bring about the early stages of the Sino-American diplomatic rapprochement, now the interactive connection between cultural exchange and high-level diplomacy flowed in the other direction: as Kissinger and Nixon backed away from their promises to Chinese leaders to withdraw from Taiwan, Beijing curtailed cultural contacts as one way to communicate their frustration with the US government.

CONCLUSION

The importance of exchange contacts in building the Sino-American relationship continued beyond the dramatic ping-pong exchanges of 1971 and 1972 and into Nixon's second term in office. This was most immediately apparent in the February 1973 agreement to establish liaison offices in Washington and Beijing – first mooted in talks with the National Committee and then designed around facilitating exchanges and trade – but exchanges had an ongoing importance beyond this single development. The spectacular successes of the Shenyang acrobatic tour of the United States and the Philadelphia Orchestra's visit to China were public celebrations of the new possibilities for cultural encounter brought by rapprochement, while the intensification of scientific contacts made the Sino-American relationship of increasing importance to China's scientific development. Even when exchanges went badly, they mattered. The horror-show of Magnuson's visit to China contributed to the fervor with

---

[114] Murray to Yost, July 26, 1974, "Subcommittee on Exchanges with China, 1972–1974," Box 131, ADBP, RBMLCU.
[115] Minutes of 25th Board Meeting of NCUSCR, May 16, 1974, Folder 73, Box 6, Series 1, DPMP, RAC.

which Zhou criticized the US bombing of Cambodia, forcing Kissinger's deferral of his next visit to Beijing. Moreover, as high-profile cultural exchanges dwindled going into 1974, their absence was powerfully felt not just by the National Committee but by the US government, too.

Nixon's second term saw the US government continue to seek influence over exchanges. US diplomats welcomed Chinese officials' willingness to agree a package of cultural and scientific exchanges directly with their American counterparts, while Kissinger worked to prevent senators and congressmen from having the authority or information to conduct meaningful negotiations while visiting the PRC. This state control was resisted, however, by actors beyond the executive branch. In 1973, both the National Committee and the Committee on Scholarly Communication mounted a concerted effort to show Washington and Beijing that they would not accept a passive role in planning the exchanges they were tasked with organizing, while Senator Magnuson bucked his restraints and demonstrated the ability of senators to think and speak for themselves when asked to participate in Sino-American diplomacy.

Both the successes and failures of rapprochement in the Nixon era were, then, attributable to a broader range of actors than has previously been suggested. Nixon's initiative had never been the one-man mission that he claimed it had been and by the time the 37th president resigned from office the relationship between his country and China was too deep and multifaceted to be managed by the president, Kissinger, and the White House alone. If this had been the case under the powerful and micromanaging Nixon, then the assumption of the presidency by the unelected Gerald Ford seemed certain to give yet greater influence over Sino-American relations to those beyond the government – for better or worse.

4

Familiarity Breeds Contempt

"Standing on the sea coast, I gaze at our Taiwan province. The blue-green waves of Sun Moon Lake ripple in my heart ... Liberate Taiwan, unite our motherland! ... The torrent of revolution cannot be held back ... We are determined to liberate our Taiwan."[1] These were the lyrics to a song, sung to the tune of a Taiwanese folk song, that caused the most high-profile Sino-American public dispute of the 1970s. The song was to be sung as part of the repertoire of an eighty-strong delegation of Chinese performing artists scheduled to visit the United States in 1975, invited by the National Committee on US-China Relations. The lyrics were indeed sung to an American audience that year – but only as part of an event organized by the US-China Peoples Friendship Association to protest the State Department's cancellation of the planned National Committee-hosted tour. That cancellation was front-page news.[2] The State Department's decision had not been made lightly: after extensive negotiations between the National Committee and the Chinese government, President Gerald Ford himself had been involved in formulating a compromise solution – editing the lyrics to express brotherhood toward Taiwan, but not plans for a violent takeover of the island – intended to salvage the tour. Beijing had rejected the US government's proposal: after all, it was Ford and his China policy that PRC leaders wanted to attack through their incendiary song.

---

[1] *China Friendship: Newsletter of the US-China Peoples Friendship Association*, July–August 1975, Vol. 1, No. 3, Folder 24, Box 17, DSUSMC, TLWLANYU.
[2] For example, "U.S. Bars Chinese Troupe," *Washington Post*, March 28, 1975.

Ford was the first American to assume the country's presidency without having been on either the top or bottom of the presidential ticket. It was no surprise, then, that he lacked domestic authority – particularly after he pardoned Nixon's crimes early in his term. This gave him no room to maneuver in negotiations with Beijing, knowing that he lacked the political capital to publicly defend further compromises toward the PRC. As we have seen, Kissinger had already been forced into fanciful proposals for a normalization deal that would permit a continued semi-official US relationship with Taiwan – something demanded by the Republican critics that came to haunt Ford. These suggestions made no more progress under Ford than they had in the twilight of Nixon's presidency. In the context of this impasse in high-level negotiations, conflicts in the exchange program took on a central importance in the overall relationship between China and the United States in 1974 and 1975.

Such conflicts were not always front-page news and rarely directly involved the US government – and certainly not the president, as the performing arts troupe clash did. An equally important development in 1974 and 1975 was the growing tension over the on-the-ground experience of American visitors to China – a cause of resentment for both visitors and hosts. The China fever that had gripped the American public in the wake of ping-pong diplomacy and the Nixon–Mao summit had prompted a clamoring for travel to the PRC and demand for invitations remained high under Ford. However, the strict choreography and ideological self-promotion that were central to China's hosting of foreign visitors began to jar with a second wave of American visitors less conscious of any role as pioneers in Sino-American people-to-people diplomacy. The truculent reaction of many of these visitors was alarming to both governments and led the tension present elsewhere in the relationship to be mirrored at the level of transnational encounter.

WUSHU AND THE CONDITION OF EXCHANGES DURING THE NIXON–FORD TRANSITION

Gerald Ford had initially been a skeptic of Nixon's rapprochement. As was the case for many of his Republican party colleagues, Ford had seen the PRC as a hostile Communist adversary with a human rights record that made Soviet gulags seem hospitable.[3] It was Ford's 1972

---

[3] Tyler, *A Great Wall*, 185.

participation in only the second congressional exchange delegation to the PRC that changed his mind. Ford's report from that visit argued that China no longer posed a threat to the United States or to the world but was instead "a land of vast human and natural resources." "[P]erhaps the most vivid [impression] of our journey [was] the reality of China's colossal potential ... this sense of a giant stirring, a dragon waking ... the clean streets, the friendly and hardworking people, the rich agricultural areas and the throbbing industrial cities are testimony to the successes of the New China in welding a nation out of the chaotic post-war period."[4]

Ford had visited China just four months after Nixon, at the height of the Sino-American honeymoon that followed the president's trip. By the time he entered office some two years later, however, rapprochement had frayed. Nonetheless, within just hours of being sworn in on August 9, 1974, Ford called in Huang Zhen, the head of the PRC Liaison Office, to reaffirm the US commitment to the Shanghai Communiqué.[5] That communiqué had, as we have seen, included the pledge by both sides "to facilitate the further development of [people-to-people] contacts and exchange," including "in such fields as science, technology, culture, sports and journalism."[6] Ford had made clear his own personal support for this aspect of the Sino-American relationship. After his own 1972 China visit, he reported to Congress that, "Among the activities which holds [*sic*] the most promise for developing understanding between our two countries is people-to-people contact and exchanges." "The exchange of people," the then-Minority Leader stated, "can be a bridge to better mutual understanding and improved political relations."[7]

Ford's recommendation for increased exchange contact had, as we have seen, been enthusiastically embraced. The Committee on Scholarly Communication had sent six delegations of American scientists to China before Ford entered office, had received eleven, and had helped fund two further scientific exchanges. The organization then sent three delegations and received two Chinese groups in just the first three months of Ford's time in office; thus, by the end of 1974, the CSCPRC had directly sent 119 American scientists to China and received 111 Chinese scientists in turn.[8] In those

[4] Boggs and Ford, *Impressions of the New China*, iii, 1–12.
[5] Editorial Note, *FRUS, 1969–1976*, Vol. XVIII, Document 85.
[6] Shanghai Communiqué, February 27, 1972, *FRUS, 1969–1976*, Vol. XVII, Document 203.
[7] Boggs and Ford, *Impressions of the New China*, 8–11.
[8] *CEN*, Vol. 5, No. 6, December 1977. The numbers of individual scientists in each direction are based on the author's tabulation from this and similar sources.

first three months of Ford's tenure, Senators William Fulbright, Jackson, and former vice president Hubert Humphrey had also all traveled to China on congressional delegations.[9] Visits by scientists and politicians were among the most politically important trips but constituted only a minority of the reportedly 8,000 Americans who had traveled to the PRC since 1972 – most of whom were of Chinese descent and thus had less need of the gatekeeping services of the CSCPRC or NCUSCR.[10] Trade, too, had rapidly expanded, partly thanks to the work of the National Council for United States-China Trade. One of the first memoranda Ford received from Kissinger correctly predicted that Sino-American trade for 1974 would surpass a billion dollars and overtake that between the United States and the Soviet Union. The United States had, from a starting point of no official trade in 1970 and just $5 million in 1971, quickly become China's second largest trading partner.[11]

Despite the setbacks described in Chapter 3, the National Committee had also expanded significantly during the Nixon era. The organization tallied a record income of $470,000 in the 1973–74 fiscal year – $130,000 of which came from the State Department, but the far greater majority from private sources – and employed a permanent staff of thirteen, with an invited membership of 434 influential Americans, up from just 60 when the organization was first established. Before their program of cultural exchanges had faltered in 1974, the NCUSCR had hosted four Chinese delegations to the United States and assisted in hosting a fifth, while sponsoring three and assisting another three delegations to China. Together, these contacts had included 203 Chinese visitors to the United States and seen 229 Americans travel to China.[12]

The most recent Chinese delegation hosted by the National Committee – one of two exchanges the organization oversaw during 1974, and an important visit given slim numbers of visits granted to the group by Beijing – was the troupe of performers of wushu. Wushu constitutes a collection of traditional Chinese martial arts with some two millennia of history that claims kung fu as what contemporary American press coverage called a "poor relation." Wushu was little known in the United States before the tour; it would achieve greater fame thanks to one of the

[9] *NFTNC*, Vol. 4, No. 4, October 1974.
[10] Mansfield, *China*, 29.
[11] Kissinger to Ford, August 15, 1974, "China Exchanges, August 9, 1974–December 31, 1974," DFWL, RG59, NACP; Talley, *Forgotten Vanguard*, 7; Mansfield, *China*, 30.
[12] NCUSCR 1974 Annual Report, NCUSCROC.

youngest but most talented members of the 1974 delegation – an eleven-year-old Jet Li. Li Lianjie, as he was then, was already a child prodigy: he began studying wushu aged just eight, having been selected to attend the Beijing Sports and Exercise School on account of his athletic ability. He would be crowned all-around youth champion in the national wushu competition in the same year he visited the United States. Li already had an eye on a future film career – he was inspired by Bruce Lee's *Fist of Fury*, which had come out in 1972 – but he was nearly recruited for a different role during the visit to the United States.[13] At a White House Rose Garden meeting with Nixon and Kissinger, the outgoing president told Li, "Young man, your kung fu is very impressive! How about being my bodyguard when you grow up?" "No," Li firmly responded, "I don't want to protect any individual. When I grow up, I want to defend my one billion Chinese countrymen!" Kissinger – perhaps now used to stern admonishments from his Chinese interlocutors – broke the awkward silence that followed: "Heavens, such a young boy and he already speaks like a diplomat!"[14]

The idea for the wushu tour had grown out of the NCUSCR-hosted 1973 Shenyang acrobatic troupe tour. The acrobats had included a short performance of wushu in their repertoire that had so impressed the National Committee and their New York City Center partners that they had together quickly proposed a tour dedicated to the Chinese art form. The content of the wushu performances was in ways a departure from the three major cultural delegations previously sent by China to the United States – ping-pong players, gymnasts, and acrobats – in that the theme of the wushu performance was martial: not only boxing but swordplay and even the use of spears, cudgels, and halberds all featured prominently. If ping-pong had been selected as the medium for the first Sino-American exchange for the unthreatening nature of its physicality, wushu showcased China's historic military strength. Critical, however, was the traditional nature of martial performance: swordplay and boxing rituals recalled an old China that had been a source of fascination and (sometimes) admiration within the United States – but never one of active fear. The last time that Chinese had deployed martial arts against American troops had been the disastrous Boxer Rebellion that had represented

[13] "What Is Wushu? How Jet Li Studied It and Made It Famous in Hong Kong Martial Arts Movies," *South China Morning Post*, November 22, 2020.
[14] "'Bruce Lee Is a Hero!' Mao Zedong Said; Nixon Admired Jet Li," *Slate*, December 22, 2010.

one of Qing China's most humiliating defeats at the hands of the United States and its allied imperial powers.[15]

The wushu troupe sent to the United States had some forty-four performers, some as young as ten years old and others in their mid-thirties.[16] The performers were accompanied by as many as twenty-five Chinese security personnel to protect against the sort of public protests that had disrupted the ping-pong return leg – and, perhaps, to ensure against defections.[17] All of the performers, the Chinese somewhat improbably claimed, were amateurs who had been selected for the visit through their triumph in a 1973 competition held in the PRC; many of the group told American reporters that they had day jobs back in China (although, when questioned, one apparent "laborer" refused to be specific about precisely what labor he was normally employed to do). The visiting performers certainly drew the large crowds one would expect for professional artists: their performances were witnessed by tens of thousands of Americans – 12,000 in San Francisco and a further 17,000 in New York alone – and the scale of the visit was indicated by its $150,000 cost. The wushu stylists had arrived in June 1974 and toured the country from Hawaii to New York, performing to fifteen sell-out audiences and garnering universal critical acclaim before the special show by Li and the two other children among the troupe for the president and Kissinger in the Rose Garden that preceded Li and Nixon's interchange.[18]

The Chinese visitors were, alongside their performances, shown the San Francisco Exploratorium and NASA's nearby Ames Research Center, treated to a day out at Honolulu's Sea Life Park (as well as the local Dole pineapple cannery), and shown another side of New York at the preserved Richmond Town on Staten Island.[19] In Columbia, Maryland,

---

[15] "Oho! This Time ... Wushu!," *Washington Post*, June 21, 1974. On changing American perceptions of Qing China, see Chang, *Fateful Ties*.

[16] "Oho! This Time ... Wushu!," *Washington Post*.

[17] Thomas B. Gold, "Critical Juncture: An American Student in China at the Dawn of Reform, 1979–1980" (unpublished book manuscript, October 2021), Chapter 5.

[18] "Wo wushu daibiaotuan di Tanxiangshan dui Meiguo jinxing youhao fangwen" [Our Wushu Delegation Arrived in Honolulu for a Friendly Visit to the United States], *Renmin Ribao*, June 24, 1974; "Wo wushu daibiaotuan fangwen Jiujinshan he Niuyue" [Our Wushu Delegation Visited San Francisco and New York], *Renmin Ribao*, July 10, 1974; "The a la Mode Was Very Good," *Washington Post*, July 10, 1974; "Notice to members," June 10, 1974, "United States-China Relations, National Committee on, 1973–", Part II: Box 817, ACLSR, LOCMD; NCUSCR Annual Report, 1974–75, NCUSCROC; Minutes of 25th meeting of NCUSCR board, May 16, 1974, "Spring 1975 Board Meeting" [sic], Box 131, ADBP, RBMLCU.

[19] NFTNC, Vol. 4, No. 4, October 1974; Gold, "Critical Juncture," Chapter 5.

Doris Lockyer was one of five private American households to host some of the performers. Lockyer cooked them apple pie – her guests did not take to the American staple – before reporters quizzed the guests. The Chinese jocularly corrected American stereotypes of China, reporting that they did, in fact, use spoons and not chopsticks to eat ice cream and watermelon (this had also been pointed out by Premier Zhou Enlai during the Nixon trip).[20] In response to the much-asked question about how hard the Chinese language was to learn, a wushu stylist pointed out that language was not so hard to learn, "even the children speak it in China." One journalist saw envy in the eyes of the Chinese as they toured the large, mod-con-equipped suburban home. "Are there homes like this in China?", the reporter asked. "No," one of the Chinese responded – and then quickly added, "But soon we will have the ability to build such a house." "Would you want to build such a house?", the American responded. A silent smile from the Chinese guest was read in the affirmative. Fifteen years after Nixon and Nikita Khrushchev's Kitchen Debate, the United States continued to pride itself on the comfort and convenience it afforded to its citizens at home.[21]

Kissinger's first visit of the Ford era took place in November 1974, four months after Li and his fellow wushu stylists returned home. That same month, Ford traveled within dozens of miles of Chinese territory to agree further arms limitation with Brezhnev at Vladivostok. Given that Chinese leaders had taken to accusing the United States of climbing on Chinese shoulders to obtain such deals with Moscow, Kissinger should not have expected a warm welcome. Nonetheless, and in spite of a specific October warning from Foreign Minister Qiao that Mao's earlier comments on the Baltic states had no relevance to normalization negotiations, the secretary of state still opened talks in Beijing by suggesting a normalization deal "on *substantially* the Japanese model." Citing domestic pressure on Ford from the public and Congress, Kissinger asked his hosts to promise a peaceful reunification with Taiwan or to allow Washington to maintain a liaison office – like the one in Beijing – in Taipei after normalization. A rehabilitated Deng Xiaoping was Kissinger's main interlocutor during the trip and told the secretary of state he would not entertain his "imaginations," which constituted a "One China and One Taiwan" policy.[22]

[20] MacMillan, *Seize the Hour*, 278.
[21] "The a la Mode Was Very Good," *Washington Post*.
[22] Memcons: Qiao, Kissinger et al., October 2, 1974, and Deng, Kissinger et al., November 26, 1974, *FRUS*, Vol. XVIII, Documents 87 and 94; ZGZYWXYJS, *Deng Xiaoping*

Deng's blunt response finally convinced Kissinger that he had been laboring under an illusion since his November 1973 trip: Beijing would not allow him to walk back from the promises he and Nixon had made about Taiwan in 1971 and 1972. With three more days of talks ahead, Kissinger shifted focus – to the relationship between American and Chinese societies. He had been encouraged to do so by George H. W. Bush, who had taken up the reins at the US Liaison Office in Beijing the month prior. Soon after his arrival, Bush had concluded that exchanges and trade boasted some of the vitality that high-level talks over normalization lacked.[23] Bush also believed that the government could be doing more to encourage such contacts. The most recent headache in exchange diplomacy was that, because of "political considerations," the Chinese were holding off confirming a previously agreed visit to the United States by the China Council for the Promotion of International Trade, set to be hosted by the National Council for United States-China Trade. Bush began using his frequent dispatches to Kissinger from Beijing to argue that, given the deadlock over the Taiwan issue, the government needed to refocus on other aspects of the relationship and that Kissinger should use his November trip to convince the Chinese to commit to a date for the CCPIT trip.[24]

After his rebuff on normalization by Deng, Kissinger had no choice but to heed Bush's suggestion. The secretary of state had already defensively returned to the topic of exchanges in his first meeting of the trip:

On the bilateral issues, if I could perhaps say one word ... bilateral exchanges and cultural agreements are essentially a symbolic aspect of our foreign policy, of our political relations, and therefore we will deal with them in this context. Frankly I am indifferent as to whether ... one [exchange] group more or less goes back and forth between the United States and China. We should use these as a symbol of our overall relationship. So when you want to settle [these issues] ... we are prepared.[25]

nianpu, 1904–1975 [Deng Xiaoping Chronicle, 1904–1975], vol. 3 (Beijing: Zhongyang wenxian chubanshe, 2009), 2069–70. Deng also referred to the possibility of Kissinger's proposed compromise as a figment of the American imagination in his discussions with a delegation from the American Society of Newspaper Editors. ZGZYWXYJS, *Deng Xiaoping sixiang nianbian*, 19–20.

[23] Bush, *China Diary*, 64–65.
[24] Bush to Scowcroft, November 20, 1974, "China Exchanges, August 9, 1974–December 31, 1974," DFWL, RG59, NACP.
[25] Memcon: Deng, Kissinger et al., November 26, 1974, *FRUS, 1969–1976*, Vol. XVIII, Document 92.

Two days later, Kissinger could no longer afford to be so aloof. He made explicit to Deng that he hoped the Chinese would reconsider their previous stance that the expansion of exchanges would have to wait until normalization, requesting that they consider "changing the pattern" of exchanges, "so that every year is not like the last year" – that is, one that had seen almost none of the high-profile cultural exchanges that the White House most valued. Doing so would avoid "expos[ing] our relationship to unnecessary speculation in the U.S.... if any special progress ha[d] been made."[26]

In the weeks before the visit, Kissinger had claimed to Bush and other colleagues that he was unconcerned by increasing public commentary that Sino-American relations had cooled.[27] Jeffrey Engel argues that this was reflective of Kissinger's general lack of concern with the public consumption of the relationship: what mattered to the secretary of state, Engel suggests, was the content and atmospherics of his personal conversations with Chinese leaders, not the press speculation that followed these secretive exchanges.[28] However, historians such as Mario Del Pero and Dominic Sandbrook have depicted Kissinger in a different light, arguing that, whatever he might say to the contrary, the secretary's actions exposed his consistent, acute consciousness of the public perception of American foreign policy, particularly to a domestic audience.[29] Kissinger's behavior during the November 1974 visit lends weight to Sandbrook and Del Pero's interpretation: although the secretary of state would clearly have preferred to discuss grand strategy, when that failed, he worked to protect the public presentation of the China initiative to which his personal reputation was so closely tied.

Pressure from Kissinger, as well as from Bush, had the effect that the USLO chief had hoped. Earlier in November, Bush complained to Chinese People's Institute of Foreign Affairs Vice President Zhou Qiuye about China shunning the NCUSCR in favor of "friendship groups" – primarily the US-China Peoples Friendship Association – saying this "hurt the

---

[26] Memcon: Deng, Kissinger, et al., November 28, 1974, *FRUS, 1969–1976*, Vol. XVIII, Document 98; ZGZYWXYJS, *Deng Xiaoping nianpu, 1904–1975*, 3:2069–70.

[27] Bush, *China Diary*, 65–66, note 40.

[28] Bush, 89. For Bush's quite different view on this, see Bush, 35–37 (note 74), 47.

[29] Mario Del Pero, *The Eccentric Realist: Henry Kissinger and the Shaping of American Foreign Policy* (Ithaca, NY: Cornell University Press, 2010); Dominic Sandbrook, "Salesmanship and Substance: The Influence of Domestic Policy and Watergate," in *Nixon in the World: American Foreign Relations, 1969–1977*, ed. Fredrik Logevall and Andrew Preston (Oxford: Oxford University Press, 2008), 85–103.

policy" of rapprochement.[30] Bush's complaint had an immediate effect: even before Kissinger arrived in Beijing, the PRC Liaison Office finally ended their silence on NCUSCR-sponsored exchanges and agreed a package of five exchanges with the National Committee.[31] Kissinger's interventions in the Chinese capital prompted Beijing to provide the National Council for United States-China Trade with a date for the CCPIT visit soon after the secretary of state returned home, with the PRC also resolving a number of trade disputes by generously overpaying American farmers to compensate for canceled agricultural deals.[32] Meanwhile, cultural exchanges were boosted when PRCLO head Huang Zhen stopped in San Francisco to arrange for an extension of a tour of Chinese archaeological artifacts to include an additional two months in the Bay Area, something the tour's American hosts had long been angling for.[33] If Kissinger and Bush's pressure on Beijing over exchanges quickly produced results, it also reaffirmed the importance of these contacts to the Ford administration – perhaps contributing to Beijing's decision to seek a range of far more intense confrontations in 1974 and 1975 that would disrupt not only to the relationship between the NCUSCR and the CSCPRC and China but also the rapprochement between the two governments.

"FLESH AND BLOOD"

As we have seen, by 1974, the Committee on Scholarly Communication was enjoying a favored position with the PRC in comparison to their sister organization, the National Committee. Yet, this did not dissuade Beijing from picking the first fight in what would turn into a running battle in the exchange program over a CSCPRC delegation scheduled to travel to China in October of that year. Just hours before a group of American linguists were set to take off from San Francisco, Xie Qimei, the go-to contact at the PRC Liaison Office for both the CSCPRC and the

---

[30] Bush, *China Diary*, 43–44; Murray to Yost, August 6, 1974, "CSCPRC – Subcommittee on Exchanges with China, 1972–1974," Box 131, ADBP.
[31] Yost to NCUSCR board members, November 26, 1974, "General Correspondence, 1974," Box 131, ADBP, RBMLCU.
[32] Solomon to Kissinger, January 27, 1975, and February 7, 1975, "China Exchanges, January 1, 1975–May 31, 1975," DFWL, RG59, NACP.
[33] Memcon: Xie and Nichols, January 28, 1975, "People's Republic of China (PRC) – Exchanges (exchange programs)" folder 2, Box 8, National Security Council East Asia and Pacific Affairs Staff Files (NSCEAPASF), 1973–76, Gerald Ford Library, Ann Arbor, MI, United States (GFL).

NCUSCR, informed the Committee on Scholarly Communication's leadership that the distinguished Princeton historian Frederick Mote's invitation to act as a translator and guide for the delegation was rescinded on account of his having "carried out illegal activities of gathering intelligence" while in China in the 1940s. Mote had previously worked for the Office of Strategic Services, the wartime precursor to the CIA, and, after the establishment of the PRC, the Communist press had accused him of smuggling radios to a pair of Catholic nuns in 1945 – something he vehemently denied.[34]

The importance of Mote's exclusion went beyond his chance to revisit China. The Committee on Scholarly Communication believed that Beijing's refusal to grant him a visa was in contravention of an important element of the structure of the exchange program as agreed in 1972: that each side would choose themselves which individuals would travel on the delegations they sent. If the CSCPRC were to agree to omit Mote, the Chinese – negotiators acutely conscious of past precedent – might begin to exclude further individual members of future delegations sent not only by the CSCPRC but by other American organizations, too. Thus, the PRC would be able to quietly return to something like its earlier position of only inviting Americans that already favored the PRC or with which Beijing wanted to directly curry favor. With behind-the-scenes approval from the State Department and the National Security Council, CSCPRC staff director Keatley thus informed Xie that the organization considered Mote's exclusion a "grave matter" – and that the delegation would not travel at all if he was not included. The show of strength worked: a day after the delegation's scheduled departure, Xie reversed course and told Keatley that if Mote had "changed his hostile attitude" toward the PRC, he was welcome on the visit. The full delegation arrived in China only a week late.[35]

The Mote dispute was a source of alarm for both the CSCPRC and the US government, but it would come to seem like small fry in comparison to the clashes over cultural exchanges that took place in 1975. The first of these was a series of headaches surrounding the tour of Chinese archaeological artifacts, scheduled to begin in March 1975 and then continue for some seven months. Lauded as "the most significant initiative"

---

[34] Keatley to The Files, October 8, 1974, "1974 – General," CSCPRCP, NAS. Mote had also been one of the fourteen founding members of the Committee on Scholarly Communication.

[35] Ibid.; Keatley to Handler, October 15, 1974, "1974 – General," CSCPRCP, NAS.

in China's cultural diplomacy of the 1970s by historian Robert Bickers, the collection arrived in the United States after two years circumnavigating the globe via Paris, Vienna, Stockholm, and Toronto, and a major stop at London's Royal Academy, where the exhibition attracted 770,000 visitors. The vast collection of relics included artifacts from China's pre-history through to the Yuan Dynasty of the thirteenth and fourteenth centuries, among them the gold-threaded jade funeral suit of Princess Dou Wan and a second-century Han dynasty bronze flying horse that became iconic – and now has a life-size replica statue on display in Lexington, Kentucky.[36] The exhibition was also inherently politically sensitive. The Cultural Revolution had given Mao's regime an international reputation as vandals of China's ancient civilization, even before the full details of that movement were widely known. The archaeological tour was an opportunity for Beijing to show that it could still unearth, preserve, and exhibit its ancient culture: all the objects had been excavated since the founding of the People's Republic.[37]

The first hiccup in the tour was a planned press preview at the National Gallery of Art, a stone's throw from Capitol Hill. The Chinese had welcomed the fanfare but had asked that journalists from Taiwan, South Africa, Israel, South Vietnam, and South Korea be barred. The gallery had predictably balked at this request and, when the Chinese refused to budge, had decided that the only viable solution was to disinvite all journalists from the event.[38] This was to the chagrin of an incensed Bush, who lamented in his Beijing diary that, by staying out of the dispute, the US government had missed an opportunity to take a firmer stance in support of freedom of the press.[39]

After the artifacts had gone on display in the American capital, the PRC Liaison Office contacted Laurence Sickman, the Director of the Nelson Gallery in Kansas City, where the relics was set to be displayed for nearly two months. PRCLO demanded that, while the tour was in Kansas City, the gallery close its permanent collection of Chinese items, which

[36] CEN, Vol. 2, No. 3, Winter 1974–75; Robert Bickers, *Out of China: How the Chinese Ended the Era of Western Domination* (Cambridge, MA: Harvard University Press, 2017), 368–69.
[37] NSC to Rockefeller, March 25, 1975, "PRC – Exchanges (exchange programs)" folder 8, Box 8, NSCEAPASF, 1973–76, GFL.
[38] Ibid.; "Meiguo Guoli Meishuguan wei wo chutu wenwu zhanlan juxing yanhui" [US National Gallery of Art Hosts Banquet for Our Archaeological Exhibition], *Renmin Ribao*, December 13, 1974; Eckstein, "Ping Pong Diplomacy," 339.
[39] Bush, *China Diary*, 117–18, 121.

included, among other valuable artifacts, a notable Tang Dynasty Buddhist relief hacked out of Henan's Longmen Caves in the 1930s. Most of
the Nelson Gallery's collection had been imported from China before the
establishment of the People's Republic; the items were thus considered by
Beijing to be ill-gotten colonial spoils.[40] As they had with the CSCPRC
and the Mote dispute, the State Department made clear to Sickman that
they would support him in rejecting the demand outright. Internally,
the Department went even further, arguing to Kissinger that, if Sickman
looked to be conceding, the government should consider convincing him
to stand up to the Chinese, such would be the embarrassment if Americans were shown to be so easily bullied.[41] Sickman stood firm without
government cajoling and, again, the Chinese backed down, allowing the
tour to proceed.[42] Their doing so ensured minimal disruption to a cultural
exchange that was in many ways fabulously successful, attracting two
million visitors to the three American host museums.[43]

The Chinese climbdown in their spat with Sickman was, however,
quickly followed by another clash, in which Beijing did not relent. The
day before Sickman informed the State Department that the Chinese had
dropped their demands of the Nelson Gallery, Kissinger was telegrammed
in Egypt – where he was negotiating the aftermath of the Yom Kippur
War – about a late change to the plan for the imminent performing arts
troupe visit to the United States.[44] The group's eighty musicians, singers,
and dancers included the famed pianist Yin Chengzong, who had memorably performed with the Philadelphia Orchestra during their tour of
China in November 1973 and was fulfilling an invitation to travel to the
United States made during that visit (Chapter 3). The troupe's expected
repertoire included classical, folk, and revolutionary music, with a mixture of contemporary pieces and others that could be dated as far back
as 300 AD. Chinese regional and ethnic minorities would be featured,
and the instruments used would include the pipa, erhu, and suona – as

[40] Bush to Kissinger, March 12, 1975, "PRC – Exchanges (exchange programs)" folder 4,
   Box 8, NSCEAPASF, 1973–76, GFL; Bickers, *Out of China*, 369.
[41] Memcon: Sickman and Zinoman, March 16, 1975, "PRC – Exchanges (exchange programs)" folder 4, Box 8, NSCEAPASF, 1973–76, GFL; Telegram, Bush to Kissinger,
   March 12, 1975, "PRC – Exchanges (exchange programs)" folder 4, Box 8, NSCEAPASF,
   1973–76, GFL.
[42] Memcon: Sickman and Zinoman, March 14, 1975, "PRC – Exchanges (exchange programs)" folder 4, Box 8, NSCEAPASF, 1973–76, GFL.
[43] NCUSCR Annual Report, 1974–75, NCUSCROC.
[44] Berris to The Record, May 23, 1975, Folder 76, Box 6, Series 1, DPMP, RAC.

well as the dizi, or bamboo flute, that had been studied by the Philadelphia Orchestra's flutist Murray Panitz. The troupe was to be the largest exchange delegation to travel in either direction since that visit.[45]

Just three weeks before the troupe were set to arrive, however, the PRC Liaison Office had informed the National Committee of an additional song to be performed by the visitors. "Compatriots of Taiwan, Our Flesh and Blood" took the tune of a Taiwanese folk song but added the new, incendiary lyrics that open this chapter. Americans had been exposed to revolutionary Chinese productions before, both in the PRC and in the United States, but a song that boasted of China's plans to "Liberate Taiwan, unite our motherland!" and promised that "The torrent of revolution cannot be held back" went beyond revolutionary tropes and amounted to an explicit threat against a treaty ally of the United States.[46]

As the Committee on Scholarly Communication and Sickman had done before, the National Committee's leadership informed the US government of the dispute and then attempted to resolve the disagreement themselves. The chances of being able to do so seemed limited, though, by indications that the PRC Liaison Office was acting on instructions from above. Arthur Rosen had recently concluded a twenty-nine-year career at the State Department to become the National Committee's president, a role he would retain until 1987.[47] When he told Xie of the National Committee's concerns about the performing arts troupe's novel content, the counsellor had replied as if he was reading from instructions, stating that Taiwan was an integral part of China and it was "only natural" for the troupe to express their feelings toward the island. Xie, who was later revealed to be employed by Chinese intelligence, flatly said the song could not be withdrawn or modified.[48]

In Washington, Habib and Lord argued to Kissinger that the United States must face down Xie and his colleagues. Following on from the Mote and Nelson Gallery disputes, Kissinger's advisors believed that the

---

[45] "Tour by Chinese Troupe Ended on Taiwan Issue," *New York Times*, March 28, 1975.
[46] "Meifang wuli quxiao woguo yishutuan fang Mei yanchu" [The US side unreasonably canceled the performance of the visiting Chinese art troupe], *Renmin Ribao*, April 3, 1975; Berris to The Record, May 23, 1975, Folder 76, Box 6, Series 1, DPMP, RAC; *China Friendship*, July–August 1975, Vol. 1, No. 3, Folder 24, Box 17, DSUSMC, TLWLANYU.
[47] Wheeler, *American NGOs in China's Modernization*, 35.
[48] Berris to The Record, May 23, 1975, Folder 76, Box 6, Series 1, DPMP, RAC; Mann, *About Face*, 64.

late inclusion of the song, after most of the troupe's program had been mutually agreed, was "obviously deliberate." Moreover, the Chinese had, since the National Committee had raised its concerns, escalated the inclusion of the song in the tour to a "matter of principle."[49] The US government was further drawn to intervene because, although the tour was organized by the NCUSCR, the exchange, like earlier high-profile visits such as the second ping-pong trip, had direct government support: the prominence and size of the delegation had necessitated Congress again appropriating federal funds to pay for official State Department security to accompany the performers across the country.[50] Habib and Lord concluded that, "If we acquiesce on [the] Taiwan item, we are quite certain it would create [a] minor storm affecting the exchange program and possibly normalization ... adverse consequences could well extend beyond exchanges programs to more substantive aspects of our relationship." Kissinger's advisors were concerned about domestic criticism of a weak response, and that rewarding Chinese brinkmanship would only empower leaders in Beijing seeking to pressure Washington via exchanges.[51]

In Beijing, Bush likewise believed that the dispute had been sought out by individual leaders advocating Sino-American confrontation. But the US Liaison Office chief argued that, for this reason, the United States should try to offer a compromise that could give cooler heads a means of climbing down without humiliation.[52] A compromise deal – approved by Ford himself, such was the importance attached to the matter – was thus presented to the PRC Liaison Office: the tour could go ahead if the PRC agreed to substitute the original song for one with lyrics that "expressed feelings of brotherhood for the people of Taiwan" but stopped short of calling for "liberation." The PRCLO's deputy chief, Han Xu, demurred, however.[53]

[49] "Meifang wuli quxiao woguo yishutuan fang Mei yanchu," *Renmin Ribao*; Gleysteen to Kissinger, March 13, 1975, "PRC – Exchanges (exchange programs)" folder 6, Box 8, NSCEAPASF, 1973–76, GFL; Berris to The Record, 23 May 1975, Folder 76, Box 6, Series 1, DPMP, RAC.

[50] Yost to Hollis, April 17, 1975, "General Correspondence – 1975," Box 131, ADBP, RBMLCU.

[51] Gleysteen to Kissinger, March 13, 1975, "PRC – Exchanges (exchange programs)" folder 6, Box 8, NSCEAPASF, 1973–76, GFL.

[52] Bush to Kissinger, March 20, 1975, "PRC – Exchanges (exchange programs)" folder 6, Box 8, NSCEAPASF, 1973–76, GFL.

[53] Memcon: Han and Habib, March 25, 1975, "PRC – Exchanges (exchange programs)" folder 5, Box 8, NSCEAPASF, 1973–76, GFL.

The US side's subsequent decision to cancel the tour surprised their Chinese interlocutors. When Habib told Han that Washington would rather have the tour called off than allow the incendiary song to be performed, Han suggested that Habib might want three more days to make a final decision. Habib was blunt: "Mr. Ambassador, you don't understand. I'm giving you a formal reply now. Tomorrow I will inform the National Committee [that the tour is cancelled]."[54] Bush soon reported that, in the wake of the cancellation, his interactions in Beijing indicated that Chinese leaders had now realized that they had "badly miscalculated" and wanted to drop the issue as soon as possible. Beijing's first public comment on the cancellation came some six days after the US government had informed PRCLO of their decision and was a low-key remark buried among coverage of the concurrent – and uncontroversial – visit by a congressional delegation that included Speaker of the House Carl Albert and House Minority Leader John Jacob Rhodes.[55] In Beijing, Deng told Albert and Rhodes that he believed that neither side wanted to step backwards in people-to-people contacts.[56] The PRC government quickly backed up its conciliatory words with actions, being forthcoming and accommodating in making arrangements to receive the largest US sports delegation to yet visit the PRC, an NCUSCR-sponsored delegation of track and field athletes that would ultimately arrive in May to be seen by some quarter of a million Chinese spectators.[57]

Beijing's efforts to temper the fallout from the dispute could not prevent the cancellation of the performing arts tour from becoming a major public spectacle in the United States, however. More than 2,000 advance tickets had been sold for performances in New York, Chicago, St Paul, and other cities and the announcement of the exchange's cancellation came just two days before the troupe was set to arrive. The US-China Peoples Friendship Association publicly protested the cancellation, holding press conferences and "educational meetings" about Taiwan in the cities that the tour had been scheduled to visit. At one event, the offending song was performed by singers who claimed to hail from Taiwan,

---

[54] Memcon: Han and Habib, March 23, 1975, "PRC – Exchanges (exchange programs)" folder 6, Box 8, NSCEAPASF, 1973–76, GFL.
[55] Bush to Kissinger, April 3, 1975, "PRC – Exchanges (exchange programs)" folder 5, Box 8, NSCEAPASF, 1973–76, GFL.
[56] ZGZYWXYJS, *Deng Xiaoping sixiang nianbian*, 11–12.
[57] Ingersoll to USLO, April 5, 1975, "PRC – Exchanges (exchange programs)" folder 7, Box 8, NSCEAPASF, GFL; NCUSCR Annual Report, 1974–75, NCUSCROC.

one of whom concluded the performance by saying that the government's actions were "doing violence to the spirit of the Shanghai Communiqué." The Friendship Association blamed the State Department for the cancellation, which they called "a slap in the face of the people of the U.S. and People's China [*sic*] who want to build genuine friendship," and leafleted those queuing to see the Chinese archaeological exhibition at the National Gallery with flyers that argued that the cancellation should be blamed on a clique of Americans who wanted to perpetuate US domination of Taiwan.[58]

It is hard to be certain of Beijing's precise motivations for seeking such a high-profile confrontation with the United States. That the dispute occurred in the context of a performing arts exchange suggests the possibility that the conflict may have been sought by one particular Chinese actor – Jiang Qing. The high-level Chinese documents that could confirm or rule out Jiang's involvement are not available, but we do know that Jiang was, in 1975, both the most high-level skeptic of rapprochement within the Chinese government and the individual with the closest control over PRC cultural policy. Jiang was herself a former Shanghai actress and her Cultural Revolution remodeling of the PRC's cultural realm had perhaps been felt most powerfully in the performing arts: under her orders, classical Beijing opera was replaced with the Eight Model Plays in which revolutionary tropes were foregrounded. Jiang had earlier used her influence over culture to try to disrupt rapprochement, ordering that coverage of the Nixon–Mao summit not be broadcast on Chinese television.[59] Jiang and her radical colleagues in Shanghai had also given a literally freezing cold reception to Kissinger's deputy, Alexander Haig, during his January 1972 visit to China to prepare for the Nixon summit, sending Haig's delegation out on Hangzhou's West Lake on an unheated boat in the depth of winter – leading to admonishments from Mao himself.[60] There is circumstantial evidence of Jiang's involvement in the exchange bust-up: in the wake of the tour's cancellation, Nancy Tang told a USLO staff member that the United States "had been causing us some trouble lately." The Brooklyn-born Tang, an influential figure in

---

[58] Berris to The Record, May 23, 1975, Folder 76, Box 6, Series 1, DPMP, RAC; *China Friendship*, July–August 1975, Vol. 1, No. 3, Folder 24, Box 17, DSUSMC, TLW-LANYU; "Phil L" [*sic*] to Harding, April 1, 1975, "PRC – Exchanges (exchange programs)" folder 5, Box 8, NSCEAPASF, 1973–76, GFL.

[59] Gong, "Chinese Decision Making," 327.

[60] MacMillan, *Seize the Hour*, 221; Baum, *China Watcher*, 62.

the Foreign Ministry and Mao's personal translator, did not specify who she meant by "us," but her Foreign Ministry colleague Ji Chaozhu later described her as acting as "Jiang Qing's eyes and ears in the Foreign Ministry" during this period.[61] Nonetheless, Jiang's personal involvement in the performing arts troupe dispute is unconfirmed, with historians so far unable to unearth decisive evidence: He Hui's coverage of the incident does not comment on why the Chinese side added the song and politicized the exchanges and cites only documents from the US side.[62]

Jiang may not have been the only culprit. Pushing US patience on exchange contacts had, throughout the Ford administration and even before, been part of the pressure Beijing sought to exert on Washington over its failure to move toward normalization. The flashpoint in the performing arts troupe dispute again revealed Beijing's particular concerns: an incendiary reminder about the PRC's plans for Taiwan was another response to Kissinger's backtracking on the US relationship with the island. Through the performing arts troupe dispute and the more minor confrontations that had preceded it, the exchange program had become another realm of Sino-American negotiation and contestation through which Beijing was seeking to push Washington toward concessions in the Sino-American relationship. There is some evidence this was successful: in the wake of the series of exchange crises of 1974 and 1975, US negotiators trod carefully in other bilateral talks for fear of igniting another public controversy.[63] Kissinger also instructed the US embassy in Taipei to make clear to the Chiang government that the US stance on the performing arts song was not an indication of any change in Washington's overall China policy.[64] If both Washington and Beijing subsequently made efforts to avoid the sort of confrontation that had led to the performing art troupe's cancellation, their attempts to patch up Sino-American exchange contacts were, however, impeded by further tensions gradually brewing between American visitors to China and those that organized the exchange program – both in the United States and on the ground in China.

[61] Bush to Kissinger, April 3, 1975, "PRC – Exchanges (exchange programs)" folder 5, Box 8, NSCEAPASF, 1973–76, GFL; Ji, *The Man on Mao's Right*, 256.
[62] He, *Dangdai Zhong Mei minjian jiaoliu shi*, 149.
[63] Harding to USLO, Beijing, April 11, 1975, "PRC – Exchanges (exchange programs)" folder 7, Box 8, NSCEAPASF, 1973–76, GFL.
[64] Kissinger to US Embassy Taipei, March 27, 1975, "PRC – Exchanges (exchange programs)" folder 5, Box 8, NSCEAPASF, 1973–76, GFL.

AMERICANS WILL BE AMERICANS

Enthusiasm among the US population for participation in exchanges with China had not waned in the years after Nixon's opening. The government continued to be bombarded by appeals from individuals and organizations, from White House interns to the Harlem Globetrotters, for sponsorship of their applications to travel to the PRC.[65] By 1975, the National Committee was responding to at least twenty to thirty separate requests a week from organizations asking for help getting to China.[66] Only a small selection of the proposed visits came to fruition, and increasingly those not selected were crying foul about being overlooked. In a meeting with Richardson, still the senior State Department officer responsible for exchanges, the Asian American academic educational psychologist, Albert H. Yee accused unsupervised "quasi-government committees" of packing delegations with amateur scholars who knew little about China and who were chosen by their friends on the selection boards. What's more, Yee, claimed, the Committees were systematically overlooking Chinese Americans. "What must they think in the PRC?", he protested.[67] (Yee was right and wrong on this point: organizations like the CSCPRC did primarily, though not exclusively, recruit from beyond the Chinese American community, but did so precisely because the PRC had other, well-worn roads into China for Americans of Chinese descent (Chapter 5). Ethnically Chinese Americans could more easily obtain visas and paid less than other foreigners for train tickets and hotels in China, although more than the local Chinese population.[68] In 1974, around 75 percent of the American scientists who traveled individually to China, rather than as part of a delegation, had names that suggested they were of Chinese descent.[69])

[65] Hasenkamp to Kissinger, November 11, 1974, "PRC – Exchanges (exchange programs)" folder 1, Box 8, NSCEAPASF, 1973–76, GFL; Greeson to Les Janka, February 26, 1975, "PRC – Exchanges (exchange programs)" folder 3, Box 8, NSCEAPASF, 1973–76, GFL.

[66] NCUSCR Annual Report, 1974–75, NCUSCROC.

[67] Yee to John Richardson, November 5, 1974, "1975 – Inquiries," CSCPRCP, NAS.

[68] Terry Lautz, *Americans in China: Encounters with the People's Republic* (New York: Oxford University Press, 2022), 100.

[69] These figures are based on the CSCPRC's attempts to record all scientific visits to China in the 1970s. See *China Exchange Newsletter* (*CEN*), Vol. 2, Numbers 1 through 3. In 1974, the Chinese government informed a visiting Senator Mansfield that, of the 8,000 US citizens that had traveled to the PRC since 1971, the majority had been of Chinese descent. Mansfield, *China*, 28.

Yee claimed that the government should take more responsibility for the "unknown sum" of public money that had funded the Committees, particularly "since the [exchange] agreement is the one tangible element of contact between Americans and people in the PRC."[70] Yee was not alone in making these complaints: another complaint came from Alfred Senft, a professor of medical sciences at Brown University, who told the Committee on Scholarly Communication he found it "disturbing" that members of scientific delegations were often close personal friends and frequent collaborators, "so that it seems that a cozy relationship is more evident than an even-handed choice of representatives."[71]

The CSCPRC's internal criteria for selecting who would travel on scientific delegations listed "scholarly merit" as the first consideration in choosing visitors. It also, however, included even vaguer criteria than this subjective assessment: "maturity and good judgement; and diplomacy."[72] The National Committee also had criteria for the selection of exchange participants that balanced "status in the field," existing influence in American society, "China expertise," and membership in the invite-only organization itself – which still only consisted of 425 individuals in 1975.[73]

In his study of the UK's scientific contacts with China in this period, Jon Agar argues that the Royal Society's role as a "gatekeeper" to the PRC allowed the organization to allocate limited invitations to China to those favored by the Society – while politically "radical" scientists were "politely turned down."[74] Meanwhile, Justine Faure has analyzed US-Soviet academic exchanges, showing the tension between those that favored American exchange participants acting "as ambassadors of the American Way of Life" and those who insisted on "scholarly excellence" as the only criterion for selection.[75] The dynamic at US exchange organizations bore similarities to both the Sino-British and US-Soviet examples. The Committee on Scholarly Communication did take seriously their own academic criteria for selecting which American scientists traveled to China: the participants in the schistosomiasis delegation that

[70] Yee to John Richardson, November 5, 1974, "1975 – Inquiries," CSCPRCP, NAS.
[71] Senft to Smith, February 12, 1975, "1975 – General," CSCPRCP, NAS.
[72] Executive Committee Meeting Minutes, May 30, 1973, "1974: Visits – Com Visit on Scholarly Exchanges," CSCPRCP, NAS.
[73] Minutes of 23rd Board Meeting of NCUSCR, October 29, 1973, Folder 73, Box 6, Series 1, DPMP, RAC; NCUSCR Annual Report, 1974–75, NCUSCROC.
[74] Agar, "'It's Springtime for Science'," 11.
[75] Faure, "Working on/Working with the Soviet Bloc," 232–33.

had prompted Senft's letter had been selected by a three-person, external committee made up of specialists in the field.[76] However, given that value judgments – including of qualities such as "maturity" and "diplomacy" – were also involved in the selection of participants, there was undoubtedly a tendency to trust those scientists who were vouched for by current and former members of the tight-knit Committee, composed of only twenty-two individuals in 1975.[77] (Meanwhile, other organizations explicitly privileged political views: Science for the People complained that applicants for a 1973 trip had "too much professionalism and not enough politics.")[78] The importance placed on the "diplomacy" of scientists selected was another consequence of the political importance of exchanges: American scholars traveled to China not only as individual researchers or even simply representatives of their institutions and fields, but also of the entirety of the US scientific establishment and their country as a whole.

The lucky few Americans who were selected for exchanges had high expectations after reading early reports from American visitors that were giddy with praise of the experience of travel in the PRC, describing "a country with few if any warts" as Doak Barnett characterized their accounts.[79] As we have seen, China's revolutionary science had been a focus of praise by early visitors such as Arthur Galston (Chapter 1). Praise went beyond Chinese science, however. Reflecting on his 1972 visit (Chapter 3), Senator Mansfield had commented on the "overwhelming" transformation of China since his experience living in the country in the 1940s. "The misery of the old China, where famines and pestilence were common and millions wandered aimlessly, is gone."[80] John Fairbank had been one of the first Sinologists to return to China, and wrote after his visit that, "The stress and even violence of 1966 to 1969 have now been succeeded ... by a sense of relaxation and euphoria that makes 1972 a happy time to be in China.... The Maoist revolution is on the whole the best thing that has happened to the Chinese people in many centuries."[81]

Visitors found China to be at once materially self-sufficient and yet still free of some of the flaws of late capitalism that had befallen the

[76] Smith to Sent, February 26, 1975, "1975 – General," CSCPRCP, NAS.
[77] Todd to Handler, January 17, 1975, "1974 – Request for Funds," CSCPRCP, NAS.
[78] Schmalzer, "Speaking about China," 326.
[79] Barnett, "There Are Warts There, Too."
[80] Mansfield and Scott, *Journey to the New China*, 34, 20.
[81] John K. Fairbank, "The New China and the American Connection," *Foreign Affairs* 51, no. 1 (1972): 39, 36.

United States. Norma Djerassi, wife of the inventor of the contraceptive pill, Carl, cited three noes – "No beggars. No ill persons. No drunks." – as a marker of how people were not left behind in Chinese society, where many were in the contemporary United States.[82] The economist, former US ambassador to India, and advisor to President John F. Kennedy, John Kenneth Galbraith, visited China in 1972. Galbraith built on the praise Arthur Galston had earlier made of China's wide provision of medical care, making the striking claim that he left the PRC "prepared to believe that Greater Shanghai ... has a better medical service than New York."[83]

Materially comfortable, the Chinese were also liberated. Gender equality was another oft-remarked feature of the PRC. Accounts of the country by American visitors before 1971 had made such claims: Shirley Graham Du Bois had said, after her 1959 visit, that "Chinese women today are, in my opinion, more the equal of men than in any country I know."[84] Similar claims were made by visitors in the 1970s: after his second, 1974 visit, Mansfield stated categorically, "Women enjoy equal rights," while Djerassi added approvingly that "Chinese women are certainly not sex objects."[85] Equality of the sexes was just one of the virtues praised by perhaps the most famous private visitor to China during the 1970s, Hollywood star Shirley MacLaine. MacLaine claimed that Chinese "women had little need or even desire for such superficial things as frilly clothes and make-up," and that, "Relationships seemed free of jealousy and infidelity because monogamy was the law of the land and hardly anyone strayed" – something that had surely been difficult to verify during a three-week visit.[86] For Djerassi and MacLaine, what some other American visitors identified as the conservative sexual politics of the PRC were in favorable contrast to some of the legacies of the American sexual revolution of the 1960s.[87] The conclusion to MacLaine's bestselling 1975 account of her 1973 trip (which was supplemented by an accompanying documentary film nominated for an Academy Award) contrasted the comfort she felt in China with the anxiety of life in the "lonely ... individualistic West." While in China, MacLaine reflected, "I

---

[82] Norma Lundholm Djerassi, *Glimpses of China from a Galloping Horse* (New York: Pergamon Press, 1974), 17–18.
[83] John Kenneth Galbraith, *A China Passage* (Boston: Houghton Mifflin, 1973), 126–27.
[84] Frazier, *The East Is Black*, 55.
[85] Mansfield, *China*, 2; Djerassi, *Glimpses of China*, 10–11.
[86] MacLaine quoted in Lovell, *Maoism*, 272.
[87] Orville Schell, *In the People's Republic: An American's First-Hand View of Living and Working in China* (New York: Random House, 1977), 161–62.

was not lonely. I almost felt at home. And I hadn't smoked a cigarette in five weeks."[88]

Not all Americans shared MacLaine's views on the condition of gender relations in China, however.[89] Paul Pickowicz recalls how the 1971 Committee of Concerned Asian Scholars delegation went as far as offering "friendly" criticism of their Chinese hosts on the subject: the visiting Americans pointed out that, in spite of Chinese claims to have eradicated gender inequality, men still vastly outnumbered women in all levels of leadership and women remained responsible for household labor in villages.[90] A 1974 Science for the People delegation also detected limitations to the changes in gender relations realized in the PRC: when the visitors asked whether husbands were allowed to stay with their wives during childbirth they were met with laughter, while questions about sexual liberation in the PRC made their hosts uncomfortable.[91]

Even when visitors did have misgivings about what they experienced in China, they often framed such feelings in a positive light, however. Mansfield stated after his 1974 trip that, "Chinese people, today, probably constitute the most ideologically sensitized and politically active population in the world" – a sideways comment on the totalitarian mobilization of Mao's China, framed in the manner in which Americans might discuss civic engagement.[92] Djerassi painted Chinese totalitarianism in even starker terms: "I believe these people have a happy, positive outlook as a result of complete thought control. They are happy because Chairman Mao has told them that they are." (Although Djerassi added the caveat that she herself could not imagine living under similar conditions.)[93] Americans were not unique in offering praise for what they witnessed when visiting China: Lovell reports that Chinese handlers of foreign delegations had, as early as the 1950s, been almost surprised at how easy it was to convince guests from non-socialist countries of the superiority of China's socialist system, while Hollander documents in detail the infatuation with the PRC experienced by visitors from a range of capitalist

[88] Shirley MacLaine, *You Can Get There from Here* (New York: W. W. Norton & Company, 1975), 243–44; Minami, "How Could I Not Love You?," 23.

[89] Minami, "How Could I Not Love You?," 21, 23–24.

[90] Pickowicz, *A Sensational Encounter*, 90, 106.

[91] Schmalzer, "Speaking about China," 327–28.

[92] Mansfield to Ford, January 6, 1975, "China – Three Years Later," "Mansfield Report on China Trip" folder, DFWL, RG59, NACP.

[93] Djerassi, *Glimpses of China*, 47.

countries during the Mao era – although he argues that Americans were exceptionally positive, even when considered in that context.[94]

Praise from early American visitors thus fueled hyperbole surrounding travel to China. But, as the numbers of those traveling on exchanges increased in 1974 and 1975, so, too, did complaints. American scholars were not used to the kind of constraints the Chinese routinely imposed upon guests. Requested itineraries were modified, with no explanation provided. Participants were ostensibly granted permission to interact freely with ordinary Chinese, but these interactions were in reality no less planned than any other aspect of their rigidly organized trips.[95] China experts who had invested so much time and effort in developing their language skills and studying the country indirectly – through refugee interviews, or by close readings of PRC propaganda – found their inability to access Chinese society more directly to be a chastening, even humiliating, experience.[96] Similarly, American scientists chafed at scientific exchanges that were, Chinese documents reveal, explicitly intended to "publicize the superiority of the Chinese socialist system."[97] Even a delegation of young political radicals, led by the Beijing-born Carma Hinton, the daughter of *Fanshen* author William Hinton, were kept on a short leash: the Chinese record of their 1975 visit notes that the Americans demanded to be allowed to "go down to the grassroots level, have contact with the masses, and observe with their own eyes." (Their hosts offered self-criticism to their superiors while reporting the Hinton delegation's complaint, but the frequency with which this complaint continued to be made suggested little changed as a result.)[98]

Attempts to circumvent restrictions imposed on exchanges generally failed: the aforementioned CSCPRC delegation of American linguists that included Frederick Mote and was led by one of the pioneers of machine translation, Winfred P. Lehmann, attempted to guarantee some direct access to the Chinese population by suggesting the group stay overnight

---

[94] Lovell, "Foreigners in Mao-Era China," 149; Hollander, *Political Pilgrims*, 278–346.

[95] Lovell, "Foreigners in Mao-Era China," 143.

[96] Author interview with Orville Schell, Oxford, UK, June 2, 2016; CSCPRC paper, "The Future of Academic Exchanges with the PRC," June 1975, "1975 – Report for Secretary of State," CSCPRCP, NAS.

[97] Reception Team [for American Delegation on Child Development and Education], "Jiedai Meiguo you'er jiaoyu daibiaotuan jihua" [Plan for Receiving an American Delegation on Child Development and Education], November 1973, Folder 153–6–42, BJMA.

[98] Foreign Affairs Group of the Shanghai Municipal Committee of the Communist Youth League Shanghai Revolutionary Committee, "Jiedai Meiguo qingnian daibiaotuan qingkuang huibao" [Report on the reception of the American youth delegation], June 27, 1975, Folder C21-3-189, SHMA.

with rural families that were hosting a portion of their trip; their Chinese hosts simply ignored the request.[99] When a bold individual visitor requested to have a mundane but unplanned interaction – say, a haircut – their minders would fall over themselves to find a reason to declare the idea "not convenient" or at least to keep the visitor constantly within their sight.[100] The PRC may have adopted these extreme levels of control from their sometime Soviet allies: an early Chinese visitor to the Soviet Union asked to "visit the home of a typical worker" but was denied because of what Jersild calls the "secrecy and paranoia of Russian life."[101]

If any spontaneous interaction did occur, consequences followed: during the NCUSCR track and field delegation, one of the American athletes had celebrated his victory in an event by running into the grandstand and shaking hands with cheering Chinese spectators. One member of the crowd had discreetly slipped a paper note into his hand, which he had glanced at incomprehensibly – it was in Chinese. The runner put the note in his jacket and forgot the incident – until two plainclothes Chinese security visited his hotel room and asked if he still had the note and knew who had handed it to them. He lied and said he had thrown the message away – but failed to allay the officers' suspicion enough to dissuade them from later breaking into his room to fruitlessly search his belongings anyway. The runner then had the political scientist Richard Baum, the NCUSCR's chosen scholar translator for the tour, decipher what they expected to surely be a covert message of dissent. It read: "Long live the friendship of the Chinese and American people."[102]

Meanwhile, Chinese hosts were frustrated that the American visitors of the mid-1970s could not always be counted on to be as unfalteringly adulatory and well mannered as the ideologically sympathetic guests of the 1960s and early 1970s had been. Particularly troublesome to the Communist government was the behavior of the small number of social scientists who managed to travel to China, often as accompanying "translators" on delegations in no way related to the social sciences, as in the case of Mote and Baum (a practice further discussed in Chapter 5). By 1975, the PRC government was complaining that these social scientists displayed a tendency to remind their Chinese counterparts that

---

[99] CSCPRC paper, "The Future of Academic Exchanges with the PRC," June 1975, "1975 – Report for Secretary of State," CSCPRCP, NAS.

[100] Author interview with Schell; Schell, *In the People's Republic*, 81–84.

[101] Jersild, *The Sino-Soviet Alliance*, 182.

[102] Baum, *China Watcher*, 73.

FIGURE 4.1 A sailing junk in the Huangpu River, photographed in 1971 by Frank Fischbeck, a photographer accompanying the US table tennis team. This junk was likely similar to that which was captured in the photograph by Orville Schell and landed the American in such trouble with his Chinese hosts. Courtesy of the University of Hong Kong Libraries.

the political system they advocated had consistently persecuted them.[103] Ill-chosen questions or observations by American guests could end with a formal complaint from Chinese hosts to the US organizer of a delegation – or with the visitor being forced into a secluded period of "illness" to avoid any contagion of such behavior to the wider visiting group.[104] The then-*New Yorker* journalist Orville Schell had discovered this when, on the youth delegation headed by Carma Hinton, he had conducted a late-night debate with his translator regarding the virtues and beauty of wind-powered boats prompted by Schell photographing some moored Chinese junks: Schell woke up the next day to a period of detention until he pledged to only record the most industrialized parts of China's modern economy (Figure 4.1).[105]

---

[103] CIA Intelligence Information Cable, "Views of the PRC concerning stalemated relations with the United States," May 24, 1975, "PRC" folder 7, Box 7, NSCEAPASF, 1973–76, GFL.
[104] Eastman to Keatley, June 20, 1976, "Eastman, Lloyd E." folder, Box 5, NASAR, BHL.
[105] Author interview with Schell; Schell, *In the People's Republic*, 172–76.

Chinese documents reveal that American visitors taking photographs of Chinese "backwardness" was of concern to their hosts on other occasions, too. A similar situation to Schell's occurred during the April 1974 visit of a delegation of members of the American Institute of Architects that included the Guangzhou-born Chinese American I. M. Pei, who would go on to design the Louvre's iconic pyramid and the Bank of China tower in Hong Kong – as well as receiving major commissions in the PRC, such as the same bank's Beijing headquarters. While visiting a commune near Shanghai, several of the architects photographed wooden boats similar to those snapped by Schell, as well as some of the older housing and alleyways. Chinese hosts "fought against" this and held multiple struggle meetings, some involving the entire visiting delegation, in which photographing China's lingering "backwardness" was criticized.[106]

The PRC's touchstone example of the tendency of Western visitors to photograph and film those parts of China not yet transformed by socialism was Michelangelo Antonioni's 1972 documentary *Chung Kuo, Cina*. The 220-minute-long film had been commissioned by the Chinese government in collaboration with the Communist Party back in Antonioni's native Italy – but then quickly attacked by both. In the discussions with the American architects, Chinese cadres sought to "expose and criticize Antonioni's despicable methods of shooting backward shots." The Chinese cadre writing the account reported that, after these discussions, the architects had become more "sensitive" to the hosts' concerns about their own photography and that the head of the delegation had assured the Chinese that they would write a "fair" report of their visit upon their return to the United States. By the final day of the delegation's visit to Shanghai, this vigorous response had led the visitors to "basically cease to shoot images of backwardness."[107]

More than a year later, Antonioni's film was still a major point of discussion with a group of American leftists on an exchange organized through the founder of China Books and Periodicals, Henry Noyes. Noyes was a Guangzhou-born, self-described "overseas Chinese" descendant of Presbyterian missionaries William D. Noyes and Mary Stevenson and a central figure in the American left's fascination with Maoist China:

---

[106] Architectural Association reception team, "Jiedai Meiguo jianzhushi daibiaotuan qingkuang jianbao" [Report on hosting US delegation of architects], April 28, 1974, Folder B246-1-692-63, SHMA.
[107] Ibid.

China Books was the first American corporation to receive US government approval for trade with the PRC and had become the largest American distributor of printed materials from the PRC, selling more than a
million copies of *Quotations from Chairman Mao Tse-tung*, commonly
known as the Little Red Book. Noyes and his visiting fellow travelers
agreed with their Chinese hosts that Antonioni's film was "indeed very
poisonous," and had been filmed from a reactionary position. The delegation reported that initially they had been very concerned by the film's
release and what the discussants believed was a depiction of a failed Chinese revolution and a country in anarchy – but that they had addressed
the situation by urgently putting on sale a book sent from China that
articulated Beijing's critique of the film. This had had a "disinfectant
effect."[108] (The PRC state finally rehabilitated Antonioni and his 1972
film in 2004, screening it at the Beijing Film Academy as part of a retro-
spective on the director that was the first time that film, or any by Antonioni, had been screened in China since 1972.)[109]

The perceived American demeaning of Chinese material progress may
have been attributable to a difference in outlook about the results of
high-modernist development: a source of pride for China; one of anxiety
for Americans. But American visitors could offer no sophisticated explanation for another common behavior while in the PRC: racism. We have
already seen how the Magnuson congressional delegation was dogged
by the senator's chauvinism. Racism was a blight on other, lower profile delegations, too: Judith Kahan, one participant in a Teamster trade
union delegation to China in September 1976, commented during the
trip that "she could use a hard-working Chinese peasant woman at home
as a domestic worker!"[110] Racism was so commonplace among American
visitors that even the avowedly anti-racist US-China Peoples Friendship
Association had accepted it as an inevitable reaction of some Americans
to China. In guidance to tour leaders, the organization advised: "Racism
toward the Chinese: First ask yourself if it is really a problem.... Recognize that most racist attitudes and behaviors come from misconceptions
or ignorance.... Your goal should be to help her/him to recognize her/his

---

[108] Shanghai People's Publishing House, "Jiedai Meiguo 'Zhongguo Shukan She' zongjingli
Hengli Nuoyisi qingkuang tongbao," May 27, 1975, Folder B244-3-657-42, SHMA;
"Chapter and Verse," *China Daily*, October 8, 2019; Kerpen, "Voices in a Silence," 147.
[109] "China Lifts Ban on Film Icon," *Globe and Mail*, December 2, 2004.
[110] Gollobin to Luxingshe [*sic*], March 8, 1977, Folder 3, Box 2, William Nuchow Papers
(WNP), TLWLANYU.

assumptions so that she/he can learn more accurately about China and the Chinese. Remember your Chinese hosts are not unused to the racist attitudes and behaviors of Westerners." There was an ambivalence to such an approach to cultural exchange: on the one hand, the optimism that simply experiencing China would help change racist attitudes; on the other, the acceptance that leaders of delegations could hardly expect anything different from American visitors.[111]

Other forms of tension were less insidious – but could still prove disruptive. Raucousness of the sort that contributed to the reputation of brash Americans abroad was evident in exchange visits of the 1970s. A banquet marking the conclusion of the May 1975 visit of the NCU-SCR-assisted US track and field team was, for example, the sight of a raucous incident of intra-American conflict that had nonetheless embarrassed Chinese hosts. The tour had, naturally, been conducted under the principle of friendship first, competition second: no team scores had been kept across the 17 different Olympic sports events (which was perhaps fortunate as the Americans, numbering among them former and current world champions, won 89 of the 90 medals awarded if not tallied). The American visitors had thoroughly enjoyed the visit: the African American sprinter Delano Meriwether was not alone in saying it had been his "best trip, by far," as shown in Meriwether shooting some forty rolls of film, while shot-putter Maren Seidler even went as far as saying that "it was the most important experience of my life.... It's hard for me to talk about it; I get tears."[112] The collegial atmosphere that defined the tour as a whole had been less evident, however, during the farewell banquet. The meal was hosted by Ambassador Bush in Beijing and attended by 200 Americans and Chinese, including the top brass of the All-China Sports Federation and several Chinese politicians (Mao's initial successor, Hua Guofeng, had attended an earlier event in the tour). During Bush's speech of thanks to the athletes and hosts, a Texas pole-vaulter loudly declared "I'm gonna kill that sonofabitch" while making a threatening advance toward Bush – before an American shot-putter tackled and physically subdued him. The Chinese hosts politely attributed this behavior to American unfamiliarity with the properties of Maotai liquor – although the cannabis the pole vaulter had reportedly been smoking might also

[111] "China Study Tours: Tour Leaders [*sic*] Handbook," USCPFA, undated but likely December 1977, Folder 2, Box 2, WNP, TLWLANYU.

[112] Baum, *China Watcher*, 69–81; "How to See China on $0.00 a Day," *Los Angeles Times*, June 3, 1975; NFTNC, Vol. 5, No. 2, July 1975.

have played a role. Baum, deputy leader of the delegation, forthrightly told the press what he concluded from the incident: that Americans will be Americans – and that Chinese hosts "will have to learn that."[113]

Chinese documents from a year prior reveal that this was not the first time an American exchange visit to China had been the scene of minor violence: a year prior, violence had also been encountered by the aforementioned visiting American architects. I. M. Pei was the first of the architects to spot why a car taking the delegation between locations had stopped: "It's a fight," he announced. While the other Americans hurriedly took pictures, the translator rushed to explain that it was no such thing and that the masses were merely apprehending an individual who had violated traffic laws (in fact, they had caught a thief). This was not the first time that the behavior of ordinary Chinese had disrupted the meticulously planned reception of foreign guests: Lovell reports an array of insensitive comments or insufficiently exuberant welcomes for guests in the 1950s and 1960s (although witnessing violence was uncommon). The internal Chinese write up of the incident with the architects ordered that, if the hosts of any future Americans noticed a similar situation, they should immediately turn the car around and travel via a different route. Street violence did not represent "the superiority of our socialist system" that the same report made clear was what the Chinese wanted to present to their guests; there was no Chinese equivalent to Baum's confidence about Americans being Americans (or, perhaps, about the masses correcting a social ill).[114]

The enduring contradiction of exchange contact encouraging both familiarity and contempt was mirrored in China's contacts with other capitalist countries in this period. Canada, for example, had normalized relations with Beijing in October 1970, before even Kissinger's first, secret visit and earlier than most of Washington's allies. Thereafter, Canada had significantly expanded their bilateral contacts with China, including exchanges. Ottawa's formal relations with the PRC meant that exchanges were, unlike Sino-American contacts, managed on a government-to-government basis. This had not, however, protected Sino-Canadian exchanges from similar disruptions to those described in this chapter: a visit by the Vancouver Symphony Orchestra planned for the

---

[113] Ibid.
[114] Architectural Association reception team, "Jiedai Meiguo jianzhushi daibiaotuan qingkuang jianbao (di yi qi)" [First report on hosting US delegation of architects], April 12, 1974, Folder B246-1-692-63, SHMA; Lovell, "Foreigners in Mao-Era China," 155.

spring of 1974 had fallen victim to the Criticize Lin Biao, Criticize Confucius political campaign, being cancelled just weeks before the orchestra's expected departure as a result of that movement's hostile reaction to Western cultural influences. Moreover, Canadian exchange participants were just as wont to complain about their treatment in China as their American cousins: more than a third of the first cohort of Canadian students to travel to the PRC on extended student exchange pulled out and returned home early.[115] Ambassador Bush met one of the returning Canadian students at a cocktail party and found them "thoroughly disillusioned, highly critical of the Chinese."[116]

That Americans were not alone in their frustrations over exchange contacts with China was little consolation to the US government. The State Department was no more willing to accept the long-term tensions over exchanges than they had been the rows over the archaeological exhibition and performing arts troupe. Instead, the government took an active stance in attempting to prevent the problems that maligned exchanges and, in turn, jeopardized the broader Sino-American relationship. State Department officers had already grown so concerned by the unreliable behavior of American exchange participants that they had taken to meeting with visitors both before and after trips in order to remind them that the exchange program had a larger, political purpose that would be undermined by overly vocal criticism of their hosts, either while in China or upon their return.[117] The US government had also begun to insist on official oversight while delegations were in China – though not always successfully. William Hitchcock was the second-most senior official at State's Department of Educational and Cultural Affairs, behind only John Richardson. During the planning for the National Committee's November 1974 delegation of university presidents (Figure 4.2), Hitchcock had railed at the NCUSCR's refusal to have a State Department minder accompany the group. "Don't all your participants understand that this is a gov't [*sic*] facilitated exchange and that we're supporting you and it?" he fumed – though without effect.[118]

[115] Berris to The Record, May 28, 1975, "General Correspondence – 1975," Box 131, ADBP, RBMLCU. For further details of the Canadian student exchange experience in China in the 1970s, see Hooper, *Foreigners under Mao*, 229–31.
[116] Bush, *China Diary*, 79.
[117] Solomon to Kissinger, July 30, 1973, *FRUS, 1969–1976*, Vol. XVIII, Document 45.
[118] Note signed "D" (likely Douglas Murray), undated, circa June 1974, Folder 130, Box 17, Series 3, RG4, NCUSCR records, RAC; Rosen to NCUSCR board of directors, March 10, 1977, "NCUSCR, 1976–77," Box 131, ADBP.

FIGURE 4.2 Part of a November 1974 delegation of US university and college presidents listen to their Chinese hosts explain traditional Chinese medicine. Among those in the photograph are Robben W. Fleming, president of the University of Michigan (seated, center), Harold L. Enarson, president of the Ohio State University (standing to right of Fleming), and scholar-escort Merle Goldman, Professor of History at Boston University (left of Enarson). Courtesy of the National Committee on U.S.-China Relations.

In reaction to the frictions caused by exchange participants in 1974 and 1975, Ambassador Bush proposed even closer government supervision of US exchange participants in China. USLO had decided that henceforth all exchange delegations be chaperoned by a foreign service officer sensitive to the "policy implications of any problems that might arise" during the trip. The USLO chief asked that the State Department make sure "that the National Committee and CSC[PRC] be told at as high a level as necessary that USG [the US government] deems it essential that USG escort be assigned to each delegation." Previously, exchange delegations had been used as a vehicle to give first-hand experience of the PRC to foreign service officers who had studied China and Chinese but had no chance to visit the mainland. Now, Bush argued that accompanying officers should be selected on the basis of their aptitude for a managerial, political role. Better official oversight would, Bush claimed, avoid the kind of "very serious" incidents that had plagued exchanges in the previous year, that "could and should have been avoided."[119]

CONCLUSION

In the fifth year of rapprochement, Sino-American familiarity was beginning to breed contempt. Both governments knew the other's negotiating position in detail and, after normalization talks stalemated during the Watergate scandal, Ford failed to reinvigorate high-level discussions. The deep frustration this prompted in Beijing pushed the PRC to find new means of protest beyond haranguing Kissinger, with Chinese leaders settling on the prominent public forum of the exchange program. American nongovernmental organizations stood firm against China playing politics in exchanges, conscious that doing otherwise would cede control of these contacts to Beijing. Able to resolve many disputes themselves, the two Committees also called on allies in the US government over the most intractable conflicts. Meanwhile, Americans were impatient for a chance to visit China but also chafed at the restrictions imposed upon them in the country. Their active resistance to these strictures alarmed both their Chinese hosts and their own government, both of whom found that a second wave of American visitors to China were not as committed to the careful exchange diplomacy of those that had broken the ice between the two sides. It was in the context of these frictions that Americans inside and outside of government concluded by 1975 that the exchange program could only continue to be successful if contacts were allowed to evolve and deepen beyond the exchange that had been possible in the first half-decade of renewed contact.

---

[119] Bush to Kissinger, April 11, 1975, "PRC – Exchanges (exchange programs)" folder 7, Box 8, NSCEAPASF, GFL. Bush's recommended changes had been implemented by 1976, if not before: see the account of Senator Hugh Scott's ill-fated visit to China in Chapter 5 and Gates to Kissinger, July 13, 1976, "Memorandums," Subject Files, 1969–1978, RG59, NACP.

5

Asking for More in Exchange

President Ford smiled at Deng Xiaoping across the negotiating table. It was the third day of the president's December 1975 visit to China and a pained silence had fallen over the cavernous Great Hall of the People. "So, do you think we have come to the end of our discussion?" Deng asked. The two men were only an hour into their first discussions of the day, but both sides knew there was nothing more to negotiate. "The only apprehension that I have, Mr. Vice Premier, is that we have gotten along so well that we have not had to take as much time this morning as we anticipated," Ford meekly responded. Kissinger attempted to fill the void with small talk, but this soon petered out. Finally, Deng found a solution: "We still have some time left … Perhaps we can chat about Tibet." And so, the vice premier explained – at length – to only the second sitting US president to ever visit China how the CCP had rescued Tibet from the "very cruel oppression" imposed by the lamas. "They had very many varieties of torture," Deng explained, "and they did not reproduce the human race."[1]

This was, then, a far cry from the week that changed the world. A year after this truncated, tepid summit, Ford left office with the United States no closer to normalization than when he took up the presidency; if anything, years of drift had pushed a deal further out of reach. This was the nadir of the Sino-American rapprochement begun by Nixon and later completed by President Carter. As we saw in the previous chapter,

---

[1] Memcon: Deng, Ford, Kissinger, et al., December 4, 1975, *FRUS, 1969–1976*, Vol. XVIII, Document 137; ZGZYWXYJS, *Deng Xiaoping sixiang nianbian*, 44–45.

the downturn in the Sino-American relationship under Ford had turned exchange visits into a new arena of contestation between the Chinese state and Americans inside and outside of government. This chapter shows how, in a related dynamic, the failure of Ford's China policy in 1975 pushed American actors beyond the Ford administration to attempt to take the initiative in negotiations with the Chinese. In particular, both the Committee on Scholarly Communication and a congressional delegation led by Senate Majority Leader Hugh Scott attempted to do what Ford had failed to and push Beijing to agree to US pressure to upgrade the Sino-American relationship. These initiatives were not immediately successful, but they did anticipate breakthroughs in both high-level and exchange diplomacy that occurred soon after Ford's exit from office and helped establish the terms on which the upgrading of Sino-American relations would take place under Carter. They were also a reminder that, as had been the case before the Nixon–Mao summit, when high-level Sino-American relations were deadlocked, Americans outside of the executive branch were willing and able to vocally dissent from the US government's China policy – and to ultimately contribute to major breakthroughs in the overall US-China relationship.

AN AURA OF FAILURE

Long before Ford arrived in Beijing on December 1, 1975, the administration had scaled back expectations for what might be achieved during the president's summit. In August of that year, Kissinger's aides described the US objective of "small, matched concessions to provide an aura of success" – most notably agreements on exchanges and trade.[2] If this "aura of success" was intended to dampen domestic and foreign skepticism about rapprochement's health, then the continued limits to the number of the most public of exchange visits – cultural contacts – was a worrying concern: in the sixteen months to November 1975, the National Committee did not receive a single Chinese delegation; the only scheduled visit had been the cancelled performing arts troupe.[3] Meanwhile, Sino-American trade for 1975 had fallen by more than half from its high point of $1.003 billion in 1974 to $493 million.[4] In July, Deng had a meeting with

---

[2] Habib, Gleysteen and Lord to Kissinger, August 4, 1975, "China Exchanges, January 1–31 May 1975," DFWL, RG59, NACP.
[3] NCUSCR Annual Report, 1974–75, NCUSCROC.
[4] Talley, *Forgotten Vanguard*, 7.

American newsmen to tell a *Wall Street Journal* reporter explicitly that Beijing would not relent in its restrictions on exchange contacts and trade until the Taiwan issue had been settled – on Chinese terms.[5]

Beijing had also returned to tactics deployed in 1971 and 1972 by undertaking what Kissinger called "a bit of nose-thumbing" toward the US government and its favored exchange organizations by showing renewed favor toward the US-China Peoples Friendship Association.[6] In the autumn of 1975 alone, that group was invited to send some six delegations to tour China, a reminder that Beijing had other channels for arranging exchanges that were beyond the influence of Kissinger and his colleagues – and that led to more consistently flattering accounts of China when the participants returned to the United States.[7] The USCPFA relied upon these tours to raise organizational funds: in the 1976–77 financial year, commissions and overages from tour participants, airlines, and travel agents amounted to more than 90 percent of the Friendship Association's $116,072 in income, for example.[8] Whether in exchange for this patronage-in-kind or because of genuine ideological conviction, or both, the organization gladly parroted Beijing's complaints about the US government's foot-dragging in normalization negotiations, making that issue the "national priority" of the group's domestic organizing from 1975 onwards.[9]

China's public relations initiatives were also defensive. Renewed American sympathy for Taiwan was posing a threat to Ford politically but this sympathy was also of concern to Beijing. The PRC was deeply alarmed at the continuing growth of American trade with Taiwan – further encouraged by Taipei's 1976 creation of a USA-ROC Economic Council – and at the ROC being allowed to open new consulates in the United States. Critics of Beijing, such as Senator Barry Goldwater, were working closely with Republic of China diplomats to argue to American audiences that rapprochement had proceeded as far as it served US interests.[10] The Beijing

---

[5] "Taiwan Issue Must Be Settled Before U.S., China Can Increase Trade, Peking Says," *Wall Street Journal*, June 3, 1975; ZGZYWXYJS, *Deng Xiaoping sixiang nianbian*, 19–20.

[6] Kissinger to Ford, October 11, 1975, "China Exchanges, October–Dec. 1975," DFWL, RG59, NACP.

[7] *NFTNC*, Vol. 5, No. 1, February 1975; Schmalzer, "Speaking about China," 313–14.

[8] USCPFA, "Income & Expense," July 1976–June 1977, Folder 10, Box 1, USCPFAR, NYPLAMD.

[9] "Minutes, [USCPFA] National Steering Committee Meeting," October 8–9, 1977, Folder 11, Box 1, USCPFAR, NYPLAMD.

[10] Habib, Gleysteen, Lord, and Solomon to Kissinger, July 3, 1975, *FRUS, 1969–1976*, Vol. XVIII, Document 112; Talley, *Forgotten Vanguard*, 18.

government sought to counter this by making use of the public platform provided by the USCPFA. The Friendship Association was the most important node in the network of American organizations and individuals still interested in China from a leftist and pro-PRC perspective in the mid-1970s.[11] Paul Lin, a respected academic at McGill University who was secretly an influential member of Beijing's intelligence network in North America, used one Friendship Association meeting to attribute the growing American sympathy for Taiwan to giveaways – bribes in kind – from the ROC government to American businessmen.[12] That same year, Beijing sent longtime-PRC resident and foreign friend Sid Engst on a twenty-five-city speaking tour across the United States, hosted by the Friendship Association and intended to further promote Beijing's foreign policy line. Engst, who had married Joan Hinton, sister of William Hinton and aunt of Carma Hinton, in Yan'an in 1949, was a former agriculture adviser to the United Nations Relief and Rehabilitation Administration (UNRRA) and had, during the Cultural Revolution, helped write a big-character poster that had won Mao's personal approval. As argued by Anne-Marie Brady and Beverly Hooper (Prologue), "foreign friends" of the PRC state were once again being put to serve Beijing's changing foreign policy goals: in 1975, this meant publicly defending rapprochement to their fellow Americans.[13]

China continued to receive National Committee cultural exchanges in 1975: the ninety-four-member track and field delegation in May and a smaller but distinguished group of eighteen specialists on international affairs in October, organized in collaboration with the influential New York-based think tank, the Council on Foreign Relations (CFR). The latter delegation was led by the vice chairman of the CFR and chairman of the Rockefeller Foundation, Cyrus Vance – who would, a year later, become Carter's first secretary of state. Others on the trip included Allen S. Whiting, who had much influence on US China policy from within and beyond the State Department in the 1960s, and the presidents of a range of influential non-governmental organizations, including the CFR, the

---

[11] Schmalzer, "Speaking about China," 330.

[12] Berris to The Record, May 22, 1975, "General Correspondence – 1975," Box 131, ADBP, RBMLCU. Paul Lin's full identity was confirmed to the author by several oral history sources. For Washington's knowledge of Lin's closeness to the Chinese government, see American Embassy Tokyo to DOS, June 19, 1970, "POL – Chicom – 6/1/70," SNF1970–73PD, RG59, NACP.

[13] Beijing had sent PRC-resident foreign friends George Hatem and Sidney Shapiro on speaking tours in the United States in 1972, too. Hooper, *Foreigners under Mao*, 24, 26, 31, 41; Brady, *Making the Foreign Serve China*, 182.

Carnegie Endowment for International Peace, the Rockefeller Foundation, and the Asia Society.[14] NCUSCR President Rosen was deputy leader of the delegation and had sought to maximize opportunities for meaningful Sino-American dialogue during the trip, successfully persuading the group's hosts, the Chinese People's Institute of Foreign Affairs, to allow the delegation to forego the usual fast-paced tours of Chinese cities and instead spend longer in the capital and hold "detailed, substantive" discussions with Chinese leaders (although Rosen did also ask that the delegation have the chance to travel to the ancient Chinese capital of Xi'an, where the first pieces of the soon-to-be world famous buried terracotta army had been unearthed that year).[15]

The talks in Beijing included a long discussion with Deng and further meetings with Acting Foreign Minister Han Nianlong and Vice Minister for Foreign Trade Yao Yilin.[16] Deng told the visitors that Sino-American relations had developed since the 1972 signing of the Shanghai Communiqué, citing cultural exchanges and trade as his only evidence and omitting any mention of high-level diplomatic negotiations. But he also said that progress had been limited.[17] Deng debated critical issues in both country's foreign policies with former deputy secretary of defense Vance – Soviet-American détente, relations with Japan and Korea, arms limitation – in a manner that anticipated their discussions after the American reentered government and become secretary of state. The delegation's discussions also foreshadowed the National Committee's later role in organizing high-ranking track-two meetings between former Chinese and US officials, such as in the wake of the crisis in Sino-American relations following both the 1989 Tiananmen crackdown and the 1999 US bombing of the Chinese embassy in Belgrade.[18]

---

[14] NCUSCR Annual Report, 1974–75, NCUSCROC.

[15] Rosen to Hsieh [Xie], September 5, 1975, Folder 110, Box 15, Series 3, RG4, NCUSCR records, RAC; "Zhou Qiuye yanqing Meiguo keren" [Zhou Qiuye hosts banquet for US guests], *Renmin Ribao*, October 7, 1975.

[16] "Han Nianlong huijian Meiguo shijie shiwu zuzhi lingdaoren daibiaotuan" [Han Nianlong meets with delegation of leaders of the US world affairs delegation], *Renmin Ribao*, October 11, 1975; Memcons: world affairs delegation meetings with Han Nianlong, and Yao Yilin, October 10 and 9, respectively, Folder 113, Box 15, Series 3, RG4, NCUSCR records, RAC.

[17] ZGZYWXYJS, ed., *Deng Xiaoping nianpu, 1975–1997* [Deng Xiaoping Chronicle, 1975–1997], vol. 1 (Beijing: Zhongyang wenxian chubanshe, 2004), 116–17.

[18] Priscilla Roberts, "'Our Friends Don't Understand Our Policies and Our Situation': Informal U.S.-China Dialogues Following Tiananmen," *Journal of American-East Asian Relations* 27, no. 1 (March 2020): 58–95; Wheeler, *American NGOs in China's Modernization*, 35.

Alongside these statesmen-like exchanges, Deng took the chance to try to settle some of the differences between Beijing and the NCUSCR. The vice premier asked Rosen why the National Committee had "refuse[d] our cultural troupe the right to sing a song that the people on Taiwan were our sisters and brothers?" Deng added that he hoped "it does not reflect ... a retreat of the entire United States government from the Shanghai Communiqué." Rosen responded that the NCUSCR did not speak for the government (even if Beijing often sought to punish the organization for Washington's policies) and in turn pressed Deng on the cancellation of a delegation of mayors that the National Committee had been planning to send to China in September. Why, Rosen asked, had Beijing refused to allow the mayor of San Juan to visit China? Was this protest against the status of Puerto Rico not just as much of an interference in America's own domestic matters as the NCUSCR preventing a Chinese troupe singing about Taiwan?[19] Beijing had its own interpretation of the cancellation, of course, having previously alleged that the United States had used the inclusion of San Juan's "colonialist" mayor as a "self-justification" of the US position in Puerto Rico that "introduces a political element into non-governmental exchanges." An ostensible violation of the ground rules of such exchanges, this was, in fact, hardly the first time that exchanges had been politicized.[20]

Back in the United States, some within the ranks of the NCUSCR echoed Deng's concerns about the consonance between the organization's stance on Taiwan and that of the US government – effectively (if privately) summarized by the founder of the National Committee, the political scientist Bob Scalapino, as a "maybe one-China, but not now" policy.[21] John S. Service was a former senior foreign service officer who had been one of the leaders of the Dixie Mission to Mao's Communists in Yan'an. Service had been born in Chengdu in 1909 and had learned to speak the Sichuanese dialect as a young boy. In the 1940s, he had correctly predicted that the CCP would win the civil war with Chiang Kai-shek's Kuomintang but had been fired after being on the frontline of those accused of "losing

[19] ZGZYWXYJS, *Deng Xiaoping nianpu, 1975–1997*, 1:116–17; Roberts, "Bringing the Chinese Back In"; Wheeler, *American NGOs in China's Modernization*, 48.
[20] "Observations by the Chinese Peoples [*sic*] Institute of Foreign Affairs," September 15, 1975, "General Correspondence – 1975," Box 131, ADBP; Baum, *China Watcher*, 63–64.
[21] Service to Barnett, September 26, 1975, "General Correspondence – 1975," Box 131, ADBP.

China" – perhaps, firebrand Senator Joe McCarthy alleged, because of political affinity with the reds.[22] He had been involved in the NCUSCR since its inception but resigned from the group in September 1975 as a protest against the continuing dominance of those who, he claimed, held either a two-China position or Scalapino's ineffectual compromise stance. Service argued that both the government and the National Committee were following an approach to the PRC-ROC dispute that was "not realistic or ... credible." Service suggested that the NCUSCR could simply become a mirror of the Chinese People's Association for Friendship with Foreign Countries – "in other words, a servant or auxiliary of the State Department." "I doubt that many of the members or directors of the Committee see themselves in this role, or would be content to stay on under these circumstances," he said. Thus, he reasoned, those individuals "do think the Committee has a public, policy influencing role.... And that policy is to serve and promote and support a two-China policy."[23] (There was diversity in the views of the National Committee's members, however: others, such as the noted expert on classical Chinese philosophy, Donald Munro, found the organization to be too pro-Beijing.)[24]

Service's resignation troubled leading NCUSCR figures such as Doak Barnett – who argued in a letter to Service that in fact the National Committee "scrupulously avoided taking any policy position itself," including on the Taiwan issue.[25] Other options than this studied neutrality were available to American cultural organizations. The United Methodist Church had deep ties to Taiwan, made possible in part by President Chiang Kai-shek's own Methodist faith. But the Church withdrew its missionaries and its funding for activities on the island in 1969, seemingly in the hope of pursuing the bigger fish of the Chinese mainland – although with little effect.[26] The National Committee, in contrast, continued to occupy the ambiguous ground that the US government, too, stood on:

---

[22] Li Hongshan, *U.S.-China Educational Exchange: State, Society, and Intercultural Relations, 1905–1950* (New Brunswick, NJ: Rutgers University Press, 2008), 198.

[23] Service to Barnett, September 26, 1975, "General Correspondence – 1975," Box 131, ADBP.

[24] Author interview with Donald Munro, Ann Arbor, MI, United States, November 21, 2017.

[25] Barnett to Service, October 21, 1975, "General Correspondence – 1975," Box 131, ADBP.

[26] Bibiana Wong, "Christian Protesters for Democracy in Taiwan: A Study of Two American Missionaries under Taiwanese Martial Law," *International Journal for the Study of the Christian Church* 16, no. 4 (October 2016): 292–93.

maintaining some level of contact with both Chinas, even as relations with the PRC were prioritized.

While the NCUSCR savored opportunities for high-level engagement through cultural exchange – even if this included frank discussions of differences – the Committee on Scholarly Communication was simultaneously pushing both the US and Chinese governments to work toward more substantive scientific exchanges. A twenty-page CSCPRC memorandum sent to Kissinger in July 1975 by the heads of the group's three sponsoring organizations – the National Academy of Sciences, the Social Science Research Council, and the American Council of Learned Societies – forcefully made the case that scientific and scholarly cooperation must now evolve beyond the current "get-acquainted period" if the exchange program was to retain the support of the American academic and commercial communities that hosted Chinese scientists. The CSCPRC wanted scientific exchanges to include opportunities not only for brief meet-and-greets but also working academic seminars on specific subjects, week-long collaborative workshops, and channels for continuing contact and cooperation in research after scientists from either side had returned to their home country after an exchange. To date, Chinese counterparts had rebuffed such suggestions: the delegation of American linguists that had traveled to China in 1974 had proposed continuing collaboration with Chinese counterparts on a joint-authored dictionary after the exchange – but had been refused. Meanwhile, both the CSCPRC and NCUSCR lobbied the two governments for scholarly exchanges, so far limited to just a few weeks in length, to begin to be extended in some cases to last months if not years. Both organizations also asked their Chinese counterparts if they would be willing to begin new types of exchange, in particular student exchanges and language training programs.[27] The United States was a laggard among capitalist countries in initiating such contacts: the first group of Italian students to study in China had arrived as early as 1957, for example, and the UK had also received a few hundred Chinese students in the early 1970s.[28]

The CSCPRC identified the second half of 1975 as a propitious moment to push for change. The CSCPRC would have direct negotiations with

---

[27] Sheldon, Lumiansky, and Handler to Kissinger, July 11, 1975, and CSCPRC paper, "The future of academic exchanges with the PRC," "1975 – Report for Secretary of State," CSCPRCP, NAS; Minutes of 28th meeting of NCUSCR executive committee, May 29, 1975, "Board of Directors Meeting, 10/28/75" [sic], Box 131, ADBP, RBMLCU.

[28] Graziani, "Youth Exchanges," 208; Roberts, "Bringing the Chinese Back In," 309.

the vice chairman of the Scientific and Technical Association of the PRC, Zhou Peiyuan, during the STAPRC's trip to the United States, before US officials had their own opportunity for talks during the Ford summit.[29] If they could earn Zhou's support, perhaps he could effect change in Beijing: he enjoyed near-peerless authority among Chinese scientists and significant influence in PRC political circles. An internationally renowned theoretical physicist before the 1949 revolution, Zhou had graduated from one of China's best educational institutions, Tsinghua, while it was still a preparatory school for study in the United States. He had then earned graduate degrees from the University of Chicago and the California Institute of Technology in the 1920s before conducting research at Princeton under Albert Einstein in the 1930s. Having broken with the Kuomintang during the Second Sino-Japanese War, Zhou returned to China in 1947 and was appointed to a succession of important posts after the establishment of the People's Republic, including leading one of China's most prestigious academic institutions, Peking University – located just a stone's throw from his alma mater, by then reconstituted as Tsinghua University. By the time of his 1975 visit to the United States, Zhou was already involved in what would become one of the PRC's most ambitious scientific undertakings: the long process of planning the Three Gorges Dam. Zhou's combination of experiences in socialist China and in the United States might, if he was persuaded, make him a powerful ally of American science in Beijing (although his time in the United States had also been a political liability for Zhou in the 1950s).[30]

The Committee on Scholarly Communication believed their leverage over Beijing was increasing because of growing Chinese appetite for American scientific knowhow and equipment. The period after Mao's death – in particular that following Deng's return to power in 1977 and 1978 – is often considered the beginning of China's opening to the world. However, recent biographies of Deng by Ezra Vogel and Alexander Pantsov have shown that the period between his rehabilitation in 1973 and his purge in January 1976 can be characterized as a dress rehearsal for the period after Deng achieved political ascendency in 1978. During this earlier period, the vice premier began trialing many of the policies

[29] Sheldon, Lumiansky, and Handler to Kissinger, July 11, 1975, "The Future of Academic Exchanges with the PRC," "1975 – Report for Secretary of State," CSCPRCP, NAS.
[30] Zhou, *Zhou Peiyuan wenji*, 405–23; Li, *U.S.-China Educational Exchange*, 190; Barrett, "China's 'People's Diplomacy'," 148–53; "Zhou Peiyuan, Physicist, Einstein Student, Dies," Associated Press, November 25, 1993.

that would be adopted during the Reform and Opening period.[31] Deng, who had a daughter who was a medical student and a son majoring in physics who would go on to do graduate work at the University of Rochester, had advocated for the value of science to China's development since the early 1960s. Thus, prominent among the changes he introduced in 1975 were those to China's science policy: a newfound stress on basic research, scientific professionalism, and importing technology.[32]

The CSCPRC tracked these changes through Chinese approaches to scientific exchange visits. By 1975, Chinese scientific interlocutors were displaying "great interest in American advanced technology," the Committee reported to Kissinger.[33] The CSCPRC had not been alone in noticing this trend: the Democratic majority whip, Senator Robert Byrd, had traveled on a congressional delegation to the PRC in August that had met Deng and reported to Ford that, whereas he was given the impression that Sino-American trade would continue to be limited, there was much Chinese interest – including from Deng himself – in expanding scientific and technological cooperation with the United States.[34] The year prior, Mao himself had told British Prime Minister Edward Heath that he was "very glad to have your help" in transferring technology that would assist in China's development. Deng hosted Heath in China in September 1975, after the Briton had left office, and told him that, in spite of the PRC's self-reliance policy, China still wanted to absorb the world's most advanced science and technology.[35]

The CSCPRC believed that American scientific expertise should not be given away cheaply. In terms that anticipated debates over the Sino-American cooperation that would emerge over later decades, the Committee on Scholarly Communication recommended that the United States contemplate "how ... exchanges affect immediate propriety [rights], as well

[31] Ezra Vogel, *Deng Xiaoping and the Transformation of China* (Cambridge, MA: Harvard University Press, 2011), 120–40; Alexander Pantsov, *Deng Xiaoping: A Revolutionary Life* (Oxford: Oxford University Press, 2015), 273–92; ZGZYWXYJS, *Deng Xiaoping sixiang nianbian*, 1–47.

[32] Greg Whitesides, *Science and American Foreign Relations since World War II* (New York: Cambridge University Press, 2019), 195–96.

[33] CSCPRC paper, "The Future of Academic Exchanges with the PRC," June 1975, "1975 – Report for Secretary of State," CSCPRCP, NAS.

[34] Memcon: President Ford and Byrd CoDel participants, September 8, 1975, [unmarked folder, likely "China Exchanges, July–September 1975"], DFWL, RG59, NACP; ZGZYWXYJS, *Deng Xiaoping nianpu, 1975–1997*, 1:85–86.

[35] Minami, "Re-Examining the End of Mao's Revolution," 366; ZGZYWXYJS, *Deng Xiaoping nianpu, 1975–1997*, 1:101.

as long-term economic interests; in what areas would it be in our national interest to transfer technology to China, thus permitting China to accelerate development; and what ... the relationship between foreign policy interests served by exchanges and economic interests affected by these programs [are]."[36]

The CSCPRC's growing concerns about knowledge transfer to China were in contrast to the US government's stance on the issue. The State Department counselled the CSCPRC to tone down its needling of the Chinese, arguing that the months before the presidential summit were a poor time to pressure Beijing – the opposite of the group's own belief that the impending visit was just the moment to speak frankly about reciprocity in exchanges.[37] The US government had shown no qualms about China accessing the most sensitive and advanced laboratories while on exchange visits. By 1975, Chinese scientists had been welcomed into, among others, the Stanford Linear Accelerator and the Fermi National Accelerator Laboratory in Chicago, as well as into research centers at industry-leading companies like Bethlehem Steel and Boeing.[38] During a 1974 visit by Chinese seismologists, Mary Brown Bullock, then a member of the CSCPRC staff and later Keatley's successor as staff director of that organization, had been surprised that "issues of national security were never raised concerning [the] visit" and that the only misgivings at the State Department about a tour of the Defense Department's Advanced Projects Research Agency – one of the most secretive laboratories in the country – had been that it might not be politic to transparently showcase US test monitoring capabilities given that the PRC opposed test-bans. (In fact, the Chinese scientists were already well aware that US seismological institutes were involved in weapons test detection and were only surprised that the American hosts felt the need to inform them of this.)[39] Indeed, if anything it seemed that the Ford administration was glad to actively facilitate the PRC acquiring advanced American technology – or so events during the president's summit trip to China suggested.

---

[36] CSCPRC paper, "The Future of Academic Exchanges with the PRC," June 1975, "1975 – Report for Secretary of State," CSCPRCP, NAS.

[37] Keatley to Sheldon, November 21, 1975, Folder 6371, Box 527, Series 1, Accession 2, SSRC records, RAC.

[38] Whitesides, *Science and American Foreign Relations*, 194.

[39] "Report on the Visit of the Chinese Seismology Delegation, April 19, 1974–May 20, 1974," "Bullock, Mary" folder, Box 2, NASAR, BHL; Fa-ti Fan, "'Collective Monitoring, Collective Defense': Science, Earthquakes, and Politics in Communist China," *Science in Context* 25, no. 1 (2012): 133–34.

FORD IN CHINA: THREE DAYS THAT DID
NOT CHANGE THE WORLD

While the CSCPRC grew increasingly confident of the leverage the United States had in negotiations over exchanges, Kissinger remained doubtful. In October, his aides noted with concern the aforementioned cancellation of the National Committee-sponsored delegation of American mayors because of Beijing's refusal to receive the mayor of San Juan, as well as a PRCLO attempt to block a US visit by a Tibetan song and dance troupe invited by the Office of Tibet in New York City, the Dalai Lama's representative in the United States and something close to a Tibetan government-in-exile. PRCLO's Xie Qimei had labelled the visit American "connivance" with "Tibetan rebels."[40] The secretary of state had previously shown limited concern about ups and downs in exchanges but, in the run up to Ford's summit, he showed himself more convinced that the Sino-American relationship now had to rest on more than simply security collaboration.[41]

Kissinger's October 1975 visit to Beijing, a preparatory trip ahead of Ford's summit, provided a chance to try to persuade Chinese leaders to cease limiting and sabotaging exchanges. In a meeting with Deng and Foreign Minister Qiao, Kissinger entreated:

We think it is important to show some vitality and forward movement in our bilateral relationship. We do not do this because we particularly care about the level of trade between the United States and China, and we believe also that China, having survived 2,000 years of its history without extensive contact with the United States, may manage to stagger on for many more years without extensive exchange between our various cultural troupes. We can even survive your favorite songs without revolution. But to us that is not the issue. To us the issue is how to be in the best position to resist hegemonial [Soviet] aspirations in the West as well as in the East. And if that is the case, it is important that we show some movement in our relationship. It is difficult to gain public support for what may have to be done if China is not an important element in American consciousness, and it cannot be unless there is some improvement in our bilateral relationship.

Perceiving all aspects of rapprochement through the lens of joint resistance to Moscow, Kissinger was arguing that, if the Sino-American

---

[40] Habib, Lord, and Solomon to Kissinger, October 6, 1975, "China Exchanges, October–Dec. 1975," DFWL, RG59, NACP; Habib to Kissinger, September 22, 1975, [unmarked folder, likely "China Exchanges, July–Sept 1975"], DFWL, RG59, NACP.

[41] Memcon: Kissinger, Habib, et al., July 6, 1975, *FRUS, 1969–1976*, Vol. XVIII, Document 113.

security and political relationship was to be preserved, public support for ties to China must be buttressed with meaningful broad contact between the two societies.[42]

Kissinger's October trip was the bitterest he experienced during his time in office: a meeting with Mao was dominated by the chairman berating Kissinger about the United States climbing on China's shoulders to reach Moscow.[43] Unable to make progress toward a draft communiqué for the forthcoming Ford summit, Foreign Minister Qiao told the secretary of state that Beijing would rather have no communiqué than meet the United States halfway.[44] Kissinger's demarche on exchanges had similarly brought little effect: a further blow was dealt to the National Committee when the Chinese stated that the number of exchanges for 1976 should remain at the *actual* level of 1975, not the number that had been planned to take place in that previous year. In the NCUSCR's case, this would mean just three exchanges – two of the five trips planned for 1975 had been cancelled.[45] In the days after his return from China, Kissinger revised down the administration's already modest expectations for the forthcoming presidential summit, talking down the likelihood of positive agreements over exchanges or trade. For the first time, he admitted to Ford that "our relationship with China has cooled."[46] USLO chief Bush had been present for the querulous talks in Beijing and was so despairing of the PRC's obstinacy that he asked Kissinger if it was not too late to just call off the president's trip. The possibility was seriously considered.[47]

Although Ford ultimately opted only to curtail and not cancel his China trip, he could not prevent the visit from being insipid from beginning to end. There was no progress in negotiations over exchanges. The final Chinese proposal for the total number of visits for the coming year was for some seventeen exchanges, with twelve of these to be managed by the Committee on Scholarly Communication. Chinese leaders had not

[42] Memcon: Deng, Kissinger, et al., October 20, 1975, *FRUS, 1969–1976*, Vol. XVIII, Document 121; ZGZYWXYJS, *Deng Xiaoping nianpu, 1975–1997*, 1:120.

[43] ZGZYWXYJS, *Mao Zedong nianpu, 1949–1976*, 6:615–16.

[44] Memcon: Qiao, Kissinger, et al., October 23, 1975, *FRUS, 1969–1976*, Vol. XVIII, Document 126.

[45] Minutes of 29th meeting of NCUSCR executive committee, October 28, 1975, Folder 78, Box 6, Series 1, DPMP, RAC.

[46] Memcon: Qiao, Kissinger, et al., October 23, 1975, *FRUS, 1969–1976*, Vol. XVIII, Document 126.

[47] Bush to Kissinger, November 5, 1975, "China Exchanges, October–Dec. 1975," DFWL, RG59, NACP.

changed their mind about reducing the role of the National Committee, insisting on their previous limit of three exchanges for that organization. Similarly, Beijing had not rectified the imbalance in the direction of CSCPRC exchanges, proposing seven Chinese delegations travel to the United States and only five be received in the PRC.[48]

Even lighthearted attempts to reflect positively on recent exchanges met barriers. Winston Lord mentioned to his Chinese counterparts one of the National Committee's few recent exchanges, the successful visit by the Chinese women's basketball team to the United States in the month before Ford's trip. Lord chatted to his hosts about tactics seen in the basketball matches. Perhaps, the Chinese suggested, tall players should all gather on one team, and leave shorter players to fend for themselves. When White House Press Secretary Ron Nessen puzzledly responded that a team could use both tall and short players, the Chinese said that perhaps, then, the divide should be between good tall players and bad short players. Lord leaned over to Nessen and warned "we [are] not talking about basketball anymore." Lord cut things off with a final riposte: "Maybe the answer is that all teams should be equal and treated as such."[49]

Meanwhile, Kissinger and Ford entreated Deng about how the American public expected the summit to lead to progress in contacts between the two societies. A December 3 article in the *Christian Science Monitor*, entitled "What Ford Can Ask from China," argued that, even though it was clear before the summit that Ford would not find agreement with the Chinese on Taiwan, progress in exchanges was necessary as "it is disturbing to many Americans that, after three years, exchanges have reached a plateau and a low plateau at that." Deng showed little concern, however, despite two direct appeals from the president, who stated that exchanges and trade were "very meaningful" in building "support from the American people for the forward movement of our overall relations."[50]

There was only one issue in bilateral ties that piqued Deng's interest: science and technology. Turning the tables on Ford, Deng argued that the US government, too, limited contacts in that field. Were there not

[48] ZGZYWXYJS, *Deng Xiaoping nianpu, 1975–1997*, 1:134–35; Berris to Rosen, Yost, and Barnett, January 13, 1976, "General Correspondence – 1975" [*sic*], Box 131, ADBP, RBMLCU.

[49] "Peking: Playing Ball," *Washington Post*, December 3, 1975.

[50] ZGZYWXYJS, *Deng Xiaoping nianpu, 1975–1997*, 1:134–35; Memcon: Deng, Ford, Kissinger, et al., December 4, 1975, *FRUS, 1969–1976*, Vol. XVIII, Document 137; "What Ford Can Ask from China," *Christian Science Monitor*, December 3, 1975.

computers "of a speed of 10 million times" that the United States refused to sell to China? the vice premier asked. Deng knew there were indeed computers that the United States would not sell: alongside the PRC's unceasing requests for visits to the most advanced American laboratories, Beijing had also sought permission to purchase what they saw, including some of the fastest computers in the world.[51] Such sales were subject to strict Cold War export controls and the US government bureaucracy had refused the most recent Chinese request to purchase top-end American computers as recently as September 23.[52] Echoing the State Department's lack of concern about Chinese access to sensitive US scientific facilities while on exchange visits, Ford ignored the US government's own self-imposed barriers to technology sales – a policy of even-handedness in technology transfers to China and the Soviet Union, and legal prohibitions on exports of weaponizable technology to Communist countries – and told Deng that "we are very anxious to be helpful in this area." In an extraordinary interchange, Ford and Kissinger now suggested that Beijing show avoid "trade channels" for technology purchase requests and instead have PRC Liaison Office chief Huang Zhen tell the State Department what they needed. Kissinger would then find computers that met Chinese requirements but also had "technical differences" from those refused to the Soviets.[53] This was not mere talk: Kissinger would personally ensure that Ford's promise to Deng was honored.

The discussion of advanced computers was one indication, though not the first, of a new direction in the Sino-American relationship – one that held out hope for the United States. Kissinger and Ford had given away for free a promise to help increase access to the products of US science, hoping to restore some goodwill and momentum to negotiations at a time when the White House was in no position to negotiate on the critical issue of Taiwan. Deng's request, however, also suggested that the United

[51] Memcon: Deng, Ford, Kissinger, et al., December 4, 1975, *FRUS, 1969–1976*, Vol. XVIII, Document 137. Deng's "10 million times" may have been in reference to the processing data rate of the computers. If so, the United States had, in fact, allowed computers of rates up to 32 million bits per second since 1974, though restrictions on the sale of yet more powerful computers remained. Hugo Meijer, *Trading with the Enemy: The Making of US Export Control Policy toward the People's Republic of China* (New York: Oxford University Press, 2016), 39.

[52] DOS paper, "PRC Economics and Trade Relations," undated, "19–23 October 1975 – PRC Briefing Book for China – Bilateral Issues (1)," Box 21, Trip Briefing Books and Cables of Henry Kissinger, 1974–77, GFL.

[53] Memcon: Huang, Kissinger, et al., May 29, 1976, *FRUS, 1969–1976*, Vol. XVIII, Document 146.

States might soon regain leverage over Beijing: scientific and technological cooperation was the one area of the relationship that the vice premier wished to expand irrespective of political progress. This has been further shown in Beijing's proposal for two thirds of the 1976 exchange program to be scientific exchanges. If Ford and Kissinger had opted against playing hardball with Deng over science and technology during an already-fraught summit, there were other Americans who were insisting that China should pay a higher price for the valuable US expertise and hardware transferred through exchanges and technology sales. It took time for such thinking to spread from the CSCPRC and the American scientific community to the White House. In the meantime, Deng underwent his second purge from office during the Mao era – in part, Chinese historian Gong Li reports, because of his interest in closer ties with the United States.[54] Following Deng's return to power in 1977, however, a new US administration was to show itself far more adroit at linking Sino-American scientific cooperation to the diplomatic relationship.

THE CSCPRC TAKES THE LEAD

While Ford and Kissinger bent over backward to provide Deng with US computer technology, the CSCPRC pursued their more forthright negotiating approach with Chinese scientists. Some progress had been achieved during the high-ranking, fourteen-person visit of the Scientific and Technical Association of the PRC to the United States led by Zhou Peiyuan in September 1975. The atmospherics of the trip were positive: visits to nine of the most prominent locations for American science – Princeton, Cambridge, and Houston among them – saw Zhou returning to old haunts, as well as again delivering lectures to American audience on his scientific research, as he had so frequently before he relocated to China in 1947. A highlight was a meeting with President Ford that Zhou considered an honor not only for the delegation but for Chinese science more broadly. Zhou had agreed to the longstanding American request that exchanges begin to move away from "survey visits" – the whistle-stop tours that moved from city to city every couple of days – and toward longer stays at a smaller number of locations that would facilitate deeper working collaboration.[55]

[54] Gong, "Chinese Decision Making," 327.
[55] Zhou, *Zhou Peiyuan wenji*, 329, 438; DeAngelis to Handler, January 8, 1976, "1976 – Exchange Agreement – Negotiations," CSCPRCP, NAS; *CEN*, Vol. 4, No. 2, April 1976 and Vol. 3, No. 4, September 1975.

Moreover, by 1975, some deeper scientific collaboration was already taking place in select fields of mutual interest, such as agriculture, seismology, plant studies, and cancer research.[56]

Meanwhile, Chinese American scientists were setting new precedents in what they achieved in their collaboration with colleagues in the PRC. One such scientist was Chen Ning Yang, a physicist at Stony Brook University in New York and one of the recipients of the 1957 Nobel Prize in physics, as well as an invited member of the National Committee. Yang had been one of the very first American scientists to travel to the PRC in summer 1971; by 1976, he had made five further trips. By that year, Yang concluded that contact between American and Chinese physicists had, over just the previous few years, "produced profound changes of outlook." Similarly, Man-Chiang Niu of Temple University had returned to China in 1972 and then, starting in 1973, began making annual summer visits to the Chinese Academy of Science's Institute of Zoology. These Chinese American scientists had advantages over some of their peers: their fluency in the Chinese language, preexisting professional networks in the PRC, and the ear of Chinese leaders (later, during Deng Xiaoping's 1979 trip to the United States, the vice premier would accept an honorary degree from Temple in part in recognition of the role Niu had played in Sino-American scientific relations). Yang and Niu were particular trailblazers with stellar scientific credentials but scientific access to China beyond the CSCPRC's organized delegations was clearly greater for Chinese Americans: among the natural scientists that the CSCPRC knew had traveled to China individually in 1975, more than 80 percent had names that suggested that they were of Chinese descent (although this was partially offset by the almost complete absence of Chinese Americans in the limited number of social scientists and humanists who found ways into the PRC, as well as, as we have seen in Chapter 4, the CSCPRC's non-exclusive focus of non-Chinese American scientists). Nevertheless, ethnicity was not all that mattered: it had been an invitation from the fellow biologist Arthur Galston that had first facilitated Niu's return to his country of birth.[57]

---

[56] CSCPRC paper, "The future of academic exchanges with the PRC," June 1975, "1975 – Report for Secretary of State," CSCPRCP, NAS.

[57] Chen Ning Yang, *Selected Papers, 1945–1980, with Commentary* (Singapore: World Scientific, 2005), 518; Li Youhua, *Shengming aomi de tansuo zhe: Niu Manjiang* [Explorer of the mystery of life: Niu Manjiang] (Beijing: Zhongguo Nongye Keji Chubanshe, 1988), 136–42; *NFTNC*, Vol. 2, No. 1, November 1971, and Vol. 6, No. 1, April 1976; *CEN*, Volumes 3 and 4, all issues through No. 5, October 1976; Zuoyue Wang, "U.S.-China Scientific Exchange: A Case Study of State-Sponsored Scientific Internationalism

These positive developments notwithstanding, the CSCPRC was deeply frustrated at continuing Chinese obstinacy in other areas. The Scientific and Technical Association of the PRC had not approved a single one of the social science and humanities delegations proposed by the US side for 1976, while, by January of that year, the balance between delegations sent in each direction had reached twenty-one received by the United States and fourteen sent to China.[58] An internal CSCPRC document now stated that the Chinese approach to exchanges was threatening to become "mutually exclusive with the purpose for which [the Committee on Scholarly Communication] was established" – that is, mutually beneficial bilateral scientific cooperation. This document argued that the group had tolerated "symbolism" and "sentiment" in its contacts with the STAPRC to date but now believed "a relationship of trust and respect with … Chinese colleagues" required "mutuality as well as realism" in the relationship.[59]

The starkest contrast in scientific exchange was in the focus of the delegations received and sent by China. The PRC continued to trumpet to visitors the low-tech science of the masses that was celebrated during the Cultural Revolution.[60] 1975 had seen the Chinese host CSCPRC-organized delegations on subjects such as paleoanthropology, schistosomiasis, rural small-scale industry, and insect control; 1974's exchange program included visits on acupuncture anesthesia and herbal pharmacology, another form of inexpensive healthcare promoted by the Chinese state in the early 1970s.[61] To be sure, these topics were of interest to many scientific visitors. As we have seen in the case of Galston and Signer, some American scientists were excited by the egalitarian potential of China's applied mass science (Chapter 1), while the quality of China's paleoanthropological collections had

---

during the Cold War and Beyond," *Historical Studies in the Physical and Biological Sciences* 30, no. 1 (January 1999): 270.

[58] DeAngelis to Handler, and Press to Han, both January 8, 1976, "1976 – Exchange Agreement – Negotiations," CSCPRCP, NAS.

[59] CSCPRC, "Discussion of 1976 Exchange Negotiations," January 30, 1976, "1976 – Exchange Agreement – Negotiations," CSCPRCP, NAS.

[60] Sigrid Schmalzer, "Labor Created Humanity: Cultural Revolution Science on Its Own Terms," in *The Chinese Cultural Revolution as History*, ed. Joseph Esherick, Paul Pickowicz, and Andrew G. Walder (Stanford, CA: Stanford University Press, 2006), 185–210; Danian Hu, "Despite or Due to the Cultural Revolution: The Development of Chinese Science, Technology, and Medicine in the 1960s and 1970s," *Endeavour* 41, no. 3 (September 2017): 78–84; Fan, "Collective Monitoring, Collective Defense."

[61] *CEN*, Volumes 2 and 3, 1974 and 1975 issues; Fang, *Barefoot Doctors and Western Medicine in China*, 99–100.

been praised by British scientists.[62] Other American scientists were interested in the potential application of the PRC's low-tech approach to, for example, insect control, at a time of growing awareness that pesticides were causing environmental damage and becoming less effective due to developing insect resistance: a conference report from the 1975 CSCPRC delegation on the subject was heard by an audience of 2,000 scientists and informed the Berkeley-based entomologist Robert van den Bosch's influential 1978 book *The Pesticide Conspiracy*.[63]

Simultaneously, however, the PRC's blinkered focus on the most advanced American technology in the topics of the delegations they sent to the United States stood out in contrast: by 1976, half of the delegations the PRC had sent to the United States had been concerned with advanced technology, in subjects such as telecommunications, petrochemicals, mining, and agricultural mechanization – all of which had direct, practical application to China's development and modernization.[64] The high-level STAPRC delegation led by Zhou Peiyuan had, in recognition of its status, even been allowed access to institutions focused on thermonuclear fusion, high-energy astrophysics, aerodynamics, and petroleum geotectonics.[65]

By 1976, the STAPRC was showing such a clear preference for visiting commercial firms and industrial laboratories and expressing such limited interest in pure academic research exchange that the Committee on Scholarly Communication had begun to wonder whether many of the delegations received even fell within the purview of a scholarly group.[66] The CSCPRC also quietly suspected China of using the access provided through scientific exchanges to obtain American industrial and commercial secrets (a suspicion shared by some in the US government, even if they seemed less immediately concerned). For example, the PRC had begun to make extensive use of American agricultural mechanization techniques – an area which had seen close Sino-American scholarly collaboration – without

[62] Agar, "It's Springtime for Science," 13.
[63] Knowledge of the problems of pest resistance and chemical toxicity encouraged the PRC's development of biological pest controls. Sigrid Schmalzer, "On the Appropriate Use of Rose-Colored Glasses: Reflections on Science in Socialist China," *Isis* 98, no. 3 (2007): 575; Schmalzer, *Red Revolution, Green Revolution*, 12–13.
[64] CSCPRC, "Discussion of 1976 Exchange Negotiations," January 30, 1976, "1976 – Exchange Agreement – Negotiations," CSCPRCP, NAS.
[65] *CEN*, Vol. 3, No. 4, September 1975; Zhou, *Zhou Peiyuan wenji*, 329, 428.
[66] CSCPRC, "Discussion of 1976 Exchange Negotiations," January 30, 1976, "1976 – Exchange Agreement – Negotiations," CSCPRCP, NAS.

acknowledging the origins of the methods used.[67] Across the Atlantic in the United Kingdom, the Royal Society also considered it to be a "trouble" that China continued to send regular visitors while limiting the number of scientists they received and that they requested to have their scientists "work in forms or organisations affected by defence or commercial security considerations." The focus of requests made to the Royal Society in 1975 overlapped with those made to the CSCPRC, including agricultural research and machine tools. West Germany and France reported similar trends in their scientific exchanges with China.[68]

The Committee on Scholarly Communication believed that China's increased demands, while burdensome, also presented an opportunity. In the wake of Ford's failure to realize change in the exchange program during his summit visit, the Committee consciously moved toward a confrontational position: imposing comparable restrictions on Chinese scientific delegations to the United States as those on American scientists visiting the PRC.[69] The CSCPRC chair, Massachusetts Institute of Technology geophysicist Frank Press, wrote to Han Xu, the deputy head of the PRC Liaison Office. Press forthrightly explained that the Committee "finds it increasingly difficult to operate" within the structure of exchanges insisted on by the Chinese: "Industrial organizations, universities, and individual scientists are reluctant to continue serving as hosts to visiting Chinese guests, frankly questioning a program in which they invest time and effort and see lessening opportunities for reciprocation." Press told Han that it was "imperative" that China agree to receive two more CSCPRC-sponsored delegations in the year ahead; doing so would bring the total number of groups sent and received into equilibrium.[70] Press did not yet reveal the CSCPRC's "back-up position": "that we will allow in only as many groups as the Chinese allow to go to China."[71]

---

[67] For a report directly reporting on US agriculture, compiled in 1978 but based in part on earlier research, see "Guanyu Meiguo siliao de kaocha baogao" [Investigative report regarding US agricultural feed], September 28, 1978, Folder 119-4-13, BJMA. CSCPRC paper, "The future of academic exchanges with the PRC," June 1975, "1975 – Report for Secretary of State," CSCPRCP, NAS; USLO to Kissinger, October 11, 1975, [unmarked folder, likely "China Exchanges, July–Sept 1975"], DFWL, RG59, NACP.

[68] Agar, "It's Springtime for Science," 13.

[69] DeAngelis to Handler, January 8, 1976, "1976 – Exchange Agreement – Negotiations," CSCPRCP, NAS.

[70] Press to Han, January 8, 1976, "1976 – Exchange Agreement – Negotiations," CSCPRCP, NAS.

[71] DeAngelis to Handler, January 8, 1976, "1976 – Exchange Agreement – Negotiations," CSCPRCP, NAS.

The US government had misgivings about the CSCPRC's aggressive stance. US officials were reticent about any action that would reduce the total number of Sino-American exchanges and that might harm the one area of bilateral cooperation in which Chinese leaders were showing an active interest. Press reported to Philip Handler, still president of the National Academy of Sciences, that the State Department was "somewhat unhappy" with the Committee's approach – although the government simultaneously stated its respect for the CSCPRC's independence and confirmed that they would do nothing to prevent the Committee having a free hand in its negotiations.[72] Beijing's response to the CSCPRC's forthrightness was less sympathetic. PRCLO and Zhou Peiyuan refused two Committee on Scholarly Communication requests for an increase in the number of delegations to China from five to seven, pushing the CSCPRC to make good on its threat: the Committee told their Chinese interlocutors that they would postpone two of the PRC's delegations – on mining and agriculture, two areas of particular Chinese interest – until 1977.[73]

For now, Beijing did not blink. Instead, the Chinese government retaliated by threatening to block the only consistent route into China for American social scientists and Sinologists: as translators for exchange delegations. The PRC had long resisted allowing Sinologists of any nationality into the country, fearing that their language skills and specialist knowledge would make them more critical consumers of the carefully choreographed of hosting foreign guests.[74] Since 1973, the CSCPRC had been operating a workaround. If Sinologists could not travel on dedicated delegations, they would instead be sent on all other delegations, traveling alongside colleagues ranging from mathematicians to paleoanthropologists under the cover of acting as translators and what the National Committee called "scholar-escorts" – even though the Chinese side provided their own translators, often (although not always) equipped with superior oral language skills than US scholars with little recent experience of speaking Chinese.[75]

---

[72] Press to Handler, January 22, 1976, "1976 – Exchange Agreement – Negotiations," CSCPRCP, NAS; CSCPRC, "Discussion of 1976 Exchange Negotiations," January 30, 1976, "1976 – Exchange Agreement – Negotiations," CSCPRCP, NAS.
[73] Keatley to Handler, January 23, 1976, and Press and Keatley to Zhou Peiyuan, January 23, 1976, "1976 – Exchange Agreement – Negotiations," CSCPRCP, NAS.
[74] Lovell, "Foreigners in Mao-Era China," 144.
[75] CEN, vol. 1, no. 3, Winter 1973–74, vol. 3, no. 1, March 1975, and vol. 4, no. 3, June 1976; NCUSCR Annual Report, 1976–77, NCUSCROC; Baum, *China Watcher*, 63.

The PRC knew of this practice; indeed, they used scientific delegations to send their own American hands to the United States.[76] Nonetheless, Beijing had made known its resistance indirectly: the historian Frederick Mote, accused of spying and uninvited (and then reinvited) as part of the 1974 CSCPRC linguistics delegation (Chapter 4), was a scholar-escort. Now, Beijing appeared to hit back at the CSCPRC's tough negotiating position by again seeking to defame – and bar – visiting Sinologists. It was in this context that Lloyd Eastman, an historian at the University of Illinois, Urbana, and Ramon Myers, an economist at the Hoover Institution at Stanford, found themselves amid controversy in the unlikely circumstances of a wheat studies delegation. Eastman and Myers had – innocently and spontaneously, they claimed – asked a Chinese geneticist how he was certain that Premier and Chairman-elect Hua Guofeng would not turn out, after all, to be a rightist deviationist. Had not Liu Shaoqi, Lin Biao, and Deng Xiaoping all enjoyed Mao's blessing before their successive falls from grace? Eastman and Myers later claimed that implying that Hua might be next was perhaps the result of the effects of jet lag, but this mea culpa did not satisfy their Chinese hosts who threatened to make Eastman and Myers the last social scientists to take part in the scholar-escort program.[77]

Meanwhile, the National Committee was unable to convince its Chinese interlocutors to cease choking cultural exchanges – a January 1976 meeting with acting PRLCO head Han Xu had little effect – and attempted to reverse its 1975 decision to jettison its public education program to focus exclusively on exchanges.[78] The National Committee thus assumed a supporting role in the most high-profile and successful Sino-American exchange of 1975: the Chinese archaeological delegation previously discussed in Chapter 4. Two million Americans visited the tour's host museums in San Francisco, Kansas City, and Washington, DC, and the NCUSCR ensured thousands more Americans benefitted from the exchange through a travel grant scheme that paid for 122 American scholars to visit the exhibitions and then host talks and slideshows

[76] Correspondence with Mary Brown Bullock, by email, January 9, 2019; Baum, *China Watcher*, 64.

[77] The Chinese had quietly dropped this hanging threat by the next year. Eastman and Myers to Keatley, June 20, 1976, "Eastman, Lloyd E." folder, Box 5, NASAR, BHL; Solomon, "Evening Report – PRC," June 16, 1976, "June 10–29, 1976" folder, Box 42, NSCEAPASF, GFL; *CEN*, Vol. 5, No. 1, February 1977.

[78] Minutes of 30th meeting of NCUSCR executive committee, February 13, 1976, "Board of Directors Meeting, 21 May 1976 [*sic*]," Box 131, ADBP.

in their local communities. Nonetheless, this was a diminished role, and the NCUSCR's income for the financial year ending in September 1976 was down more than a third.[79]

Just as the CSCPRC's confrontational approach to negotiations over exchanges had not ended the State Department's backing of that organization, renewed Chinese cold-shouldering of the National Committee did not dilute US government support for the group. A small but telling example was Ford personally meeting the NCUSCR-hosted delegation of female basketball players that had toured five American cities (and Disneyland) in November 1975. The Chinese team faced off against opponents from women's college basketball and the US National Women's Team soon after the latter's gold-medal triumph at the Pan American games. The Chinese visitors' games were watched by some 24,000 Americans – breaking records for audiences for women's basketball. In Washington, Winston Lord thought that a presidential welcome went beyond the courtesy being shown to US delegations in Beijing in 1975, but Solomon won the day by arguing that, even if Beijing's treatment of Americans had changed, the US government should maintain the protocol afforded to previous NCUSCR delegations in order to protect the National Committee's standing. Ford's time meeting the basketball players was not wasted: as we will see in the following chapter, the National Committee's prominence in cultural exchanges would be restored in 1977.[80]

That year would also see the Committee on Scholarly Communication's hard bargaining over scientific exchange bear fruit when, in February, Beijing proposed a balanced annual program of six scientific delegations in each direction, a numerically small but nonetheless significant switch from the previous ratio of five to seven in Beijing's favor.[81] Only still-inaccessible Chinese documents from the Scientific and Technical Association of the PRC and the Foreign Ministry can reveal the role of the CSCPRC's confrontational stance in this decision. Certainly, there were other factors at work. Mao's death on September 9, 1976, enthroned Hua Guofeng as the PRC's foremost leader and Hua immediately used his new power to purge the radical Gang of Four. Those far-left leaders had spent the previous decade decrying all foreign interaction

[79] NCUSCR Annual Report, 1975–76, NCUSCROC.
[80] *NFTNC*, Vol. 5, Nos. 3 & 4 [*sic*], Winter 1975; Solomon to Scowcroft, November 22, 1975, "China Exchanges, October–Dec. 1975," DFWL, RG59, NACP.
[81] *CEN*, Vol. 5, No. 1, February 1977.

and had served as a perennial counterweight to those in Beijing that sought to expand contacts such as the Sino-American exchange program. Their influence on China's science policy was still being felt even as Mao passed: a report from the day following the chairman's death described how, when receiving scientists from the West German Max Planck Society, Chinese hosts should continue to celebrate Cultural Revolution-era science policies such as that of "open-door research" (开门办科研), in which scientists shared their laboratories with workers, peasants, and soldiers – a practice Deng had been pushing back against before his purge in January 1976. After the Gang of Four were put behind bars in October 1976, however, Hua soon committed his government to greater openness to the outside world; a more active program of exchanges for 1977 was a corollary of this.[82]

What is clear, however, is that the Committee on Scholarly Communication had successfully established the terms on which expanded scientific contacts would take place. Over the next two years and beyond, Hua and Deng would both seek to use scientific cooperation with the United States as an important input to the Four Modernizations program proposed by Zhou Enlai and adopted by post-Mao leaders.[83] The CSCPRC had, through tough bargaining and a readiness to curtail American assistance, ensured that this would be a more balanced and mutually beneficial partnership than the lopsided interaction of the mid-1970s. The organization had also set an example to its government: by dissenting from Ford's willingness to provide the Chinese with access to American science at no political cost, the CSCPRC suggested that an even more significant breakthrough could be achieved by leveraging Chinese interest in American science to strengthen the US negotiating position in normalization talks.

KNOTS AND NOOSES

A breakthrough in negotiations between American exchange organizations and the PRC had to wait, then, until 1977. In the meantime, little

---

[82] Shanghai Municipal Revolutionary Committee Science and Technology Group, "Guanyu jiedai XiDe Makesi Pulangke xiehui Shitelaobo deng si wei kexuejia jihua de qingshi baogao" [Request for instructions on the plan to receive four scientists including the West German Max Planck Society member Straub], September 10, 1976, Folder C42-2-77, SHMA; Vogel, *Deng*, 188–190.

[83] ZGZYWXYJS, *Zhou Enlai xuanji*, 2:479; ZGZYWXYJS, *Deng Xiaoping sixiang nianbian*, 1.

progress was made in government-to-government talks. During Ford's final year in office, domestic distractions to both governments became more acute: Ford faced a serious primary challenge from Governor Ronald Reagan – with the president's China policy one major line of criticism – and Beijing was rocked by the deaths of Zhou and, then, Mao. Thus, the only notable episodes in Sino-American relations that took place during 1976 arose from China visits by American politicians from outside of the executive branch.

The second half of 1976 saw three high-ranking congressional delegations travel to the PRC. In July, Senate Minority Leader Hugh Scott returned to China, having previously led the first congressional delegation to the PRC in 1972. Scott's traveling companion on that earlier trip, Senate Majority Leader Mike Mansfield, separately revisited the PRC in September 1976 – Mansfield's third visit since 1972 – before another six senators traveled together in November, led by Senator Carl Curtis.[84] Congressional delegations to China were, by 1976, regular: two had traveled in 1972, one in 1973, three in 1974, and another three in 1975. But such visits were not so frequent that a place on them was not prized, both as the means to see the much-vaunted Middle Kingdom and as an indication of the guest's relative importance among peers.[85] Beijing saw an opportunity in the strong interest of US congressmen to visit the PRC. During the tense negotiations of Kissinger's October 1975 visit, both sides had agreed to maintain a rate of one official congressional delegation a year traveling to China.[86] That the actual figure for 1976 exceeded this several times over was revealing of Chinese willingness to allow a greater number of exchanges when doing so served their interests, rather than just those of the US government or American nongovernmental organizations. While governmental relations were fraught, Beijing did not want the Ford administration to draw benefit from these contacts and the PRC did not arrange additional congressional delegations through the White House. Indeed, when, in January 1976, Kissinger's aides suggested a date for the officially arranged annual congressional visit for the coming year, they found that their suggestion of April had been pre-empted by Beijing having already independently invited a congressional group for that

---

[84] *NFTNC*, Vol. 6, No. 4, December 1976.
[85] See, for example, lobbying by Senator John Sparkman in April 1976. Solomon to Friedersdorf, April 27, 1976, "April 28–30, 1976," Box 41, NSCEAPASF, GFL.
[86] Memcon: Han, Lord, Gleysteen, and Solomon, January 30, 1976, "China Exchanges, October–Dec. 1975," DFWL, RG59, NACP.

month – to be led by a Democrat, Representative Melvin Price of Illinois – without even informing, let alone consulting, the White House.[87]

The Chinese government was organizing other notable visits without the US government's involvement or approval, too. In December 1975, an ailing Zhou received as one of his final foreign guests Julie Nixon Eisenhower, the former president's daughter, and her husband, the equally blue-blooded David Eisenhower. The couple were afforded many privileges during their stay, including a meeting with Mao and discussions with Deng Xiaoping in which the vice premier lamented China's economic weakness.[88] Beijing showed further appreciation for the Nixon family when Mao received the former president himself in February 1976.[89] The trip had been arranged behind the back of the Ford administration when PRC Liaison Office head Huang Zhen had secretly traveled to Nixon's California home in August 1975.[90] Nixon's visit was calculated by Beijing to publicly contrast the dramatic breakthroughs in Sino-American relations achieved under the former president with the slowdown in governmental relations under his successor: in a cutting dismissal of Ford's summit trip of December 1975, an internal Chinese party publication claimed that Nixon's visit was "the most noteworthy event in U.S.-PRC relations since the establishment of liaison offices in 1973," while also reveling in the claim that, as "a direct result" of Nixon's presence in Beijing, Ford had lost votes in the New Hampshire presidential primary contest with Reagan.[91] The trip had also been an opportunity for Beijing to rehash old arguments in exchange diplomacy: Jiang Qing treated the Nixons to a performance of "Taiwan Compatriots, Our Flesh and Blood," the controversial song at the heart of the 1975 cancellation of the Chinese performing arts troupe delegation (Chapter 4). In spite of Jiang's thunderous applause, Nixon rose off his seat only enough to avoid disrespecting his host; Pat Nixon, however, fell for Jiang's ploy and gave a standing ovation.[92]

[87] Kissinger to USLO, January 31, 1976, "China Exchanges, October–Dec. 1975," DFWL, RG59, NACP.
[88] ZGZYWXYJS, *Mao Zedong nianpu, 1949–1976*, 6:630–32; ZGZYWXYJS, *Deng Xiaoping sixiang nianbian*, 46.
[89] ZGZYWXYJS, *Mao Zedong nianpu, 1949–1976*, 6:638–39.
[90] Solomon to Kissinger, August 23, 1975, "August 1975," Box 40, NSCEAPASF, GFL.
[91] Solomon, "Evening report – PRC," June 22, 1976, "June 10–29, 1976" folder, Box 42, NSCEAPASF, GFL.
[92] Solomon, "Briefing Item," February 23, 1976, "February 1976," Box 41, NSCEAPASF, GFL.

The White House's reaction to Nixon's trip was complex. On the one hand, the government recognized that Nixon's travel had been an embarrassing reminder of lackluster Sino-American ties under Ford and shared Beijing's view that it had hurt the president politically. On the other hand, Solomon read the trip as a reassuring indication of continuing Chinese interest in rapprochement: Beijing would hardly have bothered to bring Nixon and his significant secret service detail over to the PRC if Chinese interest in rapprochement had truly ceased.[93]

Senator Scott's congressional delegation to China in July had the formal approval and support of the White House that the unofficial trips by the Nixon family lacked. This officiality may help explain why the trip proved so fractious. The more cordial moments of the visit offered further reminders of the changing focus of Sino-American relations: Scott's senior-most host at his farewell banquet was physicist Zhou Peiyuan, who was also involved in the discussions between Scott and Foreign Minister Qiao Guanhua.[94] The less cordial moments were reminders of acerbic high-level relations. Scott had made his return to China – his twelfth trip, after wartime service in the Pacific and his 1972 visit – on a presidential plane, bearing a letter of introduction from Ford, and, he publicly claimed on the president's "request."[95] In spite of the air of formality this lent to the envoy, Thomas S. Gates Jr., the new USLO chief, had been careful to warn the senator that his visit did not come at an opportune moment for discussing sensitive matters of substance with his Chinese interlocutors. Ignoring this warning and spurned on by his companion Robert Barnett – by then director of the Asia Society, which had taken over the NCUSCR's public education programming the year prior – Scott had self-importantly (and incorrectly) informed politburo standing committee-member Zhang Chunqiao that the letter from Ford provided him personal authority to negotiate the key issues in Sino-American relations, including the status of Taiwan.[96] Zhang's response to Scott's attempt to

[93] Ibid.

[94] "Sikete canyiyuan he furen zai Jing juxing gaobie yanhui" [Senator Scott and his wife held a farewell banquet in Beijing], *Renmin Ribao*, July 15, 1976; "Qiao Guanhua waizhang huijian bing yanqing Meiguo canyiyuan Gonghedang lingxiu Sikete he furen" [Foreign Minister Qiao Guanhua met and hosted a banquet for the Senate Republican leader Scott and his wife], *Renmin Ribao*, July 13, 1976.

[95] Solomon to Scowcroft, June 22, 1976, "May 27–28, 1976," Box 41, NSCEAPASF, GFL; "Hugh Scott to Visit China July 10–24," *Washington Post*, July 3, 1976.

[96] Gates to Kissinger, July 13, 1975, "Memorandums," Box 4, Subject Files, 1969–1978, RG59, NACP; "Zhang Chunqiao fuzongli huijian Meiguo canyiyuan Gonghedang

re-open talks over Taiwan was stark: he made clear that there would be no negotiation whatsoever with the United States over the island and that the renegade province could only be liberated by force. In what Scott later described to Ford as a "chilling" comment, Zhang went as far as describing Taiwan as "a noose around the neck of the United States" – and threatened that, if the United States did not take the noose off, the Chinese army would gladly "cut it off."[97]

In pushing his Chinese hosts on Taiwan, Scott was only doing what dozens of senators and congressmen thought the executive branch should be doing. As the Nixon–Mao summit receded into the past, and with images of South Vietnam's final collapse fresh in American minds, a groundswell of political and public opinion had risen up in 1975 and 1976 that held that the Ford administration was too meek in accepting Beijing's line on Taiwan: a *New York Times* editorial from June had argued for finding ways to improve relations with the PRC "short of abandoning 14 million Taiwanese."[98] This public mood was powerfully demonstrated in August 1976 when, much to the discomfort of the White House, the Republican Party added to the party's official platform for that year's election explicit support for "the freedom and independence of our friend and ally, the Republic of China."[99] By October, the Republican governor of Pennsylvania, William Scranton, had gone as far as saying that Taiwan was a sovereign nation and should be invited back to the UN. Under this pressure from within his own party, Ford himself even publicly – and incorrectly – implied that the Shanghai Communiqué had included a commitment by the PRC to use peaceful means to reunify the country.[100] Beijing had not failed to notice the renewed support for the Republic of China among the US government and influential Americans, while also continuing to observe Americans' lingering habit of confusing the PRC and ROC – something documented by Zhou Peiyuan during his 1975 trip to the United States.[101] Thus, for the same reason that Scott felt

lingxiu Sikete" [Vice Premier Zhang Chunqiao meets with US Senate Republican leader Scott], *Renmin Ribao*, July 14, 1976.

[97] Bush to Kissinger, July 14, 1976, "China, unnumbered items (31) 12–14 July 1976," Box 6, Kissinger-Scowcroft West Wing Office Files, 1974–77 (KSWWOF1974-77), GFL.

[98] "The China Knot," *New York Times*, June 17, 1976.

[99] "1976 Republican Platform: United States-Chinese Relations," available at www.fordlibrarymuseum.gov/library/document/platform/china.htm. Accessed June 21, 2021.

[100] Memcon: Qiao, Kissinger, et al., October 8, 1976, *FRUS, 1969–1976*, Vol. XVIII, Document 157.

[101] Zhou, *Zhou Peiyuan wenji*, 136; Memcon: Huang Zhen, Kissinger, et al., August 18, 1976, *FRUS, 1969–1976*, Vol. XVIII, Document 152.

confident taking a forthright position on the issue, his Chinese interlocutors found themselves compelled to bite back fiercely against this reverse tide in American public discourse.

The Scott incident was another example of the unresolved contradiction, present throughout both the Nixon and Ford years, between the White House's desire to build political support for the Sino-American relationship on the Hill while also preserving complete control over negotiations with Beijing. Ford knew from his own 1972 trip how visiting the PRC could help build political support for rapprochement (Chapter 4).[102] But senior figures like Scott – leader of the Republicans in the Senate, as well as a long-time friend of China and of rapprochement – expected to be able to hold frank, meaningful talks with their Chinese interlocutors while on such trips, just as Senator Magnuson had assumed would be possible (Chapter 3). Since Nixon's resignation, Kissinger had further exacerbated this tension: in his attempts to find some kind of flexibility in normalization negotiations, the secretary of state had used congressional visits as a way of testing the water for future negotiating positions. In 1975, the State Department had briefed politicians traveling to China with novel formulations on the Taiwan problem to slip into conversation to measure the Chinese response. Simultaneously, Kissinger would personally tell the Chinese that these same delegations had no authority to negotiate, thereby distancing himself from any adverse reaction from Beijing. The passivity of US China policy since the Ford summit seems to have meant that Scott himself had not been tasked with sounding his interlocutor out over Taiwan – he did so on his own volition. Nonetheless, it was unsurprising that Chinese leaders eventually reacted angrily to propositions which contradicted Beijing's firmly stated stance on the issue.[103]

If Kissinger's approach to Congressional exchanges was flawed, Beijing's approach often achieved the PRC's desired ends. Shaken by Zhang's acerbic rhetoric about a noose around an American neck, Scott returned from China newly conscious of Beijing's opposition to the United States maintaining active relations with regimes on both sides of the Taiwan Strait. His report to the Senate, submitted in early 1977, argued that the United States "should press ahead with the process of cutting the Gordian knot" with Taiwan – consciously or unconsciously continuing Zhang's

---

[102] Boggs and Ford, *Impressions of the New China.*
[103] Talking points, drafted by Brooks, included in materials for July 22, 1975 meeting, "1973 Briefing" [*sic*], Subject Files, 1969–1978, RG59, NACP.

motif of ties to be severed – and soon after the November election he publicly advocated that the Carter administration should finalize normalization where Ford had not.[104] Huang Zhen could hardly hide his satisfaction when asking a sultry Kissinger what he made of Scott's report.[105] Other senators that traveled on congressional delegations during the Ford era were also influenced by their experiences in China. After Senator Byrd returned from his 1975 visit, he told Ford that, although he "went there somewhat antagonistic," he had come home "impressed" by a China "not a threat to our way of life" and with which "we have much in common" – not least, "countering the Soviet Union" (although Byrd also said he would "put my money" on China outstripping the Soviets in the long run, with a concurring Kissinger adding that the PRC "could be a pretty scary outfit" within twenty years).[106]

Ford's promised sale of computers to China came four months after Scott's visit and the month after Mao's death and was the only notable step forward in the government-to-government relationship in 1976. After a Chinese request to buy the most powerful computer manufactured by Burroughs Corporation had been refused in May – in spite of Kissinger working with Burroughs's chairman, Ray MacDonald, to realize a sale – August saw government approval of the sale of a Control Data Corporation system intended for seismic oil exploration.[107] Assistant Secretary of State Arthur Hummel was sure to make clear in a meeting at the PRC Liaison Office that the sale had been "exceptional" and that "administrative difficulties" had only been overcome because of the agreement made between Deng and the president.[108] Deng had been purged before the sale materialized, but he would soon return to the Chinese government and redouble his efforts to gain access to the benefits of American science.

Despite honoring the promise to provide powerful computers to the PRC, Kissinger had abandoned hope of moving relations forward before the election. In October, he admitted to Foreign Minister Qiao that,

[104] Hugh Scott, *The United States and China: A Report* (Washington, DC: United States Government Printing Office, 1976); "Hugh Scott Says He Urged Ford to Cut Taiwan Tie," *New York Times*, August 18, 1977.

[105] Memcon: Huang, Kissinger, et al., August 18, 1976, *FRUS, 1969–1976*, Vol. XVIII, Document 152.

[106] Memcon: Ford, Senator Byrd CoDel participants, September 8, 1975, [unmarked folder, likely "China Exchanges, July–Sept. 1975"], DFWL, RG59, NACP.

[107] Habib and Greenwald to Kissinger, May 10, 1976, "1974–78 NSD 246 and 247," Subject Files, 1969–1978, RG59, NACP.

[108] Aubert to USLO, October 21, 1976, "China, unnumbered items (36) 12–29 October 1976," KSWWOF1974–77, GFL.

"speaking frankly, there has been a certain deterioration in our relationship." The secretary lamented that it was a "mistake" for there not to be more active societal contacts. "Whose fault is it?", asked Qiao. "Frankly, it depends on your viewpoint," Kissinger argued, "if you say there can be no progress in this area until normalization, then the fault lies with us. But if you say that we need to progress in this area to create the basis for normalization, then we both have responsibility."[109] It was one of Kissinger's final interchanges with a Chinese interlocutor before he left office – and a stark departure from his earlier bullishness about the comparative insignificance of exchanges when compared to Sino-American strategic cooperation.

CONCLUSION

The twilight of the Ford and Kissinger era had seen all vitality sapped from Sino-American state-to-state negotiations over normalization. Into that vacuum had flowed other actors and interactions: the Committee on Scholarly Communication had negotiated hard with their Chinese interlocutors about what the PRC should offer in return for their unfettered access to American science, while Senator Scott sought to conduct his own independent negotiations with leaders in Beijing. Scott was bluntly rebuffed and the CSCPRC did not achieve their immediate objectives – although, as the next chapter will show, their efforts had not been in vain. Indeed, the period between the Ford summit of December 1975 and Carter's inauguration in January 1977 would, in spite of the deadlock in normalization negotiations, ultimately prove to be a transitional moment. Critical elements of the relationship that emerged in this period – above all, active and deepening scientific cooperation negotiated by both non-governmental and governmental actors – would rapidly develop during Carter's time in office and soon play an important role in the exchange and diplomatic relationship.

Nor did the strained atmospherics of the high-level relationship in this period wholly poison mutual goodwill during exchange encounters. In October 1976, while Qiao and Kissinger threw mutual accusations at one-another, Chinese and American volleyball players ended a game in Berkeley with a spontaneous exchange of shirts to cheers from an audience

---

[109] Memcon: Qiao, Kissinger, et al., October 8, 1976, *FRUS, 1969–1976*, Vol. XVIII, Document 157.

of 7,000 spectators.[110] The next month, a delegation of American gymnasts concluded a successful tour of China weighed down with thirty bags of souvenirs from a country that had enchanted them.[111] At the very same time, a Chinese astronomy delegation was being welcomed into a Texan home to sample enchiladas, refried beans, and apple pie, seated alongside the children and families of their American colleagues.[112] The hard work of the NCUSCR and CSCPRC in executing these successful exchanges – even as their negotiations with Beijing became strained – continued to build American public support for rapprochement, irrespective of the condition of high-level governmental contacts.

---

[110] "Wo paiqiu daibiaotuan fangwen Meiguo" [Our volleyball Delegation Visited the United States], *Renmin Ribao*, October 14, 1976; *NFTNC*, Vol. 6, No. 4, December 1976.

[111] de Keijzer, "U.S. Gymnastics Delegation to China," January 1, 1977, "NCUSCR, 1976–77," Box 131, ADBP, RBMLCU.

[112] *CEN*, vol. 4, no. 6, December 1976.

6

Political Science

Jimmy Carter was elected as the forty-eighth US president less than a month after China's radical quadrumvirate, the Gang of Four, had been arrested. The near-simultaneous changing of the guard in Beijing and Washington in October and November 1976 was to have a profound impact on Sino-American relations. The positive developments that were to follow were anticipated in the very first moments of the Carter presidency, when Chinese hosts provided radios to members of a National Committee gymnastics delegation touring China, tuning the devices to the Voice of America so that the gymnasts could list to election results being counted at home – despite the PRC government's official ban on the station within its borders. During the same visit, an accompanying State Department representative was permitted to spend hours wandering around Shanghai photographing the big character posters that used a different medium to herald China's own political changes of late 1976.[1]

The Gang of Four was, in the short term, replaced by Hua Guofeng, but their downfall soon cleared the way for the return of Deng Xiaoping. Hua's enthronement and Deng's return paved the way for closer Chinese engagement with the outside world. Equally importantly, this chapter will show, Carter's election brought new thinking and personnel to US China policy. In 1977 and 1978, policymakers in Washington paid increasing attention to how Chinese leaders – in particular, Deng – were urgently seeking access to US scientific knowledge and technology

---

[1] de Keijzer, "U.S. Gymnastics Delegation to China," January 1, 1977, "NCUSCR, 1976–77," Box 131, ADBP, RBMLCU.

in order to expedite China's modernization. This interest manifested most consistently through the transnational scientific relationship and the exchange program, as well as in Chinese requests to buy US technology. Prompted by American scientists, Carter's administration would ask a higher price for this access than Ford or Kissinger had. Where Ford and Kissinger had promised Deng US computers without asking anything in return, Carter's lead foreign policy advisor, Zbigniew Brzezinski, worked with the top American scientists within and beyond the US government to link scientific assistance for Deng's urgent modernization efforts to diplomatic negotiations toward normalization – an innovation that helped to secure a final agreement in December 1978, on US terms. Meanwhile, the CSCPRC played the central role in facilitating the scientific cooperation promised by Brzezinski, managing a rapidly expanding exchange program, preparing for the beginning of student exchanges, and advising the US government on which areas of Chinese science would offer the most fecund ground for deeper Sino-American cooperation. Thus, as had been the case with the initial breakthrough rapprochement under Nixon and Mao, it was a combination of governmental and nongovernmental actors that helped realize Carter and Deng's final normalization agreement of 1978.

ONE STEP BACKWARD

Carter ultimately achieved great success in upgrading both the diplomatic and exchange relationships between the United States and China. This outcome seemed an unlikely one in 1977, however. While one of Ford's very first actions upon entering the White House had been to affirm his commitment to Sino-American rapprochement as it had been constructed under his predecessor, Carter showed no haste in making such an assurance. Indeed, the president-elect initially caused alarm in Beijing when he called Chiang's regime on Taiwan "China" in a *Time* magazine interview and pledged to maintain the island's independence from the PRC.[2] Ambiguity about the US relationship with Taipei was accompanied by uncertainty within the administration about how to square rapprochement with Carter's interest in human rights: one of the new administration's

---

[2] Brzezinski to Carter, February 4, 1977, "MR-NLC-98-215," Box 40, China Vertical File (CVF), JCL; Memcon: Huang, Kissinger, January 8, 1977, David P. Nickles, ed., *Foreign Relations of the United States, 1977–1980*, vol. XIII, China (Washington, DC: United States Government Printing Office, 2013), Document 2.

earliest memoranda on China concerned the PRC's forced labor camps that detained perhaps hundreds of thousands of Chinese citizens.[3] A month after Carter took office, the US-China Peoples Friendship Association had grown sufficiently concerned with the new president's China stance that they asked all of their 7,000 members to make use of Carter's appearance on a phone-in TV talk show to directly and publicly ask him why he was not pursuing normalization more ardently.[4]

The challenges posed to rapprochement by Carter's uncertainty toward China policy were offset by who the new president recruited to manage relations with Beijing. While the broached idea of Kissinger remaining as secretary of state was ultimately rejected, a remarkable number of Carter's China team already had direct experience of dealing with the PRC – through the exchange program and the Committees that oversaw it. Kissinger's replacement as secretary of state, Cyrus Vance, had first traveled to China as head of the National Committee's international affairs delegation in October 1975 (Chapter 5). In the secretary of state's first meeting with Foreign Minister Huang Hua, Vance recalled how that trip had strongly shaped his understanding of the PRC. Another of Carter's cabinet appointments, W. Michael Blumenthal, had even closer links with the NCUSCR. Blumenthal's family had fled to Shanghai during the Second World War, where he had lived under Japanese occupation in the Shanghai ghetto. The Chinese he had learned there, including the Shanghai dialect, had been one reason for him being selected to chair the National Committee from 1972 to 1975. He was still on the NCUSCR's board when Carter made him his treasury secretary.[5] Other National Committee members appointed to Carter's staff included NCUSCR board member Michel Oksenberg, who became lead China advisor to the National Security Council, and Leonard Woodcock, Carter's choice to head up the US Liaison Office in Beijing. (All National Committee members appointed to government office became temporarily inactive within that group while in public service.) The rotating door between the NCUSCR and US foreign policymaking simultaneously swung in the other

[3] Oksenberg to Brzezinski, June 20, 1977, RACP: NLC-15-41-6-1-3, JCL.

[4] USCPFA National Normalization Committee to all USCPFA locals and organizing committees, February 23, 1977, Folder 8, Box 1, USCPFAR, NYPLAMD.

[5] *NFTNC*, Vol. 7, No. 1, March 1977; Memcon: Huang, Kissinger, January 8, 1977, *FRUS, 1977–1980*, Vol. XIII, Document 2; W. Michael Blumenthal, *From Exile to Washington: A Memoir of Leadership in the Twentieth Century* (New York: The Overlook Press, 2013), especially 66–115, 244–67.

direction: Oksenberg replaced Richard Solomon at the NSC, and Wood-cock took up the post held by Thomas Gates and previously by George Bush; in turn, Solomon, Gates, and Bush all became NCUSCR members soon after leaving office, with Solomon and Barbara Bush, George's wife, joining the Committee's board.[6]

The number of Carter appointees drawn from the higher ranks of the National Committee again demonstrated the nexus between that group and official China policy. Ultimately of even greater significance, how-ever, was Carter's recruitment from the Committee on Scholarly Com-munication with the PRC. The president made the chair of that group, Frank Press, his lead science advisor. Press was one of the brightest lights in American science: he had discovered how to measure earthquakes out at sea and designed the seismographs that American astronauts had placed on the moon. But his qualifications for leading, first, the CSCPRC and, then, the White House's Office of Science and Technology Policy went beyond his research: Press was also an effective political opera-tor. Seismology was the key to monitoring underground nuclear tests, and this had won a thirty-three-year-old Press pride of place in disarma-ment negotiations with Soviet nuclear specialists during a 1958 Geneva summit.[7]

Press, whose mother had once lived in the northeastern Chinese city of Harbin, had first traveled to the PRC when he led a Committee on Scholarly Communication seismology delegation there in 1974.[8] Seismol-ogy was also one of the PRC's most active scientific disciplines in the 1970s: it was one of the few subjects that fit within the epistemic val-ues of both the Cultural Revolution focus on applied, "people's" science and the more orthodox basic scientific research that Chinese scientists increasingly returned to over the course of the decade – and that was of more interest to elite American scientists. As Fa-ti Fan has shown, after the 1966 Xingtai earthquake killed 8,000, Zhou Enlai visited the disas-ter site and launched a "war against earthquakes" through which the PRC attempted to master the ability to accurately predict major quakes. A State Seismological Bureau was founded in 1971, and the number of local seismological stations increased from just a handful to some 250 by

[6] NCUSCR Annual Report, 1976–77, NCUSCROC.

[7] "President's Science Adviser: Frank Press," *New York Times*, May 19, 1977.

[8] Interview of Frank Press by Ronald Doel on July 1, 1997, Niels Bohr Library and Archives, American Institute of Physics, College Park, MD, United States, electronic ver-sion available at www.aip.org/history-programs/niels-bohr-library/oral-histories/6929-1. Accessed December 13, 2021.

the mid-1970s. China's massive investment in seismology attracted the attention of American scientists such as Press, who had long been keen to add China's vast territorial space to their global seismological data sets and were at the time, like their Chinese counterparts, interested in the possibility of earthquake prediction. That interest had only intensified after China's seismologists successfully predicted the 1975 Haicheng earthquake, saving as many as 100,000 lives. (Although the failure to then predict the far more devastating Tangshan earthquake of the following year had dented the reputation of Chinese seismology.)[9]

Press joined the White House directly after two years chairing the CSCPRC, in which he had led the organization's strained but ultimately successful negotiations with Beijing over imbalances in the exchange program (Chapter 5).[10] He took with him into the White House his closest colleague at the Committee, Anne Keatley. Having served as staff director of the Committee on Scholarly Communication since the early 1970s – taking up the role when that was the CSCPRC's only full-time staff position – Keatley entered government in 1977 as perhaps the American with the single-most experience negotiating scientific cooperation with the PRC. Together, these two hires anticipated the central role that China would play in Carter's science policy and the critical role that science would have in Carter's China policy. Press and Keatley's official appointments also transferred years of nongovernmental experience of negotiating scientific cooperation with China into the White House; soon, the government would adopt a strategy in negotiating scientific cooperation with Beijing that was deeply similar to that pursued by the CSCPRC while under Press and Keatley's leadership.[11]

Even before Carter's new appointees had their feet under the table, cultural exchanges were recovering after the perilous years of the Ford ere. The National Committee's seven exchanges for 1977 constituted the largest annual package of contacts the organization had ever overseen and was, Doak Barnett commented to NCUSCR President Rosen, "certainly the most

---

[9] Fan reports that some Chinese seismologists claimed to have detected warning signs of the Tangshan earthquake but that these were ignored. Fan, "'Collective Monitoring, Collective Defense'," 131–34, 147–48; Schmalzer, "Reflections on Science in Socialist China," 576; "Report on the Visit of the Chinese Seismology Delegation, April 19, 1974–May 20, 1974," "Bullock, Mary" folder, Box 2, NASAR, BHL.
[10] Keatley to Handler, January 14, 1975, "1975 – General," CSCPRCP, NAS; "President's Science Adviser," *New York Times*.
[11] Author interview with Anne Solomon (previously Keatley); CEN, Vol. 5, No. 1, February 1977.

encouraging development affecting the National Committee for a very long time."[12] The exchanges would cover a range of themes: sporting tours by an American tennis team and a Chinese soccer team, an education delegation in each direction, and a group of up-and-coming young American politicians. A third National Committee board delegation was scheduled for October, and, perhaps most significantly of all, the NCUSCR would, in June, host a delegation from the Chinese People's Institute of Foreign Affairs, the first time the organization had sent a delegation to any foreign country. Among the lowest ranked members of that delegation was a Foreign Ministry staff member who also acted as an interpreter: a twenty-seven-year-old Yang Jie-chi, later Chinese ambassador to the United States, Foreign Minister – and today the highest-ranking foreign policymaker under Xi Jinping.[13]

The Committee on Scholarly Communication had a full program planned for 1977, too. Six groups would travel in either direction that year, finally bringing the number of delegations the organization was permitted to send to China in line with the number it was asked to receive. American astronomists, linguists, and cancer specialists would go in one direction, while China sent chemists, metrologists, and three delegations with a more applied focus: on geological drilling, tunnel boring, and hematite ore beneficiation.[14] The CSCPRC had been deeply relieved to achieve this parity in exchange numbers: Robert Lumiansky, the president of the American Council of Learned Societies, told the *New York Times* in June 1977 that the CSCPRC had come close to pulling out of the exchange program altogether before the Scientific and Technical Association of the PRC had finally addressed the Committee's complaints.[15]

If the parity in the number of exchanges in each direction mollified the CSCPRC, the organization was still receiving complaints from key US institutions – MIT, the National Bureau of Standards, AT&T's Bell Laboratories – that the PRC was offering few opportunities for their researchers while continuing to make great demands on American hosts. Sympathetic to this pressure, in 1977, the CSCPRC again pushed for changes that would increase the scientific value of exchanges. One

[12] Barnett to Rosen, April 15, 1977, "NCUSCR, 1976–77," Box 131, ADBP, RBMLCU.
[13] "Meiguo wuqing Wansi huijian wo waijiao xuehui daibiaotuan" [US Secretary of State Vance meets with the delegation of the Chinese People's Institute of Foreign Affairs], *Renmin Ribao*, June 30, 1977; NCUSCR Annual Report, 1976–77, NCUSCROC.
[14] *CEN*, Vol. 5, No. 1, February 1977; *CEN*, Vol. 7, No. 1, February 1979.
[15] "China Rebuffs U.S. Bid to Widen Scholarly & Scientific Visits," *New York Times*, June 29, 1977.

alteration urgently sought was curtailing China's tendency to use all exchanges, irrespective of ostensible subject matter, as "opportunities to demonstrate the achievements of the PRC" through days of sightseeing at historical sites and model factories and communes and evenings in front of China's latest model operas.[16] Such sightseeing hardly maximized opportunities for scientific cooperation and was notoriously burdensome: a group of Teamster Union labor officials planning an exchange in 1976 had been told to expect an itinerary that was "extremely arduous and taxing to the extent that many travelers have been unable to endure its physical demands." The participants in that trip were made to obtain medical certificates that certified they were fit "for long hours on [their] feet, little rest and constant activity."[17]

As well as seeking to reduce the nonacademic content of visits to China, the CSCPRC also intensified its efforts to begin ongoing research collaboration. The group took heart from the recent success of James Andreasen, an aquaculturalist who worked on the US government's hydroelectric dams, in initiating an exchange of fish specimens with the Chinese Academy of Sciences in October 1976.[18] However, the Chinese government remained a suspicious collaborator. Chinese scientists had previously brought seed samples to the United States to exchange with American scientists but seed samples taken to China by the 1976 CSCPRC wheat studies delegation had been largely destroyed by Chinese authorities because of their (likely unfounded) fears of smut fungus spore contamination.[19] Other scientific delegations were often kept away from the Chinese specialists they would benefit most from meeting: a delegation focused on schistosomiasis, or snail fever, was barred from seeing the same snail colonies that their hosts showed a group of American doctors a week later, while a medical delegation that included American psychiatrists met no Chinese psychiatrists, even though a delegation of surgeons did.[20]

---

[16] He, *Dangdai Zhong Mei minjian jiaoliu shi*, 136; DeAngelis, CSCPRC press release on interdisciplinary delegation to China, June 1977, "1977 – Visits – Committee Visit on Scholarly Exchanges," CSCPRCP, NAS.

[17] William Nuchow to members of the China trip, May 19, 1976, Folder 12, Box 1, WNP, TLWLANYU.

[18] *CEN*, Vol. 5, No. 1, February 1977.

[19] For more details on Chinese concerns about the risks of contamination from American smut fungus, see Folder B135-4-649, SHMA; Gold, "Critical Juncture," Chapter 5; DeAngelis, CSCPRC press release on interdisciplinary delegation to China, June 1977, "1977 – Visits – Committee Visit on Scholarly Exchanges," CSCPRCP, NAS.

[20] DeAngelis, CSCPRC press release on interdisciplinary delegation to China, June 1977, "1977 – Visits – Committee Visit on Scholarly Exchanges," CSCPRCP, NAS.

If frustrations continued to be felt about American access to Chinese science, there was also, in 1977, cause for hope in scientific contacts. In May of that year, an exchange delegation from Rockefeller University invited their Chinese hosts to reverse the dynamic of previous scholarly interchanges and to ask questions of their visitors, rather than listen to the Americans give a one-way monologue. Frederick Seitz, the president of the university, was overwhelmed with the response: "Whereas … this procedure would not have been very fruitful two years ago, it turned out to induce a much livlier [*sic*] discussion in the present climate which seems to represent something in the nature of substantial thaw. In fact, by the time our journey ended in Canton many of the conversations took the form of normal scientific exchange." At one lecture in Shanghai, local hosts had even insisted that all dialogue be conducted in English.[21]

The CSCPRC had also taken heart from a Beijing radio broadcast of a speech by Zhou Peiyuan that had criticized the Gang of Four's obstruction of scientific research and that had recalled Mao's personal praise of Chinese American physicist Chen Ning Yang's suggestions for improving Chinese scientific development made during the Nobel laurate's 1972 PRC visit. The Committee on Scholarly Communication had also noted that the PRC was increasing the number of young scientists it was sending to be trained in Western countries such as the United Kingdom and West Germany. The United States could be next: China's scientific exchange relationship with the United States was already one of its most active, even when compared to countries that had established formal diplomatic relations with Beijing.[22]

These changes were felt before the return of Deng Xiaoping to policymaking in July 1977 – not least because Deng and Hua Guofeng were united in prioritizing the PRC's scientific development.[23] Nonetheless, Deng's return hastened the pace: the restored vice premier soon argued that self-isolation had left China lagging behind the West and that China should again seek to "make the foreign serve China," the 1956 Mao quotation that, as we saw in Chapter 2, had been deployed from 1972 to justify rapprochement and the people-to-people contacts that had accompanied that changed policy.[24] By July, Deng had added that science

---

[21] Seitz to Handler, June 1, 1977, "1977 – General," CSCPRCP, NAS.

[22] CSCPRC working paper, "The Importance of Expanding U.S.-China Scientific and Technical Relations," March 23, 1977, "1977 – Exchange Agreement – Negotiations," CSCPRCP, NAS; Zhou, *Zhou Peiyuan wenji*, 59; Agar, "'It's Springtime for Science'," 17.

[23] Pantsov, *Deng*, 328.

[24] ZGZYWXYJS, *Deng Xiaoping nianpu, 1975–1997*, 1: 157–59; ZGZYWXYJS, *Deng Xiaoping sixiang nianbian*, 48–49, 56–57; Pantsov, *Deng*, 327–28.

did not have an inherent class element and could serve all classes, an important departure from Maoist diatribes against science that was more "expert" than "Red."[25]

It was against this propitious backdrop that both the Committee on Scholarly Communication and the US government sought to achieve a significant advancement in scientific exchange relations during the Committee's June visit to China. The seventeen-member group was the highest-ranking delegation the organization had ever dispatched.[26] Social Science Research Council President Eleanor Sheldon returned to China, alongside ACLS President Lumiansky, together representing the most august American humanities and social sciences institutions. Most notably, Secretary of State Vance personally asked NAS President Handler to head the trip, believing that his experience of pioneering high-level scientific cooperation with the Soviets would enable him to realize a breakthrough with Beijing, too. Frank Press and National Security Advisor Brzezinski also urged Handler to lead the visit, with Keatley writing to her old boss that the visit had "implications ... for the broader country to country relationship" and that US governmental support for the visit would "send a political signal to the other side."[27] Handler and his colleagues used the visit to propose lengthening exchanges to as many as three months in duration, beginning student exchanges, and intensifying ongoing research collaboration beyond the conclusion of individual visits. The leaders of the delegation told Zhou Peiyuan, "Both the American public and our scholarly community expect that U.S.-Chinese scholarly relations will be expanded in scope and made more intensive as a result of the [CSCPRC] visit."[28]

In many ways, the Committee on Scholarly Communication visit offered further grounds for optimism about China's scientific opening to the world. Handler and Sheldon wrote to Vance that they had witnessed a "renaissance" in the five universities and twenty research institutes they had visited. "By the end of our visit we became convinced that China's current internal priorities are conducive to establishment

---

[25] ZGZYWXYJS, *Deng Xiaoping nianpu, 1975–1997*, 1: 164–65.

[26] He, *Dangdai Zhong Mei minjian jiaoliu shi*, 139.

[27] Keatley to Handler, March 9, 1977, and Keatley to Handler, March 21, 1977, "1977 – Visits – Committee Visit on Scholarly Exchanges," CSCPRCP, NAS; Handler to Seitz, April 12, 1977, "1977 – General," CSCPRCP, NAS; Wolfe, *Freedom's Laboratory*, 185–91.

[28] Handler and Sheldon to Zhou, May 4, 1977, "1977 – Visits – Committee Visit on Scholarly Exchanges," CSCPRCP, NAS.

[*sic*] of significant new relationships with the United States and other foreign countries in fields of science and technology."[29] The MIT biophysicist Walter A. Rosenblith had been allowed to visit an officially closed Tsinghua University (and Handler had even had a – somewhat extracurricular – request for a tour of Beijing's vast underground bomb shelter system granted).[30] The main objective of the visit had not been achieved, however: Chinese interlocutors had rejected proposals for deepening exchanges and negotiations over exchanges had been "tense and strained." Keatley's replacement as CSCPRC staff director, Mary Bullock, later recalled that the talks were the worst she ever experienced throughout a career of dealing with Chinese interlocutors. Handler had found it "extraordinarily difficult to get [the Chinese] even to discuss the relatively simple matters we had placed before them," with the talks "dominated by repeated reference to the failure of the United States to implement the Shanghai Communiqué." Vice Premier Ji Dengkui had "repeatedly referred, rather harshly" to the issue of Taiwan and "explicitly stated" that any expansion of scientific cooperation would have to wait until normalization. Handler was so frustrated at the lack of progress that he almost stormed out of Beijing before the scheduled end of the trip.[31]

During a CSCPRC-sponsored China visit of a delegation focused on applied linguistics three months later, the Chinese communicated a similar message directly to American academics beyond the upper echelons of the CSCPRC. An internal Chinese report stated that, in a private conversation, the delegation's leader, the distinguished Berkeley scholar of Chinese literature and language, John Jamieson, agreed with his hosts as to where the blame lied for the impasse in academic exchanges: five years after the Shanghai Communiqué, the US government had still not

[29] "Ji Dengkui fuzongli huijian Mei Zhong Xueshu Jiaoliu Weiyuanhui daibiaotuan' [Vice Premier Ji Dengkui Meets with CSCPRC Delegation], *Renmin Ribao*, June 17, 1977; Handler and American Council of Learned Societies to Vance, August 5, 1977, Folder 6372, Box 527, Series 1, Accession 2, SSRC records, RAC.

[30] Handler to Seitz, June 27, 1977, "1977 – General," CSCPRCP, NAS.

[31] "Fang Yi fuyuanzhang zhuchi yi Guo Moruo yuanzhang mingyi juxing de yanhui huanying Mei Zhong Xueshu Jiaoliu Weiyuanhui daibiaotuan" [Vice President Fang Yi presides over banquet hosted by President [of the Chinese Academy of Sciences] Guo Moruo to welcome CSCPRC delegation], *Renmin Ribao*, June 14, 1977; Handler to Panofsky, June 27, 1977, "1977 – Visits – Committee Visit on Scholarly Exchanges," CSCPRCP, NAS; Handler and Sheldon to Vance, August 5, 1977, Folder 6372, Box 527, Series 1, Accession 2, SSRC records, RAC; author interview with Mary Brown Bullock, by telephone, April 25, 2018, and correspondence with Bullock, by email, 9 January 2019.

normalized relations with Beijing. Jamieson's interlocutors promised the American academic that, once normalization occurred, the PRC was willing to upgrade scientific exchanges, welcoming historians, linguists, and literature scholars – that is, the long-resisted social scientists and humanists – into China.[32] The Chinese government knew that figures in the NCUSCR also believed, like Jamieson, that US recognition of Beijing was overdue. PRC records from an October NCUSCR-sponsored delegation of state-level American education officials cite a conversation with the deputy leader of the group, William A. Delano. Delano, a lawyer who had been the Peace Corps's first general counsel, was a long-standing NCUSCR member and served on the Committee's executive committee. He told his hosts that the Carter administration was being held back from normalization by the continuing influence of the Taiwan lobby's propaganda machine and by the strength of conservative forces in the US Congress. Delano had been in China in 1945 as an Army Chinese interpreter and had met CCP supporters in China's wartime capital of Chongqing. Now, he admitted to his Chinese hosts that he believed the United States should have diplomatically recognized the People's Republic as early as 1949 – thus implying that finally doing so was significantly overdue.[33]

Acute Chinese pressure during the CSCPRC's summer visit was, Handler concluded, applied with a target in mind: Secretary of State Vance's own trip to China, set for a month later.[34] The tactic worked: soon after their return, the CSCPRC leadership lobbied Vance and the State Department, channeling the pressure from both Beijing and the American scholarly community on to the government. The CSCPRC made clear that the more substantive exchanges the government knew American scientists desired were predicated on Washington convincing Beijing of its commitment to advancing Sino-American rapprochement.[35] Moreover, this private lobbying was accompanied by ACLS President Lumiansky going public regarding the "tough" and "blunt" communication from Beijing

[32] Shanghai Education Bureau Revolutionary Committee, "Meiguo yingyong yuyanxue daibiaotuan zai Hu qingkuang huibao" [Report on the US applied linguistics delegation in Shanghai], undated but likely September 1977, Folder B105-9-50-134, SHMA.
[33] Shanghai Education Bureau Revolutionary Committee, "Jiedai Meiguo zhou he difang jiaoyujie fuzeren daibiaotuan de qingkuang" [Report on hosting delegation of US state and local educators], November 24, 1977, Folder B105-9-48, SHMA.
[34] Handler to Seitz, June 1, 1977, "1977 – General," CSCPRCP, NAS.
[35] Handler and Sheldon to Vance, August 5, 1977, Folder 6372, Box 527, Series 1, Accession 2, SSRC records, RAC.

and the reality that the exchange relationship could not move forward without political progress first.[36]

In spite of their Chinese interlocutor's focus on diplomatic normalization as necessary for any upgrading of scientific exchanges, the CSCPRC did not simply pass responsibility for resolving this impasse to the US government. Upon his return from China, Handler told Vance that the most important outcome of the CSCPRC trip had been that the US side had been able to "state clearly" the problems in the exchange program and how the CSCPRC wanted the Chinese to respond to these issues. "The Chinese were informed firmly" that repeated survey visits to institutions such as MIT and Bell Laboratories "are becoming a burden" and that continued access to these institutions would only be possible if China agreed to send a smaller number of its scientists for longer stays that would be better suited to truly collaborative research. The CSCPRC had also hinted to their hosts that American scientists were wise to the true purpose of ever-increasing Chinese requests to see America's best high-technology facilities; he dismissed Chinese claim that such delegations were primarily to promote binational friendship, which were "fatuous when we receive delegations concerned specifically with 'hematite ore dressing' or 'advanced drilling technology'."[37]

Handler's threats to curtail Chinese access were not idle talk: in the months after the visit, Handler internally pushed for the Committee on Scholarly Communication to begin restricting the topics of Chinese exchange delegations to academic subjects alone, "avoiding any visits concerned with advanced technology," as half of the delegations sent in 1977 did.[38] Handler elaborated, "If [the Chinese] do, indeed, pursue only a 'more of the same' course I would object to their sending a half-dozen delegations interested in advanced technology in exchange, for example, for such subjects as ... medical care by 'barefoot doctors' to rural people (irrelevant to the American scene), molecular biology (of which they have very little) and astrophysics (even less)."[39] Handler hoped that these restrictions would act as a "nudge, to remind them

---

[36] "China Rebuffs U.S.," *New York Times*.

[37] Handler and Sheldon to Vance, August 5, 1977, Folder 6372, Box 527, Series 1, Accession 2, SSRC records, RAC.

[38] Handler to Sheldon and Lumiansky, September 15, 1977, Folder 6372, Box 527, Series 1, Accession 2, SSRC records, RAC.

[39] Handler to Branscomb, October 25, 1977, "1977 – General," CSCPRCP, NAS.

of what it is they seek from this country and that they can be denying themselves while they deny us."[40]

Handler and the CSCPRC believed that, over time, these new restrictions would hurt the PRC and prompt a change in Beijing's approach to exchanges. In the meantime, Vance traveled to China in August. The president did briefly consider using Vance's trip to make a significant push for a quick normalization deal and the secretary of state even carried with him a draft of the communiqué that would announce the agreement, ready if negotiations were successful. However, an unexpected breakthrough in talks over the Panama Canal treaties prompted the president to rescind these instructions at the last minute. Instead, he ordered Vance to put forward the maximum version of US normalization terms – including the United States being allowed to maintain governmental representation in Taipei – and was unsurprised when the Chinese deemed this a nonstarter.[41]

Vance also used the trip to reaffirm to Beijing the US government's support for an expansion of the exchange relationship, with the secretary of state again recounting his own NCUSCR-sponsored visit to China in 1975 to underline how important he personally considered the exchange program to be and stated that the US government "want to make it clear that we favor" the push by the CSCPRC and the NCUSCR for more substantive exchanges. Vance also lamented the downturn in Sino-American trade in the previous years: after a peak of just over a billion dollars, two-way trade had dwindled to $349 million by 1976. Foreign Minister Huang Hua responded that, given the lack of progress in normalization negotiations, "The level and scope of exchanges we have achieved so far perhaps will remain for some years to come" and that trade levels would continue to fluctuate.[42]

Vance's visit to the PRC has been remembered as a failure: historians such as Harding have concurred with Deng's judgement, made shortly after Vance left, that the visit was a "step backwards."[43] In his memoirs, Huang similarly suggests that Beijing was unmoved by the proposals put forward by the secretary of state.[44] Back in the United States, the US-China

---

[40] Handler to Branscomb, November 22, 1977, "1977 – Exchange Agreement – Negotiations," CSCPRCP, NAS.

[41] Cyrus Vance, *Hard Choices: Critical Years in America's Foreign Policy* (New York: Simon and Schuster, 1983), 79–82; ZGZYWXYJS, *Deng Xiaoping sixiang nianbian*, 69.

[42] Carter to Vance, August 18, 1977, *FRUS, 1977–1980*, Vol. XIII, Document 43; ZGZYWXYJS, *Deng Xiaoping sixiang nianbian*, 72; Huang, *Memoirs*, 344–46; Talley, *Forgotten Vanguard*, 7.

[43] ZGZYWXYJS, *Deng Xiaoping sixiang nianbian*, 75; Harding, *Fragile Relationship*, 75.

[44] Huang, *Memoirs*, 344–46.

Peoples Friendship Association claimed that Vance's trip "revealed that the Carter Administration ... is still clinging to the hope of maintaining U.S. military and diplomatic intervention in China." The Friendship Association extolled its membership that, "We must organize a campaign among Americans of all walks of life that will prove Carter and Vance wrong" in believing that the American public wanted the government to maintain a relationship with "the Taiwan regime."[45] Certainly, the visit did not lead to an immediate breakthrough in the exchange program: the National Committee's board traveled to China in October and had its own efforts to expand and deepen the exchange program rebuffed, with the Chinese saying that "present U.S.-China relations" meant that exchanges should remain at the level of the previous year.[46] This notwithstanding, Brzezinski noted in Washington that Deng had made no comment when Vance stated that the United States would continue to provide Taiwan with arms after normalization.[47] Enrico Fardella argues that this "loud silence" suggested for the first time that Beijing might ultimately accept a post-normalization US-Taiwan relationship that would meet the terms Carter had set out internally as his red lines before Vance departed.[48]

1977 proved, then, to be a false start in both exchange and high-level governmental diplomacy. Nonetheless, in that year, the conditions for the dramatic breakthroughs of 1978 were falling into place. Accounts of Carter's achievement of normalization by Harding, Fardella, and Ezra Vogel all stress the importance of the visit of Frank Press to China in July 1978 in precipitating a final normalization deal.[49] As we will see, that moment was indeed critical. But Press's proposals for scientific cooperation were not new: they were almost identical to those made by the CSCPRC during their summer 1977 visit. This similarity was no coincidence: Press had personally overseen similar negotiations as Committee

[45] "National Campaign for Normalization," undated but from 1977, Folder 10, Box 1, USCPFAR, NYPLAMD.

[46] "Huang Hua waizhang huijian Mei Zhong Guanxi Quan Wei Hui Lishihui daibiaotuan' [Foreign Minister Huang Hua meets with the NCUSCR delegation], *Renmin Ribao*, October 23, 1977; Memcon: Jian and Yost, October 22, 1977, Folder 98, Box 13, Series 3, RG4, NCUSCR records, RAC.

[47] Brzezinski to Carter, August 25, 1977, "Armacost Chrono File, 8/16–25/77," Box 4, National Security Affairs – Staff Material – Far East Files (NSASMFEF), JCL.

[48] Enrico Fardella, "The Sino-American Normalization: A Reassessment," *Diplomatic History* 33, no. 4 (September 2009): 551.

[49] Harding, *Fragile Relationship*, 96; Fardella, "Sino-American Normalization," 554, note 27; Vogel, *Deng*, 322–23.

on Scholarly Communication chair up until his entry to the White House and he and Keatley continued to enjoy close relations with their previous employer after entering government service.[50] Moreover, the CSCPRC had shared their negotiating position with the White House, after which it was, as will be shown below, heavily drawn upon by the National Security Council, including by National Security Advisor Brzezinski. The Committee had aimed for just such an outcome: documents prepared for their 1977 visit described how "expanded scientific ... relations with China would have immediate and long-term benefit for U.S. foreign policy" and that realizing such an expansion "would be valuable at this stage in which formulas for the establishment of diplomatic ties are being studied."[51] Thus, once again, nongovernmental exchange organizations were laying the groundwork for agreements in the high-level diplomatic relationship, even if such agreements also needed a more dynamic governmental approach than that offered during Vance's visit.

TWO STEPS FORWARD

Even if Vance's trip had seemingly failed to make headway toward normalization, Brzezinski had concluded from the secretary of state's discussions with Deng that there was now a leader in Beijing who might be persuaded to accede to Washington's conditions for normalization. Following Vance's trip, the national security advisor and his staff identified facilitating greater Chinese access to US science and technology as a means to show American interest in deepening the bilateral relationship – as well as a way to increase US leverage in normalization negotiations. Washington was already acutely aware that the PRC was utilizing exchanges as one way of accessing American scientific knowledge – not least because of the Committee on Scholarly Communication's vocal complaints about the burdens this placed on American industry and academic institutions. The month after Vance's trip, Deng had further told the visiting National Committee board of his interest in utilizing scientific cooperation with the outside to advance his modernization goals:

---

[50] The closeness of this relationship is not only clear from the documents but also attested to in oral history recollections of the period. Author interviews with Anne Solomon (previously Keatley), June 25, 2018, and Mary Brown Bullock, 25 April 2018, and email exchanges with Mary Brown Bullock, January 2019.

[51] CSCPRC working paper, "The importance of expanding U.S.-China scientific and technical relations," March 23, 1977, "1977 – Exchange Agreement – Negotiations," CSCPRCP, NAS.

"We must make things foreign serve China," he told NCUSCR President Charles Yost, adding that "We lag behind," "especially in science and technology." The PRC must "absorb the advanced experience" of other countries, Deng said. In response to Deng's enthusiasm, Yost promised that the United States – and the NCUSCR – was prepared to help: "We ... think that exchanges can make more of a contribution ... in the transfer of science and technology," to which Deng expressed "our thanks."[52] Beijing was simultaneously showing intensifying interest in purchasing the physical technology seen during these exchanges. In a memorandum to Carter sent the same month as the NCUSCR's visit, Frank Press linked these two developments and made the case that the US government should encourage and respond positively to Chinese interest.[53]

As discussed in Chapter 5, Chinese attempts to buy US technology had not been without problems. Ford's remarkable promise during his 1975 China summit to facilitate Chinese access to the fastest American computers had only encouraged Chinese interest in further purchases: by 1978, the PRC was awaiting US government decisions on export licenses for thirty different high-technology items.[54] Sales of such technologies to Communist countries were, however, subject to strict controls, and some government departments – Defense and Energy, most recently – had been slow in approving sales to the PRC. In late 1977, Press appealed to the president to intervene. Press's memorandum appealed to Carter's political priorities by suggesting that, for example, providing technology to improve China's natural resource extraction capabilities could help with the global energy crisis that dogged Carter's America.[55] But, "perhaps most important," Press argued, was that technology sales would support

[52] "Deng Xiaoping fuzongli huijian Meiguo Mei Zhong Guanxi Quan Wei Hui Lishihui daibiaotuan" [Vice Premier Deng Xiaoping meets with the NCUSCR delegation], *Renmin Ribao*, October 24, 1977; Memcon: Deng and Yost, October 23, 1977, Folder 98, Box 13, Series 3, RG4, NCUSCR records, RAC.

[53] Press to Carter, October 14, 1977, *FRUS, 1977–1980*, Vol. XIII, Document 64.

[54] Ibid.; Zbigniew Brzezinski, *Power and Principle: Memoirs of the National Security Advisor 1977–1981* (New York: Farrar, Straus, Giroux, 1983), 200.

[55] Press to Carter, October 14, 1977, *FRUS, 1977–1980*, Vol. XIII, Document 64. For concurrent Chinese interest in Western knowledge in this area, see ZGZYWXYJS, *Deng Xiaoping sixiang nianbian*, 97. For more on encouraging Chinese energy extraction, in particular its oil reserves, see Minami, "Oil for the Lamps of America?" For similar arguments of the long-term value of Sino-American scientific cooperation, including in energy production, see CSCPRC working paper, "The importance of expanding US-China scientific and technical relations," March 23, 1977, "1977 – Exchange Agreement – Negotiations," CSCPRCP, NAS.

"establishing long-term ties between China and American industry, as well as our scientists and engineers." US commercial interest was important: the PRC had not been shy about buying competing technology from Japan or Western Europe when the United States refused to sell (although Chen Ning Yang, who knew more than most about Chinese scientific priorities, believed that the PRC preferred working with the United States over Japan or Western Europe, on account of American openness during scientific exchanges).[56] In spite of objections from Vance – who worried about Moscow's reaction – Carter agreed to Press and Brzezinski working to expedite licensing decisions. By February 1978, a small committee had secretly changed the government's policy on dual-purpose technology sales – items that could have military as well as civilian use – making it easier to sell such items to China than to the Soviet Union.[57]

Meanwhile, China's modernization efforts only gained in urgency. In March, the PRC Central Committee called the country's first National Science Conference since 1950, an event of grand scale attended by China's top leadership and a staggering 6,000 scientists, researchers, and cadres.[58] Hua Guofeng told this largest ever assembly of China's scientists that science and technology was the most important of the Four Modernizations and that the PRC could only catch up to the West in this area through greater interaction and exchanges with the outside world. Brzezinski noted Deng's opening speech, too, in which the vice premier had said that science and technology was the "crux" of successfully modernizing China. Brzezinski wrote to Carter that, "After 20 years in search of a distinctive path to modernity, the Deng-administered regime appears to be joining the rest of the world."[59] Meanwhile, internal CSCPRC research likewise reflected on the conference approvingly, concluding that the outcome was that "China's scientists, intellectuals and technicians have been cast in the role of vanguard in modernizing their country."[60] Unbeknownst to American observers, Deng had also

---

[56] CIA report, "U.S.-China Trade Relations," September 30, 1977, RACP: NLC-6-8-4-4-9, JCL; Press to Carter, October 14, 1977, *FRUS, 1977–1980*, Vol. XIII, Document 64; Yang, *Selected Papers*, 518; Vance, *Hard Choices*, 113.

[57] Oksenberg to Brzezinski, February 17, 1978, RACP: NLC-15-41-10-4-5, JCL; Vance, *Hard Choices*, 78.

[58] ZGZYWXYJS, *Deng Xiaoping sixiang nianbian*, 110–13.

[59] Brzezinski to Carter, April 7, 1978, "Weekly Reports, 53–60," Box 41, Zbigniew Brzezinski Collection, JCL; *CEN*, Vol. 6, No. 2, April 1978. In this analysis, Brzezinski was echoing a long-standing discourse within the US government of China as a, to use Goh's term, "troubled modernizer." Goh, *Constructing the U.S. Rapprochement with China*, 47.

[60] *CEN*, Vol. 6, No. 2, April 1978.

made an important practical step toward his modernization goals when, on March 13, the politburo approved creating a select group of leaders to manage imports of foreign technology into the PRC.[61]

Even before these historic milestones, China was changing its approach to scientific exchanges. The pressure put on China by Handler in the wake of the CSCPRC's unsuccessful summer 1977 visit had, by 1978, had a positive effect. Three months after the CSCPRC's summer 1977 leadership delegation to the PRC, staff director Bullock reflected that the six groups that the organization had sent to China in 1977 had been provided with programs "far superior to those arranged in previous years." As the Committee on Scholarly Communication had requested, sightseeing had been minimized and substantive scientific discussions maximized. Many more of the American requests for content had been granted, while the Chinese had also made other encouraging changes on their own initiative: the astronomy delegation had been involved in joint seminars on solar physics, galaxies, and stellar evolution with their professional counterparts in China, while a cancer research delegation had also been involved in seminars on research problems with fellow specialists from the Chinese Medical Association that included "extended, prolonged discussions [in which] every effort was made to facilitate serious, non-political inquiry" – or, in other words, less lecturing about the virtues of Chinese socialism, more sincere attempts to swap scientific findings.[62] It was in this period, too, that the CSCPRC observed that the steady stream of letters that American scientists had been sending their counterparts in China since the early 1970s and even the late 1960s had finally begun to be meaningfully answered, a first step toward the desired exchange of data and serious, ongoing research collaboration that would, ultimately, become an important facet of the Sino-American scientific relationship by the mid-1980s.[63]

China's desire to use its contacts with the outside world to expedite its modernization efforts, as well as the possibility that Handler and the National Academy could curtail valuable access to American science, motivated Beijing to add greater substance to exchanges – even before any change in the diplomatic relationship between the two governments. Chinese leaders' interest in utilizing exchanges to accelerate their country's development was simultaneously apparent in exchanges overseen by

---

[61] ZGZYWXYJS, *Deng Xiaoping nianpu, 1975–1997*, I: 279.
[62] Bullock to Handler, October 28, 1977, "1977 – General," CSCPRCP, NAS.
[63] Smith, "Role of Scientists," 127; Harding, *Fragile Relationship*, 8.

the National Committee. In November 1977, the NCUSCR had received a Chinese delegation focused on higher education that they had expected to be made up of administrators. In fact, however, Beijing sent a group of their senior-most Western-trained scientists – indeed, the highest-ranking Chinese educators to ever be sent to the United States – who used the trip to study US academic and scientific institutions for insights into how to improve China's largest universities. The visitors also asked for guidance on this question from senior American scientists involved in earlier exchanges, such as physicist Chen Ning Yang.[64] Similarly, a January 1978 delegation of Chinese petroleum experts hosted by the National Council for United States-China Trade acted both as a shopping trip for high-end American technology and as a chance for knowledge transfer between US experts in oil extraction and their Chinese counterparts. The importance Beijing attached to this delegation was indicated by the inclusion of Li Renjun, director of the State Planning Commission, the highest-ranking PRC government official to have ever officially visited the United States.[65]

If the changing domestic priorities in Beijing were propitious to again deepening Sino-American ties, so, too, were Washington's internal politics: the Panama Canal treaties that had been prioritized over normalization proposals at the time of the Vance trip had passed the Senate in March and April. Indeed, there were growing signs of political pressure on Carter to move the relationship with Beijing forward: the influential senior Democrat Senator Jackson returned from a congressional delegation hosted by the Chinese People's Institute of Foreign Affairs in February. Deng had told the visiting senator of his hope to "import modern technology and experience from around the world" and that "Sino-American trade can become much faster" after normalization.[66] Upon his return, Jackson commented publicly that he had "detected a new spirit in China" and that he believed that the Carter administration should dedicate more time to solving outstanding differences with the PRC.[67]

---

[64] "Wo gaodeng jiaoyu daibiaotuan jieshu fang Mei huiguo" [Our higher education delegation ended their visit to the United States], *Renmin Ribao*, December 12, 1977; *CEN*, Vol. 6, No. 2, December 1977; Bullock to Handler, 2 December 1977, "1977 – Visits – General," CSCPRCP, NAS.

[65] Trips by Deng and others to the United Nations that required transiting through New York were not considered official visits to the United States. *CEN*, Vol. 6, No. 2, December 1977.

[66] Minami, "Re-Examining the End of Mao's Revolution," 371.

[67] Statement by Jackson, February 22, 1978, "Armacost Evening and Weekly Reports File, 1978/7–8," Box 1, NSASMFEF, JCL.

Meanwhile, an on-the-ground campaign to bolster public support for normalization – and increase pressure on Carter to realize that end – had become the focus of the US-China Peoples Friendship Association. The Friendship Association was producing materials that lauded the potential benefits of normalization for "both the American and Chinese people" – greater cultural exchanges, the beginning of student exchanges, the stationing of reporters in each country, and direct US flights to China – and highlighted that the United States had become "the only major country in the world not to have diplomatic relations with China."[68] (The group daringly claimed that normalization would even benefit Taiwan, prompting the island to begin negotiating unification with a munificent PRC.[69]) The USCPFA's political lobbying wing sought a full-court press on the Carter government to realize normalization: they organized a "Normalization Conference" that attracted nearly 400 people, sought to get as many as 30,000 signatures on a petition to the government, encouraged people to write to Carter and to their local congressman or senator, had unions declare themselves in favor of normalization, and leafleted the public during exchange visits such as the NCUSCR-hosted October 1977 tour of a Chinese All-Star Soccer Team. The group even mass-produced pin buttons and some 3,000 bumper stickers for its members that read "One China, U.S. Out of Taiwan." (The USCPFA was so vociferous in its support of Beijing's position on normalization that they were even censured by their PRC contacts for being too uncompromising: the slogan "One China, U.S. Out of Taiwan," the Chinese said, was misleading as in fact the PRC was prepared to tolerate a continuing unofficial American presence on the island after normalization.)[70]

The Friendship Association had, with the encouragement of Beijing's state-run travel agency, the China International Travel Service, introduced a new type of exchange visit to China – the "China Study

[68] USCPFA document, "Full Diplomatic Relations with China Now!," 1977 (otherwise undated), Folder 11, Box 1, WNP, TLWLANYU; "An Open Letter on Normalization," *US-China Review*, Vol. 2, No. 1, January–February 1978, located at Folder 9, Box 1, WNP, TLWLANYU.

[69] "Carter Should Complete Normalization," *US-China Review*, Vol. 2, No. 4, July–August 1978, located at Folder 9, Box 1, WNP, TLWLANYU.

[70] "National Office Report – 1/77–4/77," Folder 7, Box 1, USCPFAR, NYPLAMD; McCart, Normalization Outreach Committee of USCPFA, to Members, September 19, 1977, Folder 5, Box 71, James Forman papers, LOCMD; Report, "One China: Normalization Conference," undated but from 1977, Folder 9, Box 1, USCPFAR, NYPLAMD; National Campaign for Normalization, undated but from late 1978, Folder 10, Box 1, USCPFAR, NYPLAMD; Dasso to Selden, June 2, 1977, Folder 10, Box 1, USCPFAR, NYPLAMD.

Tour" – that had as one of its explicit objectives working toward normalization. Where previous USCPFA delegations had been made up of members of the Friendship Association who were deemed already sympathetic toward the PRC, now the China International Travel Service told the organization to cast a wider net: "A few individuals in the (CST) [sic] groups might be bad but the vast majority would be OK. We have faith in the majority of the people and feel that 90–95% of the people will be friendly to China and not influenced by the 1–2% who might create any serious trouble." Beijing was ever more confident of winning over most Americans who had contact with China; indeed, the standout advice to leaders of these new tours was "LET CHINA SELL ITSELF! Do not try to talk tour members out of their politics or sell them China's."[71] In a July 1978 briefing, the president of the Chinese People's Association for Friendship with Foreign Countries directly encouraged the USCPFA in this direction: "It is our hope," the Chinese official said, "that the USCPFA as an organization can be expanded so that it can be an organization that plays an important role in the political life of the American people."[72] By 1979, the Friendship Association had grown to some 10,000 members across 125 local chapters – although this broadening of the organization was at the expense of the organization's previous political cohesion, with many previously active leftist members resigning.[73]

The PRC government was even prepared to engage with Carter's human rights agenda if this helped improve China's image in the United States. Having previously dismissed Carter's emphasis on human rights as a gimmick, Beijing now began to make at least a token effort to adapt to this new facet of US foreign policy: several low-level officials were prosecuted in 1978 explicitly for depriving people of their human rights. That this was primarily for the benefit of foreign observers was indicated by the publicity given to the cases in China's English-language press.[74] Later in the year, Deng even consented to answering questions gathered from democracy protestors by the American columnist Robert Novak. Portentously, the vice premier praised the protests but also compared

[71] "China Study Tours: Tour Leaders [sic] Handbook," USCPFA, undated but likely December 1977, Folder 2, Box 2, WNP, TLWLANYU.

[72] "Foreign Policy Briefing with President of Youxie [Chinese People's Association for Friendship with Foreign Countries]," July 8, 1978, Folder 10, Box 1, WNP, TLWLANYU.

[73] Deane to "China Trip Friends," August 26, 1979, Folder 14, Box 1, WNP, TLWLANYU; Schmalzer, "Speaking about China," 336–37.

[74] Oksenberg to Brzezinski, March 30, 1977, RACP: NLC-26-39-6-17-7, JCL; CIA report, "Human Rights in East Asia," 31 October 1978, RACP: NLC-28-17-15-10-6, JCL.

them to Mao's Hundred Flowers campaign – which ended with a vicious purge orchestrated by Deng himself.[75]

In the White House, President Carter knew, however, that any normalization deal would have critics as well as supporters. The Republic of China government in Taipei continued to invest heavily in lobbying and the Taiwan lobby had even personally targeted Carter's relatives and neighbors in his hometown of Plains for expenses-paid trips to Taiwan that came with gifts and lavish hospitality – in return for guests encouraging Carter to drop any plans for finalizing normalization.[76] Whether because of Taiwanese lobbying or a sense of loyalty to "Free China," broad American public opinion was strongly against any deal that sacrificed Taiwan to establish relations with Beijing (even as it supported a deepening of American contact with the PRC). A *U.S. News and World Report* opinion poll conducted in 1978 found that 58 percent of respondents were opposed to recognizing Beijing as the sole legitimate Chinese government if this meant de-recognition of Taiwan, with only 20 percent in favor of such a course of action.[77]

Meanwhile, the growth in trade with China since 1971 was beginning to cause resentment among American workers who found themselves competing with a new source of cheap labor: in February 1978, the American Clothing and Textile Workers Union claimed that nearly 3,000 jobs had been lost as a result of the United States importing a million pairs of cotton work gloves from China "made under slave labor conditions" and not subject to bilateral trade quotas.[78] The Carter administration hoped that the technology sales it was seeking to make to the PRC might help with this domestic political obstacle: Brzezinski's chief China aide, Oksenberg, co-authored a paper that proposed that, as normalization talks moved forward, China should be encouraged to make major technology and grain purchases that would be announced in the run up to the announcement of the deal, "demonstrating to the U.S. public the tangible benefits to be derived from normal relations" with Beijing.[79]

---

[75] ZGZYWXYJS, *Deng Xiaoping sixiang nianbian*, 194–95; Rowland Evans and Robert Novak, "An Interview with China's Teng Hsiao-ping," *Washington Post*, November 28, 1978.

[76] Jimmy Carter, *Keeping Faith: Memoirs of a President* (Fayetteville, AR: University of Arkansas Press, 1995), 192.

[77] Jonathan Manthorpe, *Forbidden Nation: A History of Taiwan* (New York; Basingstoke: Palgrave Macmillan, 2009), 215.

[78] "Union Asks Curb on Chinese Work Gloves Flooding U.S. Market," *AFL–CIO News*, February 9, 1978, Folder 11, Box 1, WNP, TLWLANYU.

[79] NSC paper, "A Proposal for Asian Policy Adjustments," undated, *FRUS, 1977–1980*, Vol. XIII, Document 84.

Brzezinski was sensitive to the changing of complex American public sentiment toward China, as well as the simultaneous shifts in Beijing's domestic priorities. But Carter's national security advisor's interest in China was driven above all by his perceptions of the Cold War. In this regard, too, 1978 seemed to be the moment to attempt to finally realize normalization. By the spring of that year, Carter was questioning whether he should remain committed to superpower détente – for it seemed that Moscow certainly was not. 1977 had seen the stationing of SS-20 missiles in Europe, continued Soviet and Cuban involvement in Angola, and a massive Russian intervention in the Ethiopia–Somalia conflict. In April 1978, the Soviet-backed coup d'état in Afghanistan caused further, serious alarm in Washington (and Beijing, too).[80] From the beginning of 1978, Brzezinski, a long-standing Cold Warrior, pointed to China as an opportunity for Washington to offer a firm response. Carter indicated his support for Brzezinski's case when, in February, he overruled protests from his secretary of state and allowed Brzezinski to accept an outstanding invitation to travel to China.[81]

Keen to exploit the opportunity provided by this visit, Brzezinski and his NSC staff set out a strategy and timetable for seeking a normalization agreement. One of Brzezinski's conclusions from the 1977 Vance visit had been that it had been naive for the administration to think it could reach a quick deal with Beijing on normalization without developing other aspects of the relationship.[82] Oksenberg and Michael Armacost, Brzezinski's two China advisors, suggested in March "a strengthened China connection" as a response to the newfound Soviet aggression that would include "formal diplomatic relations, expanding exchanges and trade, and fuller strategic consultations." This, they argued, "is the most effective card we have, and the sooner we play it the better."[83] In devising their strategy for normalization, Brzezinski and Oksenberg actively sought to learn from what had and had not worked under Kissinger,

[80] Breck Walker, "'Friends, But Not Allies' – Cyrus Vance and the Normalization of Relations with China," *Diplomatic History* 33, no. 4 (September 2009): 588; Odd Arne Westad, "The Fall of Détente and the Turning Tides of History," in *The Fall of Détente: Soviet-American Relations during the Carter Years*, ed. Odd Arne Westad (Oslo: Scandinavian University Press, 1997), 28.

[81] Brzezinski to Carter, February 9, 1978, "Weekly Reports, 42–52," Box 41, Zbigniew Brzezinski collection, JCL.

[82] Brzezinski, *Power and Principle*, 201.

[83] NSC paper, "A Proposal for Asian Policy Adjustments," undated, *FRUS, 1977–1980*, Vol. XIII, Document 84.

with Oksenberg leading a systematic review of negotiations during the Nixon and Ford administrations.[84] One important conclusion made by the NSC staff was that Kissinger had been wrong to think that geopolitics was the only determinant of the health of the relationship. "In addition to global affairs, domestic conditions in both countries and the climate of the bilateral relationship – the rhetoric each had been using about the other, the state of the trade relationship, the tone of cultural and scientific exchanges – shaped the atmosphere and substance of [each] visit" by Kissinger to China. Given this conclusion, Oksenberg told Brzezinski to take heart as, "Not since 1973 has the bilateral relationship been as satisfactory." The positive developments in the exchange program that had occurred since the CSCPRC June 1977 visit had been accompanied by an upturn in trade – $391 million in 1977 rising to $1.23 billion in 1978 – as well as growing tourism that Beijing was using to raise funds for technology purchases from Western countries.[85]

Brzezinski had the opportunity to put into practice his holistic approach to the Sino-American relationship when he traveled to China in May 1978. He took as a gift a piece of the moon retrieved by American astronauts, and this symbol of US scientific prowess anticipated a critical theme of the trip.[86] Efforts to use the visit to deepen Sino-American scientific cooperation had begun even before the national security advisor arrived in Beijing. A week before he had set off, Brzezinski had arranged a meeting in Washington between deputy Liaison Office chief Han Xu and Frank Press in which the US side made the case to Han for the Chinese receiving "a very high-level delegation of scientists and engineers" to follow in the wake of Brzezinski's trip.[87]

Brzezinski had, upon arrival in China, immediately told Deng that the United States had "made up its mind" to reach a normalization agreement. In counterpart talks between Huberman and Jiang Nanxiang, the vice chairman of the State Science and Technology Commission, Jiang spoke at length about how the recent Chinese National Science

[84] Brzezinski, *Power and Principle*, 198.
[85] NSC Scope Paper for May, 1978 Brzezinski China Trip, otherwise undated, *FRUS, 1977–1980*, Vol. XIII, Document 106; Talley, *Forgotten Vanguard*, 7; CIA report, "China and Global Issues," April 1978, RACP: NLC-26-49-7-2-1, JCL; ZGZYWXYJS, *Deng Xiaoping sixiang nianbian*, 55, 90, 92–93.
[86] Memcon: Hua, Brzezinski, et al., May 22, 1978, *FRUS, 1977–1980*, Vol. XIII, Document 111.
[87] Memcon: Han, Brzezinski, et al., May 15, 1978, *FRUS, 1977–1980*, Vol. XIII, Document 105.

Conference opened "brighter prospects ... for further exchanges" with the United States. Jiang also recounted to Huberman that the Gang of Four had opposed international scientific cooperation as "following the slavish comprador philosophy" and gave an account of when, in 1974, Mao's wife Jiang Qing had successfully sabotaged the purchase of an American color television plant by claiming that the US supplier's courtesy gift of glass snails was a calculated insult intended to mock the slow pace of China's economic development. "They made use of this incident to put a lot of labels on the persons concerned and such an act was absurd and silly." Jiang Nanxiang was making clear that China was making a decisive break with the past. He also pushed for the US government to adopt "new measures" toward technology sales to China, something Deng raised directly with Brzezinski.[88] With Carter's approval, Brzezinski encouraged this interest.[89]

Brzezinski stopped short of proposing normalization terms during the trip but, in addition to repeatedly telling Deng that the United States had "made up its mind" to strike a deal, the national security advisor informed the vice premier that US Liaison Office chief Woodcock was ready to begin serious negotiations from June.[90] Deng and Brzezinski's other Chinese interlocutors were careful not to offer immediate concessions in talks with the visiting American, but Brzezinski enjoyed a long dinner with Deng in which the vice premier chose not to rebut the national security advisor's statements on Washington's relations with Taiwan. The two men exchanged numerous toasts and Deng "smilingly accepted" when Brzezinski offered to reciprocate the vice premier's hospitality by hosting Deng at a dinner in his home in Washington; that dinner would come to fruition in January 1979, as part of the first official visit by a PRC leader to the United States. The changes underway in China that provided the backdrop to Brzezinski's negotiations were felt even in the entertainment provided: the visiting American's trip to the Beijing Opera was not to see one of the model operas shown to so many exchange visitors before 1978, but instead a traditional opera reminiscent of the pre-Cultural Revolution era.[91]

---

[88] Memcon: Jiang, Huberman, Gleysteen, May 21, 1978, China: MR-NLC-98-215, Box 40, CVF, JCL; Memcon: Deng, Brzezinski, May 21, 1978, *FRUS, 1977–1980*, Vol. XIII, Document 110; Teiwes and Sun, *End of the Maoist Era*, 163.

[89] Brzezinski, *Power and Principle*, 208, 212.

[90] Memcon: Hua, Brzezinski, et al., May 22, 1978, *FRUS, 1977–1980*, Vol. XIII, Document 111; Brzezinski to Carter, September 11, 1978, "China MR-NLC-98-215 [3]," Box 41, CVF, JCL; Brzezinski, 215.

[91] Brzezinski, *Power and Principle*, 210, 212–15.

SCIENTIFIC BREAKTHROUGH

Brzezinski returned to Washington to a jubilant welcome from Carter. The success of the national security advisor's China visit began a final phase in Sino-American negotiation toward normalization. Fardella has argued that Carter and Brzezinski's achievement of normalization in December 1978 was due to Brzezinski's "remarkable ability" and the opportunity provided by both disintegrating Soviet-American détente and China's rapid post-Mao reorientation "from 'class struggle' to 'socialist modernization'." This section argues that a further important – and underacknowledged – variable that determined the Carter administration's success in finally reaching the deal that had eluded Nixon, Kissinger, and Ford was the Carter government's successful exploitation of science and technology cooperation – not least through scientific exchanges – as a means of eliciting political progress and negotiating flexibility from Beijing.[92]

In the weeks after Brzezinski returned to Washington, his staff worked feverishly to capitalize on Chinese receptiveness to the proposed follow-up visit by Press and to address Chinese complaints about delays to technology sales. On June 1, Oksenberg protested to Brzezinski of "an interminable bureaucratic morass" that continued to prevent the granting of licenses for technology sales.[93] In his memoirs, Brzezinski suggests that one way that he successfully overcame these internal bureaucratic barriers was cultivating allies within the bureaucracy, citing Frank Press as a key example. In fact, the former CSCPRC head had his own long-standing motivations for fostering Sino-American relations: Press jumped at the chance to revisit China and needed little convincing about the merits of pushing for normalization in 1978.[94]

The planning for the Press delegation had been made with an eye to Deng's modernization agenda: the proposals for new scientific cooperation drawn up by Keatley, Press, and the NSC targeted those areas of Chinese development identified as a priority by Deng and Fang Yi, who had been made the minister overseeing China's State Science and

---

[92] Fardella recognizes a connection between scientific cooperation and the final steps toward normalization; I deepen his analysis by placing this in the broader context of scientific exchanges throughout the 1970s.

[93] Oksenberg to Brzezinski, June 1, 1978, "China (PRC), 1978/6–8," Box 8, National Security Affairs – Zbigniew Brzezinski material – Country Files (NSAZBMCF), JCL; Oksenberg to Brzezinski, June 2, 1978, RACP: NLC-26-1-3-5-4, JCL.

[94] Brzezinski, *Power and Principle*, 226.

Technology Commission in March 1978, during the National Science Conference. In devising their proposals, Keatley and Press drew on their experience at the CSCPRC: in 1978, the Chinese leadership prioritized projects in agriculture, materials science, computers, laser science, and high-energy physics – all of which had been the foci of CSCPRC-sponsored exchanges.[95] Press's trip was thus consciously intended to confirm to Deng's domestic political audience that his policy of reaching out to the West would bring a positive response and tangible results. It is important to recognize that, in 1978, the rapid and seemingly inexorable modernization that China achieved in the subsequent forty years was not inevitable – indeed, it seemed an unlikely outcome given the PRC's stuttering development to that point. Oksenberg told Brzezinski that Deng's opening to the West could be as fleeting as previous periods of openness in Chinese modern history – and could be followed by a subsequent turn inwards. "These xenophobic phases [in modern Chinese history] have always been detrimental to U.S. policy interests in East Asia ... one cannot help but wonder whether a forthcoming Western response to this most recent Chinese turn outward might not reduce somewhat the amplitude in China's cyclical pattern of development."[96]

Brzezinski and Oksenberg also saw an anti-Soviet aspect to Press's trip. The Chinese had surprised everyone in Washington but Brzezinski in opting to receive Press in July rather than August. The key reason behind this decision was that Carter's science advisor was set to travel to Moscow later that month. Beijing would like to "stick its finger in Moscow's eye" by hosting Carter's science advisor as the head of the most high-ranking delegation of American science personnel ever sent

---

[95] Reconstituted in 1977, the State Science and Technology Commission had taken over managing China's science and technology cooperation with Western countries from the Chinese Academy of Sciences. Oksenberg to Brzezinski, June 30, 1978, "China (PRC), 1978/6–8," Box 8, NSAZBMCF, JCL; Fang Yi, *Fang Yi wenji* [Collected Works of Fang Yi] (Beijing: Renmin chubanshe, 2008), 147–68; ZGZYWXYJS, *Deng Xiaoping sixiang nianbian*, 110–13; Chenxi Xiong, "Deng Xiaoping's Views on Science and Technology: Origins of the Sino-U.S. Science and Technology Cooperation, 1977–1979," *Journal of American-East Asian Relations* 28, 2021, no. 2 (2021): 167–68, 178; "1978–1985 Nian quanguo kexue jishu fazhan guihua gangyao (cao'an)" [National Science and Technology Development Plan, 1978–1985 (draft)], available at www.most.gov.cn/ztzl/gjzcqgy/zcqgylshg/200508/t20050831_24438.html. Accessed November 22, 2021.

[96] In an oral history interview, Brzezinski was careful to make clear that he was no more certain than Oksenberg that Deng would get his way in shaping Chinese domestic politics and transforming China. Author interview with Zbigniew Brzezinski, Washington, DC, United States, January 19, 2010; Oksenberg to Brzezinski, June 30, 1978, "China (PRC), 1978/6–8," Box 8, NSAZBMCF, JCL.

to another country – just weeks before Press took a smaller contingent of scientists to the Soviet Union.[97] Indeed, Moscow loudly denounced Press's trip: Soviet state media claimed that scientific cooperation was being used as a front for technology transfers to help Beijing upgrade its military and claimed that the trip had a "dangerous character for the cause of peace and for the national interests of the U.S."[98]

The Press delegation's primary objective was reaching an agreement for the beginning of systematic government-to-government scientific exchanges. Since 1977, direct government involvement in exchanges had been gradually increasing. Departments of the federal government – for example, Education – had begun to directly fund individual exchanges, in addition to State's continuing support of the overall budgets of the NCUSCR and the CSCPRC, and the indirect government funding of the CSCPRC through the National Science Foundation. The government had also begun adding their own specialist personnel to Committee on Scholarly Communication visits, with Department of Agriculture staff accompanying a June 1977 delegation. Meanwhile, government institutions such as the National Bureau of Standards were receiving a growing number of Chinese delegations as part of their US tours. Most significant of all, in January 1978, the Department of Energy had, alongside the National Council for United States-China Trade, hosted the first ever government-to-government exchange between the PRC and the United States in the form of the aforementioned group of high-ranking Chinese specialists on oil.[99] The Chinese had permitted these piecemeal changes in exchange contacts even as they had maintained that it was still premature to begin full-scale official exchanges negotiated directly between the two governments. The Press trip sought to test whether Beijing could be persuaded to sign agreements that would formalize government involvement and management of exchanges and that would therefore significantly upgrade the intensity of bilateral cooperation between the two governments.

This did not mean, however, that the US government expected or desired an end to the "facilitated" exchange program overseen by the

[97] Oksenberg to Brzezinski, June 30, 1978, "China (PRC), 1978/6–8," Box 8, NSAZB-MCF, JCL; Brzezinski, *Power and Principle*, 226.
[98] "Soviets Assail China Visit by U.S. Scientific Delegation," *Washington Post*, July 6, 1978.
[99] NCUSCR Annual Report, 1976–77, NCUSCROC; *CEN*, Vol. 5, No. 1, February 1977, and Vol. 6, No. 2, December 1977; "U.S.-China scientific relations advance," *Chemical & Engineering News*, May 16, 1977.

CSCPRC and the NCUSCR. In fact, plans for government-to-government exchanges were intended as an expansion of, and supplement to, the existing exchange program. Indeed, the briefing material prepared by Oksenberg for the group stated explicitly that the primary purpose of the trip was to, "Encourage an expanded science and technology program with China at all levels, particularly recognizing the important role to be played by the facilitating organizations" – that is, the NCUSCR, the CSCPRC, and the National Council for United States-China Trade. Thus, the specific proposals made by Press were for cooperation in agriculture, resource extraction, seismology, high-energy physics, public health, and space exploration – all but the last of which had been foci for the Committee on Scholarly Communication's exchange program to date. Likewise, Oksenberg instructed Brzezinski to "emphasize" to the Press delegation that, as the CSCPRC had long been arguing, "the S&T [*sic*] relationship we seek with China must be mutually beneficial and reciprocal."[100] Moreover, the areas of potential future cooperation that Oksenberg identified as most useful to American science – earthquake prediction and biological control of insects, for example – were just those that CSCPRC chairs – Lewis Branscomb and then Press himself – had targeted over the previous years for deeper cooperation between American and Chinese scientists.[101] The PRC hosting of the Press delegation indicated their own interest in building on earlier scientific exchanges: officials and scientists in the fields of agriculture, energy, medical care, geology, and metrology met the delegation – every single area of which had been the subject of earlier exchanges.[102]

The Chinese response to the Press visit, and to accelerating governmental and nongovernmental scientific cooperation, further confirmed Brzezinski and the Carter administration's belief that deeper cooperation in science and technology could precipitate a closer overall Sino-American relationship and more salubrious diplomatic contacts. Fang Yi suggested in his welcoming remarks to Press that the link ran in the other direction: "If the obstacle of the lack of normalization of Sino-U.S. relations is removed, vast vistas will open up for the expansion of scientific

---

[100] Oksenberg to Brzezinski, June 30, 1978, "China (PRC), 1978/6–8," Box 8, NSAZB-MCF, JCL.

[101] Branscomb to Handler, November 17, 1977, "1977 – Exchange Agreement – Negotiations," CSCPRCP, NAS; Pines to Press and Smith, March 11, 1975, "1975 – General," CSCPRCP, NAS.

[102] Xiong, "Deng Xiaoping's Views on Science and Technology," 178.

and technological exchanges and cooperation."[103] Other, less public comments by the Chinese government suggested, however, that the bait of US scientific assistance was working: soon after the Press delegation returned home, a PRC embassy official in a third country told their American colleague that Press's delegation had been considered in Beijing to have been a "major success," both in terms of encouraging further science and technology exchanges and in moving toward normalization. The official said that the trip had made the Chinese aware both of the need "to improve the flow of S&T [*sic*] information by increasing the amount of information coming in and upgrading the quality as well." The official indicated that the Chinese knew the most expedient way to do so: there was a "need to turn to the U.S., as the technological leader of the world, to increase and upgrade the technological information coming into China." The official had said that the delegation had been taken as an important sign in Beijing that the US government was sincere in moving rapidly toward normalization and confirmed that, as a direct result of the visit, Sino-American exchanges would presently increase.[104]

That month, Vice Premier Gu Mu returned from a five-week tour of Western Europe and became another powerful voice arguing for utilizing foreign expertise to catch up with the West, strengthening the Chinese domestic coalition in favor of the scientific cooperation proposed by Press. One of the arguments made by Gu after this trip, as well as by other influential Chinese leaders who visited Japan and other Western countries in 1978, was that buying off-the-shelf Western technology – as China had been doing since the early 1970s – would not alone be sufficient; there needed to be accompanying imports of human knowledge from the West, such that the PRC could itself begin to innovate and develop its own technology.[105] Press's trip had also seen progress on that front, with his Chinese hosts finally agreeing to a student exchange program. In a moment that would come to occupy a place in the folklore of the Sino-American exchange relationship, Press had called his president at 3 a.m. Washington time. "Frank, what's happened, [has] another

[103] "High Level Science & Technology Delegation to People's Republic of China Returns to United States," Center for US China Relations Newsletter, Folder 11, Box 1, WNP, TLWLANYU.

[104] Memorandum, The Situation Room to David Aaron, July 28, 1978, RACP: NLC-1-7-3-41-5, JCL.

[105] Gu Mu, *Huiyilu* [Memoirs] (Beijing: Zhongyang wenxian chubanshe, 2009), 293–309; ZGZYWXYJS, *Deng Xiaoping nianpu, 1975–1997*, 1: 335; Xiao Donglian, "Zhongguo gaige chuqi dui guowai jingyan de xitong kaocha he jiejian [The Systematic Investigation

Mount Etna ... exploded?" "No, I'm in China with Deng Xiaoping," Press responded, "Deng ... insisted I call you now to see if you would permit 5,000 Chinese students to come to American universities." Before slamming the phone down, Carter barked: "Tell him to send 100,000." Within five years, Deng had.[106]

THE FLOODGATES OPEN

Press's delegation thus achieved its immediate objective: beginning a program of government-to-government exchanges to supplement the contacts that were already taking place below the state level. In analyzing the connection between high diplomacy and exchanges in Sino-American relations, it is important to recognize that, after years of insisting that deeper exchanges must follow normalization, ultimately, Beijing agreed to a substantial enhancement of the exchange program nearly half a year before normalization was agreed. Three formal governmental agreements on exchanges – on agriculture, space technology, and student and scholarly exchanges – were all signed in the months between the Press visit and the final normalization deal of December 1978.[107]

It was not only the new program of official exchanges that benefitted from the Press trip. The Committee on Scholarly Communication sent another delegation of its leadership to China in August 1978. This delegation received a very different reception to that which Handler had led in June 1977. "Almost their first official words to me were that they now agree to end the period of 'scholarly tourism', and begin more substantive scholarly encounters," CSCPRC staff director Bullock reported. Her Chinese hosts gave "due recognition" that the CSCPRC had been pushing for such a change "for years" and now stated explicitly that, "We quite agree, after six years experience [*sic*], that there is a need to deepen scientific exchanges. We quite agree to turn our scientific tourism into a more substantive exchange program." Bullock reported that the Press trip "had made a deep impression on Chinese scientists and their institutions, not just in terms of initiating new governmental programs

and Use for Reference of Foreign Experience in the Early Days of Reform]," *Zhonggong Dangshi Yanjiu*, no. 4 (2006): 23–27.

[106] Carter speech, "What Can the U.S. and China Do Together?," November 10, 2013, available at www.cartercenter.org/news/editorials_speeches/jc-what-us-china-can-do-together.html. Accessed August 21, 2019.

[107] *CEN*, vol. 6, no. 5, December 1978; Smith, "Role of Scientists," 128.

but in strengthening ties with the American scholarly community." At every banquet and institution – even those in far-flung Harbin – the Chinese made reference to "a new era in Chinese-American [sic] scholarly relationships, a new sense that it would be possible to embark upon a wide variety of scholarly projects." Bullock concluded: "There was no question but that Frank Press's trip had reaffirmed a central role for the CSCPRC and the NAS in substantive scholarly exchanges."[108] The continued importance of the Committee on Scholarly Communication to Sino-American exchanges beyond the Press visit had been confirmed before his plane had even returned home: Oksenberg had called Bullock during the return flight to arrange to have her meet the plane at Andrews Air Force to urgently discuss how the CSCPRC could help the government substantiate the bold proposals made during Press's visit.[109]

Although Kissinger had always harbored an interest in bringing exchanges directly under the government's control, when the Carter administration was given the option to do so by Beijing's lifting of its objection to government-to-government exchange contacts, the White House instead opted to continue a public-private partnership in Sino-American exchanges. This was a reversion to type in the US government's broad approach to exchange diplomacy during the Cold War: Kissinger's desire to closely control Sino-American exchange contacts was the exception to the rule.[110] The government certainly increased its own involvement in exchange contacts from late 1978, but the Carter administration simultaneously asked both the CSCPRC and the NCUSCR to expand their activities, too. Press himself approached the CSCPRC in late August to ask the organization he had chaired to act as a conduit of information to the American academic community about the new program of student and scholar exchanges. Two weeks later, an Inter-Agency Task Force set up to initiate the newly agreed educational exchanges requested that the CSCPRC prepare a tender proposal to go a step further and manage the selection and sending of American students and scholars to China.[111]

---

[108] Bullock to Handler, August 11, 1978, "1978 – General," CSCPRCP, NAS; CSCPRC memorandum, "Conversation with Huang Kun-yi," August 8, 1978, "1978 – General," CSCPRCP, NAS.

[109] Author interview with Bullock.

[110] Krenn, *United States Cultural Diplomacy*, 7.

[111] Handler to Press, September 18, 1978, "1978 – Student Exchange Program – General," CSCPRCP, NAS.

The initiative for the Committee on Scholarly Communication having such a central role in these new exchanges came from the US government. Indeed, Bullock revealed to her Chinese counterparts that the organization, while excited by the expansion of the exchange of scientific researchers, was comparatively less interested in a direct role in student exchanges (even if the organization had worked on proposals for just such contacts in previous years).[112] Accordingly, the CSCPRC's tender proposal for managing student contacts made clear that, as the group had been asked by the government to run the program, the CSCPRC was not expecting to draw on any of its own funds to support the new exchanges. Instead, the organization asked the government for $287,000 in funding just to cover the CSCPRC's own costs in managing the program during the year ahead; further government funds were also expected to cover the stipends and travel costs of Americans traveling to China. The CSCPRC could set such conditions – and request such a substantial budget – because the Committee's leadership knew that, by 1978, it had become invaluable to the exchange program. Only the CSCPRC had the necessary institutional knowledge to be able to quickly realize such an ambitious expansion of exchange contact – experience accrued from managing visits involving hundreds of American and Chinese academics since 1972. The close relationship that the government and the Committee on Scholarly Communication had developed since that year made it natural that the government would turn to the organization to facilitate novel but familiar forms of contact. This new role would also facilitate the wider transmission of the CSCPRC's hard-earned institutional knowledge into a broader American academic community that had, until 1978, had to rely on the Committee as the primary gatekeeper to scholarly exchange with China.[113]

Chinese memoir accounts and archival documents reveal that Beijing similarly believed that nongovernmental contacts with Americans would continue to be an important conduit of scientific and technical

---

[112] CSCPRC memorandum, "Conversation with Chien Hao," August 11, 1978, "1978 – General," CSCPRCP, NAS; Handler and Sheldon to Zhou Peiyuan, May 4, 1977, "1977 – Visits – Committee Visit on Scholarly Exchanges," CSCPRCP, NAS.

[113] Handler to Press, September 18, 1978, "1978 – Student Exchange Program – General," CSCPRCP, NAS; CSCPRC paper: "Students Exchanges with the People's Republic of China: A Statement of Capabilities and Management Options," July 23, 1978, Folder 6374, Box 527, Series 1, Accession 2, SSRC records, RAC.

knowledge.[114] For example, plans for the November 1978 hosting of a delegation from the American Society for Metals specifically identified expanding channels of nongovernmental exchanges of technical knowledge as a priority for the visit. Metallurgy had been an area in which the PRC had been importing substantial foreign equipment since the early 1970s, such as through the "Four-Three Program" – so named because it involved US$4.3 billion of imports of such equipment.[115] Chinese hosts noted the global standing of the American Society of Metals as a nongovernmental professional and academic society. That standing was reflected in the delegation's composition, which included a combination of top figures from US companies, including the Ford Motor Company and US Steel, and academics such as the delegation leader, the Columbia-based, Chongqing-born Chinese American expert in high-temperature alloys, John Kai Tien.[116] The contrast between this visit and those of a year prior was stark: there were no complaints about normalization by either side, and an "utterly friendly and harmonious" atmosphere was the backdrop for Ye Zhiqiang, a vice minister in the Ministry of Metallurgical Industry, telling Tien of the "vast" prospects for exchanges and trade in the future.[117]

The American Society for Metals visit was just one example of a 1978 exchange that included the communication of technical, expert knowledge of immediate benefit to China's upgrading of its technology. The American visitors were reportedly positively impressed with some aspects of the Shanghai No. 5 Steel Plant, located in the Baoshan District that would soon become one of the hearts of Chinese steel manufacturing in the Reform and Opening period. The Americans also, however,

[114] Li Qi, "Ji 1978 nian Zhou lao shuai Zhongguo jiaoyu daibiaotuan fang Mei [Remembering Zhou Peiyuan's Leading of the 1978 Education Delegation to the United States]," in *Zongshi jujiang biaoshuai kaimo – – jinian Zhou Peiyuan wenji* [Grand Master and Role Model: Anthology Commemorating Zhou Peiyuan (Beijing: Xueyuan Press, 2002), 102.

[115] Chen Donglin, "Kaifang de qianzou: 'Sisan fang'an' jiqi dui Gaige Kaifang de yingxiang [A Prelude to Opening-up: The Four-Three Program and its Influence on Reform and Opening]," *Journal of National Museum of China*, no. 1 (2019): 10–19.

[116] Shanghai Metallurgical Industry Bureau Revolutionary Committee, "Guanyu jiedai Meiguo yejin xuehui fang Hua tuan de qingshi baogao" [Request for instructions on receiving the delegation from the American Society for Metals], November 16, 1978, Folder B122-3-15, SHMA.

[117] Shanghai Metallurgical Bureau Reception Team, "Jiedai Meiguo yejin xuehui daibiaotuan jianbao" [Report on hosting delegation from the American Society for Metals], November 22, 1978, Folder B122-3-15, SHMA.

worked with their Chinese hosts on where foreign technology could be best deployed to upgrade the facilities, for example, by replacing technology imported during the 1960s with computer-equipped facilities as used in the United States. Techniques for the use of this technology were also shared during a symposium: one of the visiting Americans offered a detailed, practical presentation that included five precise suggestions for how to better make use of vacuum metallurgy in steel processing that the Chinese report described as "of great research value to us."[118]

The exchange came on the back of a National Council for United States-China Trade-hosted visit to the United States by China's Society of Metals in August through September that had been led by Xu Zhi, the vice minister of metallurgy. During that exchange, the Chinese visitors had stressed their interest in a US role developing China's mining industry.[119] Like the US government, then, the PRC saw the beginning of governmental cooperation in science and technology as complementary to continuing nongovernmental contacts, rather than negating the need for such exchanges. Indeed, with greater opportunities for importing advanced American technology, scientific exchanges took on an added importance as a means by which Chinese scientists could identify and then learn to make best use of the cutting-edge, foreign technology with which they were often comparatively unfamiliar.

An exchange with the American Society for Metals was still a scientific exchange of the sort that predominated before 1978, even if it clearly had immediate practical benefits to Chinese industry. Further Chinese records from 1978 reveal that other contacts that came under the rubric of "technical exchanges" reflected newfound Chinese interest in technology purchases: they were often dominated by attempts by American manufacturers to sell their technology and, as importantly, their processes to the PRC. One such trip was by an engineer from the US company Miles Laboratories and focused on what was, in 1978, still a new technology that the company had developed only two years earlier: high-fructose corn syrup. In a detailed report on "mechanical efficiency," water consumption, and "technical requirements," the Shanghai Food Industry Corporation described the "far-reaching significance" of introducing the process into China's food production industry and suggested that a 150,000-ton-capacity syrup plant could be built in two years or less.

---

[118] Ibid.
[119] *NFTNC*, Vol. 8, No. 2/3, Summer/Fall 1978.

The Miles engineer used the example of his company's recent exports of the technology and processes of producing high-fructose corn syrup to Hungary as a reference point for how China could introduce the technique into its agricultural processing.[120] Handler and his colleagues at the CSCPRC had earlier worried that the PRC was using scientific exchange visits to the United States to learn American agricultural modernization techniques on the sly; in post-Mao China, the PRC could avoid this circuitous route and buy directly from the source.[121]

The Chinese records on hosting scientific exchanges from 1978 are distinct from earlier records: where before the politics of exhibiting socialism were the dominant trope, with scientific knowledge primarily discussed within such terms, by 1978, internal Chinese government communication on scientific contact with the United States was explicitly focused on what China could gain through exchange. For sure, as this book has argued, this was always an important consideration in the scientific delegations China sent to the United States. However, the profound changes in China of 1978 were evident in the transparently utilitarian approach to receiving American scientists that year: gone were concerns about propaganda and promoting socialist science, now Chinese cadres unabashedly reported the utility of learning from Americans visiting the PRC.[122]

These changes were also evident in 1978's reversal of the long-standing dynamic in negotiations between the CSCPRC and the Chinese government: where before, it had almost always been the Americans pressing Beijing to agree to greater contacts, now Chinese science officials proposed an expansion of contacts that stretched the capacity of both the Committee on Scholarly Communication and of American scientific and educational institutions. In negotiations over expanding the exchange of research scholars, Huang Kunyi, who represented both the Scientific and Technical Association of the PRC and China's State Science and Technology Commission, told Bullock during the CSCPRC leadership delegation of August that Beijing wanted to send as many scholars as possible to the

---

[120] Shanghai Food Industry Corporation, "Yu Meiguo Maiersi Gongsi zuotan qingkuang huibao" [Report on discussions with US Miles Company], November 23, 1978, Folder B189-2-1840, SHMA.

[121] For a later, related development, see Charles Kraus, "More than Just a Soft Drink: Coca-Cola and China's Early Reform and Opening," _Diplomatic History_ 43, no. 1 (January 2019): 107–29.

[122] British scientists and their government simultaneously observed this new trend in China's approach to scientific cooperation. Agar, "'It's Springtime for Science'," 16–17.

United States, at any expense. Bullock, however, cautioned that she could not produce "some magic number" of how many researchers American universities could absorb, emphasizing that each individual academic must be matched with an appropriate American colleague.[123]

PRC leaders were equally anxious to begin student exchanges. Jian Hao, another State Science and Technology Commission representative, knew Bullock well after a month spent traveling together during the Chinese seismology delegation sent to the United States in 1974. Now, during Bullock's August 1978 visit to the PRC, Jian revealed that his ministry was under great pressure to rapidly expand exchange contacts in order to serve the ambitious domestic development agenda being set by Deng. China had initially proposed sending as many as 500 students to the United States by the very next month, but Jian admitted that they simply could not find enough suitably qualified students in such a short space of time, with the Chinese official particularly concerned about the fluency of the students' English. Ultimately, fifty-two Chinese scholars would arrive in the United States before the end of 1978, with the remaining 450 arriving by the end of the 1978–79 academic year. There was a slant toward older students, described by the Chinese side as graduate students or research fellows – or simply, and deliberately ambiguously, "visiting scholars." In fact, however, many of those sent had received their education prior to the beginning of the Cultural Revolution in 1966; China had only reopened its universities in 1977. Thus, many of the Chinese sent in 1978 and 1979 undertook study rather than research in the United States, using their time in American universities to offset education they had missed earlier in their life.[124]

Exchanges that directly served Chinese modernization were certainly Beijing's priority in 1978, but the National Committee was also adjusting to Beijing's newfound enthusiasm for expanding contacts. The NCU-SCR had been involved in a series of recent blockbuster exchanges. With Madison Square Gardens, the National Committee co-hosted a Chinese national basketball team that featured the 7-foot-six-inch "Great Wall" Mu Tiezhu, who anticipated the equally tall – but ultimately far more talented – future star Yao Ming. The NCUSCR had sent an American

[123] CSCPRC memorandum, "Conversation with Huang Kun-yi," August 8, 1978, "1978 – General," CSCPRCP, NAS.
[124] CSCPRC memorandum, "Conversation with Chien Hao," August 11, 1978, "1978 – General," CSCPRCP; Li, "Ji 1978 nian Zhou lao shuai Zhongguo jiaoyu daibiaotuan fang Mei," 101–02, 104.

tennis team, sponsored by Pepsi, to China in October 1977 that played
to nearly 10,000 spectators, the largest ever crowds for that sport in
China, before sending a volleyball delegation in June 1978 and their first
ticketed paid-for delegations for their members (further discussed in the
epilogue).[125] The highlight of the National Committee's 1978 program
was receiving the largest ever cultural troupe to be sent by the PRC to
any country. The delegation of 150 performers from the Performing Arts
Company of the PRC – a belated replacement for the cancelled 1975
troupe (Chapter 4) – had arrived in July on two of the US-made Boeing 707s bought by the PRC earlier in the decade. The performers had
been personally welcomed to the United States by Carter and Brzezinski
before meeting with Martha Graham and undertaking an "enormously
popular" tour co-hosted by the New York Metropolitan Opera House.[126]
The opening night alone attracted an audience of 4,000 to New York's
Lincoln Center, with the spectators witnessing both modern and classical
works, ranging from revolutionary ballet and folk dance, through traditional Beijing opera, to solo Western-style singers and a pianist, with
performers including Guo Zhihong, son of Guo Moruo. Some of the
visitors' repertoire had previously been banned by the Gang of Four but
now reintroduced into the troupe's program for the visit.[127]

With the end of Jiang Qing and the Gang of Four's control over Chinese culture in 1977, new forms of Sino-American cultural collaboration
seemed possible. In January 1978, the Austrian-born American film and
theatre director, Otto Preminger, was invited to China to discuss the possibility of filming a biopic of Norman Bethune, the Canadian surgeon
who had become a household name in the PRC after being eulogized
by Mao himself for his medical work alongside the People's Liberation
Army. Mao's 1939 essay "In Memory of Norman Bethune" held the surgeon up as a paragon of revolutionary internationalism and was read by

---

[125] "Zhongguo lanqiu daibiaotuan li Jing fu Mei" [Chinese basketball delegation leaves
Beijing for the United States], *Renmin Ribao*, November 10, 1978; NCUSCR Annual
Report, 1977–78, NCUSCROC; "Chinese Hoping Sky Is Limit for Their Man Mu,"
Washington Post, November 16, 1978.

[126] "Wo yishutuan zai Huashengdun juxing shou chang yanchu" [Our performing arts
troupe held its first performance in Washington], *Renmin Ribao*, July 22, 1978; NCU-
SCR Annual Report, 1977–78, NCUSCROC; NCUSCR "Program Summary: January-June, 1978," "NCUSCR – Board Meeting, 1978," Box 131, ADBP, RBMLCU;
Gold, "Critical Juncture," Chapter 9.

[127] "Meiguo guanzhong relie huanying Zhongguo yishutuan yanchu" [An American audience warmly welcomes the performance of the Chinese arts troupe], *Renmin Ribao*, July
7, 1978; Gold, "Critical Juncture," Chapter 9.

practically all Chinese children during their schooling, even as Bethune was comparatively unknown in North America. Preminger had asked to visit China to shoot the biopic in 1972, but his request had apparently been rebuffed by Jiang Qing.[128]

Preminger was warmly welcomed in 1978, but Chinese officials remained uncertain as to how to effectively host an American director who had twice been nominated for the Academy Award for Best Director. Those tasked with hosting Preminger in Shanghai had been informed by the central state-owned China Film Corporation that Preminger had been invited as a businessman; only later did they realize he was a film director – and a famous one at that (they quickly organized a Chinese film director of their own to act as his escort).[129] It was, then, perhaps little surprise that Preminger's biopic was not quickly realized: the director died in 1986, four years before a version of his proposed film was released in the form of *Bethune: The Making of a Hero*. The 1990 film was the first co-production between the PRC and any Western country, and at the time the most expensive Canadian film ever made. Its five-year production had, however, been dogged by delays, not least when the entire forty-person Canadian crew staged a walk-out from filming in Yan'an in protest at poor working conditions (an apt location for such a protest).[130] Preminger's 1978 visit was notable, then, as a first step toward Chinese cinematic cooperation with the West – but there was still much ground to be covered before such cooperation bore fruit.

NORMALIZATION

Brzezinski's strategy of incorporating Chinese interest in American science and technology into Washington's push for normalization had helped to bring an agreement into sight by the final months of 1978. Chinese interest in realizing a normalization agreement with the United

---

[128] Shanghai Revolutionary Committee Foreign Affairs Office, "Jiedai Meiguo dianying daoyan jian zhipianren Puleimingge de qingkuang" [Report on receiving US film director and producer Otto Preminger], January 20, 1978, Folder B177-4-670, SHMA; Hooper, *Foreigners under Mao*, 14; Brady, *Making the Foreign Serve China*, 145; Jay Leyda, "China's Dr. Bethune," *Film Quarterly* 32, no. 2 (1978): 63–64.

[129] Shanghai Revolutionary Committee Foreign Affairs Office, "Jiedai Meiguo dianying daoyan jian zhipianren Puleimingge de qingkuang," January 20, 1978, Folder B177-4-670, SHMA.

[130] *Bethune: The Making of a Hero* entry in the Canadian Film Encyclopedia, available at http://cfe.tiff.net/canadianfilmencyclopedia/content/films/bethune-the-making-of-a-hero. Accessed January 12, 2021.

States now appeared to be at least as motivated by the beneficial effects this would have on their domestic modernization as they were the PRC's international security. Huang Hua recalls in his memoirs that Deng was pushing for improvements in ties with Washington in 1978 at least in part because "this was ... necessary with regard to the economy."[131] Li Jie, a Chinese historian with access to party records, has persuasively argued that, because "the United States was clearly the main sources of advanced ideas and technology" for China's modernization drive, "the smooth normalization of relations [became] a key component in China's opening to the world."[132]

As the White House pushed for normalization, government officials were mindful that the influence of scientific exchanges on normalization talks could run in the other direction: that the CSCPRC's practice of hard-nosed negotiating with Beijing could hurt the momentum toward normalization. Oksenberg had reported to Brzezinski in August that the Chinese were impatient to begin student exchanges but that any flaunting of American superiority in science could revive xenophobia in Beijing. The NSC advisor argued that, "How we handle the student exchange program should take into account [D]eng's vulnerabilities. We want to make sure that the Chinese students are qualified and that the program entails reciprocity, but the way we achieve these objectives must not intrude on Chinese definitions of sovereignty."[133] The government knew that the Committee on Scholarly Communication was worried about the possibility of the PRC sending underqualified scholars and students with poor English – worries fueled when Jian Hao had shared his own concerns about China having no choice but to do so with Bullock. Moreover, the Committee's long-standing concerns about disparity in levels of access during scientific exchanges had only begun to be addressed in 1978.[134] Oksenberg pushed the CSCPRC to take a light touch on both issues – at least until normalization was agreed.[135]

[131] Harding, *Fragile Relationship*, 349.
[132] Li Jie, "China's Domestic Politics and the Normalization of Sino-U.S. Relations," in *Normalization of U.S.-China Relations: An International History*, ed. William Kirby, Robert Ross, and Gong Li (Cambridge, MA: Harvard University Asia Center, 2007), 82.
[133] Oksenberg to Brzezinski, August 11, 1978, *FRUS, 1977–1980*, Vol. XIII, Document 128; Oksenberg to Brzezinski, August 7, 1978, "Armacost Evening and Weekly Reports File, 1978/7–8," Box 1, NSASMFEF, JCL.
[134] CSCPRC memorandum, "Conversation with Chien Hao," August 11, 1978, "1978 – General," CSCPRCP, NAS.
[135] Brzezinski to Mondale, August 18, 1978, "China (PRC), 1978/6–8," Box 8, NSAZB-MCF, JCL.

If there remained areas of unresolved tension in exchange diplomacy that could have complicated normalization negotiations, overall, the new heights reached in exchanges in late 1978 buttressed accompanying high-diplomatic talks and offered a harbinger of a new era in the Sino-American relationship. In October, Zhou Peiyuan led a delegation to Washington that negotiated an agreement to begin student and scholar exchanges with the National Science Foundation's director, psychologist Richard C. Atkinson.[136] Zhou and his colleagues were working frantically to meet Deng's call in June 1978 to have as many as 3,000 or 4,000 Chinese students enroll at foreign universities in 1978 – and as many as 10,000 the following year – and hoped the United States could accept many of these students. With normalization not yet agreed, the delegation was officially nongovernmental, with Zhou using only his title of president of Peking University and acting chairman of the China Association for Science and Technology, a mass organization representing Chinese scientists and engineers on a nongovernmental basis. However, Li Qi, who then worked for the PRC State Council on science and education, recalls that one of the objectives of the visit was to begin official state-to-state scientific exchanges and thus to aid progress toward normalization. Li recalls that the delegation simultaneously sought to broaden contacts with US universities and nongovernmental scientific research institutions.[137]

Meanwhile, the Committee on Scholarly Communication estimated that 1978 had seen a year-on-year tripling of the number of total exchanges between the United States and China, with many of the American visitors to China being provided levels of access unprecedented since 1949.[138] Meanwhile, the NCUSCR had sponsored nine exchanges that year – a total number of trips just one short of the tally for the previous two years combined.[139] In addition, long-delayed technology licenses were finally receiving approval from the more reluctant departments within the US government and Beijing had been persuaded to make the large grain purchases that, it was hoped, would help make normalization attractive to US domestic audiences thinking of their pocketbooks.[140]

---

[136] Zhou, *Zhou Peiyuan wenji*, 438.

[137] Li, "Ji 1978 nian Zhou lao shuai Zhongguo jiaoyu daibiaotuan fang Mei," 99–101.

[138] *CEN*, vol. 6, no. 5, December 1978.

[139] NCUSCR Annual Reports, 1977–78 and 1978–79, NCUSCROC.

[140] Brzezinski to Carter, September 11, 1978, "China MR-NLC-98-215 [3]," Box 41, CVF, JCL.

Indeed, American businesses reported unprecedented interest in trade from their Chinese counterparts, including in sectors long eyed by corporate America, such as China's off-shore oil reserves.[141]

As Brzezinski had predicted, normalization negotiations had been buoyed by flourishing exchanges and trade and were proceeding apace. A key meeting had occurred between Carter and PRCLO chief, Chai Zemin, on September 19, in which the president made clear that the United States would continue a full range of "commercial contacts" – in other words, arms sales – to Taiwan after normalization. Chai protested – but did not rule out proceeding with a deal under such conditions.[142] On November 2, the United States presented a draft normalization communiqué to the Chinese.[143] That same day, Deng pressed his Politburo to seize the opportunity at hand and strike a deal with Washington.[144] Deng and USLO chief Woodcock hammered out the final terms in the first two weeks of December: Washington would terminate its Mutual Defense Treaty with Taiwan by activating a one-year cancellation clause and not sell arms to the ROC during that period – although the US side made clear that such sales would resume thereafter. This last point had been resisted by Chai but Deng – the ultimate Chinese arbiter – had grudgingly agreed to normalize relations anyway. Ambassadors would be exchanged in March 1979, and Deng himself would visit the United States beginning in January – the first top leader of the PRC to officially do so. The deal was announced in Beijing and Washington on December 15, 1978.[145]

The efforts by both the Chinese and US governments to boost American popular support for normalization in 1978 paid off: pollsters reported the highest popular support for recognizing the PRC on record, with 66 percent of Americans in favor to 25 percent opposed. Another poll conducted in the wake of normalization found that 45 percent of Americans believed the PRC was friendly to the United States compared to 23 percent who saw Beijing as unfriendly, far superior numbers to views of the

---

[141] Oksenberg and Huberman to Brzezinski, August 31, 1978, RACP: NLC-26-53-5-10-9, JCL; Brzezinski to Carter, September 11, 1978, "China MR-NLC-98-215 [3]," Box 41, CVF, JCL.

[142] Memcon: Carter and Chai, September 19, 1978, "China MR-NLC-98-215 [3]," Box 41, CVF, JCL.

[143] Brzezinski, *Power and Principle*, 229.

[144] Wang Taiping, ed., *Zhonghua renmin gongheguo waijiao shi: 1970–1978* [A Diplomatic History of the People's Republic of China, 1970–1978], vol. 3 (Beijing: Shijie zhishi chubanshe, 1999), 378.

[145] Fardella, "Sino-American Normalization," 566–70.

Soviet Union – 21 percent friendly to 31 percent unfriendly. The tactics of 1978 surely helped the public reception of normalization, but polling also suggested that the long-term process of building broad support for Sino-American relations, not least through exchange contacts, had paid off: the 1978 figure of 66 percent public approval for recognition was the highest yet recorded, but only a slight improvement on the 62 percent in favor from 1977, whereas these figures were night-and-day different to the 39 percent in favor/45 percent opposed of a decade earlier. Cultural exchanges were even more popular than diplomatic ties: a separate poll in October 1977 found that more than three-quarters of Americans favored increased cultural and sporting exchanges, with only an eighth of people opposed, higher figures than support for greater trade.[146]

There is, of course, no comparable data for the reception of the agreement among the Chinese population, but an internal Shanghai Office of Propaganda report dated Christmas Day 1978 offers insight into how the PRC state presented the agreement to the Chinese populace and the citizenry's apparent response. The report reveals that, when the news had been announced, the local government had organized mass meetings to listen to radio broadcasts or watch television reports on the agreement. Some of the audience apparently remarked that the television reports were akin to an "atomic bomb that shocked the entire world," with others reading poems to mark the event. In what the report claimed was a "free discussion" between cadres and the masses, myriad benefits of normalization were cited, from "isolating the Chiang clique" to "combatting Vietnam's petty hegemonism" – a harbinger of the PRC's attack on Vietnam less than two months later. The discussion included an examination of why the two countries had established diplomatic relations "so quickly" – glossing over eight years of negotiation since ping-pong diplomacy and instead highlighting the rapid breakthroughs of 1978 – in which expanding scientific and cultural exchanges and trade were highlighted as incentives for both sides to have reached a normalization deal. "The people of both countries strongly demand an increase in contact and exchange and the further development of friendship," the report claimed.[147]

---

[146] Connie de Boer, "The Polls: Changing Attitudes and Policies toward China," *Public Opinion Quarterly* 44, no. 2 (Summer 1980): 269–73.

[147] CCP Shanghai Municipal Committee Office of Propaganda, "Sixiang dongxiang: Zhong Mei jianjiao de xiaoxi fabiao hou ben shi ganbu he qunzhong xuexi taolun de qingkuang" [Ideological trends: Report on study and discussions with cadres and

The document bridged the rhetoric of the pre- and post-Deng eras: trade was talked about as mutually beneficial, although some Marxian logic came through in the claim that the United States needed China as a market because of the country's excess in goods and capital. The authors in the Shanghai government's propaganda department struck a confident tone, but the document also made explicit that China would benefit from deeper ties, citing the need to import advanced scientific knowledge and equipment from the West to serve the Four Modernizations. In a more defensive passage, the report admitted that Beijing and Washington had not fully agreed on the issue of arms sales to the ROC and even aired internal disagreements over the wording of the normalization agreement on the issue of Taiwan: the authors stated that Gan Bo, a local cadre from Shanghai's Yangpu District, was wrong to worry that the United States had been insufficiently explicit about its plans to withdraw from Taiwan – and went as far as saying that the remaining presence of hundreds of American troops on the island would prevent it falling under the influence of the Soviet Union. Citing the virtues of a continued American military presence on Taiwan seemed a remarkable walk back from the PRC's earlier hardline positions on US withdrawal from the island and was a striking testament both to Carter's successful negotiations and to the powerful transformation in PRC priorities in Sino-American relations under Deng's guidance.[148]

CONCLUSION

The final weeks of 1978 were a symbolic turning point for modern China: after the December 15 announcement of a normalization agreement, December 18 to 22 saw the Third Plenum of the Eleventh Congress of the CCP at which Deng was confirmed as having usurped Hua Guofeng as China's paramount leader and at which his agenda for modernization through Reform and Opening Up was adopted. As this chapter has argued, these developments were not unrelated. After more than seven years of normalization negotiations, the Carter administration finally achieved a deal with Deng in part as a result of Brzezinski placing scientific cooperation at the center of the Sino-American relationship and connecting negotiations over assistance to the PRC's ambitious modernization

---

the masses on the establishment of Sino-American diplomatic relations], December 25, 1978, Folder A22-4-14-64, SHMA.
[148] Ibid.

agenda to normalization talks. Chinese impatience to secure access to US science and technology had already seen Beijing compromise on its previous stance that an upgrading of scientific exchanges had to wait for normalization: in fact, both nongovernmental and governmental exchanges had evolved to a new level in 1978, many months before a final normalization deal was struck. This evident hunger for American scientific expertise and technology had simultaneously emboldened Carter to set forth strong normalization conditions. The CSCPRC had long argued that science and technology gave the United States leverage over China and the ultimate proof of this was offered in Deng's decision to compromise on previously sacrosanct normalization terms, establishing formal relations with Washington despite knowing that the US government would cease to sell arms to Taiwan for only a short one-year grace period. Thus, where cultural exchanges had kick-started Sino-American rapprochement, in 1978, scientific cooperation – not least through exchanges – helped bring about a normalization agreement on terms that served Deng and the PRC's immediate interests but also Carter and Washington's long-term desire to protect Taiwan.

Epilogue

The New Normal

Normalization had a profound effect on the Sino-American exchange program and interactions between the societies of China and the United States more broadly. The unusual characteristics of exchanges from 1971 to 1978 had been a result of the unique relationship between the Chinese and US governments: a partnership intense and important but also unofficial and incomplete. This had made the informal diplomacy of the National Committee, the Committee on Scholarly Communication, and their Chinese counterparts of great consequence and ensured that exchange organizations were recognized by both governments as key actors in the Sino-American relationship. Both the NCUSCR and CSCPRC celebrated normalization, an achievement they had consciously contributed to since the mid-1960s; both were feted by the Chinese government for the contribution they had made to that achievement.[1] But the formalization of Sino-American diplomatic ties also posed a challenge to the two nongovernmental Committees. Beijing had previously insisted that Sino-American government-sponsored exchanges had to await normalization; now that normalization had been achieved, the NCUSCR and CSCPRC had to find purpose and support in a changed political environment. This epilogue briefly considers the landscape of the exchange program as and after normalization was realized. It argues that, despite the changes in the Sino-American diplomatic relationship, there were as many continuities as there were changes between pre- and

---

[1] "Wo zhu Mei lianluochu juxing zhaodaihui qingzhu Zhong Mei jianjiao" [Our Liaison Office in the United States Held a Reception to Celebrate the Establishment of Diplomatic Relations between China and the United States], *Renmin Ribao*, January 3, 1979.

post-normalization exchange contacts, at least in the immediate wake of the upgrading of the governmental relationship.

EXCHANGES AND THE STATE

The most important change in Sino-American exchange contacts to occur post-normalization was the beginning of major direct involvement of both governments in exchanges. As early as 1977, there had begun to be a gradual increase in government participation in facilitated exchanges, particularly through the inclusion of government employees from both sides in exchange trips. This had intensified in the wake of the Frank Press trip of July 1978. This earlier official participation in exchanges notwithstanding, the array of formal government-to-government exchange agreements that began to be signed from late 1978 afforded the US government unprecedented involvement in exchange contacts and made Chinese government involvement official and explicit. For the first time, the two governments acted as the official sponsors and organizers of exchanges. This was a function that had on the US side previously been the almost exclusive domain of private organizations (with the exception of congressional delegations and a very small number of other officially sponsored exchange delegations).[2] However, as has been argued over the course of this book, this was not a change from the government being uninvolved in exchanges to being deeply involved; instead, it was only the manner of involvement that changed. Both governments had always been deeply interested in exchanges since 1971; the difference had been that, before normalization, the US government had exercised its influence indirectly and largely out of sight, while the Chinese government had preferred to negotiate exchange contacts primarily with US nongovernmental organizations.

---

[2] The summer and autumn of 1978 had seen a range of government employees involved in exchange visits: China had sent a delegation of municipal administrators, many of whom were senior party members as well as government officials; a delegation of US educators had included the executive deputy commissioner of the Office of Education; an NCU-SCR civic and world affairs delegation had included Donna Shalala of the Department of Housing and Urban Development; and the director of the High Energy Physics Division of the Department of Energy, Dr. W. A. Wallenmeyer, had given a lecture tour in China. Minutes of 32nd meeting of NCUSCR board, July 5, 1978, "NCUSCR – Board Meeting, 1978," Box 131, ADBP; *CEN*, vol. 6, no. 5, December 1978; Shalala to Rosen, October 24, 1978, Folder 92, Box 12, Series 3, RG4, NCUSCR records, RAC; NCUSCR "Program Summary: January-June, 1978," "NCUSCR – Board Meeting, 1978," Box 131, ADBP.

This led to a recasting of the formal definition of the exchanges overseen by the CSCPRC and the NCUSCR. Since 1972, the exchanges overseen by the two groups had been classed as "facilitated exchanges." Although China maintained that contacts arranged through the two groups and the National Council for United States-China Trade were with the American people, their use of the term "facilitated exchanges" was a reminder that, in fact, Beijing (and Washington, too) saw these exchanges as more than unofficial contacts and instead as a program that was nongovernmental and private in execution but partially facilitated by officials. Revealingly, in 1978, the Chinese government explicitly stated that they considered contacts with the National Committee and Committee on Scholarly Communication to now be exclusively "people-to-people" contacts, and no longer "facilitated." In doing so, Beijing effectively relieved the organizations of their previous role as government-endorsed facilitators of exchanges and placed them in the same category as other private organizations with no close links to government that were involved in transnational interaction with China.[3] This action contradicted repeated Chinese claims made earlier in the decade that Beijing could not endorse anything other than people-to-people contacts until normalization. It was, then, indicative of the true Chinese understanding of the liminal nature of exchange contacts in the unique circumstances of Sino-American rapprochement before 1979.

As had already become clear in the second half of 1978, however, this more direct state involvement in exchange contacts would not end the CSCPRC and NCUSCR's role in exchanges with China. Shortly after normalization took place, Brzezinski wrote to National Committee Chairman Charles Yost, saying, "I recognize that your Committee has legitimate questions to ask concerning your role in the post-normalization period," but assured Yost that, "if anything, the opportunities for your organization to play a vital role in Sino-American relations will expand."[4] Indeed, in the late 1970s, 1980s, and even into the 1990s, both groups increased their exchange activities with China. The National Committee continues to be heavily involved in Sino-American transnational contacts to this day, although the organization's formal exchanges were wound down in the 1990s as private travel to China became commonplace. The Committee on Scholarly Communication closed its Washington office in

---

[3] CSCPRC memorandum, "Conversation with Chien Hao," August 11, 1978, "1978 – General," CSCPRCP, NAS.
[4] Brzezinski to Yost, January 9, 1979, Folder 15, Box 1, Series 1, DPMP, RAC.

1996, although a scholar exchange program was, until just a few years ago, continued out of the American Council of Learned Societies and a CSCPRC Beijing office.

After normalization, both Committees continued organizing Sino-American exchanges with enthusiastic government support. In January 1978, the National Committee's board removed a previous restriction on the proportion of the organization's budget that could be drawn from public funds; that year was the first in which more than half of the Committee's budget (55 percent, or $290,000) would come from the government. The following year the absolute and relative figures of state support went up further. Norton Wheeler's study of the NCUSCR in the 1980s and 1990s states that government funding for the group continued to grow in real terms, if not in proportional terms, into the 1980s and amounted to 25–30 percent of the NCUSCR's (larger) budget in that period. This public support dropped off only in the 1990s, when other sources of income grew substantially (and the administrative burden associated with applying for government grants grew).[5]

The Committee on Scholarly Communication likewise continued to receive substantial government support after 1978. Funding was received indirectly through the National Science Foundation but also through direct support, including the funding secured to oversee the student exchange program that was launched in 1978. The vast expansion of scientific and technical contacts that the group would oversee from 1979 meant that the group's budget was expected to balloon to $1.5 million for that year, a significant portion of which was provided by the US government.[6] However, the White House's Office of Science and Technology Policy was not prioritized for budgetary funding in the years that followed, which encouraged the CSCPRC to also continue to seek private funding.[7]

THE PLURALIZATION OF EXCHANGES

Another important change that began in 1977 and 1978 but intensified after normalization was the pluralization of the organizations involved in

---

[5] Minutes of 31st meeting of NCUSCR board, January 16, 1978, "NCUSCR – Board Meeting, 1978," Box 131, ADBP, RBMLCU; NCUSCR Annual Reports, 1977–78 and 1978–79, NCUSCROC; Wheeler, *American NGOs in China's Modernization*, 30; author interview with Berris, New York, United States, August 27, 2017.

[6] NAS council minutes, "Report of the Foreign Secretary," October 29, 1978, "1978 – Student Exchange Program – General," CSCPRCP, NAS.

[7] Suttmeier and Simon, "Conflict and Cooperation," 155.

Sino-American exchanges and thus the decentralization of such contacts. Between 1971 and 1978, most exchanges had been organized by a small number of organizations and institutions on both sides. On the Chinese side, the Scientific and Technical Association of the PRC, the Chinese People's Institute of Foreign Affairs, the Chinese People's Association for Friendship with Foreign Countries, and a small number of other government-run, Beijing-based organizations had managed exchanges centrally. The US side of the exchange program likewise had strong central organization: as has been shown, the National Committee, the Committee on Scholarly Communication, and the National Council for United States-China Trade managed the most high-profile exchanges, with only the US-China Peoples Friendship Association offering a competing set of regular contacts (and those of a lower political profile). The centrality of these exchange organizations notwithstanding, exchanges could, before 1978, be arranged directly with other organizations in the United States in a way that was not possible with Chinese institutions. As we have seen, during the 1970s, Beijing negotiated ad hoc individual or occasional visits with an array of US companies, professional societies, research institutions, and public figures in a manner that, before 1978, they would not have permitted in reverse. (Often, these groups would then turn to the NCUSCR or CSCPRC for advice or funding, even as they also planned their visit directly with the Chinese.)

This relatively streamlined system of managing Sino-American societal contact was atomized on both sides beginning in early 1978. From China's March 1978 National Science Conference onwards, institutions throughout the PRC were permitted to begin negotiating exchange contacts directly with US groups without necessarily coordinating with their own central government.[8] Moreover, while receiving exchange delegations and other visitors continued to be an important part of China's foreign relations, the PRC government began to switch its focus from high-profile visits planned in Beijing to more localized initiatives throughout the country that did not always have to be coordinated with the central government.[9] In turn, this helped precipitate a similar decentralization on the US side. Stanford University, which had been the first stop on Zhou Peiyuan's October 1978 visit to the United States (Chapter 6), was the first American university to directly agree an exchange program with the PRC when they signed a deal to swap students and scholars with

[8] Smith, "Role of Scientists," 128.
[9] Brady, *Making the Foreign Serve China*, 190.

the Chinese Academy of Sciences and other Beijing-based institutions. The agreement was negotiated by Douglas Murray, the former NCUSCR vice president, during Zhou's trip, with Stanford receiving their first students from the PRC within a month. By the end of the year, Berkeley and Temple University – home to the Chinese American scientist Man-Chiang Niu – also had Chinese scholars resident on their campuses.[10] This was only the beginning of a process that would see a huge expansion in the number of Chinese students and scholars participating in a multitude of US academic programs over the following decades.

The pluralization of exchange organizations and the accompanying loosening of restrictions of travel to the PRC that occurred in 1978 might, like the US government's direct involvement in managing exchanges, have spelt the end for the NCUSCR and CSCPRC's prominent role in contacts with China. Previously, both groups had derived power and support from their role as gatekeepers of access to China and had specialized in overseeing a limited number of carefully planned exchange delegations, formed from hand-picked individuals who were among the most prominent in their respective sectors and fields. This change happened rapidly: whereas in 1976 reportedly only 1,500 Americans traveled to China (other than to the Canton Trade Fair), many on NCUSCR or CSCPRC trips, in 1978 around 10,000 Americans were invited to the PRC, with an even greater number traveling in the years after normalization was agreed.[11] Thus, as individual travel and a greater array of organized trips were increasingly practicable, the two Committees appeared to have been deprived of their raison d'être.

In the event, however, both the CSCPRC and the NCUSCR found a purpose in a post-normalization landscape of Sino-American contact by expanding and diversifying their programs. As discussed in Chapter 4, the opaque process by which the Committee on Scholarly Communication selected participants in its exchanges had been a source of criticism; for the 1979 program, the organization began to accept applications for participation in their exchanges. The CSCPRC also branched out beyond its previous role as a facilitator of exchanges: the organization's program for 1979 included not only the exchange delegations that were the groups mainstay but also a reciprocal traveling lecture program, the aforementioned longer

---

[10] Li, "Ji 1978 nian Zhou lao shuai Zhongguo jiaoyu daibiaotuan fang Mei," 100; *CEN*, vol. 6, no. 5, December 1978; author interview with Murray.

[11] "So You're Going to the People's Republic of China!," undated USCPFA publication, Folder 9, Box 1, WNP, TLWLANYU.

term exchanges of researchers and students, and two bilateral scientific symposia, one in the United States and another in China.[12]

The scholarly contacts overseen by the Committee on Scholarly Communication were likely to continue to benefit from institutional oversight; the National Committee's program of more amorphous cultural contacts seemed more directly threatened by an opening China. Tourism to the country had begun to rapidly expand in 1978, when Western cruise ships began docking in China for the first time since 1949; by 1990, 2.5 million Americans had traveled to the PRC as tourists.[13] One of the NCUSCR's responses to new opportunities for tourism in China was to introduce "members' trips" – essentially small, high-end tour groups organized by the National Committee in collaboration with the China International Travel Service. However, take-up for this new initiative was low, perhaps because the NCUSCR was late to the game of tour groups to China: over the 1970s, such trips had increasingly become the focus of the US-China Peoples Friendship Association, and in 1978 alone, that group was overseeing eight such tours.[14] As early as 1977, the Friendship Association was issuing promotional leaflets that called China "the world's prime tourist destination," and, by 1980, an internal document stated that there had been a "basic shift in USCPFA tours work from selection to sales" and that "selling more tours" was the organization's priority – a stark contrast to the group's origins connecting American leftists with the PRC.[15] Thus, although the National Committee ran two members' trips in 1978 and three in 1979, the organization decided against diverting significant energy toward on-demand delegations.[16]

[12] *CEN*, vol. 6, no. 5, December 1978.

[13] Earlier in the 1970s, some cruise ships that had docked in Hong Kong had been allowed to send small groups of American tourists on a tour of Guangzhou, then the nearest major mainland Chinese city. *NFTNC*, Vol. 7, No. 1, March 1977; Mansfield, *China*, 29; Harding, *Fragile Relationship*, 9.

[14] Minutes of National Steering Committee, USCPFA, May 21–22, 1977, Folder 7, Box 1, USCPFAR, NYPLAMD.

[15] "So You're Going to the People's Republic of China!," undated USCPFA publication, Folder 9, Box 1, WNP, TLWLANYU; "Tour Leader Opportunities," January 30, 1980, Folder 3, Box 2, WNP, TLWLANYU. The Friendship Association simultaneously also took on a new post-normalization role when it was asked by the PRC government to recruit English-language teachers from among its network of young Americans with a known interest in China. Author interview with Judith Shapiro, Beijing, China, January 3, 2018; Williams to USCPFA members, July 25, 1979, Folder 29, Box 5, DSUSMC, TLWLANYU.

[16] Rosen to Members of the National Committee, May 22, 1978, "United States-China Relations, National Committee on, 1973–," Part II: Box 817, ACLSR, LOCMD;

Instead, it seemed that the NCUSCR's best chance for finding a continuing purpose was to stick to what it did best. The PRC Performing Arts Company delegation of 1978 had acted as a potent and timely reminder that, even as small-scale tourism to China became easier, it took significant expertise to pull off a high-profile cultural exchange visit. The National Committee enjoyed the connections needed to help finance hosting a 150-member delegation: the NCUSCR arranged for the National Endowment of the Arts to underwrite the exchange to the value of $100,000, and negotiated sponsorship from Coca-Cola, Pan American Airways, and the Bank of America. Substance was added through professional exchanges with American performers at the Juilliard School of Music and the American Ballet Theatre School; some stardust sprinkled in meetings at Universal Studios in Hollywood and with President Carter.[17] In the years to come, the National Committee continued to focus on being a – probably the – leading US organization for just such high-profile, high-quality visits, both in the cultural sphere but also increasingly on civil society and political topics.[18]

RECIPROCITY IN EXCHANGES

During the first seven years of US-PRC exchanges, a number of irritants had emerged in the exchange relationship which had prevented the deepening of the relationship and had, at times, bred resentment. Some of these issues were resolved or at least ameliorated in 1978; others, however, continued to linger. Perhaps, the most fundamental source of acrimony in the exchange program was the lack of equivalence and reciprocity in the programs offered by both sides: as detailed in Chapters 5 and 6, the Committee on Scholarly Communication had come close to pulling the plug on scientific exchanges over the perceived one-sided benefits that China was receiving from scientific cooperation without offering sufficient access

---

Minutes of 32nd meeting of NCUSCR board, July 5, 1978, "NCUSCR – Board Meeting, 1978," Box 131, ADBP, RBMLCU; "NCUSCR exchanges, 1972–79," September 14, 1979, Folder 16, Box 1, Series 1, DPMP, RAC.

[17] The tour had its origins in discussions during the Philadelphia Orchestra's visit in 1973. Minutes of 31st meeting of NCUSCR board, January 16, 1978, "NCUSCR – Board Meeting, 1978," Box 131, ADBP, RBMLCU; NCUSCR Annual Report, 1977–78, NCUSCROC.

[18] Wheeler, *American NGOs in China's Modernization*, 30–49; Roberts, "Informal U.S.-China Dialogues Following Tiananmen."

in return; as Chapter 4 showed, Americans had long resented draconian controls on American exchange visitors to China that contrasted with the great freedom afforded to Chinese visitors to the United States.

Equality in exchanges was not established in 1978; instead, these contacts became even more lop-sided after normalization. The first fifty-two PRC scholars to take up long-term residencies at US universities departed China on Boxing Day of that year – six days before formal diplomatic recognition occurred on January 1, 1979 – with another ten arriving later that same month; only six American researchers traveled in the opposite direction – a ten-to-one ratio.[19] In just the next few years, thousands of Chinese students and scholars traveled to the United States to benefit from the country's education system, with only hundreds of Americans going in the other direction – to speak of only one particular disparity.

However, the *tension* created by this asymmetry was significantly reduced in 1978 as a result of Chinese recognition of the imbalance in Sino-American exchanges. Previously, Beijing had insisted that cultural and scholarly contacts were reciprocal and that a balance in the overall number of delegations in each direction constituted equality. Chinese officials and scientists had maintained this stance even as they asked for ever larger numbers of delegations to be received in America's most advanced laboratories and factories – all while simultaneously refusing access to China for the scholars that would gain most from travel to the country. In August 1978, however, a senior Chinese scientific official, Huang Kunyi, had come clean. In a key meeting, Huang asked CSCPRC staff director Bullock, "In your opinion, does [the program of scholarly contacts] need to be balanced?"[20] Beijing showed newfound frankness in admitting that the PRC government knew that China was gaining more from scholarly contacts than it could give. Chinese recognition of the lopsided benefits of the exchange program was not merely rhetorical. In a significant change to previous policy, from 1978, PRC officials offered to pay for all the costs of aspects of the exchange program that were not wholly reciprocal: if the United States agreed to train more students and young researchers, or if the Americans agreed to send a greater number of senior academics to pass on their knowledge while in China, Beijing

[19] Qian Ning, *Chinese Students Encounter America*, trans. T. K. Chu (Seattle, WA: University of Washington Press, 2002), 95; Li, "Ji 1978 nian Zhou lao shuai Zhongguo jiaoyu daibiaotuan fang Mei," 104; "Scholarly Exchange Chronology," undated, Folder 6, Box 14, USCPFAR, NYPLAMD.
[20] CSCPRC memorandum, "Conversation with Huang Kun-yi," August 8, 1978, "1978 – General," CSCPRCP, NAS.

would gladly foot the bill.[21] Richard Suttmeier and Denis Simon are among the scholars of post-normalization scientific contacts that analyze this "benefitting side pays" formula, although they do not mention that the Chinese recognition of imbalance in scientific exchange was a substantial break with the PRC's approach before 1978.[22]

Chinese scientists were, from 1978, candid about the reasons for the imbalance in the program: they told their American counterparts that the conditions of Chinese laboratories were still not of a standard that would allow China to productively receive a larger number of American scholars. Beijing promised to take in as many students and scholars as it could and showed a willingness to remove some of the previous restraints on those American academics it did receive, in particular the social scientists that had long been pushing for access to China: the Chinese Academy of Social Sciences had been established in 1977, and the CSCPRC welcomed a delegation from that organization to the United States the year after normalization had been agreed, while the PRC received a delegation of American specialists on the Han dynasty in October 1978, one of the first delegations of humanists to travel from the United States.[23]

The American side effectively accepted the exchange relationship remaining unbalanced when, in 1979, the US government agreed to grant an unlimited amount of visas for Chinese who were accepted onto bona fide university programs in their country, irrespective of the numbers of students and scholars the PRC accepted.[24] Washington knew that, in doing so, they were surrendering the bargaining chip of reciprocity, a tool powerfully wielded by the Committee on Scholarly Communication and, then, the US government itself in the run up to normalization.[25] The decision to forego this leverage paved the way for deep collaboration between the two societies and removed a source of tension that had strained the relationship in the 1970s: by 1990, 100,000 Chinese students and scholars had received visas to study or research in the United

---

[21] Li, "Ji 1978 nian Zhou lao shuai Zhongguo jiaoyu daibiaotuan fang Mei," 103; *CEN*, vol. 6, no. 5, December 1978.

[22] Suttmeier and Simon, "Conflict and Cooperation," 147–48.

[23] CSCPRC memorandum, "Conversation with Huang Kun-yi," August 8, 1978, "1978 – General," CSCPRCP, NAS; *CEN*, vol. 6, no. 5, December 1978.

[24] David Lampton, Joyce Madancy, and Kristen Williams, *A Relationship Restored: Trends in U.S.-China Educational Exchanges, 1978–1984* (Washington, DC: National Academy Press, 1986), 70.

[25] Author unknown, "Position Paper: Security and Technological Transfer," circa September 1978, RACP: NLC-26-52-2-1-3, JCL.

States.[26] These vast flows simply could not have been on the basis of like-for-like reciprocity. Perhaps, then, there was no point in laboring such a point – although, forty years hence, it seems that China did rather better out of the bargain.[27] More recently, resentment has resurfaced in the United States at the apparent one-sided benefits of Sino-American scientific exchange since the 1970s. The causes of that resentment can be traced back to the decisions of the 1970s – although, when we do so, we realize that US decisions were as important as Chinese requests in creating the asymmetrical flows of people and knowledge of the 1980s and later.

TAIWAN AND EXCHANGES AFTER NORMALIZATION

The most long-standing and fundamental barrier to greater exchanges – US ties to Taiwan – was, in 1978, effectively resolved. During rapprochement, Beijing had objected not only to the US government's continuing diplomatic connection with Taipei but also to links between the societies of the United States and Taiwan, as exemplified by PRC protests at contacts between the National Academy of Sciences and Taiwanese scholars and to the National Committee's promotion – however indirectly – of cultural links between the United States and the island. Normalization, of course, helped defuse this issue. But, earlier in 1978, Chinese officials had already suggested that their anxiety regarding Taiwan had eased. In her August 1978 meeting with Jian Hao of the State Science and Technology Commission, Bullock asked whether Chinese scientists might be interested in international symposia jointly hosted by their respective academies of science, similar to those the Chinese were then developing with the Australian Academy of Sciences. Jian "immediately asked" whether the National Academy of Sciences continued to have a relationship with counterparts in Taiwan, and if these contacts were under a "formal agreement." Bullock said that the NAS had not ended its relationship with counterparts on the island and asked if that would prevent such cooperation between the two academies. "In the past that was the case, but now I am not entirely sure," Jian replied.[28]

---

[26] Harding, *Fragile Relationship*, 9.

[27] A similar point is made in Suttmeier and Simon, "Conflict and Cooperation," 147–48.

[28] CSCPRC memorandum, "Conversation with Chien Hao," August 11, 1978, "1978 – General," CSCPRCP, NAS.

Just as Carter and Brzezinski made clear in their political negotiations that the US government would maintain contacts – not to mention arms sales – with the Republic of China after normalization, so, too, did Bullock make explicit to Jian that the National Academy of Sciences, and many of the US universities the Chinese were increasingly working with, would continue their programs with Taiwan. "China would be unrealistic [to] think otherwise."[29] Jian moved the conversation on and the symposia were agreed just a few months later and timetabled to begin in 1979, without the National Academy of Sciences ending its ties to Taiwan.[30] The Taiwan issue had never been clear-cut: the Chinese had initially refused to work with the NAS in any way due to the organization's links with Taiwan, but thereafter had developed a close, productive relationship with the Academy – without any change in its relationship with Taiwan's scientific community. Clearly, then, PRC officials were capable of quietly compromising their position if they saw other good reasons to pursue contacts with a US organization. In the wake of normalization, the PRC diluted its position yet further and effectively dropped the issue of scientific links between the United States and Taiwan.

SCIENTIFIC AND TECHNOLOGICAL COOPERATION AFTER NORMALIZATION

Over the course of the 1970s, both governmental and nongovernmental actors in the United States had grown concerned that the exchange program was being exploited by China to gain access to America's scientific, technological, and industrial secrets. The significant expansion of exchanges and cooperation from 1978 necessarily increased the risks of the PRC exploiting these contacts to upgrade their science and technology sector on the cheap (even as the concurrent spike in Chinese purchases of American technology assuaged the US business community about how Sino-American partnership would affect their propriety interests). Farsighted American officials recognized that there were long-term risks to charitably assisting China's modernization: Oksenberg reminded Brzezinski in June 1978 that the PRC considered the United States a long-term adversary. The NSC staff member stopped short of stating that the United States should in turn see China in the same way, but he did argue

---

[29] Ibid.
[30] *CEN*, vol. 6, no. 5, December 1978.

that the United States should "not ... play Santa Claus" when it came to exchanges.[31]

The US government took the risk of intellectual property theft seriously and linked this commercial risk to national security concerns. A government paper from the autumn of 1978 outlined the government's plans to respond to the heightened risk of espionage brought by the greater number of exchanges that would follow normalization. The COMEX – Committee on Exchanges – system would advise on the intelligence and counter-intelligence implications of the exchange program, with membership of the committee being granted to representatives from the CIA and the departments of Defense, State, and Commerce. The committee could wall-off certain laboratories to exchange scholars or place restrictions – for example, banning access to computer production facilities – on individual scholars under suspicion. COMEX sought to liaise not only with government agencies but also with private organizations involved in exchanges, an arrangement that worked well in the case of contacts with the Soviets and was expected to be transferrable to the expanding relationship with China.[32]

The still-classified authors of this paper admitted frankly, "We are well aware of the intense sensitivity in the academic community toward the intrusion of security agencies into scholarly activity," and thus sought to avoid adverse reactions that could endanger the exchange program or have "even larger political concerns."[33] This concern was well-placed: within a year of the new counter-intelligence measures being introduced, the FBI was causing alarm by hassling American hosts of even seemingly mundane Chinese delegations such as a group on women's issues.[34] In the decades to come, one of the most serious challenges to the exchange program would be cases where Chinese researchers fell under suspicion of using their access to American research to unfairly assist China's industry

---

[31] Oksenberg to Brzezinski, June 30, 1978, "China (PRC), 1978/6–8," Box 8, NSAZB-MCF, JCL. According to Oksenberg's White House colleague Anne Keatley, the injunction not to play Santa Claus originated in a marginalia response to a memorandum written by President Carter himself. Author interview with Anne Solomon (previously Anne Keatley), New York, United States, January 17, 2020.

[32] Author unknown, "Position Paper: Security and Technological Transfer," circa September 1978, RACP: NLC-26-52-2-1-3, JCL.

[33] Ibid.

[34] Edward Friedman (signed "Ed") to Rosen, July 10, 1979, Folder 92, Box 12, Series 3, RG4, NCUSCR records, RAC; "Youyi zhi shu chang qing" [The Tree of Friendship Grows Evergreen], *Renmin Ribao*, 3 July 1979.

and military, as alleged, for example, in the infamous 1999 Cox Report that alleged that stolen American secrets had aided the development of the PRC's nuclear arsenal.[35]

As Chapters 5 and 6 showed, from 1975 through 1978, the transfer of physical technology began to be an important accompaniment of the knowledge transfers that occurred through exchange visits. Technology sales continued to be of close interest to Beijing beyond normalization. However, it was nonetheless the case that, even into the 1980s, the physical transfer of technology was no replacement for the continuing transfer of knowledge and expertise through the exchange program. One reason for this was the continuation of limits on technology transfers beyond normalization: Brzezinski had won the bureaucratic battle to expand Chinese access to technology (Chapter 6), but even he believed in limits to what should be sold to the PRC.[36] Normalization did not remove these barriers and, even into the 1980s, the US government would remain reluctant to permit the sale of the most advanced and sensitive technology to China (although the Soviet invasion of Afghanistan in December 1979 further eased restrictions on Chinese access to weaponizable technology).[37]

Even if the PRC had been provided unrestricted access to US technology, the Chinese knew that their contacts with American academics and researchers were of great significance to their modernization efforts; human knowledge was at least as important as hardware. During their isolation from the global scientific community in the Cultural Revolution era, China had missed out on the advances brought by the information revolution and significant advances in management science – just two areas that became a priority interest for China in Sino-American scientific exchanges.[38] This technology could not be sold in a box and was instead achieved through exchanges and joint initiatives such as the National Center for Industrial Science and Technology Management Development, established in Dalian in Northeast China in 1979 and staffed by a

---

[35] United States Congress and Christopher Cox, *U.S. National Security and Military/Commercial Concerns with the People's Republic of China* (Washington, DC: United States Government Printing Office, 1999); Suttmeier and Simon, "Conflict and Cooperation," 152.

[36] Press to Carter, October 13, 1978, *FRUS, 1977–1980*, Vol. XIII, Document 144; Harding, *Fragile Relationship*, 7.

[37] Mann, *About Face*, 110–11.

[38] Suttmeier and Simon, "Conflict and Cooperation," 145; NCUSCR Annual Report, 1977–78, NCUSCROC; *CEN*, vol. 6, no. 5, December 1978; USLO to SOS, November 18, 1978, RACP: NLC-26-24-7-5-4, JCL.

combination of Americans and Chinese.[39] This transfer of technical practice would be critical to China's learning of the information revolution
techniques that would drive the surge in economic growth in Western
economies in the 1980s and beyond.[40]

(EX)CHANGING UNDERSTANDING

There remained, then, ongoing tensions in the exchange program after
normalization, even as other long-standing irritants were resolved.
These strains did not, however, prevent exchanges continuing to serve
an important and constructive role in the Sino-American relationship
beyond 1978. This book has made the case that the unique conditions
of the diplomatic relationship between China and the United States
between 1971 and 1978 gave the exchange program a greater significance than might have been the case in less unusual circumstances.
Nonetheless, true "normalization" of the Sino-American relationship
could not be achieved with a stroke of a pen. Exchanges continued to
serve a critical role in building understanding between the peoples of
those two countries, long isolated from one another and having only
begun the process of again becoming reacquainted by 1978. Indeed, it
is important not to overstate how familiar Chinese and Americans were
in 1979. Great strides had been made in the preceding eight years – perhaps most significantly through exchange contacts – but much remained
to be done.

An example from March 1978 is revealing. In that month, the China
International Travel Service sent a delegation of its leadership to the
United States. The exchange was a success, with the visitors being reunited
with many of the Americans that they had themselves hosted on earlier
exchange visits to the PRC.[41] The Chinese delegation was particularly
enthused about visiting several rural destinations and smaller American
cities. Given their reaction to this portion of the tour, the National Committee asked the visitors why they had initially only requested trips to the
largest cities. The group of professional Chinese travel agents replied that

[39] Lampton, Madancy, and Williams, *A Relationship Restored*, 64–66. For other cooperation in this area, organized through the NCUSCR, see Xue Yuqiao, "Meiguo shi ruhe
peiyang jingji guanli renyuan de" [How Does the United States Train Economic Manag-
ers], *Renmin Ribao*, March 14, 1980.

[40] Suttmeier and Simon, "Conflict and Cooperation," 145.

[41] "Waishi wanglai" [Foreign Affairs], *Renmin Ribao*, March 30, 1978; *NFTNC*, Vol. 8,
No. 1, Spring 1978.

these were the only places in the United States they could name.[42] Into the 1980s and beyond, then, exchanges continued to be one of the principal means by which the people of each country learned about the other, and the NCUSCR and CSCPRC's contribution to this continuing process of building understanding was critical.

In the 1980s, the National Committee expanded its role in building Sino-American understanding beyond exchange visits. With the number of Chinese traveling to the United States soaring from 1978, and American public interest in the country again surging, the NCUSCR responded to the combination of American interest in and ignorance about China by returning to its earlier role of providing public education activities – now to both Americans and Chinese.[43] The organization's orientation programs for newly arrived Chinese students and scholars became a mainstay of the group's activities in the 1980s and into the 1990s.[44]

Reducing mutual ignorance was one important continuing function of the National Committee; another was managing and resolving conflict in the relationship. Despite the abundant mutual goodwill that accompanied the upgrading of Sino-American relations in 1978, exchanges in that year came up against similar challenges to those that had rocked the relationship in years gone by. An NCUSCR volleyball delegation in June 1978 was one such example. Tensions over a delay in granting a visa to a coach who was an Israeli citizen had boiled over when the men's coach had called a press conference in which he said that the trip had been disrupted by the political "whims" of the Chinese. A *New York Times* story quoted the coach as saying the Chinese "shenanigans" were "a slap in the face," leading a PRCLO official to tell the National Committee of "his extreme displeasure" at the coach's behavior. The public controversy resulted in a rescheduling and downsizing of the delegation – though not, thanks to significant behind-the-scenes work by the NCUSCR, to the cancellation of the visit.[45] The NCUSCR's careful diplomacy in this and many other cases ironed out many such controversies (usually before they made it into the papers) and the value of having experienced organizations that enjoyed the trust of their Chinese colleagues continued to be proven beyond the 1970s. Meanwhile, Sino-American high diplomacy

---

[42] NCUSCR "Program Summary: January–June, 1978," "NCUSCR – Board Meeting, 1978," Box 131, ADBP.

[43] NCUSCR Annual Report, 1977–78, NCUSCROC.

[44] Wheeler, *American NGOs in China's Modernization*, 34.

[45] Berris and Henderson to The Record, June 23, 1978, Folder 91, Box 12, Series 3, RG4, NCUSCR records, RAC.

was itself not without controversy after 1979 and, at times of conflict between the two governments and people, exchange organizations, first among them the NCUSCR, became important Sino-American mediators, brokers, and cross-cultural communicators. The origins of this important role lay in the relationships that were carefully built in the 1970s.[46]

EXCHANGES IN PRC FOREIGN RELATIONS
IN THE DENG ERA AND AFTER

If the changes in China's relationship with the United States altered the PRC's exchange diplomacy with the United States, so, too, did the changing of the guard in Beijing and the profound changes in domestic and foreign policy that followed Deng's ascent to power in 1978. This change in the domestic order of power was directly felt in China's exchange contacts with the outside world. Among the many Americans to visit China after 1979, some had also traveled between 1971 and 1978. These visitors were often taken aback by the change in how the PRC was presented to foreign guests: where Cultural Revolution mass participation in politics and economics had previously been celebrated, after the Mao era, the same policies were blamed for anarchy and China's economic stagnation. Occasionally, Americans even asked their hosts to explain this sea-change in the narratives accompanying visits to what were often the same factories or work units as shown to visitors before 1978 – sometimes even by the same Chinese guides. The ubiquitous answer was that the previous specious explanations for Chinese achievement had been the result of the insidious Gang of Four – the universal scapegoat in post-Mao China – who had poisoned the thinking of the guide.[47] Other aspects of the exchange experience in China changed slowly, however: Richard Baum, the translator for the NCUSCR's 1975 track and field delegation (Chapter 4), recalls that, during a return visit to China in late 1978, the party state still continued to resist any spontaneous interaction between visiting Americans and local Chinese – especially ordinary Chinese who had not been politically vetted – even as other aspects of exchanges were being liberalized as described in Chapter 6.[48]

---

[46] Wheeler, *American NGOs in China's Modernization*, 35–37; Roberts, "Informal U.S.-China Dialogues Following Tiananmen."
[47] For an indicative example, see Baum, *China Watcher*, 73–75.
[48] Baum, 75.

China's changing domestic politics were also felt in the shifting political inflection of exchange contacts with the American people. Beijing's earlier preference for developing ties with radical leftist Americans that was explored in this book's prologue had already faded in the rapprochement era. The remainder of the Mao period and even the years immediately after the chairman's death had nonetheless still seen some Chinese interest in leftist Americans, hosted alongside the more apolitical or centrist visitors that this book has focused upon. In the wake of Deng's ascent to power, however, any lingering connection between the PRC state and American leftists was severed, to be replaced by converse Chinese priorities. As Frazier has shown, contacts between Black Americans and China had been dominated by shared revolutionary convictions before 1971; already by 1980, however, businessmen had become Beijing's favored constituency among the US Black community.[49] Post-Mao Sino-American business ties were facilitated in part by many Americans who had first visited China in the 1970s or even before. The most remarkable example was surely Sidney Rittenberg, the American who had first gained the CCP's favor in Yan'an before spending a decade of his more than three-decade PRC residency in prison for his pro-Cultural Revolution activism (Chapter 1). In 1980, he set up a US-based business consultancy for American firms wanting to break into the China market, thus completing a personal odyssey not so dissimilar to some contemporaneous PRC officials. If Rittenberg changed with the CCP, other American leftists refused to, and many American foreign friends broke ties with the PRC in the wake of Deng's reforms.[50]

Even in the era of Chinese breakneck economic growth, business and economics were not the only priority of the PRC state, however; other forms of exchange continued to serve a function for Beijing, too. Sporting diplomacy had played a central role in Sino-American rapprochement and continued to have a place in Deng-era PRC foreign relations. Where table tennis had been used to break the ice with the United States (and with other countries such as Japan before that), tennis was at the center of PRC efforts to build rapprochement with South Korea and with Taiwan in the 1980s and 1990s. If sport was still used as a bridge in diplomacy, more broadly the PRC changed its approach to international sporting competition in that era, quietly abandoning "friendship first,

---

[49] Frazier, *The East Is Black*, 209; Harding, *Fragile Relationship*, 13.
[50] Hooper, *Foreigners under Mao*, 242–44, 14.

competition second" and focusing on winning glory for China through medal tallies at the Olympics and other tournaments.[51]

Meanwhile, the PRC continued to engage in musical exchanges of the sort that had been so successful during the Philadelphia Orchestra's tour of 1973. Like the country's sporting diplomacy, the nature of China's musical diplomacy changed over time: during the 1970s, the PRC had sent performing arts delegations in return for American classical musicians, reflecting the focus of Chinese arts in the 1970s. By the 2000s, however, classical music had become central to the PRC's musical exchanges abroad, as reflected in major tours of Taiwan, Japan, and Korea by the Chinese Philharmonic Orchestra soon after its establishment in 2000.[52] Meanwhile, the PRC became a favorite spot for touring American orchestras: the Philadelphia Orchestra returned to China in 1993 and 2001, and then, in the 2010s, began making almost yearly visits to the country.[53] Not dissimilarly to the PRC's changing approach to international sports, post-Mao China increasingly sought recognition on the same terms of artistic accomplishment as other countries – as a producer and an audience for the most internationally prestigious forms of music – rather than pursuing its own distinct approach to cross-cultural musical encounter. Thus, as Brady has argued in her analysis of post-1978 Chinese *waishi* foreign relations management more broadly, there was a peculiar mixture of continuity and change in post-Mao exchange contacts with the United States, with much continuity and many echoes from the rapprochement period being experienced against a backdrop of rapid and profound change under Deng.[54]

CONCLUSION

For all the change caused by normalization, much remained the same in Sino-American exchanges. Diplomatic recognition allowed government-to-government exchanges, but this was far from the first government involvement in Sino-American exchange diplomacy. The NCU-SCR and CSCPRC adapted their programming in recognition of new possibilities for governmental and nongovernmental contact, but both

---

[51] Wang, "'Friendship First'," 135, 151–52; Xu, *Olympic Dreams*, 162–63.
[52] Gienow-Hecht, "The World Is Ready to Listen," 28.
[53] Lin and Mullally, *Beethoven in Beijing*.
[54] Anne-Marie Brady, "'Treat Insiders and Outsiders Differently': The Use and Control of Foreigners in the PRC," *The China Quarterly* 164, no. 4 (2000): 949.

Committees remained important brokers between the two societies into the 1980s. Flows of people in both directions increased, with reciprocity remaining important in a new period of comparative openness, but redefined in terms of access, rather than tallies of visitors. Mutual familiarity grew, but much remained to be learned. China changed, but legacies of the first period of intense contact between the PRC and the United States long lingered.

Conclusion

Ties That Bind?

The final Sino-American normalization agreement made in 1978 again highlighted the close connection between exchange diplomacy and the US government's long campaign to achieve normalization. Brzezinski, Frank Press, and the Committee on Scholarly Communication with the PRC had reversed the long-standing dynamic of American desire for deeper exchanges and Chinese pressure for US commitments in diplomatic negotiations. Now it was Deng Xiaoping and Beijing that wanted to thicken the Sino-American exchange relationship and begin governmental exchanges. Doing so was the means by which China would gain access to the American knowledge and technology that could expedite Chinese modernization. The Americans were happy to oblige – but Brzezinski took a leaf out of the CSCPRC's book and demanded a price for this assistance. Normalization would open the gates for a flood of American knowledge and technology into China and Carter and his national security advisor drove a hard bargain, ultimately convincing Deng to accept the president's conditions for normalization – including continuing US arms sales to Taiwan after 1979.

Scientific exchanges, then, helped unlock the final prize of normalization. That prize would not have been within reach in 1978 had it not been for the positive influence of the exchange program at earlier junctures in the rapprochement. Under Nixon's watch, exchange diplomacy had been used by both sides to indicate their initial interest in dialogue. The breakthrough of ping-pong diplomacy had taken Sino-American contact from backchannels to the front of US newspapers and the American public's attention. In the wake of Nixon's trip, exchanges – of acrobats, musicians, and athletes – had provided a direct, personal experience of rapprochement to thousands of Americans who had watched the president's summit from afar. These early exchanges had also confirmed what Nixon could only suspect: that decades of hysteria about a red, yellow peril were over and that Americans were prepared to make friends with people who had been viewed with more suspicion than any other Cold War foe.

Without exchanges, rapprochement might not have survived until Carter's term. Nixon's resignation had rocked the Sino-American relationship and Kissinger and Ford were impotent in their efforts to restore momentum to high-level diplomatic negotiations during the truncated term of Nixon's successor. The White House had fixed on exchange contacts as a sustaining tie that might obfuscate the stale diplomatic talks that plagued Ford's time in office. Chinese leaders were wise to this tactic: Beijing knew that the United States was using exchanges to puff Sino-American relations after Nixon's fall and that sabotaging cultural ties would increase pressure on Washington to give ground in diplomatic negotiations. But exchanges, for the most part, continued during the tense Ford years and the specific targeting of the National Committee's cultural exchanges while scientific contacts remained largely unmolested betrayed that Beijing had found their own uses for those exchanges managed by the Committee on Scholarly Communication. The Republicans were not to survive long enough in office for Ford and Kissinger to work out how to turn this Chinese interest in US science into leverage in Sino-American relations, but their Democratic Party successors would not miss the trick.

Cultural and scientific exchanges, then, exercised a powerful influence on the Sino-American diplomatic relationship. It could be tempting to consider the quality of these contacts as merely representative and derivative of high-level talks. Certainly, there was a connection between the two and, naturally enough, salubrious diplomatic meetings eased exchanges between the two peoples, just as deadlock in normalization negotiations strained the exchange program. But causation ran in both directions. Consider an alternative outcome to a number of critical moments. A first ping-pong visit that had been publicly decried in the United States would have cooled Nixon's enthusiasm for extending the olive branch to Beijing – an initiative he was never certain would win public approval. A calamitous return leg of the table tennis exchange might have dissuaded Chinese leaders from a broad reopening to not only the US government but also American society, too. The cessation of exchanges under Ford would likely have taken the final wind out of rapprochement's sails, removing the last substance from an enervated relationship. Carter and Brzezinski's 1978 push for normalization may well have proved as ineffective as Vance's tepid 1977 visit had it not been for Washington's bargaining chip of US scientific assistance to a reforming China. In all these moments and more, exchanges were the difference between make and break in the Sino-American relationship. A full understanding of the success, failures, and course of the Sino-American relationship in the 1970s thus requires understanding this second track of diplomacy and its influence on high diplomacy between Washington and Beijing.

Exchanges were, then, an important, variable in the condition of the relationship. This was the case, not least, because they were overseen by organizations and individuals outside of the control of the leadership of either country. The National Committee's first contribution to rapprochement was to demonstrate that the American public had lost patience with containing China without any prospect of engagement or dialogue and then to form a chorus of Americans demanding a change in US policy toward Beijing. The organization subsequently made perhaps its most critical single contribution to rapprochement by arranging and successfully hosting the first delegation of PRC citizens to the United States in ping-pong diplomacy's return leg. This trip showcased and confirmed the critical and unique role that the National Committee would play in rapprochement: a private organization sufficiently unofficial to satisfy Beijing's refusal of government-run exchanges and, at the same time, competent, cooperative, and committed to many of the same broad objectives as Washington in the new relationship with the PRC.

The Committee on Scholarly Communication played a quieter role in the first years of exchange diplomacy. It took time to convince Beijing to deal with a group run out of the National Academy of Sciences, a Washington institution both physically and institutionally closer to government than the heavily privately funded, New York–based NCUSCR. In a way that was not true of the National Committee, the CSCPRC owed their privileged position in exchange contacts to sponsorship from the government (and the NCUSCR). However, as a new phase of exchange diplomacy dawned after Deng's (temporary) return to power in 1973, the Committee on Scholarly Communication gained in confidence as it oversaw a successful program of scientific contacts that was clearly of growing importance to the PRC. The organization demonstrated its independent agency by expertly managing Chinese ardor for access to American scientific expertise and technology – at a time when the US government's own policy of generous technological assistance to China won little benefit for the United States. Pulled in different directions by their constituents in the American scientific community and their counterparts in Beijing, the CSCPRC indulged Chinese requests for extensive access to America's scientific crown jewels – the advanced labs at MIT, the cutting-edge industrial technology at AT&T, the country's finest scientific minds – but never ceased reminding PRC officials and scientists that, through their requests, they were accruing a debt.

By avoiding parsimony, the Committee on Scholarly Communication facilitated a grander bargain whereby their scientific constituency's much-desired access to Chinese scientific space was won not by point scoring but through political progress. The CSCPRC saw this bigger picture before the US government did and, by then working hand-in-glove with Brzezinski and donating their most experienced talent – Press and Keatley – to government service, they made an immeasurable contribution to moving both the diplomatic and exchange relationship to a higher stage under Carter. The CSCPRC thus helped initiate the deep, substantive cooperation between the academic and scientific communities of the United States and China that it had sought since 1966.

Throughout the long road to normalization, the NCUSCR, the CSCPRC, and many other individuals and groups involved in the exchange program were thus powerful nongovernmental allies in Washington's diplomatic campaign to consummate rapprochement with Beijing. From an early stage in the exchange relationship, the NCUSCR and the CSCPRC made explicit that they were not prepared to act as supplicants. If they were expected to manage and organize exchange visits, such trips must be those most desired by the American constituencies the two groups represented. Throughout this period, the NCUSCR and the CSCPRC expected their government's support – financially and politically – but insisted that they should be free to negotiate directly with their Chinese counterparts and the government in Beijing. Moreover, the two Committees did not truck interference in the content of exchanges from either government and showed, on multiple occasions, that they would not permit periodic Chinese attempts to politicize these contacts to their own ends. The important cooperation toward building Sino-American rapprochement offered by both organizations was always conditional.

Both governments knew this. Beijing had defined the dynamic of Sino-American exchange visits of the 1970s by insisting that even the most significant of these contacts be conducted on an ostensibly people-to-people basis. While this decision guaranteed a critical role for organizations such as the NCUSCR and CSCPRC, it quickly became clear that neither government intended to stay aloof from contacts that were so politically important. Chinese leaders up to and including Mao and Zhou had been personally involved in the invitation to US ping-pong players to visit China and thereafter the premier and even the chairman continued to be directly involved in the planning and execution of Beijing's exchange diplomacy, seeking to ensure it played a critical, complementary role in the PRC's policy toward the United States. Beijing often claimed that exchanges were a matter for the American and Chinese people – but there was, of course, no private realm in a highly mobilized totalitarian Maoist society, and the Chinese state was omnipresent during American visits to the PRC. Exchanges were put to other ends by the PRC government, too: as a signal of their frustrations at stalled rapprochement under Ford, as a means to push senators and congressmen to lobby their own government on normalization, and as a conduit of American scientific knowledge in the years immediately before and after Mao's death.

Beijing's deep involvement in exchange diplomacy was mirrored in Washington. Ping-pong diplomacy had made Kissinger nervous: he was convinced that the American athletes would upset his carefully crafted backchannel signals to the Chinese leadership (they did not, of course).[1] Having been taken off guard by that event, the US government resolved to thereafter proactively involve itself in exchange diplomacy. Drawing on a long history of American public-private cooperation in cultural and exchange contacts with the outside world, a framework for public-private cooperation in Sino-American exchanges was established in 1972 and 1973.[2] When contacts proceeded painlessly, the State Department was content to take a backseat, providing funding and encouragement to these organizations but leaving them to work with Chinese counter-parts and the American public to promote rapprochement. However, the government did not sit idly when the exchange program was not serving this purpose. In the first years of rapprochement, this meant Washington lobbying hard for the PRC government to end its preference for working with American groups on the political left and instead switching their focus to the elite-led, politically centrist organizations – the CSCPRC and NCUSCR – that had US government approval. Under Ford, US government activism took the form of efforts to defuse repeated clashes and ongoing friction in exchange contacts. Finally, under Carter, the White

---

[1] Author interview with Berris, August 27, 2017.
[2] Krenn, *United States Cultural Diplomacy*; Cull, "How We Got Here," 26.

House threw its weight behind the CSCPRC's efforts to deepen scientific and technological cooperation with China, incorporating a long-standing goal of that private group into official policy toward Beijing. Exchanges were never wholly instrumental – interactions on the ground were, as we have seen, too complex and varied to be wholly controlled by either government – but the contours of Sino-American exchange diplomacy were of equal importance to both Beijing and Washington's foreign policy toward the other.

KISSINGER'S VISION OF RAPPROCHEMENT

In his memoirs, as well as his meetings with his Chinese interlocutors, Kissinger often derided exchange diplomacy as a sideshow that bore little relevance to the inner workings of rapprochement.[3] Nixon's right-hand man did not bother to hide his satisfaction at having switched from being an ivory-tower academic advising policymakers to being at the core of government decision-making, and this colored his dealings with those who sought to influence Sino-American relations from outside of government. Kissinger always presented rapprochement as driven entirely by two factors: the global, geostrategic balance of power and the secretive negotiations he and Nixon had initiated with China's very highest leaders. He did so because he believed that he and the US government could control these variables. Thus, in Kissinger's reading, the rapprochement with Beijing had been effected solely by him, Nixon, Mao, and Zhou. It had been these men that had perceived the opportunity of triangular diplomacy and then exploited that opening through carefully orchestrated negotiations during summit trips.

Kissinger's vision of rapprochement through triangular diplomacy was a powerfully effective one – initially. The consciously nonideological approach that he and Nixon adopted allowed the two men to identify the opportunity to powerfully shift the global balance of power through just a few short visits to China. However, this fundamental change could only be realized once; no matter how regular Kissinger's calls on the Chinese leadership were, none would ever have the impact that the president's first, ground-breaking visit had. It took Kissinger some time to recognize this reality. As the relationship lost momentum in 1973 and 1974, Kissinger

---

[3] Bush to Scowcroft, November 20, 1974, "China Exchanges, 9 August 1974–31 December 1974," DFWL, RG59, NACP; Kissinger, *White House Years*, 705.

dismissed as "stupid" any suggestion – even from his own advisors – that the relationship was influenced by actors beyond his grasp.[4] He reacted to the slowdown in rapprochement by attempting to intensify security collaboration with the PRC. When this only made matters worse, Kissinger repeated like a mantra his belief that Beijing would not pull away from rapprochement so long as the Soviets continued to threaten China and the United States was able to offset this challenge.

This book has made the case that Kissinger's view of Sino-American diplomacy was incomplete. The Sino-American rapprochement cannot, this work argues, be fully understood with reference only to summitry, secret talks, and strategic strengths and weaknesses. The slowdown in the diplomatic relationship in the mid-1970s revealed that security cooperation was an insufficient foundation for ties between the two countries. The Chinese expressed their preference for an alternative repeatedly and clearly: the United States should consummate the relationship and normalize its diplomatic ties with Beijing on China's terms. This, however, was not seriously considered as a possibility by US leaders during the course and aftermath of Watergate. Thus, a diplomatic relationship that began with a ping-pong trip became conditioned as much by the ups and downs in exchange contacts as it was Kissinger's sagging negotiations in Beijing. Spectacular visits such as that by the Philadelphia Orchestra offered some of the vitality that high-level talks lacked, while confrontations such as the 1975 performing arts troupe dispute provided the American public glimpses into the fissures that had emerged in the secret talks between the two country's leaders. The final proof of Kissinger's failure of vision came in 1977 and 1978: Carter and Brzezinski did what Kissinger refused to and recognized the interactive connection between exchange diplomacy and high-level relations. Their holistic approach of treating exchanges as not simply symbolic and derivate of governmental talks but instead a substantive aspect of the US relationship with the PRC helped realize the normalization deal that Kissinger could not.[5]

---

[4] Memcon: Kissinger, Scowcroft, Lord, Solomon et al., July 19, 1973, "China Exchanges, July 10-October 31, 1973," DFWL, RG59, NACP.

[5] After Kissinger left office in 1977 – never to formally return to government service – he changed his estimation of the importance of nongovernmental Sino-American contacts, especially as he became an influential individual in such contacts. Kissinger would, in the early 2010s, call the NCUSCR – an organization he was closely involved in his post-government career – "an indispensable part of any long-range approach to China." Wheeler, *American NGOs in China's Modernization*, 28.

EXCHANGE DIPLOMACY IN INTERNATIONAL
AND TRANSNATIONAL HISTORY

There is a broader implication to the limit of Kissinger's realist view of Sino-American relations. Kissinger believed that the transnational facets of the Sino-American relationship – exchanges, trade, and other societal contacts – had no bearing on high diplomacy. In arguing against this, this book not only offers a counter-narrative about the Sino-American relationship in the 1970s but also makes a broader case for the relevance of transnational history to diplomatic history. This book offers a further case study in harmony with a chorus of historians who argue for the productive compatibility between these two sub-fields. A decade ago, Thomas Zeiler observed that diplomatic and in particular international history had enthusiastically embraced transnational history and, in doing so, brought new life to what many saw as a tired field.[6] This book draws on the insights made by Zeiler and by the scholars he cites to show that a holistic history of the Sino-American relationship in the 1970s requires considering both diplomatic and transnational perspectives simultaneously. Nongovernmental, transnational actors helped develop the relationship between the Chinese and American people and also their governments, while the actions of the two governments not only created the possibility of transnational connections but also actively influenced such interactions. Explicating either relationship cannot be done without proper attention to the other.

Transnational historians have often sought to write histories that shed light on nonstate actors who have been too often overlooked in classical diplomatic histories. This book is just such a history: an argument for the role of exchange participants and organizations as leading agents of rapprochement. However, this work also shows that transnational history ignores the state at its peril. Judging by the example of Sino-American relations in the 1970s, transnational actors were rarely able to ignore the state. As Zeiler argues, "the state is relegated to a secondary role in ... history at the peril of losing a sense of the nature of power, who captures it, who loses it, and how it is deployed." Zeiler cites diplomatic history and its methodology as having relevance to transnational history: "by investigating both private and public archives, and nation-states as well as transnational exchanges, [diplomatic historians] appreciate how power functions at home and abroad."[7]

---

[6] Zeiler, "The Diplomatic History Bandwagon," 1053.
[7] Ibid., 1056.

The importance of power and the question of who wields it is borne out in the case study offered by this book. Exchanges were moments of cross-cultural communication, performance, and learning, and helped create or resurrect transnational epistemic communities. But they were also a form of diplomacy. The visits overseen by the National Committee, the Committee on Scholarly Communication, and other exchange organizations had a direct bearing on the high-level Sino-American diplomatic relationship. Both governments knew this and their concerted efforts to shape the exchange program toward their foreign policy ends highlight the importance that these contacts had on the government-to-government relationship. In turn, the NCUSCR and CSCPRC – but also their leftist rivals in the Committee of Concerned Asian Scholars and the US-China Peoples Friendship Association – knew that the US and Chinese governments exercised a powerful influence over transnational contacts. The National Committee and the Committee on Scholarly Communication worked tirelessly to preserve their independence of action from both governments and to protect the interests of their members and broader public constituencies. But to do so, they had to build effective relationships of trust with both governments because ultimately their core objective – facilitating contact with China – relied on cooperation with the two governments. Thus, this work simultaneously demonstrates the influence of nongovernmental, transnational actors on high diplomacy and shows the impact of state actors on transnational interactions. In doing so, it posits that there is great analytical value in connecting our transnational and diplomatic histories.

Of course, the circumstances of Sino-American diplomacy in the 1970s were unique and perhaps peculiar. The narrow relationship between the societies of the United States and China in that decade afforded great power to each government to control flows between their two countries, a power that was, as explored in the epilogue, diluted from 1979. This power to control societal interactions might be considered unusual. As is the case with so many historiographical innovations, the recent predilections of transnational history are in part a representation of our present: a post-Cold War world where, having helped topple Communism in Eastern Europe and spark a global environmentalist movement, transnational actors now seem to move fluidly between highly integrated societies (even if they, too, still pay close attention to government policy).[8]

---

[8] For how the present reality of transnational actors influences our analysis, see Risse-Kappen, "Bringing Transnational Relations Back In," 3–4.

Thus, transnational history, with its focus on the person, idea, or object in motion, often focusses on flows that seem relatively unencumbered. But historically contacts between societies have not been wholly free: for as long as states have exercised control within their borders, they have likewise aspired to control what passes across those frontiers. Even within the time frame of this book, broad contacts between free societies were the exception, not the norm. Socialist countries across the world controlled their people's contacts with the outside world using many of the same methods as employed by Beijing; authoritarian states that sided with the United States in the Cold War also sought to set the parameters for transnational influence on their societies. The power that the US and Chinese governments were able to wield over exchange contacts was, then, significant – but not unique. I suspect, therefore, that the vast majority of transnational organizations in history were deeply concerned with their relations with the state: it seems likely that they would have recognized that a combative relationship with a state could prevent them exercising agency while effective relationships with states could enhance their agency. We should bear this in mind particularly when studying the transnational in a past that was distinct from the integrated world of our present.

LESSONS FOR NOW

Contemporary Sino-American relations have entered a period of friction and even confrontation as China's rise challenges unquestioned US global hegemony. In the face of this renewed tension between the two countries, exchange contacts and other societal contacts may again take on the preeminent importance they did in the 1970s – and may prove to be the clinching argument for cooperation instead of conflict. The connections between US and Chinese societies are now on a scale that would have been unimaginable in the Nixon or even Carter era, even as they have been interrupted by the COVID-19 pandemic.[9] Millions of Americans and Chinese have traveled between the two countries; many thousands have made lives that span the two; academic cooperation is now deep and constant; trillions of dollars are invested and earned as a result of economic connections. These transnational connections offer a powerful argument against any conflict that would endanger them – although

---

[9] Even architects of normalization such as Brzezinski could not envisage the development of the relationship that would follow. Author interview with Brzezinski.

history has proven that arguments against conflict, however compelling, do not always prevent it.

Nonetheless, contemporary transnational contacts also contain much friction – as they did in the 1970s – and, as this book has shown, familiarity can breed contempt. Since the Tiananmen crackdown of 1989, Americans have been deeply, bitterly disappointed that China's opening to the world that began in the 1970s has not been followed by an opening of their society to liberal values.[10] Chinese that have traveled to and lived in the United States have not always come away convinced of that society's virtues (even if many have, often voting with their feet by opting to remain in the country).[11] Likewise, economic interaction and interdependence has bred resentment: Donald Trump was just the most recent American political leader to highlight the apparent costs of China's economic rise to the American economy. The issue of reciprocity in Sino-American exchange – a source of much tension in the 1970s – is now being raised again after the fact, with Americans blaming an earlier generation of compatriots for facilitating the rise of a potential adversary through access to US knowledge, technology, and wealth – and pledging to end cooperation that, they allege, lopsidedly benefits China.

The 1970s contain lessons for this critical moment. The most important of these is that the relationship between the people and societies of these two countries is both deeply important and closely connected to the diplomatic relationship – even if, as this book has shown, neither the transnational nor diplomatic aspect of the relationship determines the other. What this suggests is that we are mistaken if we think that the economic and societal interconnectedness of the two countries will determine cooperation at the diplomatic level. But we are also right to take heart that the deep, broad connections between the Chinese and American people can have a positive – perhaps corrective – influence on strained diplomatic ties. They have before. "Decoupling" is not unprecedented in Sino-American relations; the mutual isolation of 1950 and 1971 was far more total than any that is likely to occur in the 2020s. As this book has argued, exchanges helped build a relationship from that

---

[10] See, for example, Madsen, *China and the American Dream*; Miriam London, "The Romance of Realpolitik," in *The Broken Mirror: China after Tiananmen*, ed. George Hicks and Asai Motofumi (Harlow: Longman, 1990), 246–56.

[11] R. David Arkush and Leo O. Lee, *Land without Ghosts: Chinese Impressions of America from the Mid-Nineteenth Century to the Present* (Berkeley, CA: University of California Press, 1989).

low starting point. Similar interactions could help repair the relationship after the artificial barriers of the pandemic are lifted.

As this book has shown, exchange diplomacy is no more straightforward than governmental relations. Nor is it always a source of shared understanding. Thus, just as it may not be enough to rely on Sino-American societal connections to prevent conflict between the two governments, so, too, is it not sufficient to blindly promote greater transnational interaction in the interests of improving and sustaining the relationship. The lesson from the experience of the National Committee and the Committee on Scholarly Communication in the 1970s is that mutual understanding does not come automatically and instead requires hard thinking and hard work. Often, those two Committees had the most powerful influence on the relationship when they were prepared to leverage the trust they had built over years of cooperation in order to speak frankly to their Chinese counterparts. If we wish to protect and promote Sino-American relations through contemporary exchanges and transnational interactions, we need to work through difficulties and misunderstandings in the relationship just as much as we celebrate successes to date. We should do so honestly: as other historians of cultural diplomacy have recently shown, the best transnational diplomats are those who speak truthfully, about both their home and host countries.[12]

Doing so could offer a transnational route to making sense of – and a success of – China's rise. In the 1970s, few expected China to become like the United States. American visitors to the PRC in the 1970s tried to understand the country on its own terms and expected China to remain culturally and ideologically distinct from their own society. The momentous changes that followed Deng's emergence as China's paramount leader in 1978 changed that view: soon, Americans grew confident – perhaps complacent – that the PRC was converging with the United States, not only economically and socially but also politically. Tiananmen challenged this view, but the end of the Cold War – and, according to at least one American scholar, of history – allowed Americans to again slip into thinking that China could only rise by conforming to the liberal teleology of capitalistic democracy. It is now clear that this view was wrong. China is, by some measures, already a larger economy than the United States; by any measure, it is a behemoth whose meteoric economic growth is comparable only with the twentieth century rise of America or the original

---

[12] Cohn, "'In between Propaganda and Escapism'," 420.

Industrial Revolution in Northwest Europe.[13] That growth was built on an economic model that drew on capitalist examples but also maintained government intervention in the economy on a scale unrivalled by other modern capitalist economies. China also has an authoritarian government that in recent years has further confirmed its commitment to indefinite one-party – even one-man – rule and to tightening its grip over all aspects of Chinese society, including on previously autonomous areas of its periphery. If China might one day liberalize politically, such an outcome would be a profound reversal of current trends. We are back to where we were in the 1970s when it comes to forecasting the PRC's future: the country will likely remain powerfully distinct from the US example.

How to effectively respond to China's rise is the most important geopolitical challenge facing the United States in our time – as has been increasingly recognized in the 2020s. It is also a test for millions of Americans outside of government – not only those whose businesses and livelihoods rely on a functioning relationship with the Chinese but also all those working toward the United States having a constructive role in international society and the world. Efficacious engagement with the PRC is more challenging now than at any time since the period discussed in this book (bar, perhaps, the very immediate aftermath of the 1989 crackdown). China's authoritarianism obstructs the interchange of ideas and controls its citizens' interactions with the outside world – even, alarmingly, when they are on US campuses.[14] Beijing's treatment of its own citizens – whether in Xinjiang, Hong Kong, or in its most prestigious universities – has brought into the question the morality of working with Chinese partner institutions altogether.[15] Meanwhile, as in the 1970s, some Americans have begun to question whether Chinese access to the United States should remain comparably unfettered when Americans are subject to intense surveillance (and sometimes worse) while in the PRC.[16]

---

[13] By, for example, purchasing power parity. See the CIA's World Factbook for 2021 at www.cia.gov/the-world-factbook/field/real-gdp-purchasing-power-parity/country-comparison. Accessed December 9, 2021.

[14] "On Campuses Far from China, Still under Beijing's Watchful Eye," *New York Times*, May 4, 2017.

[15] "China has silenced American academics for years. Now they're pushing back," *Washington Post*, September 23, 2018; "Cornell decision adds to growing climate of fear on Chinese campuses," *South China Morning Post*, October 29, 2018.

[16] David Shambaugh, "Opinion: Nobody Wins in a U.S.-China Visa War," *Inkstone News*, April 23, 2019.

But understanding the PRC – without explaining away objectionable policies – is fundamental not only to avoid any destiny of war but also to the United States finding its way in the world after the moment of global hegemony that followed the Soviet collapse but then faded in the sands of Iraq and the mountains of Afghanistan.[17] The contradictions between transnational engagement with China and resisting the long arm of China's authoritarianism seem almost irreconcilable. But difficult choices in Sino-American transnational relations are not new: the challenge of building a constructive relationship with the revolutionary Communist Chinese society of the 1960s and 1970s seemed an impossibly large task.[18] This book has documented how Americans rose to that challenge – ultimately with hard-won success. Negotiating the complex compromises necessary in contemporary Sino-American transnational initiatives – from cultural exchanges such as the Philadelphia Orchestra's now-frequent tours of China to more ambitious enterprises such as joint-venture universities – will not be easy. But doing so is essential if Americans are to understand a China that is now a competitor but also a peer, and if the United States still hopes to exercise influence in a China no longer rising but risen.

---

[17] Graham T. Allison, *Destined for War: Can America and China Escape Thucydides's Trap?* (Boston, MA: Houghton Mifflin Harcourt, 2017). Such arguments were still being made by leading figures in the PRC's foreign policy establishment in 2009, although these voices have increasingly been drowned out by so-called "wolf warrior" diplomats in more recent years. Zhao, "You minjian waijiao dao gonggong waijiao."

[18] Doak Barnett's speech for "containment without isolation" in 1966 would hardly seem out of place today. "U.S. and China: Policy Shift Based on 'Containment Without Isolation'," *New York Times*, July 27, 1969.

Bibliography

PRIMARY SOURCES

Archives

Beijing Municipal Archives, Beijing, China (BJMA)
Bentley Historical Library, University of Michigan, Ann Arbor, MI, United States (BHL)
    Alexander Eckstein papers (AEP)
    Michel Oksenberg papers
    National Archive on Sino-American Relations (NASAR)
Gelman Library, The George Washington University, Washington, DC, United States
    Committee on Scholarly Communication with the PRC papers
Gerald Ford Library, Ann Arbor, MI, United States (GFL)
    Kissinger–Scowcroft West Wing Office Files, 1974–77 (KSWWOF1974-77)
    National Security Council East Asia and Pacific Affairs Staff Files (NSCEAPASF)
    Trip Briefing Books and Cables of Henry Kissinger, 1974–77
    Trip Briefing Books and Cables of President Ford, 1974–77
Guangdong Provincial Archives, Guangzhou, China (GDPA)
Harvard University Archives, Cambridge, MA, United States (HUA)
    John K. Fairbank papers (JKFP)
Jimmy Carter Library, Atlanta, GA, United States (JCL)
    China Vertical File (CVF)
    National Security Affairs – Staff Material – Far East Files (NSASMFEF)
    National Security Affairs – Zbigniew Brzezinski material – Country Files (NSAZBMCF)
    Remote Access Collection Program (RACP) (listed by reference number, e.g. NLC-2-6-17-7-6-1)
    Zbigniew Brzezinski collection

Manuscript Division, Library of Congress, Washington, DC, United States (LOCMD)
  American Council of Learned Societies records (ACLSR)
  Francis R. Valeo papers
  James Forman papers
  Joseph and Stewart Alsop papers
National Academy of Sciences archives, Washington, DC, United States (NAS)
  Committee on Scholarly Communication with the PRC papers (CSCPRCP)
National Committee on United States-China Relations office collection, New York, United States (NCUSCROC)
New York Public Library Archives and Manuscripts Division, New York, United States (NYPLAMD)
  US-China Peoples Friendship Association records (USCPFAR)
Rare Book and Manuscript Library, Columbia University, New York, United States (RBMLCU)
  A. Doak Barnett papers (ADBP)
Richard Nixon Library, Yorba Linda, CA, United States (RNL)
  Kissinger Files – Country Files – Far East (HAKCFFE)
Rockefeller Archive Center, Sleepy Hollow, NY, United States (RAC)
  Douglas P. Murray papers (DPMP)
  Social Science Research Council (SSRC) records
  National Committee on United States-China Relations (NCUSCR) records
Shanghai Municipal Archives, Shanghai, China (SHMA)
Tamiment Library and Robert F. Wagner Labor Archive, New York University, New York, United States (TLWLANYU)
  David Sullivan US Maoism collection (DSUSMC)
  Oral History of the American Left collection
  William Nuchow papers (WNP)
Tianjin Municipal Archives, Tianjin, China
United States National Archives II, College Park, MD, United States (NACP)
  Record Group 59: Records of the Department of State (RG59)
    Director's Files of Winston Lord (DFWL)
    Subject Files, 1969–1978
    Subject Numeric Files, 1970–73, Political & Defense (SNF1970-73PD)

PUBLISHED DOCUMENTS AND DOCUMENT COLLECTIONS

Ahlberg, Kristin L., ed. *Foreign Relations of the United States, 1917–1972.* Vol. VIII, Public Diplomacy, 1969–1972. Washington, DC: United States Government Printing Office, 2018.

Nickles, David P., ed. *Foreign Relations of the United States, 1969–1976.* Vol. XVIII, China, 1973–1976. Washington, DC: United States Government Printing Office, 2007.

Nickles, David P., ed. *Foreign Relations of the United States, 1977–1980.* Vol. XIII, China. Washington, DC: United States Government Printing Office, 2013.

Phillips, Steven E., ed. *Foreign Relations of the United States, 1969–1976*. Vol. XVII, China, 1969–1972. Washington, DC: United States Government Printing Office, 2006.

Phillips, Steven E., ed. *Foreign Relations of the United States, 1969–1976*. Vol. E-13, Documents on China, 1969–1972. Washington, DC: United States Government Printing Office, 2006.

United States Congress and Christopher Cox. *U.S. National Security and Military/Commercial Concerns with the People's Republic of China*. Washington, DC: United States Government Printing Office, 1999.

Zhonggong zhongyang wenxian yanjiushi [CCP Central Committee Document Research Office], ed. *Deng Xiaoping nianpu, 1904–1975* [Deng Xiaoping Chronicle, 1904–1975]. Vol. 3. Beijing: Zhongyang wenxian chubanshe, 2009.

Zhonggong zhongyang wenxian yanjiushi [CCP Central Committee Document Research Office], ed. *Deng Xiaoping nianpu, 1975–1997* [Deng Xiaoping Chronicle, 1975–1997]. Vol. 1. Beijing: Zhongyang wenxian chubanshe, 2004.

Zhonggong zhongyang wenxian yanjiushi [CCP Central Committee Document Research Office], ed. *Deng Xiaoping sixiang nianbian* [Chronicle of Deng Xiaoping Thought]. Beijing: Zhongyang wenxian chubanshe, 2011.

Zhonggong zhongyang wenxian yanjiushi [CCP Central Committee Document Research Office], ed. *Jianguo yilai Mao Zedong wengao* [Mao Zedong's Manuscripts since the Founding of the PRC]. Vol. 13. Beijing: Zhongyang wenxian chubanshe, 1987.

Zhonggong zhongyang wenxian yanjiushi [CCP Central Committee Document Research Office], ed. *Mao Zedong nianpu, 1949–1976* [Mao Zedong Chronicle, 1949–1976]. Vol. 6. Beijing: Zhongyang wenxian chubanshe, 2013.

Zhonggong zhongyang wenxian yanjiushi [CCP Central Committee Document Research Office], ed. *Mao Zedong waijiao wenxuan* [Selected Works of Mao Zedong on Diplomacy]. Beijing: Zhongyang wenxian chubanshe, 1994.

Zhonggong zhongyang wenxian yanjiushi [CCP Central Committee Document Research Office], ed. *Zhou Enlai nianpu, 1949–1976* [Zhou Enlai Chronicle, 1949–1976]. Vol. 3. Beijing: Zhongyang wenxian chubanshe, 1997.

Zhonggong zhongyang wenxian yanjiushi [CCP Central Committee Document Research Office], ed. *Zhou Enlai waijiao wenxuan* [Selected Works of Zhou Enlai on Diplomacy]. Beijing: Zhongyang wenxian chubanshe, 1990.

Zhonggong zhongyang wenxian yanjiushi [CCP Central Committee Document Research Office], ed. *Zhou Enlai xuanji* [Selected Works of Zhou Enlai]. Vol. 2. Beijing: Renmin chubanshe, 1984.

MEMOIRS AND TRAVEL ACCOUNTS

Arkush, R. David, and Leo O. Lee. *Land without Ghosts: Chinese Impressions of America from the Mid-Nineteenth Century to the Present*. Berkeley, CA: University of California Press, 1989.

Baum, Richard. *China Watcher: Confessions of a Peking Tom*. Seattle: University of Washington Press, 2010.

Berris, Jan Carol. "The Evolution of Sino-American Exchanges: A View from the National Committee." In *Educational Exchanges: Essays on the Sino-American Experience*, edited by Joyce K. Kallgren and Denis Fred Simon, 80–95. Berkeley, CA: University of California Press, 1987.

Blumenthal, W. Michael. *From Exile to Washington: A Memoir of Leadership in the Twentieth Century*. New York: The Overlook Press, 2013.

Boggs, Hale, and Gerald Ford. *Impressions of the New China: Joint Report to the United States House of Representatives*. Washington, DC: United States Government Printing Office, 1972.

Bruce, David. *Window on the Forbidden City: The Beijing Diaries of David Bruce, 1973–1974*. Hong Kong: University of Hong Kong Press, 2001.

Brzezinski, Zbigniew. *Power and Principle: Memoirs of the National Security Advisor 1977–1981*. New York: Farrar, Straus, Giroux, 1983.

Bush, George H. W. *The China Diary of George H. W. Bush: The Making of a Global President*. Edited by Jeffrey Engel. Princeton, NJ: Princeton University Press, 2008.

Carter, Jimmy. *Keeping Faith: Memoirs of a President*. Fayetteville, AR: University of Arkansas Press, 1995.

Committee of Concerned Asian Scholars. *China! Inside the People's Republic*. New York: Bantam Books, 1972.

Djerassi, Norma Lundholm. *Glimpses of China from a Galloping Horse*. New York: Pergamon Press, 1974.

Eckstein, Ruth. "Ping Pong Diplomacy: A View from Behind the Scenes." *Journal of American-East Asian Relations* 2, no. 3 (1993): 327–42.

Fang, Yi. *Fang Yi wenji* [Collected Works of Fang Yi]. Beijing: Renmin chubanshe, 2008.

Galbraith, John Kenneth. *A China Passage*. Boston, MA: Houghton Mifflin, 1973.

Galston, Arthur. *Daily Life in People's China*. New York: Crowell, 1973.

Galston, Arthur. "Shih-Wei Loo Remembered." *Plant Science Bulletin* 45, no. 2 (1999).

Gu, Mu. *Huiyilu* [Memoirs]. Beijing: Zhongyang wenxian chubanshe, 2009.

Han, Suyin. *My House Has Two Doors*. London: Triad, Grafton Books, 1980.

Hinton, William H. *Fanshen: A Documentary of Revolution in a Chinese Village*. New York: Monthly Review Press, 1966.

Huang, Hua. *Memoirs*. Beijing: Foreign Languages Press, 2008.

Ji, Chaozhu. *The Man on Mao's Right: From Harvard Yard to Tiananmen Square, My Life inside China's Foreign Ministry*. New York: Random House, 2008.

Kissinger, Henry. *Diplomacy*. New York: Simon & Schuster, 1994.

Kissinger, Henry. *White House Years*. Boston, MA: Little, Brown and Company, 1979.

Kissinger, Henry. *Years of Upheaval*. London: Weidenfeld & Nicolson, 1982.

Liu, Kin-ming. *My First Trip to China: Scholars, Diplomats, and Journalists Reflect on Their First Encounters with China*. Hong Kong: East Slope Publishing Limited, 2012.

MacLaine, Shirley. *You Can Get There from Here*. New York: W. W. Norton & Company, 1975.

Magnuson, Warren G. *China Report: Report of a Special Congressional Delegation*. Washington, DC: United States Government Printing Office, 1973.

Mang, Robert A., and Pamela Mang. "A History of the Origins of the National Committee on United States-China Relations." Prepared for the Christopher Reynolds Foundation, Inc., January 1976. Available at www.ncuscr .org/wp-content/uploads/2016/06/page_attachments_NCUSCR-Early-History-Mang.pdf. Accessed June 24, 2022.

Mansfield, Mike. *China: A Quarter Century after the Founding of the People's Republic: A Report*. Washington, DC: United States Government Printing Office, 1975.

Mansfield, Mike, and Hugh Scott. *Journey to the New China: April-May 1972*. Washington, DC: United States Government Printing Office, 1972.

Murray, Douglas P. "Exchanges with the People's Republic of China: Symbols and Substance." *The Annals of the American Academy of Political and Social Science* 424, no. 1 (1976): 29–42.

Nixon, Richard M. *The Memoirs of Richard Nixon*. Vol. 2. New York: Warner Books, 1979.

Phillips, Warren H., and Robert Keatley. *China: Behind the Mask*. Princeton, NJ: Dow Jones Books, 1973.

Pickowicz, Paul. *A Sensational Encounter with High Socialist China*. Hong Kong: City University of Hong Kong Press, 2019.

Rockefeller, David. *Memoirs*. New York: Random House, 2002.

Schell, Orville. *In the People's Republic: An American's First-Hand View of Living and Working in China*. New York: Random House, 1977.

Scott, Hugh. *The United States and China: A Report*. Washington, DC: United States Government Printing Office, 1976.

Song, Shixiong, *Zishu: Wo de tiyu shijie yu ying ping chunqiu* [Autobiography of Song Shixiong: My Sports World and Days on Screen]. Beijing: Zuojia chuban she, 1997.

The National Security Council Project Oral History Roundtables: China Policy and the National Security Council. Interview by Ivo Daalder and I. M. Destler, April 11, 1999.

Theroux, Eugene. "The Founding of the Council." *The China Business Review* 20, no. 4 (1993): 2.

Vance, Cyrus. *Hard Choices: Critical Years in America's Foreign Policy*. New York: Simon and Schuster, 1983.

Wu, Xiuquan. *Zai waijiaobu ba nian de jingli, 1950.1–1958.10: Waijiao huiyilu* [Eight Years in the Foreign Ministry: Memoirs of Diplomacy]. Beijing: Shijie zhishi chubanshe, 1983.

Xiong, Xianghui. *Wo de qingbao yu waijiao shengya* [My Career in Intelligence and Diplomacy]. Beijing: Zhonggong dangshi chubanshe, 1999.

Yang, Chen Ning. *Selected Papers, 1945–1980, with Commentary*. Singapore: World Scientific, 2005.

Zhou, Peiyuan. *Zhou Peiyuan wenji* [Collected Works of Zhou Peiyuan]. Beijing: Daxue chubanshe, 2002.

ORAL HISTORY INTERVIEWS

Anne Solomon (previously Anne Keatley), New York, United States, June 25, 2018
Anne Solomon (previously Anne Keatley), New York, United States, January 17, 2020
Charles (Chas) W. Freeman Jr, telephone interview, January 7, 2011
Donald Munro, Ann Arbor, MI, United States, November 21, 2017
Douglas Murray, New York, United States, September 9, 2015
Eleanor Sheldon, New York, United States, January 17, 2020
Eugene Theroux, Washington, DC, United States, September 21, 2015
Jan Berris, New York, United States, August 15, 2015
Jan Berris, New York, United States, August 27, 2017
Jan Berris, New York, United States, January 17, 2020
Jan Berris, New York, United States, June 19, 2019
Jan Berris, New York, United States, June 26, 2018
Judith Shapiro, Beijing, China, January 3, 2018
Mary Brown Bullock, email exchanges, January 2019
Mary Brown Bullock, telephone interview, April 25, 2018
Orville Schell, Oxford, UK, June 2, 2016
Paul Pickowicz, telephone interview, November 11, 2020
Robert Keatley, Washington, DC, United States, September 2, 2015
Susan Shirk, Beijing, PRC, December 17, 2017
Thomas Gold, email exchanges, December 15, 2021
William R. Smyser, Washington, DC, United States, August 12, 2015
Winston Lord, telephone interview, January 14, 2011
Zbigniew Brzezinski, Washington, DC, United States, January 19, 2010

NEWSPAPER SOURCES AND PERIODICAL PUBLICATIONS

Chemical & Engineering News
China Daily
China Exchange Newsletter (CEN)
China Friendship: Newsletter of the US-China Peoples Friendship Association
Christian Science Monitor
Committee of Concerned Asian Scholars (CCAS) Newsletter
Foreign Affairs
Guardian
Los Angeles Times
National Geographic
New York Review of Books
New York Times
News from China
Newsweek
Notes from the National Committee (NFTNC)
Peking Review
Renmin Ribao [People's Daily]
Washington Post

SECONDARY SOURCES

Agar, Jon. "'It's Springtime for Science': Renewing China-UK Scientific Relations in the 1970s." *Notes and Records of the Royal Society of London* 67, no. 1 (2013): 7–24.

Aijazuddin, F. S. *From a Head, through a Head, to a Head: The Secret Channel between the US and China through Pakistan.* Oxford: Oxford University Press, 2000.

Allison, Graham T. *Destined for War: Can America and China Escape Thucydides's Trap?* Boston, MA: Houghton Mifflin Harcourt, 2017.

Barber, Sue Ellen. "Music and Politics: The Philadelphia Orchestra in the People's Republic of China." Master's thesis, University of Michigan, 1977.

Barnouin, Barbara, and Yu Changgen. *Chinese Foreign Policy during the Cultural Revolution.* London: Kegan Paul International, 1998.

Barrett, Gordon. "China's 'People's Diplomacy' and the Pugwash Conferences, 1957–1964." *Journal of Cold War Studies* 20, no. 1 (2018): 140–69.

Bayly, C. A., Sven Beckert, Matthew Connelly, Isabel Hofmeyr, Wendy Kozol, and Patricia Seed. "AHR Conversation: On Transnational History." *The American Historical Review* 111, no. 5 (2006): 1441–64.

Bickers, Robert. *Out of China: How the Chinese Ended the Era of Western Domination.* Cambridge, MA: Harvard University Press, 2017.

Boer, Connie de. "The Polls: Changing Attitudes and Policies toward China." *Public Opinion Quarterly* 44, no. 2 (1980): 267–73.

Brady, Anne-Marie. *Making the Foreign Serve China: Managing Foreigners in the People's Republic.* Lanham, MD: Rowman & Littlefield, 2003.

Brady, Anne-Marie. "'Treat Insiders and Outsiders Differently': The Use and Control of Foreigners in the PRC." *The China Quarterly* 164, no. 4 (2000): 943–64.

Brown, Keisha A. "Blackness in Exile: W.E.B. Du Bois' Role in the Formation of Representations of Blackness as Conceptualized by the Chinese Communist Party (CCP)." *Phylon* 53, no. 2 (2016): 20–33.

Bullock, Mary Brown. "American Exchanges with China, Revisited." In *Educational Exchanges: Essays on the Sino-American Experience*, edited by Joyce K. Kallgren and Denis Fred Simon, 23–43. Berkeley, CA: University of California Press, 1987.

Burr, William. "'Casting a Shadow' over Trade: The Problem of Private Claims and Blocked Assets in U.S.-China Relations, 1972–1975." *Diplomatic History* 33, no. 2 (2009): 315–49.

Busch, David S. "The Politics of International Volunteerism: The Peace Corps and Volunteers to America in the 1960s." *Diplomatic History* 42, no. 4 (2018): 669–93.

Caute, David. *The Fellow-Travellers: Intellectual Friends of Communism.* Revised edition. London: Yale University Press, 1988.

Chang, Gordon H. *Fateful Ties: A History of America's Preoccupation with China.* Cambridge, MA: Harvard University Press, 2015.

Chen, Donglin. 'Kaifang de qianzou: "Sisan fang'an" jiqi dui Gaige Kaifang de yingxiang [A Prelude to Opening-Up: The Four-Three Program and Its

Influence on Reform and Opening]'. *Journal of National Museum of China*, no. 1 (2019): 10–19.

Chen, Dunde. *Mao Zedong Nikesong zai 1972* [Mao Zedong and Nixon in 1972]. Beijing: Kunlun chubanshe, 1988.

Chen, Jian. *Mao's China and the Cold War*. Chapel Hill, NC: University of North Carolina Press, 2001.

Chen, Jian. "Zhou Enlai yu 1973 nian 11 yue Jixinge fang Hua [Zhou Enlai and Kissinger's November 1973 Visit to China]." *Journal of East China Normal University (Philosophy and Social Sciences)*, 2014: 15–26.

Chu, T. K., and Qian Ning. *Chinese Students Encounter America*. Seattle, WA: University of Washington Press, 2002.

Cohen, Warren I. "While China Faced East: Chinese-American Cultural Relations, 1949–71." In *Educational Exchanges: Essays on the Sino-American Experience*, edited by Joyce K. Kallgren and Denis Fred Simon, 45–46. Berkeley, CA: University of California Press, 1987.

Cohn, Deborah. "'In between Propaganda and Escapism': William Faulkner as Cold War Cultural Ambassador." *Diplomatic History* 40, no. 3 (2016): 392–420.

Cull, Nicholas J. "How We Got Here." In *Toward a New Public Diplomacy: Redirecting U.S. Foreign Policy*, edited by Philip Seib, 23–47. New York: Palgrave Macmillan, 2009.

Del Pero, Mario. *The Eccentric Realist: Henry Kissinger and the Shaping of American Foreign Policy*. Ithaca, NY: Cornell University Press, 2010.

Dudziak, Mary L. *Cold War Civil Rights: Race and the Image of American Democracy*. Princeton, NJ: Princeton University Press, 2000.

Engerman, David C. *Know Your Enemy: The Rise and Fall of America's Soviet Experts*. New York: Oxford University Press, 2009.

Evangelista, Matthew. 'Transnational Organizations and the Cold War'. In *The Cambridge History of the Cold War*, edited by Melvyn P. Leffler and Odd Arne Westad. Vol. 3, 400–21. Cambridge: Cambridge University Press, 2010.

Evangelista, Matthew. *Unarmed Forces: The Transnational Movement to End the Cold War*. Ithaca, NY: Cornell University Press, 1999.

Fan, Fa-ti. "'Collective Monitoring, Collective Defense': Science, Earthquakes, and Politics in Communist China." *Science in Context* 25, no. 1 (2012): 127–54.

Fang, Xiaoping. *Barefoot Doctors and Western Medicine in China*. Rochester, NY: University of Rochester Press, 2012.

Fardella, Enrico. "The Sino-American Normalization: A Reassessment." *Diplomatic History* 33, no. 4 (2009): 545–78.

Faure, Justine. *Working on/Working with the Soviet Bloc: IREX, Scholarly Exchanges and Détente*. Edited by Ludovic Tournès and Giles Scott-Smith. Oxford: Berghahn Books, 2017.

Frazier, Robeson Taj. *The East Is Black: Cold War China in the Black Radical Imagination*. Durham, NC: Duke University Press, 2015.

Gao, Wenqian. *Zhou Enlai: The Last Perfect Revolutionary: A Biography*. Translated by Peter Rand and Lawrence Sullivan. New York: Public Affairs, 2007.

Gao, Yunxiang. "W. E. B. and Shirley Graham Du Bois in Maoist China." *Du Bois Review: Social Science Research on Race* 10, no. 1 (2013): 59–85.

Gienow-Hecht, Jessica C. E. "The World Is Ready to Listen: Symphony Orchestras and the Global Performance of America." *Diplomatic History* 36, no. 1 (2012): 17–28.

Goh, Evelyn. *Constructing the U.S. Rapprochement with China, 1961–1974: From "Red Menace" to "Tacit Ally."* Cambridge: Cambridge University Press, 2004.

Gong, Li. 'Chinese Decision Making and the Thawing of U.S.–China Relations'. In *Re-examining the Cold War: U.S.-China Diplomacy, 1954–1973*, edited by Robert Ross and Jiang Changbin, 321–60. Cambridge, MA: Harvard University Press, 2002.

Gong, Li. *Kuayue honggou: 1969–1979 nian Zhong Mei guanxi de yanbian* [Bridging the Divide: The Evolution of Sino-American Relations from 1969 to 1979]. Zhengzhou: Henan renmin chubanshe, 1994.

Graziani, Sofia. "The Case of Youth Exchanges and Interactions between the PRC and Italy in the 1950s." *Modern Asian Studies* 51, no. 1 (2017): 194–226.

Griffin, Nicholas. *Ping-Pong Diplomacy: Ivor Montagu and the Astonishing Story behind the Game That Changed the World*. London: Simon & Schuster, 2014.

Gu, Zixin. "Why Your Devotion to People-to-People Diplomacy – An Interview with CPAFFC Vice President Li Xiaolin." *Voice of Friendship*, no. 4 (2005): 18–23.

Harding, Harry. *A Fragile Relationship: The United States and China Since 1972*. Washington, DC: Brookings Institution, 1992.

He, Hui. *Dangdai Zhong Mei minjian jiaoliu shi: 1969–2008 nian* [Contemporary Chinese and American Folk Exchange History (1969–2008)]. Beijing: Kexue chubanshe, 2017.

Hilton, Brian. "'Maximum Flexibility for Peaceful Change': Jimmy Carter, Taiwan, and the Recognition of the People's Republic of China." *Diplomatic History* 33, no. 4 (2009): 595–613.

Hollander, Paul. *Political Pilgrims: Travels of Western Intellectuals to the Soviet Union, China, and Cuba, 1928–1978*. New York: University Press of America, 1990.

Hong, Zhaohui, and Yi Sun. "The Butterfly Effect and the Making of 'Ping-Pong Diplomacy'." *Journal of Contemporary China* 9, no. 25 (2000): 429–48.

Hooper, Beverley. *Foreigners under Mao: Western Lives in China, 1949–1976*. Hong Kong: Hong Kong University Press, 2016.

Hu, Danian. "Despite or Due to the Cultural Revolution: The Development of Chinese Science, Technology, and Medicine in the 1960s and 1970s." *Endeavour* 41, no. 3 (2017): 78–84.

Jersild, Austin. *The Sino-Soviet Alliance: An International History*. Chapel Hill, NC: University of North Carolina Press, 2014.

Ji, Chongji. *Zhou Enlai zhuan* [Zhou Enlai Biography]. Edited by ZGZYWXYJS. Vol. 2. Beijing: Zhongyang wenxian chubanshe, 2008.

Jin, Ge. "Zai Waijiaobu 'duoquan' qianhou [Before and After the Seizure of Power in the Foreign Ministry]." In *Zhou Enlai de Zuihou Suiyue, 1966–1976*

[Zhou Enlai's Final Years, 1966–1976], edited by An Jianshe, 237–77. Beijing: Zhongyang wenxian chubanshe, 1995.

Johnson, Matthew D. "From Peace to the Panthers: PRC Engagement with African-American Transnational Networks, 1949–1979." *Past & Present* 218, Supplement 8 (2013): 233–57.

Kerpen, Karen Shaw. "Voices in a Silence: American Organizations That Worked for Diplomatic Recognition of the People's Republic of China by the United States, 1945–1979." PhD dissertation, New York University, 1981.

Kirby, William, Robert Ross, and Gong Li, eds. *Normalization of U.S.-China Relations: An International History*. Cambridge, MA: Harvard University Asia Center, 2007.

Klein, Christina. *Cold War Orientalism: Asia in the Middlebrow Imagination, 1945–1961*. Berkeley, CA: University of California Press, 2003.

Kramer, Paul. "Is the World Our Campus? International Students and U.S. Global Power in the Long Twentieth Century." *Diplomatic History* 33, no. 5 (2009): 775–806.

Kraus, Charles. "More than Just a Soft Drink: Coca-Cola and China's Early Reform and Opening." *Diplomatic History* 43, no. 1 (2019): 107–29.

Krenn, Michael L. *The History of United States Cultural Diplomacy: 1770 to the Present Day*. New York: Bloomsbury Academic, 2017.

Lampton, David, Joyce Madancy, and Kristen Williams. *A Relationship Restored: Trends in U.S.-China Educational Exchanges, 1978–1984*. Washington, DC: National Academy Press, 1986.

Lanza, Fabio. *The End of Concern: Maoist China, Activism, and Asian Studies*. Durham, NC: Duke University Press, 2017.

Lautz, Terry. *Americans in China: Encounters with the People's Republic*. New York: Oxford University Press, 2022.

Lebovic, Sam. "From War Junk to Educational Exchange: The World War II Origins of the Fulbright Program and the Foundations of American Cultural Globalism, 1945–1950." *Diplomatic History* 37, no. 2 (2013): 280–312.

Leyda, Jay. "China's Dr. Bethune." *Film Quarterly* 32, no. 2 (1978): 63–64.

Li, Hongshan. *U.S.-China Educational Exchange: State, Society, and Intercultural Relations, 1905–1950*. New Brunswick, NJ: Rutgers University Press, 2008.

Li, Jie. "China's Domestic Politics and the Normalization of Sino-U.S. Relations." In *Normalization of U.S.-China Relations: An International History*, edited by William Kirby, Robert Ross, and Gong Li, 56–89. Cambridge, MA: Harvard University Asia Center, 2007.

Li, Lingxiu, and Zhou Minggong. *Tiyu zhizi: Rong Gaotang* [Son of Sport: Rong Gaotang]. Beijing: Xinhua chubanshe, 2002.

Li, Mingde. "Zhong Mei keji jiaoliu yu hezuo de lishi huigu [A Historical Review of Sino-American Science and Technology Exchanges and Cooperation]." *Meiguo yanjiu*, no. 2 (1997): 144–47.

Li, Qi. 'Ji 1978 nian Zhou lao shuai Zhongguo jiaoyu daibiaotuan fang Mei [Remembering Zhou Peiyuan's Leading of the 1978 Education Delegation to the United States]'. In *Zongshi jujiang biaoshuai kaimo – jinian Zhou Peiyuan wenji* [Grand Master and Role Model: Anthology Commemorating Zhou Peiyuan]. Beijing: Xueyuan Press, 2002.

Li, Yongan, and Zhang Yingqiu. "Pingpang waijiao de wenhua fenxi [A Cultural Analysis of Ping Pong Diplomacy]." *Tiyu wenhua dao kan*, no. 1 (2012): 139–41.

Li, Youhua. *Shengming aomi de tansuo zhe: Niu Manjiang* [Explorer of the Mystery of Life: Niu Manjiang]. Beijing: Zhongguo Nongye Keji Chubanshe, 1988.

Lin, Jennifer R., and Sharon Mullally. *Beethoven in Beijing*. Documentary. History Making Productions, 2020.

Lin, Mao. "'To See Is to Believe?' – Modernization and U.S.–China Exchanges in the 1970s." *The Chinese Historical Review* 23, no. 1 (2016): 23–46.

Loayza, Matt. "'A Curative and Creative Force': The Exchange of Persons Program and Eisenhower's Inter-American Policies, 1953–1961." *Diplomatic History* 37, no. 5 (2013): 946–70.

London, Miriam. "The Romance of Realpolitik." In *The Broken Mirror: China after Tiananmen*, edited by George Hicks and Asai Motofumi, 246–56. Harlow: Longman, 1990.

Lovell, Julia. *Maoism: A Global History*. London: The Bodley Head, 2019.

Lovell, Julia. "The Uses of Foreigners in Mao-Era China: 'Techniques of Hospitality' and International Image-Building in the People's Republic, 1949–1976." *Transactions of the Royal Historical Society* 25 (2015): 135–58.

Lu, Hanchao. "Versatility, Interdisciplinarity, and Academic Collaboration: Paul Pickowicz's Insights on Chinese Studies." *The Chinese Historical Review* 27, no. 1 (2020): 50–66.

Lumbers, Michael. *Piercing the Bamboo Curtain: Tentative Bridge-Building to China during the Johnson Years*. Manchester: Manchester University Press, 2008.

Lüthi, Lorenz M. *Cold Wars: Asia, the Middle East, Europe*. Cambridge: University Press, 2020.

Lüthi, Lorenz M. "Restoring Chaos to History: Sino-Soviet-American Relations, 1969." *The China Quarterly* 210 (2012): 378–97.

Ma, Jisen. *The Cultural Revolution in the Foreign Ministry of China*. Hong Kong: Chinese University Press, 2004.

MacMillan, Margaret. *Seize the Hour: When Nixon Met Mao*. London: John Murray, 2006.

Madsen, Richard. *China and the American Dream: A Moral Inquiry*. Berkeley, CA: University of California Press, 1995.

Mann, James. *About Face: A History of America's Curious Relationship with China from Nixon to Clinton*. New York: Alfred Knopf, 1999.

Manthorpe, Jonathan. *Forbidden Nation: A History of Taiwan*. New York; Basingstoke: Palgrave Macmillan, 2009.

Mao, Joyce. *Asia First: China and the Making of Modern American Conservatism*. Chicago, IL: University of Chicago Press, 2015.

Meijer, Hugo. *Trading with the Enemy: The Making of US Export Control Policy toward the People's Republic of China*. New York: Oxford University Press, 2016.

Millwood, Pete. "An 'Exceedingly Delicate Undertaking': Sino-American Science Diplomacy, 1966–78." *Journal of Contemporary History* 56, no. 1 (2021): 166–90.

Millwood, Pete. "(Mis)Perceptions of Domestic Politics in the U.S.-China Rapprochement, 1969–1978." *Diplomatic History* 43, no. 5 (2019): 890–915.

Minami, Kazushi. "'How Could I Not Love You?': Transnational Feminism and US-Chinese Relations during the Cold War." *Journal of Women's History* 31, no. 4 (2019): 12–36.

Minami, Kazushi. "Oil for the Lamps of America? Sino-American Oil Diplomacy, 1973–1979." *Diplomatic History* 41, no. 5 (2017): 959–84.

Minami, Kazushi. "Re-Examining the End of Mao's Revolution: China's Changing Statecraft and Sino-American Relations, 1973–1978." *Cold War History* 16, no. 4 (2016): 359–75.

Munteanu, Mircea. "Communication Breakdown? Romania and the Sino-American Rapprochement." *Diplomatic History* 33, no. 4 (2009): 615–31.

Ninkovich, Frank. "The Rockefeller Foundation, China, and Cultural Change." *The Journal of American History* 70, no. 4 (1984): 799–820.

Oberdorfer, Don. *Senator Mansfield: The Extraordinary Life of a Great American Statesman and Diplomat*. Washington, DC: Smithsonian Books, 2003.

Oyen, Meredith. *The Diplomacy of Migration: Transnational Lives and the Making of U.S.-Chinese Relations in the Cold War*. Ithaca, NY: Cornell University Press, 2015.

Pachetti, Federico. "The Roots of a Globalized Relationship: Western Knowledge of the Chinese Economy and U.S.–China Relations in the Long 1970s." In *China, Hong Kong, and the Long 1970s: Global Perspectives*, edited by Odd Arne Westad and Priscilla Roberts, 181–203. Cham: Palgrave Macmillan, 2017.

Pang, Xianzhi, and Jin Chongji. *Mao Zedong zhuan, 1949–1976* [Mao Zedong Biography, 1949–1976]. Vol. 2. Beijing: Zhongyang wenxian chubanshe, 2003.

Pantsov, Alexander. *Deng Xiaoping: A Revolutionary Life*. Oxford: Oxford University Press, 2015.

Passin, Herbert. *China's Cultural Diplomacy*. London: China Quarterly, 1962.

Perlmutter, David D. *Picturing China in the American Press: The Visual Portrayal of Sino-American Relations in Time Magazine, 1949–1973*. Lanham, MD: Lexington Books, 2007.

Preston, Andrew, and Douglas Rossinow. "Introduction." In *Outside in: The Transnational Circuitry of U.S. History*, edited by Andrew Preston and Douglas Rossinow, 1–18. New York: Oxford University Press, 2017.

Qian, Jiang. *Xiaoqiu zhuandong daqiu: "Pingpang waijiao" muhou* [Little Ball Moves Big Ball: Behind the Scenes of Ping-Pong Diplomacy]. Beijing: Dongfang chubanshe, 1997.

Qian, Jiang. "Zhou Enlai xu xie 'pingpang waijiao' huazhang [Zhou Enlai Writes Another Chapter in China's Ping-Pong Diplomacy]." *Dangshi bolan*, no. 8 (2017): 45–48.

Risse-Kappen, Thomas. "Introduction." In *Bringing Transnational Relations Back in: Non-State Actors, Domestic Structures and International Institutions*, edited by Thomas Risse-Kappen, 3–35. Cambridge: Cambridge University Press, 1995.

Roberts, Priscilla. "Bringing the Chinese Back in: The Role of Quasi-Private Institutions in Britain and the United States." In *China, Hong Kong, and the Long*

1970s: Global Perspectives, edited by Priscilla Roberts and Odd Arne Westad, 303–25. Cham: Palgrave Macmillan, 2017.

Roberts, Priscilla. "'Our Friends Don't Understand Our Policies and Our Situation': Informal U.S.-China Dialogues Following Tiananmen." *Journal of American-East Asian Relations* 27, no. 1 (2020): 58–95.

Romano, Angela, and Valeria Zanier. "Circumventing the Cold War: The Parallel Diplomacy of Economic and Cultural Exchanges between Western Europe and Socialist China in the 1950s and 1960s: An Introduction," *Modern Asian Studies* 51, no. 1 (2017): 2–3.

Ross, Robert. *Negotiating Cooperation: The United States and China, 1969–1989*. Stanford, CA: Stanford University Press, 1995.

Ross, Robert and Jiang Changbin, eds. *Re-Examining the Cold War: U.S.-China Diplomacy, 1954–1973*. Cambridge, MA: Harvard University Press, 2001.

Sandbrook, Dominic. "Salesmanship and Substance: The Influence of Domestic Policy and Watergate." In *Nixon in the World: American Foreign Relations, 1969–1977*, edited by Fredrik Logevall and Andrew Preston, 85–103. Oxford: Oxford University Press, 2008.

Schmalzer, Sigrid. "Labor Created Humanity: Cultural Revolution Science on Its Own Terms." In *The Chinese Cultural Revolution as History*, edited by Joseph Esherick, Paul Pickowicz, and Andrew G. Walder, 185–210. Stanford, CA: Stanford University Press, 2006.

Schmalzer, Sigrid. "On the Appropriate Use of Rose-Colored Glasses: Reflections on Science in Socialist China." *Isis* 98, no. 3 (2007): 571–83.

Schmalzer, Sigrid. *Red Revolution, Green Revolution: Scientific Farming in Socialist China*. Chicago, IL: University of Chicago Press, 2016.

Schmalzer, Sigrid. "Speaking about China, Learning from China: Amateur China Experts in 1970s America." *Journal of American-East Asian Relations* 16, no. 4 (2009): 313–52.

Sher, Gerson S. *From Pugwash to Putin: A Critical History of US-Soviet Scientific Cooperation*. Bloomington, IN: Indiana University Press, 2019.

Shuman, Amanda. "Learning from the Soviet Big Brother: The Early Years of Sport in the People's Republic of China." In *The Whole World Was Watching: Sport in the Cold War*, edited by Christopher Young and Robert Edelman, 163–74. Stanford, CA: Stanford University Press, 2019.

Smith, Kathlin. "The Role of Scientists in Normalizing U.S.-China Relations: 1965–1979." *Annals of the New York Academy of Sciences* 866, no. 1 (1998): 114–36.

Snow, Edgar. *The Long Revolution*. New York: Random House, 1972.

Song, Min. "A Dissonance in Mao's Revolution: Chinese Agricultural Imports from the United States, 1972–1978." *Diplomatic History* 38, no. 2 (2014): 409–30.

Su, Jingjing. "Diplomatie de La Médecine Traditionnelle Chinoise En République Populaire de Chine: Un Atout Dans La Guerre Froide." *Monde(s)* 20, no. 2 (2021): 141–61.

Su, Jingjing, and Zhang Daqing. "Xin Zhongguo shouci fu Mei yixue daibiaotuan zhi tanjiu [An Exploration of New China's First Medical Delegation to the United States]." *Zhongguo keji shi zazhi* 32, no. 3 (2011): 395–405.

Suttmeier, Richard, and Denis Simon. "Conflict and Cooperation in the Development of U.S.–China Relations in Science and Technology: Empirical Observations and Theoretical Implications." In *The Global Politics of Science and Technology*, edited by Maxmillan Mayer, Mariana Carpes, and Ruth Knoblich. Vol. 2, 143–59. Berlin: Springer, 2014.

Talley, Christian. *Forgotten Vanguard: Informal Diplomacy and the Rise of United States-China Trade, 1972–1980*. Notre Dame, IN: University of Notre Dame Press, 2018.

Tao, Wenzhao. *Zhong Mei Guanxi Shi, 1972–2000* [A History of Sino-American Relations, 1972–2000]. Vol. 3. Shanghai, 2004.

Teiwes, Frederick, and Warren Sun. *The End of the Maoist Era: Chinese Politics during the Twilight of the Cultural Revolution, 1972–1976*. Armonk, NY: ME Sharpe, 2007.

Tucker, Nancy Bernkopf. *Strait Talk: United States-Taiwan Relations and the Crisis with China*. Cambridge, MA: Harvard University Press, 2009.

Tucker, Nancy Bernkopf. "Taiwan Expendable? Nixon and Kissinger Go to China." *The Journal of American History* 92, no. 1 (2005): 109–35.

Tudda, Chris. *A Cold War Turning Point: Nixon and China, 1969–1972*. Baton Rouge, LA: Louisiana State University Press, 2012.

Tyler, Patrick. *A Great Wall: Six Presidents and China: An Investigative History*. New York: Public Affairs, 1999.

Unschuld, Paul U. *Medicine in China: A History of Ideas*. Berkeley, CA: University of California Press, 1985.

Vogel, Ezra. *Deng Xiaoping and the Transformation of China*. Cambridge, MA: Harvard University Press, 2011.

Volland, Nicolai. "Translating the Socialist State: Cultural Exchange, National Identity, and the Socialist World in the Early PRC." *Twentieth-Century China* 33, no. 2 (2008): 51–72.

Von Eschen, Penny. "Locating the Transnational in the Cold War." In *The Oxford Handbook of the Cold War*, edited by Richard H. Immerman and Petra Goedde, 451–68. Oxford: Oxford University Press, 2013.

Walker, Breck. "'Friends, But Not Allies' – Cyrus Vance and the Normalization of Relations with China." *Diplomatic History* 33, no. 4 (2009): 579–94.

Wang, Jiyu. 'Shenyang zaji tuan: wushi nian licheng [50 Years of the Shenyang Acrobatic Troupe]'. *Zaji yu moshu*, no. 5 (2001): 19–21.

Wang, Guanhua. "'Friendship First': China's Sports Diplomacy during the Cold War." *Journal of American-East Asian Relations* 12, no. 3–4 (2003): 133–53.

Wang, Taiping, ed. *Zhonghua renmin gongheguo waijiao shi: 1970–1978* [A Diplomatic History of the People's Republic of China, 1970–1978]. Vol. 3. Beijing: Shijie zhishi chubanshe, 1999.

Wang, Zuoyue. "Controlled Exchanges: Public-Private Hybridity, Transnational Networking, and Knowledge Circulation in US-China Scientific Discourse on Nuclear Arms Control." In *How Knowledge Moves: Writing the Transnational History of Science and Technology*, edited by John Krige, 368–410. Chicago, IL: University of Chicago Press, 2019.

Wang, Zuoyue. "Transnational Science during the Cold War: The Case of Chinese/American Scientists." *Isis* 101, no. 2 (2010): 367–77.

Wang, Zuoyue. "U.S.-China Scientific Exchange: A Case Study of State-Sponsored Scientific Internationalism during the Cold War and Beyond." *Historical Studies in the Physical and Biological Sciences* 30, no. 1 (1999): 249–77.

Wei, Shiyan. "Jixinge di er ci fang Hua [Kissinger's Second Visit to China]." In *Xin Zhongguo waijiao fengyun* [Winds and Clouds in New China's Diplomacy], edited by Waijiaobu waijiaoshi bianjishi [Foreign Ministry Editorial Office on Diplomatic History]. Vol. 3, 59–70. Beijing: Shijie zhishi chubanshe, 1990.

Westad, Odd Arne. "The Fall of Détente and the Turning Tides of History." In *The Fall of Détente: Soviet-American Relations during the Carter Years*, edited by Odd Arne Westad, 28. Oslo: Scandinavian University Press, 1997.

Wheeler, Norton. *The Role of American NGOs in China's Modernization: Invited Influence*. London: Routledge, 2013.

Whitesides, Greg. *Science and American Foreign Relations since World War II*. New York: Cambridge University Press, 2019.

Wilcox, Emily. "Performing Bandung: China's Dance Diplomacy with India, Indonesia, and Burma, 1953–1962." *Inter-Asia Cultural Studies* 18, no. 4 (2017): 518–39.

Wolfe, Audra J. *Freedom's Laboratory: The Cold War Struggle for the Soul of Science*. Baltimore, MD: Johns Hopkins University Press, 2018.

Wong, Bibiana. "Christian Protesters for Democracy in Taiwan: A Study of Two American Missionaries under Taiwanese Martial Law." *International Journal for the Study of the Christian Church* 16, no. 4 (2016): 288–304.

Xia, Yafeng. "China's Elite Politics and Sino-American Rapprochement, January 1969–February 1972." *Journal of Cold War Studies* 8, no. 4 (2006): 3–28.

Xia, Yafeng. *Negotiating with the Enemy: U.S.-China Talks during the Cold War, 1949–1972*. Bloomington, IN: Indiana University Press, 2006.

Xiao, Donglian. "Zhongguo gaige chuqi dui guowai jingyan de xitong kaocha he jiejian [The Systematic Investigation and Use for Reference of Foreign Experience in the Early Days of Reform]." *Zhonggong Dangshi Yanjiu*, no. 4 (2006): 22–32.

Xiong, Chenxi. 'Deng Xiaoping's Views on Science and Technology: Origins of the Sino-U.S. Science and Technology Cooperation, 1977–1979'. *Journal of American-East Asian Relations* 28, no. 2 (2021): 159–85.

Xu, Guoqi. *Chinese and Americans: A Shared History*. Cambridge, MA: Harvard University Press, 2014.

Xu, Guoqi. *Olympic Dreams: China and Sports, 1895–2008*. Cambridge, MA: Harvard University Press, 2008.

Yang, Kuisong. "The Sino-Soviet Border Clash of 1969: From Zhenbao Island to Sino-American Rapprochement." *Cold War History* 1, no. 1 (2000): 21–52.

Yang, Kuisong, and Yafeng Xia. "Vacillating between Revolution and Détente: Mao's Changing Psyche and Policy toward the United States, 1969–1976." *Diplomatic History* 34, no. 2 (2010): 395–423.

Yi, Guolin. "The 'Propaganda State' and Sino-American Rapprochement: Preparing the Chinese Public for Nixon's Visit." *Journal of American-East Asian Relations* 20, no. 1 (2013): 5–28.

Zeiler, Thomas W. "The Diplomatic History Bandwagon: A State of the Field." *The Journal of American History* 95, no. 4 (2009): 1053–73.

Zhang, Baijia, and Jia Qingguo. "Steering Wheel, Shock Absorber, and Diplomatic Probe in Confrontation Sino-American Ambassadorial Talks Seen from the Chinese Perspective." In *Re-Examining the Cold War: U.S.-China Diplomacy, 1954–1973*, edited by Robert Ross and Jiang Changbin, 173–99. Cambridge, MA: Harvard University Press, 2002.

Zhao, Qina. "Meiguo zhengfu zai Taiwan de jiaoyu yu wenhua jiaoliu huodong (1951–1970) [US Governmental Educational and Cultural Exchange Activities in Taiwan (1951–1970)]." *Ou-Mei yanjiu* 31 (2001): 79–127.

Zhao, Qizheng. "You minjian waijiao dao gonggong waijiao [From People's Diplomacy to Public Diplomacy]." *Waijiao pinglun* 26, no. 5 (2009): 1–3.

Index

Printed in the USA
CPSIA information can be obtained
at www.ICGtesting.com
LVHW040249300823
756703LV00003B/79